GETTING INTO LOCAL POWER

Studies in Urban and Social Change

Published by Blackwell in association with the *International Journal of Urban and Regional Research*. Series Editors: Harvey Molotch; Linda McDowell; Margit Mayer; Chris Pickvance

The Blackwell Studies in Urban and Social Change aim to advance debates and empirical analyses stimulated by changes in the fortunes of cities and regions across the world. Topics range from monographs on single places to large-scale comparisons across East and West, North and South. The series is explicitly interdisciplinary; the editors judge books by their contribution to intellectual solutions rather than according to disciplinary origin.

Published

Getting Into Local Power: The Politics of Ethnic Minorities in British and French Cities
Romain Garbaye

Cities of Europe
Yuri Kazepov (ed.)

Cities, War, and Terrorism
Stephen Graham (ed.)

Cities and Visitors: Regulating Tourists, Markets, and City Space
Lily M. Hoffman, Susan S. Fainstein and Dennis R. Judd (eds)

Understanding the City: Contemporary and Future Perspectives
John Eade and Christopher Mele (eds)

The New Chinese City: Globalization and Market Reform
John R. Logan (ed.)

Cinema and the City: Film and Urban Societies in a Global Context
Mark Shiel and Tony Fitzmaurice (eds)

The Social Control of Cities? A Comparative Perspective
Sophie Body-Gendrot

Globalizing Cities: A New Spatial Order?
Peter Marcuse and Ronald van Kempen (eds)

Contemporary Urban Japan: A Sociology of Consumption
John Clammer

Capital Culture: Gender at Work in the City
Linda McDowell

Cities After Socialism: Urban and Regional Change and Conflict in Post-Socialist Societies
Gregory Andrusz, Michael Harloe and Ivan Szelenyi (eds)

The People's Home? Social Rented Housing in Europe and America
Michael Harloe

Post-Fordism
Ash Amin (ed.)

Free Markets and Food Riots
John Walton and David Seddon

Fragmented Societies
Enzo Mingione

Urban Poverty and the Underclass: A Reader
Enzo Mingione

Forthcoming

Eurostars and Eurocities: Free-Moving Urban Professionals in an Integrating Europe
Adrian Favell

Cities and Regions in a Global Era
Alan Harding (ed.)

Urban South Africa
Alan Mabin

Urban Social Movements and the State
Margit Mayer

Social Capital Formation in Immigrant Neighborhoods
Min Zhou

GETTING INTO LOCAL POWER

THE POLITICS OF ETHNIC MINORITIES IN BRITISH AND FRENCH CITIES

Romain Garbaye

Blackwell
Publishing

BLACKWELL PUBLISHING
350 Main Street, Malden, MA 02148–5020, USA
9600 Garsington Road, Oxford OX4 2DQ, UK
550 Swanston Street, Carlton, Victoria 3053, Australia

The right of Romain Garbaye to be identified as the Author of this Work has been asserted in accordance with the UK Copyright, Designs, and Patents Act 1988.

First published 2005 by Blackwell Publishing Ltd

1   2005

Library of Congress Cataloging-in-Publication Data

Garbaye, Romain.
     Getting into local power: the politics of ethnic minorities in British and French cities / Romain Garbaye.
          p. cm.—(Studies in urban and social change)
     Includes bibliographical references and index.
     ISBN-13: 978-1-4051-2697-7 (hardback: alk. paper)
     ISBN-10: 1-4051-2697-3 (hardback: alk. paper)
     ISBN-13: 978-1-4051-2694-6 (pbk.: alk. paper)
     ISBN-10: 1-4051-2694-9 (pbk.: alk. paper)
     1. Local elections—France—Case studies.   2. Minorities—France—Political activity—Case studies.   3. France—Ethnic relations—Political aspects—Case studies.   4. Local elections—Great Britain—Case studies.   5. Minorities—Great Britain—Political activity—Case studies.
6. Great Britain—Ethnic relations—Political aspects—Case studies.   7. Birmingham (Eng.)—Politics and government.   8. Lille (France)—Politics and government.   9. Roubaix (France)—Politics and government.   I. Title.   II. Series.
     JS4975.G37 2005
     323.141′09173′2 – dc22   2005005880

A catalogue record for this title is available from the British Library.

Set in 10½ on 12 pt Baskerville
by SNP Best-set Typesetter Ltd, Hong Kong
Printed and bound in India
by Replika Press, Pvt. Ltd, India

The publisher's policy is to use permanent paper from mills that operate a sustainable forestry policy, and which has been manufactured from pulp processed using acid-free and elementary chlorine-free practices. Furthermore, the publisher ensures that the text paper and cover board used have met acceptable environmental accreditation standards.

For further information on
Blackwell Publishing, visit our website:
www.blackwellpublishing.com

Contents

List of Maps ix

Foreword by Patrick Weil x

Series Editors' Preface xiv

Acknowledgements xv

Introduction 1
    The Election of Ethnic Minorities on European City
    Councils 1
    Comparing Ethnic Minority Politics in Britain and France 3
    Contrasting Levels of Representation and Modes of Access in
    the 1980s and 1990s 6
    Towards an Analysis of Local Political Processes 13

1 Historical Institutionalism and the Comparison of Local Cases 20
    Strategies of Management of Ethnic Conflict and Historical
    Institutionalism 20
        Strategies of management of ethnic conflict 21
        Historical institutionalism 25
        Central and local factors 26
    Birmingham, Lille and Roubaix, 1980s–2001 29
    The Main Propositions and the Outline of the Book 32

*The framing of debates on immigration and integration in national
politics: 1945–2001*   32
Contrasting local political systems   34

2 The British Policy Framework: Liberal Citizenship Regime,
   Depoliticization and the Race Relationism of British Cities   37
   1948–1958: Pressure on Local Authorities and National
   Indifference   39
   The beginning of mass migration   39
   National apathy and local agitation   41
   1958–1968: The Birth of the British Race Relations Policy
   Framework   44
   Depoliticization   44
   1965–1968: the first 'race relations' policies ·   46
   *Consequences of the race relations framework on later patterns of
   minority participation*   49
   The 1970s and 1980s: The Legacy of the 1960s Settlement   50
   The polarization of the 1970s   50
   The Labour Party as the minorities' party – until 2001?   51
   The 1980s onwards: local Labour activism   54
   The 'Race Relationism' of British Cities in the 1980s and 1990s   57
   *Equal opportunities policies, city networks and the election of
   non-white councillors*   57
   Local variations   59
   Conclusion   61

3 The French Policy Framework: Planned Migration, Xenophobic
   Politics and Durable Political Exclusion   63
   1945–1973: State Planning and Unintended Effects   64
   The 1945 framework and the generation gap   65
   The unexpected arrival of extra-European immigrants   68
   The management of North African populations by the central state   69
   1974–1983: The Bureaucratic Management of Political
   Incertitude   70
   From migrants to minorities   70
   Struggling to define immigration policy   71
   1983–1997: National and Local Politicization of Immigration
   in Xenophobic Terms   73
   The Socialist Party and the failure of the Beur movement   74
   *The rise of the Front National and the contradictory reactions of
   party elites*   78
   The Construction of Consensus after 1997   86
   Socialist policy innovations   86
   The 2001 local elections   89
   Conclusion   90

4 Birmingham, 1980s–2001: Inner-city Labour Politics and
   Pluri-ethnic Government   92
      From Indifference to Multi-ethnic Coalition: The Birth of Ethnic
      Politics in Birmingham   95
         Birmingham government: polycentric and partisan   95
         A large, diverse and disadvantaged ethnic minority population   97
         From indifference and hostility to pluri-ethnic government: 50 years of
         ethnic politics   103
      Institutions and Activists: How Ethnic Minorities Penetrated the
      Labour Party   116
         Styles of community organization   117
         The political institutions of the inner city   122
         Three styles of co-optation in Labour ward-level politics: from vote
         brokerage to independent councillors   125
      Conclusion   142

5 Lille, 1980s–2001: Machine Politics and Exclusion of Minorities
   in the French Municipal System   144
      Introduction   144
         The Lille–Roubaix comparison   144
         A strategy of avoidance and denial   145
      Lille's Double Strategy of Externalization and Political Exclusion   147
         The emergence of a North African minority   147
         The municipality's policy of gentrification   150
         The persistence of a social and ethnic 'problem' in Lille   152
         Social discontent in the political arena: Front National, republican
         universalism and minority disorganization   155
      The French Municipal System, Machine Politics and Minority
      Exclusion in Lille   159
         Municipal institutions in Lille   161
         The 1980s: municipal politics and the failure of the Beur movement 164
         The 1990s: machine politics and the marginalization of North
         African dissent   169
         Relations between municipality and North African groups in the 1990s:
         patronage and dependence   179
      Conclusion   185

6 Roubaix, 1980s–2001: Inclusion Through Neighbourhood Groups
   and an Open Municipal Game   187
      Introduction   187
      Urban Crisis, Migrations and the Political Management of
      the Crisis   188
         From 'Holy City of the Proletariat' to post-industrial crisis   188
         A large population of Algerian descent   189

Roubaix identity, Front National vote and pro-minority policies 191
Institutions and generations of activists 195
Roubaix Political History and Immigrant Incorporation in the
1990s 196
*Cross-party government and inclusion of migrants in the municipal
community* 197
North African activists in an open political game 206
Conclusion 209

Conclusion 211
Strengths and Limitations of Historical Institutionalism in Ethnic
Minority Studies 211
The End of the Path: Muslim Anger in Britain and the
Lingering Burden of Beur Failure in France 213
Ethnic Minorities and the Decline of the European Left 217
Local Strategies and their Unintended Effects 218

Appendix: Interviews and Sources 221

Notes 223

Bibliography 240

Index 256

Maps

Map 1   Birmingham wards and constituencies in October 1996   xvii

Map 2   Percentage of population of black and minority ethnic
groups in Birmingham by ward, 1991   xviii

Map 3   Percentage of population of ethnic Pakistani group in
Birmingham by ward, 1991   xix

Map 4   The neighbourhoods of Lille   xx

Map 5   Concentration of foreigners in the neighbourhoods of
Roubaix   xxi

Foreword

Patrick Weil, Directeur de Recherches, CNRS-Université Panthéon-Sorbonne (Paris I)

It was a challenge, for a young French graduate student, to leave France seven years ago to work towards a PhD in the United Kingdom on French and British local politics, drawing on an American, new institutionalist approach. It was an additional challenge to return successfully to the French academic system, given the relative lack of interest of the French in institutionalist political science and given their traditional distrust of comparative studies.

Yet Romain Garbaye has successfully carried off these challenges, and I am happy to introduce the result. Trained at Oxford University, he is now Assistant Professor at the Sorbonne (University of Paris-IV). In his dissertation that is now published as this book, he compares the politics of ethnic minorities in three cities: a British one, Birmingham, and two French ones, Lille and Roubaix. Examining how ethnic minorities 'get into local power', he asks why they have successfully entered Birmingham politics while remaining shut out of Lille politics and slowly gaining ground in Roubaix. Is it because the French are faithful to their republican ideology while the British have embraced multiculturalism? Or should one point to more persistent racism and intolerance in France than in Britain? Neither of these. Using historical institutionalism as a tool of enlightenment, he demonstrates instead that it is features of local political systems such as central–local relations, modes of local party organization and styles of local government that have shaped different patterns of access to political representation across countries and cities.

With these premises, the book unfolds a rigorous, clear and penetrating comparison of 40 years of minority politics on either side of the Channel. In doing so, it constitutes a welcome addition to the field of European migration studies where comprehensive and truly comparative studies are still rare. It also illustrates the pertinence of institutionalist approaches by detailing how political institutions deeply rooted in the history of nations and cities shape in complex ways the birth of multicultural societies in western Europe. It combines an interest in immigration politics with a focus on the workings of urban political systems.

The book highlights the far-reaching consequences of Britain's peculiar citizenship regime in the post-war period, which, by granting citizenship rights to all migrants upon arrival in the United Kingdom, greatly encouraged minority participation and durably shaped 40 years of minority politics. Symmetrically, the book retraces the linkage between the French nationality regime, under which most first-generation migrants have lived in France as foreigners, and the persistent pattern of manipulation and exclusion that afflicted minority politics in the 1980s and 1990s. It goes on to demonstrate more clearly than has been done before how the disastrous failure of North African secular politics in the 1980s had a lasting impact on the place of ethnic minorities in the French polity, alienating them from the political left, and indeed from the political system as a whole, in the 1990s, with signs of a timid surge in participation appearing only now.

Imagine for a moment that instead of becoming citizens immediately upon their arrival in the United Kingdom, immigrants from the New Commonwealth had been granted the status of foreigners with non-automatically renewable permits; is it not likely, as happened in France, that the restrictionists and ethnocentrists would have insisted that their stay was only temporary, and would have asked their government to focus its political agenda on the immigrants' return? This is precisely what many French politicians and policy-makers did, and what the British could not do, because immigrants into Britain were citizens of the UK upon their arrival, for better and for worse. Therefore, the restrictionists focused instead on stopping new immigration and reforming the nationality regime. They succeeded, and, in exchange for their acceptance of this policy objective, the Labour Party was able to create anti-racist policies. Romain Garbaye shows how these developments set the institutional framework of British immigration and integration policy for the next 40 years, framing minorities' demands and shaping political alliances in cities.

In France, the restrictionists did not worry – in the 1960s – about stopping immigration, because they were sure that, whenever it became necessary, they could send immigrants back home. Indeed, they tried to do just that after the 1974 oil shock. Former President Giscard d'Estaing headed an attempt to deport 500,000 legal Algerian immigrants. The left reacted forcibly, as did the

Gaullists. This was a battle that lasted from 1974 until 1998, during which the right to settle and then to acquire French citizenship easily was at stake for numerous immigrants and their children. At that time, the Front National picked up Giscard d'Estaing's programme and campaigned for repatriation. It was not a good time for integrating ethnic minorities into local politics, and the book details how the negative consequences of these poisonous debates were experienced on the ground, at the level of neighbourhood and city politics in France's deprived post-industrial areas.

The book also analyses the capacity of city governments to react to social and ethnic changes. When New Commonwealth immigrants settled in the UK, immediately becoming citizens, they tended to concentrate in certain urban areas, and in the 1980s started to acquire a degree of recognition and influence in local politics. This was so not only because they were citizens, but also because local councils are elected by ward. Ethnic minorities became intimately, though conflictually, involved in the politics of the local Labour Party in Birmingham, becoming one of the pillars of a strong pluri-ethnic coalition that governed the city in the 1980s and 1990s.

In France, immigrants have also lived in ghettoized areas, although patterns of segregation are often less pronounced than in Britain. However, in these areas, they were not until recently the majority of the citizens; this is because, while being in the majority, they were not citizens. The book shows how this handicap translated into lasting political exclusion in the context of the French local political system. For those naturalized immigrants who became French, their electoral weight was feeble in the context of city-wide electoral districts, and they were confronted with powerful and entrenched networks that perpetuated established modes of government without adapting to social change. One of the most penetrating lessons of the book deals with the place of local political elites in the national political system. In France, local mayors can be national figures, nurturing presidential ambitions, as is the case in Lille. This explains why their local policies are scrutinized by the national press and can have a national impact, and therefore why they pursue politics that are traditional to the extreme, while a lesser-known mayor such as Roubaix's can have a wider margin to innovate in ethnic politics.

Romain Garbaye's book also opens perspectives for the future. At a time when some British Muslims are using their vote against the Labour Party to vent their anger against its Iraq policy, the book traces the origins of Muslim discontent to disappointment with Labour inner-city policy in the late 1990s. The disastrous failure of North African secular politics in 1980s France alienated them from the political left, and indeed from the political system as a whole, in the 1990s. The signs now appearing of a new, timid resurgence of minorities into city councils reflect not only demographic changes but also the continuing hold of local partisan elites over political representation. As France starts to move towards new approaches to resolving its lingering immigrant integration crisis, such as positive action policies and the institutionalization of Islam, it is worthwhile keeping this political backdrop in mind.

Series Editors' Preface

The Blackwell *Studies in Urban and Social Change* series aims to advance theoretical debates and empirical analyses stimulated by changes in the fortunes of cities and regions across the world. Among topics taken up in past volumes and welcomed for future submissions are:

- Connections between economic restructuring and urban change
- Urban divisions, difference, and diversity
- Convergence and divergence among regions of east and west, north, and south
- Urban and environmental movements
- International migration and capital flows
- Trends in urban political economy
- Patterns of urban-based consumption

The series is explicitly interdisciplinary; the editors judge books by their contribution to intellectual solutions rather than according to disciplinary origin.

Proposals may be submitted to members of the series Editorial Committee:

Harvey Molotch
Linda McDowell
Margit Mayer
Chris Pickvance

Acknowledgements

This book is a revised version of a DPhil thesis defended at Oxford University. Thanks are due above all to David Goldey and Desmond King, my DPhil supervisors, for their constant encouragement and support. I am also grateful to all the local politicians, activists and social workers who answered my questions in France and Britain. Their cooperation and good will were invaluable to me. Interviews with them often worked as personal lessons on political struggle, which I was privileged to receive.

I have been financially supported during my years of graduate work by the Besse scholarship of my college at Oxford, Worcester, where I have spent four fulfilling years of research and teaching. I am grateful in particular to Kate Tunstall and Alan Ware. The Philip Williams fund of the Pôle Européen of Sciences Po in Paris provided crucial financial backing for the field research in Birmingham and Lille. The Department of European Studies at Aston University, Birmingham, functioned as a logistical base and a source of advice, and for that I am grateful to Anne Stevens and to John Gaffney. John Rex and Danièle Joly of CRER at the University of Warwick encouraged my work in its early stages. In Lille, the Centre d'Études et de Recherches Administratives, Politiques et Sociales de Lille (CERAPS), Université de Lille-II, has also been an invaluable source of material and intellectual support. I am grateful to Patrick Hassenteufel for facilitating my connection with CERAPS, and to Frédéric Sawicki, its director, for welcoming me. My stays there provided the opportunity for many inspiring discussions on Lille politics with

Rémi Lefebvre and on French Islam with Nancy Venel. I extend my warmest regards to them here. Marie Poinsot at ADRI in Paris provided precious indications on minority politics in Lille. I thank John Solomos and Les Back for their kind permission to discuss in detail parts of their wonderful book, *Race, Politics and Social Change* (Routledge, 1995). I also thank Taylor and Francis for their permission to reproduce here as chapter 2 a revised version of an article that I published in *Immigrants and Minorities*, 22, 2/3 (2003), available online at tandf.co.uk.

The preparation of this book has also been made possible by my stay at the Robert Schuman Centre for Advanced Studies at the European University Institute in Florence, where I held a Jean Monnet post-doctoral fellowship in 2001–2. I benefited from the excellent research atmosphere there and I am grateful to the director of the centre, Helen Wallace, for welcoming me and for her encouragement. At the Université Paris IV-Sorbonne I found a stimulating and friendly academic environment in which to prepare the final version of the book.

Many people have helped in this project, through their advice and guidance. In particular I wish to thank here Patrick Weil, Sophie Body-Gendrot, Randall Hansen, Adrian Favell, Virginie Guiraudon, Peter John, Patrick Le Galès, Yves Mény and Martin Schain. Participation in collective research projects led by Paul Statham and Ruud Koopmans, and by Karen Kraal, Marco Martiniello, Rinus Penninx, Alisdair Rogers, Jean Tillie, and Steve Vertovec, has provided an excellent opportunity for me to learn about on-going research in Europe, and to develop various aspects of the work leading to this book, for which I am extremely grateful. I also wish to thank all friends and colleagues who have helped and contributed in various ways, in particular Lionel Arnaud, Françoise de Barros, Marie-Claude Blanc-Chaléard, Erik Bleich, Hassan Bousetta, Jacques Carré, Alistair Cole, Véronique Dimier, Meindert Fennema, Catherine Fieschi, Andrew Geddes, David Howarth, Riva Kastoryano, Jonathan Laurence, Jonathan Lipkin, Rahsaan Maxwell, Damian Moore, Lorena Ruano, Sonia Tebbakh, Jean Tillie, Valérie Sala-Pala, and John Solomos. I am also grateful to Harvey Molotch for his advice on the preparation of the book. I thank Jacqueline Scott, Angela Cohen and Brigitte Lee at Blackwell for their help with the production of the book. Of course, any mistakes are my responsibility.

Finally, I express my gratitude to my parents Jean and Françoise, to my sister, Anne, and to my friends in Oxford, London and Paris, who supported me as the years passed. Linda shares my life. Thank you for your love, your enthusiasm and your staunch support.

Vincent Wright's supervision of the early stages of the project was extremely inspiring and friendly. This book is dedicated to his memory.

Map 1 Birmingham wards and constituencies in October 1996.
Source: Birmingham City Council, 1996

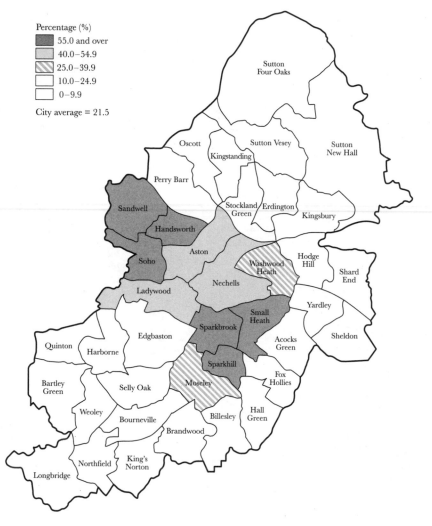

Map 2 Percentage of population of black and minority ethnic groups in Birmingham by ward, 1991.
Source: 1991 census; Information Team, Department of Planning and Architecture, Birmingham City Council, 1991

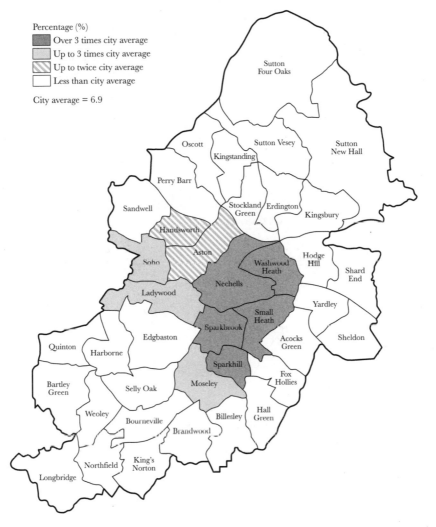

Percentage (%)

- Over 3 times city average
- Up to 3 times city average
- Up to twice city average
- Less than city average

City average = 6.9

Sutton Four Oaks

Oscott

Kingstanding

Sutton Vesey

Sutton New Hall

Perry Barr

Sandwell

Stockland Green / Erdington

Kingsbury

Handsworth

Aston

Washwood Heath

Hodge Hill

Shard End

Soho

Nechells

Ladywood

Yardley

Small Heath

Sparkbrook

Acocks Green

Sheldon

Edgbaston

Quinton

Harborne

Sparkhill

Fox Hollies

Bartley Green

Selly Oak

Moseley

Hall Green

Weoley

Bourneville

Billesley

Brandwood

Longbridge

Northfield

King's Norton

Map 3 Percentage of population of ethnic Pakistani group in Birmingham by ward, 1991.
Source: 1991 census; Information Team, Department of Planning and Architecture, Birmingham City Council, 1991

Map 4 The neighbourhoods of Lille.
Neighbourhoods where ethnic minority concentration was the highest in 1990 were Lille-Sud (19.3 per cent), Faubourg de Béthune (18.5 per cent), Moulins (14 per cent), Fives (10 per cent) and Wazemmes (9.2 per cent).
Source: Ville de Lille, 1998, based on INSEE 1990 census data

Map 5 Concentration of foreigners in the neighbourhoods of Roubaix.
Source: Giblin-Delvallet, 1990

Introduction

The Election of Ethnic Minorities on European City Councils

Western European societies in the twentieth century were delimited by, and organized within, the structure of the nation-state. This model has entailed a congruence of national cleavages with state boundaries and has ensured the stability of European societies. The result was the relatively low salience of ethnic cleavages as sources of political conflict in these societies (apart from peripheral conflicts such as the Basque conflict or Northern Irish conflict, or such as the Belgian case). But the state-national model has increasingly been challenged by various trends, foremost among which is extra-European immigration, along with European integration and the renewed vitality of regional politics. It is precisely the dominance of the nation-state as a geographically bounded group of people that makes movements of populations a political phenomenon;[1] and the scale of these movements has turned them into a potential 'challenge to the nation-state' in its role as the framework for European politics (Joppke, 1998).

In particular, the participation of ethnic minorities in politics is a new phenomenon that brings far-reaching changes. Immigrant populations have morphed into well-settled ethnic minorities, that is to say, in political terms, populations which share an interest in agendas of struggle against racial discrimination and for the recognition of cultural and religious differences in various policy areas, for instance education or the construction of custom-built places of worship.[2] Political institutions such as trade unions, elected

\...lies and political parties, which used to represent and articulate \...flicts within ethnically homogeneous societies, now find themselves faced with agendas related to ethnic diversity. The reaction has often been one of refusing access to minority individuals and interests. This book studies the processes through which western European political systems react to ethnic diversity, in what conditions they react to it or ignore it, how they resist pressures to take on board minority agendas, and why and how they embrace them when they do. It focuses on one particular aspect which is deemed a revealing 'flash point': the election of individuals from an ethnic minority background on city councils, and the political careers of these activists that lead to election.

Cities are at the forefront of attempts by ethnic minority populations to participate in urban politics, as is reflected by a growing body of comparative research.[3] The already long history of immigrant politics, then black and Hispanic politics, in American cities since the 1960s hints at a similarly durable relevance of cities in European immigrant politics.[4] The intensity of ethnic minority participation at the local level has often stood in contrast to its absence or weakness in national scenes. In Britain, for instance, where immigrants of post-colonial background have traditionally voted in all elections, national and local, the number of ethnic minorities has risen much faster in local councils than in the House of Commons.[5] National policies have also channelled the participation of minorities into city politics: in countries where immigrants have no formal national citizenship, they are often granted local voting rights, as in Ireland in 1963, Sweden in 1976, Denmark in 1981, Norway in 1982 and the Netherlands in 1986. That the European Union (EU) gives its citizens the right to vote in the local elections of member countries in which they are resident, but not in national elections, reflects a similar trend.

The importance of locality for the study of minority politics is also linked to the web of relations that exist between citizenship, community, locality and ethnicity. Cities have always been a central arena for the definition of citizenship, as the etymological link between the two words indicates (see Holsten and Appadurai, 1996). An important reason for this is that territorial proximity encourages feelings of shared interests and common involvement in public affairs: 'outside the workplace, neighbourhoods are the most important forum for political mobilization' (Keating, 1991, p. 40). Urban territories and participation are closely connected to the emergence of ethnic communities (Lowndes, 1995, p. 162). The high spatial concentration of ethnic minorities in neighbourhoods encourages feelings of shared identities and interests among immigrants of particular neighbourhoods, which in turn provides incentives for them to become actors on the local political scene.

The participation of ethnic minorities in city politics follows a cycle that sees them moving from positions of outsiders of a system to positions of insiders, going through several stages, from political apathy to informal mobilization over specific issues, then to more formal modes of association. In turn, this is usually correlated with participation in formal representative politics, when rules of enfranchisement permit, which entails not just electoral participation but also activism in party politics (see Vertovec, 1998, p. 211). Participation in representative politics, in turn, ultimately leads to the election of councillors of ethnic minority background on city councils.

In which conditions can ethnic minorities be elected on city councils? When they are kept off these councils, why and how does this happen? Why are there sometimes large numbers of ethnic minorities on councils, and why at other times or in other cities is their presence largely tokenistic, limited to one or two isolated individuals? What kinds of political careers do these ethnic minority councillors follow, and how do these careers lead to election? Once they are elected, to what extent do they seek to create and maintain racially or ethnically conscious policies, and with what degree of success? What do all these questions tell us about the openness or closedness of European political systems to ethnic minorities?

Beyond these questions, the focus on city council politics makes it possible to contribute to other related lines of questioning. It documents processes of change in the social composition of ruling groups in cities, and it provides analyses of the workings of urban political systems. The promotion of ethnic diversity as an asset is a feature of some European cities emerging from the crisis of the Fordist economy and trying to manage the social, cultural and political transformations that follow; others have been more reluctant to acknowledge their diversity. The political forces that accompany the processes of redefinition of local identities need to be analysed.

The ethnic minority councillors discussed in this book are predominantly affiliated to left-wing parties, because ethnic minorities are frequently supporters of these parties' stance in defence of workers. Therefore another central theme of the book is the question of relations between ethnic diversity and left-wing parties. This feeds directly into an important object of speculation, which is the relative importance of ethnicity and class as sources of cleavage, with the possibility that ethnicity, along with other 'postmodern' issues, may become more salient, while other sources of cleavage, such as social class, might be losing their long-time prevalence as the main organizing principles of European politics (Kitschelt, 1997).

Comparing Ethnic Minority Politics in Britain and France

The British–French comparison is a fruitful one in immigration and ethnic minority studies because the two countries present intriguing parallels (see notably Lapeyronnie, 1993; Favell, 1998; Bleich, 2003). Regarding the participation of ethnic minorities in urban politics, the comparison reveals significant cross-national differences within broadly similar trajectories. While cities in both countries are clearly following similar evolutions towards increasing levels of representation of ethnic minorities, the timing of that process, the channels of access to council seats, the political processes that open or close these channels and the significance of these councillors in terms of policy change all present variations.

France and Britain are both old centralized nation-states with stable, democratic political institutions, developed economies, large welfare systems and similar patterns of post-war migration. In both countries, the main mass immigration movements started in the mid-1940s and were mostly economic, with migrants seeking employment, and France and Britain looking for manpower to sustain the reconstruction of their economies after the war. These migratory waves originated for the most part in colonies, then former colonies, although in each case there were also migrants from European countries: Irish migrants in Britain or Portuguese workers in France (the largest immigrant population in France, comparable to the Algerian population). In Britain, post-colonial, extra-European immigration originated, first, from the West Indies, mainly in the 1940s and 1950s, then from Asian members of the New Commonwealth: India, Bangladesh and Pakistan. In France, it came mainly from former North African colonies: Morocco, Tunisia and Algeria, then from former colonies in black Africa: Senegal and Mali (Frybes, 1992; Joly, 1992).

Comparing statistics on ethnic minority populations in each country is complicated because of the differing approaches to ethnic categorization, legal constraints on ethnic counts in France[6] and differing methods of survey. Nevertheless, all attempts do suggest minority populations of comparable sizes in the last two decades, around 6 per cent to 8 per cent of the total population of each country. In Britain, the 2001 census indicated 7.9 per cent of the total population (or 4,630,000 people) as 'ethnic minority', on the basis of declaration of ethnicity by the respondents.[7] This excluded foreigners. In France, counts of foreigners exclude the significant number of people born in a foreign country who have become French through naturalization. A more comparable category to Britain is that of French residents born outside of France who were born outside the European Union,[8] which amounted to 6.9 per cent of the population in 1999.

This post-colonial immigration wave in both countries was more or less desired and controlled; but the permanent settlement of immigrants in their host country, instead of their returning home after a period of work, was not anticipated by the authorities. In both countries, post-colonial migrants and their offspring are characterized by cultural and religious difference from mainstream society, and they are for the most part plagued by high unemployment rates and spatial concentration in derelict areas of cities.[9]

The cultural and religious characteristics of the ethnic minority populations also present many similarities. In each case there is a significant Muslim population, although it is difficult to estimate its size with precision.[10] In Britain, the 2001 census counted 3.1 per cent of self-described Muslims in the total population (or around 1,500,000 people); the survey published by a team led by Tariq Modood and Richard Berthoud in 1997 strongly suggests that this population was largely congruent with the Britons who described themselves as Pakistani or Bangladeshi in the 2001 census.[11] In France, the Muslim population is difficult to evaluate because, like ethnicity, religion is not a question in the national census. The most credible estimate, given by demographer Michèle Tribalat, is 3.7 million people who are 'possibly Muslims' (i.e. because they originate in predominantly Muslim countries); only a third of those interviewed in a 1995 survey declared themselves to be 'believers' and to attend a mosque on a regular basis.[12]

As for the African and African-Caribbean population in both countries, it is predominantly from a Christian background. The political preoccupations of important sub-groups of both populations were for a long time focused on their country of origin, especially in the case of the Algerians in France and of the Indians and Pakistanis in Britain, with a strong influence from groups that reflected internal and home-grown divisions. For parts of the Muslim communities in both countries, religion has been an important way of mobilizing, often through demands for the construction of mosques, sometimes with the financial support of Middle Eastern countries.

Another important element is the combination of ideological, legal and organizational rules with which these populations are accommodated by their host states within the general juridical and welfare system, what might be called the 'incorporation framework'. This framework plays a direct role in allowing, framing and limiting opportunities for participation of ethnic minorities. Here again, the two countries have broad similarities. Stephen Castles, in a 1995 typology of ways in which 'nation-states respond to immigration and ethnic diversity', focusing on ideologies and policies, grouped them together as two examples of an 'assimilationist model', as opposed to a 'differential exclusion model' (Japan and Germany) or a 'pluralist model' (the United States and Australia) (Castles, 1995). In particular, the author points to the laissez-faire attitude regarding immigration-related problems that prevailed in both countries at the beginning of the immigration wave in the 1950s: in both countries, it was thought that immigrants were to assimilate through existing institutions such as the school system (Castles, 1995).

Soysal points in the same direction when she characterizes Britain as focused on an individualistic style of representation and mediation of interest between society and the state, as opposed to more corporatist polities, such as Sweden or the Netherlands (Soysal, 1994, p. 5). She does not include France in Britain's category, but in many ways one could, because the

French polity is also constructed around a liberal, individualist conception of the individual. In both France and Britain, immigrants are expected to fit into the participatory framework of the state primarily as individuals, and, if they are to form groups, these are not institutionalized branches of the state, as for instance in the Swedish corporatist system, but rather voluntary associations.

Indeed, both countries have extended access to welfare to all immigrants on a territorial and individual basis. Both countries can also be considered as presenting a 'liberal' model of formal citizenship, as opposed, for instance, to Germany, where accession to political citizenship was almost impossible before the 1990s for the large population of foreign 'guestworkers' (Brubaker, 1992). By contrast, France and Great Britain have traditionally made access to citizenship easier. In France, access to French nationality is granted on liberal terms, at least in theory (Weil, 2002), and, in Britain, there has been a tradition of full political citizenship for New Commonwealth immigrants entering British territory. The developments that have taken place in this British post-colonial model over the last 40 years have been in the direction of a convergence with the French framework, linking nationality and citizenship. Finally, Lapeyronnie stresses the similarity in the evolution of social structures in both countries. In both, according to him, the traditional institutions of the working class which used to link individuals to the national polity, such as unions and left-wing parties, have been gradually losing influence over the last few decades, hence the descent into social marginalization, violence and 'ethnicization' of a new underclass of unemployed workers and migrants, the 'excluded' (Lapeyronnie, 1993, 'La crise des institutions', pp. 51ff.).

Contrasting Levels of Representation and Modes of Access in the 1980s and 1990s

The book focuses on the representation of ethnic minorities on British and French councils in the 1980s and 1990s,[13] more precisely until 2001. The book deals with post-September 11, 2001 and Iraq war developments in Britain as the closing episode of this era, because these events entail a brutal and far-reaching break in the logic of British ethnic minority politics.

In the period under discussion, a process of increase in the number of ethnic councillors has been taking place in the two countries. But it has differed sharply in its timing, its scale, and in the political conditions and modes of accession to elected office. In Britain, it was visible as early as the late 1970s, followed by an ascending curve in the 1980s and 1990s, and was largely linked to political movements demanding recognition of ethnic diversity and anti-discrimination policies. In France, the election of councillors on a significant level only appeared to emerge for the first time in the 2001 municipal elections, after the 1989 and 1995 municipal elections had witnessed the failure of coordinated political enterprises aiming at imposing North African councillors on councils. In 2001, those who were elected were often local personalities or individuals hand-picked by local party leaders, and most of the time they did not articulate specific claims, in a continuing contrast with Britain.

The contrast between the two countries placed them at opposite ends of the spectrum of western European countries faced with similar migration waves. While Britain is the European country with one of the earliest and most extensive phenomenon of minority inclusion on councils, ahead of Denmark, Sweden and the Netherlands, France is one of the last large European countries to follow.

In Britain, the movement was initiated in London. In 1974, there were four ethnic minority councillors in London boroughs; this figure had risen to 35 by 1978, had more than doubled to 79 by 1982, and continued to rise in the early 1990s with 193 sitting ethnic minority councillors in London, comprising 10 per cent of London councillors overall in 1990 (Adolino, 1998, p. 45).[14] Cities in other urban areas across the country followed a few years later, starting from close to zero in the late 1970s, and increasing steadily throughout the 1980s, with an estimated 170 in 1985 (Geddes, 1993, p. 43). In 1996, it was estimated that there were around 600 local councillors of ethnic minority background in Britain out of a total of around 25,000, or around 3 per cent of the total (LGIU, 1996). Five years later in 2001, that number was roughly stable, with a slight decline to 2.5 per cent,[15] probably attributable to the unpopularity of the Labour Party during Tony Blair's second term.

Although even 3 per cent of local councillors appear to leave the British minority population still under-represented (compared to around 8 per cent of the UK population), their representation was in fact much higher if one considers that many of the 25,000 or so British local councillors represent rural areas with a negligible minority population. More indicative statistics are those made by Michel Le Lohé on 15 provincial cities (table 0.1), which indicate in most cases a representation on local councils for Asians that was proportionate to their percentage of the local population. 'In the seven local authorities outside London where the Asian population exceeds 10 per cent, Asians provide 13 per cent of all councillors. This is just 1 per cent lower than the average Asian population in these authorities – thus the representation is almost exactly proportionate' (Le Lohé, 1998, p. 73). In many instances 'black' populations were also represented, although less well.

Whether of Asian or black descent, these councillors have been active in local politics or local community work before their election, and owe their election to activism and political struggle, often against competing interests in

Table 0.1 Population and representation outside London (percentages)

City	Asian		Black	
	Population	*Councillors*	*Population*	*Councillors*
Birmingham	13.5	13.7	5.9	3.4
Blackburn	14.2	10.0	0.4	0.0
Bradford	13.6	12.2	1.1	0.0
Coventry	9.3	13.0	1.6	1.9
Kirklees	8.3	5.6	1.8	0.0
Leicester	24.7	23.2	2.4	0.0
Luton	13.6	16.7	4.9	6.3
Manchester	5.9	4.0	4.6	3.0
North Beds	5.6	5.7	2.8	0.0
Nottingham	4.8	12.7	4.6	5.5
Pendle	9.7	7.8	1.0	0.0
Preston	8.3	3.5	1.2	0.0
Sandwell	10.6	11.1	2.4	0.0
Slough	22.6	30.0	5.1	0.0
Wolverhampton	12.3	5.0	5.1	0.0

Source: Le Lohé, 1998, p. 89; sources for population the 1991 census; for councillors Le Lohé's research.

their own party. It is also frequently the case that their election campaign was fought on a platform that explicitly mentioned racism and diversity as relevant issues. In fact many were elected as part of more or less coordinated campaigns designed to impose anti-racist agendas on local councils.

They have frequently become well established in the councils where they sit and in the urban, low-income communities that they have represented. Despite frequent accusations of tokenism and patronage, they have managed to participate actively in the decision-making processes of the councils in which they have sat, regularly rising to positions of prominence, for instance as chairs of council committees. It is also important to note the existence of important contrasts between cities: for both blacks and Asians, the levels of representation vary sometimes largely from one city to another.

This steady process in Britain in the 1980s and 1990s has a symbolic dimension, with the cities putting forward their openness to cultural diversity as an asset to promote themselves as modern and vibrant communities. It has also been closely correlated with the development of policies against racial discrimination in local councils and the institutionalization of ethnic minority-run social services by councils. Beyond election on councils, there has also been in Britain a process of 'incorporation', measured here in Bobo and Gilliam's sense as the 'extent to which a group has achieved significant representation' coupled with their actual ability to exert 'influence in political decision-making' (1990, p. 378).

In France, there is no exhaustive survey of the number of ethnic minority councillors, but, by all accounts, North African populations have been under-represented in cities. In the 1989 municipal election, when mobilization in favour of local North African representation reached a peak in France, a nationwide initiative launched by the association France Plus managed to get only around 100 elected, according to one study;[16] another estimate put the figure at around 200, but even that remained very low.[17] After the 1995 elections, a survey carried out on a representative sample of French municipalities[18] found that only 4 per cent of the candidates surveyed were of 'immigrant' ('*immigré*') background, and that even among these, most were of European immigrant background, typically Portuguese or Spanish (Oriol, 1998). While the proportion of those candidates who actually succeeded in getting elected was not specified, it is highly probable that it was small, thus making extra-European ethnic minorities extremely under-represented in that election. Indeed, North African councillors were rare in France between 1995 and 2001, and the very few that were elected were almost always kept in subordinate or isolated positions. The complaint that only 'token Arabs'[19] were elected was universally heard in that period.

Only in 2001 did the trend change: in the municipal election that year, some 3.5 per cent of the newly elected councillors in the 109 French cities with more than 50,000 people were of Maghrebi background (Geisser and Oriol, 2001). As in the British case, these figures must be treated with caution. Many of these cities are either centres or suburbs of larger urban areas, notably of the Paris and Lyon area, which have many large suburbs. These cities most of the time have large ethnic minority populations. The proportion of 3.5 per cent therefore suggests a continuing level of under-representation in many of these cities, where the percentage of French men and women of North African background may often be much higher (and even more so if one adds the percentage of North African nationals who reside there). At any rate, 3.5 per cent indicates clear under-representation when juxtaposed with the proportion of 6.9 per cent of the total population. Still, compared to the very low number of candidates in 1995, it suggests a trend in the early 2000s in the direction of increasing representation.

While in Britain there had been pressure from the grassroots of the party to impose ethnic minority candidates, in France it was mostly party leaders who approached local personalities or leaders of associations to ask them to be candidates (*Le Monde*, 8/03/01). Many minority councillors were placed in lower positions on their party's lists, often in barely electable positions, and were therefore elected narrowly (see *Libération*, 02/03/01: 'Integrated, but at the end of the list'[20]). Accession to elected positions rarely meant accession to symbolic and powerful positions, such as the meaningful post of adjunct or mayor in medium or large cities. There was no notable change or innovation in the cities' attitudes towards their disadvantaged areas and populations after 2001.

As in Britain, the situation in France in 2001 differed often dramatically from one city to another. The largest cities, Lyon or Paris, still lagged behind other cities, while the third French city, Marseille, was among those with the most diverse city councils (Geisser and Oriol, 2002). There were also large variations among medium-sized or small cities. All of this suggests that, in both France and Britain, there was a chronological evolution from absence to inclusion of minorities on city councils in the 1980s and 1990s, but that it followed a distinctive path in the two countries:

1   It has taken place much earlier in Britain.
2   British minority councillors frequently have a career as party activists behind them, while their French counterparts are more frequently hand-picked among local personalities with little political clout.
3   The process appears irreversible and meaningful in terms of participation in actual decision-making in Britain, but there is still little sign of this in France.
4   The election of councillors was accompanied by the formulation and implementation of anti-discrimination policy agendas in Britain, which is not the case in France.

To these contrasts one must add differences between cities in the two countries. There are several reasons for these differences: the time lag between the migration processes, the differences between citizenship regimes, sociological and cultural differences between the minority populations of the two countries, all come into play.

Post-war immigration tended to peak approximately 10 years earlier in Britain than in France, with the strongest population flows arriving in Britain just before and just after the first restrictive Act in 1962 and in 1974, while a similar peak in migration occurred in France in the years preceding the official end of planned migration at the time of the first oil shock in 1974.[21] In 1966, the Survey of Race Relations estimated the total number of non-whites in Britain at around 924,000, while the number of foreigners from Africa in France (overwhelmingly from a Maghreb country) was only 428,160 in 1962, and 652,096 in 1968 (or about a third less than in Britain at the same period, for a comparable total population). In the first years of the 1970s the gap was closing, with an estimated 1.5 million people of New Commonwealth ethnic origins in Britain in 1971, or around 2.5 per cent of the population,[22] while in France in 1975 there were 1,192,300 foreigners from African countries (again almost all from Algeria, Morocco or Tunisia), or 2.26 per cent of the total population of France.

This time lag may account for some of the differences, in particular of course the fact that processes of inclusion on councils started earlier in Britain. Many of the political and social policy developments associated with immigration seem to have occurred in similar ways in both countries, but often earlier in Britain than in France, suggesting that it is simply following in the footsteps of Britain (argued by Lapeyronnie, who talks of the convergence of political agendas [1993, pp. 143–59]). First, the issue became politicized as early as the late 1950s in Britain, with riots and clear tendencies in the electorate to support xenophobic candidates, while both urban unrest and a racist vote only appeared in France some 25 years later, in the early 1980s. Similarly, Britain was first confronted with multiculturalist demands in the late 1960s, such as the desire of Sikhs to be able to wear traditional clothes at their workplace (Beetham, 1970), while comparable controversies over Muslim headscarves started to occur in France from 1989 onwards. The mobilization of left-wing and ethnic minority groups against racism and for minorities' rights in the 1970s in Britain can appear to be the precursor the Beur movement.[23] This was a nationwide protest movement of second-generation North Africans in the early and mid-1980s against exclusion and racism. Recent events in France, such as the remodelling of anti-discrimination policy after the British example of the 1960s and 1970s, also lend credence to this interpretation.

The difference between citizenship regimes is the other fundamental factor. Ethnic minorities from the New Commonwealth[24] who arrived in Britain before the restrictive acts passed from the early 1970s onwards have enjoyed full citizenship upon entry into Britain by virtue of the British Nationality Act of 1948. It perpetuated for the citizens of the New Commonwealth (ex-colonies) a tradition of free access to the British territory, and free exercise of voting rights, for all subjects of the British crown.[25] This very liberal policy, which changed only in 1981 with the British Nationality Act of 1981, has made the immigrant population a potentially powerful sub-group of the electorate since their arrival in the 1950s and 1960s. They have used their voting rights to significant effect at least since the mid-1970s, when they started being noted by political parties for registering and turning out in large numbers for elections (Community Relations Commission, 1975). In the 1990s, their registration rates were equal to those of whites for Asians, and significantly lower for blacks;[26] this difference is probably one factor that accounts for the higher number of Asian councillors compared to blacks. Whether black or Asian, they have tended overwhelmingly to support the Labour Party,[27] and indeed most of the ethnic minority councillors in Britain sit on Labour benches.

In France, by contrast, first-generation immigrants do not as a rule have the vote and cannot stand for election. This is obviously a fundamental explanation for their lack of representation. Only the North African second generation, which does have French citizenship, constitutes a pool of voters. It has taken time for many of them to become adults and to start to use their voting rights, in particular if one bears in mind the time lag between the two countries.

There are also differences between the organization of the immigrant communities of France and Britain that may account for their greater participation in Britain. Most ethnic minorities in Britain, whether from the West Indies or Asia, come from democracies, and have brought with them well-established participatory traditions. In the case of African-Caribbeans, there has been in particular a tradition of church-based mobilization and of sympathy for the American civil rights movement which has influenced political organization of that community in Britain. In the case of Indians and Pakistanis, a strong Marxist and left-wing culture among migrant workers led to the early establishment of strong Labour movements in the 1960s, such as the Indian Workers' Association (IWA), as well as a tendency to participate in native British trade union activity.

North Africans in France come largely from two countries, Morocco and Algeria, which have weak democratic traditions. Their governments have sought for a long time to control their populations through community organizations, the Amicales, which are linked to their networks of consulates in France's main cities. As a result, participation in union activities or political parties does exist (for instance, Moroccans have long been active in student unions) but is limited. In the case of Algerians, the war of independence against France from 1954 to 1962, when a large community was already settled in the north of France, made them a suspicious population that was closely watched by the French police and secret services. This made it difficult for them and their members to develop ties with French unions and parties, although some of the latter were in favour of Algerian independence and staged rallies and demonstrations to support it (Mouriaux and Wihtol de Wenden, 1987). The difficulty was compounded by violent conflict between competing factions of the independence movement (Mouvement National Algérien [MNA] against the Front de Libération Nationale [FLN]), in which several thousand members of the Algerian community in France were killed in the 1950s (Freeman, 1979, pp. 41ff.; Stora, 1992; Genty, 1999).

One can also note that the socio-economic stratification of the groups in each country is different, and the development of an ethnic minority middle class seemed to occur earlier in Britain, among blacks as well as Asians (Cashmore, 1992; Deakins and Ram, 1996). This may explain greater access to conventional politics on the part of British minorities, in particular in the case of the Indian community, part of which originates in wealthy business *milieux* in India and East Africa. However, the hypothesis of a correlation between higher income and success in local elections is not very persuasive, since communities with very low economic status in Britain, such as Pakistanis in inner cities, frequently obtain high levels of representation on city councils.

Towards an Analysis of Local Political Processes

To these explanations of the British–French contrast, the book seeks to add an additional, and more wholly persuasive, explanation, based on an institutional perspective on ethnic minority politics. The main rationale for this is that since the election of city councillors is by definition a political subject, it is necessary to examine its political context and determinants in order to understand not just its timing, but also the paths of access to election, the factors that explain the influence of councillors, or lack thereof, once they are elected, and the direction in which this influence is exerted. The differences in the levels and styles of election on councils between cities within one country suggest that it is also tributary to the organizational and political features of localized political processes that can be explained even less by nationwide demographic trends. The contention of the book is that institutional and political factors, and the ways in which they have combined and created specific local political dynamics, have compounded demographic, legal and sociological factors to reinforce the contrast between the two countries as well as to shape local variations.

Lapeyronnie's suggestion of a parallel evolution in the two countries is based on a comparison of broad socio-economic tendencies because his overarching thesis posits a decline of traditional institutions of socialization of the working class, across all countries in western Europe. As such it views developments related to immigration as one element that fits into these broader, parallel transformations. But comparing modes of election of ethnic minorities between countries and cities requires a more precise analysis. Many of those events in France that seem to emulate British developments in fact take different directions: the racist far right in Britain has only had temporary successes, while the French Front National blossomed from 1983 into a major national force well entrenched in grassroots politics across the country, even spectacularly recovering from a split after 1998. Crowley and Weil noted a decade ago that the comparison of the two trajectories could very well be turned on its head, with French developments announcing possible British changes:

> Some common features between France today and Britain a decade or two ago (preoccupation with immigration control, the 'youth' issue, Le Pen/Powell, Hijab/Turban, etc.) suggest that France might move towards a British situation. On the contrary, one could argue that France's adoption (in the 1970s) and sub-

sequent abandonment of multiculturalism shows that community-based integration does not work and points to an inevitable evolution in British thinking.
(1994, p. 124)

Most importantly for this book, the Beur movement of the 1980s focused from
the start on issues of citizenship and recognition of cultural difference for
second-generation migrants, issues which are quite distinct from those of anti-
racist struggle and relations between races on which black and Asian activists
focused in the 1970s. In addition, if the Beur movement had been destined
to emulate the anti-racist movements of the 1970s in Britain, this would have
translated into lasting political and policy change as it did in Britain; instead,
however, the movement met with failure and almost entirely disappeared at
the end of the 1980s. Why did it manage to lead to the election of around
200 councillors in 1989, and why were all these councillors marginalized in
their councils and not subsequently re-elected in the following 1995 elections?
Why were those elected in 2001 not radical and anti-racist activists, as was
the case for the black and Asian Britons elected in the early 1980s, but in
many cases somewhat apolitical or inexperienced individuals hastily chosen
by parties from the local community? Why are they still under-represented,
and why are local policies not reflecting a clear dedication to anti-discrimination policies? And how can we explain differences among cities in the two
countries?

The fact that a majority of immigrants were deprived of voting rights must
also not be overestimated because the residential concentration of these
populations in certain urban areas has given at least some weight to these
electors. One must also add to electors the first-generation immigrants who
do have a vote through naturalization or dual nationality (around 15 per cent
of Moroccans and 8 per cent of Algerians[28]). The electoral significance of
minority populations in city politics has been visible since 1989, when the
interest of political parties in putting Beur candidates on their lists was to a
large extent motivated by electoral considerations. Their electoral weight
varied from city to city according to their level of residential concentration
and according to the mix of ethnic origin in each city. But Kelfaoui (1996)
also notes that the levels of registration of North African French men and
women depended largely on whether local authorities or local political parties
were actively or not promoting their participation. Why there was such active
promotion of their participation in some cities, but not in most, is something
that needs to be explained.

It must also be noted that those European countries that granted voting
rights in local elections to their foreign migrant populations often did so very
early on in the migration process, in the 1970s or early 1980s. This means
that by the late 1980s and early 1990s there was in all these countries some
sort of ethnic minority representation in local councils (Le Cour de Grand-

maison and Wihtol de Wenden, 1993). In sharp contrast, the proposal has never gained much currency in France despite repeated campaigns. The proposal was dropped in the early 1980s after being agitated by the Socialist Party in the 1981 presidential election campaign, and it was dismissed again by a Socialist government in 2000 when proposed by their Green coalition partners. Between these two moments the idea was often put forward but it was always intently ignored by major political parties. These repeated dismissals have perpetuated for a particularly long – and continuing – period the disenfranchising effects of the French citizenship regime on first-generation migrants, and constitute one more puzzle on the French side.

The differences between the two countries are to some extent shaped by differences between aforementioned 'incorporation frameworks', which have reverberated with the factors discussed above. While Britain and France have both displayed in the past a tendency to rely on assimilationist stances to integrate migrants, their frameworks have also presented variations. Brubaker (1992) has argued that French and German historical legacies keep the nationality and citizenship regimes of these two countries in separate tracks, and Schnapper (1991, 1992) has argued that France is characterized by a specific model of incorporation, namely incorporation through assimilation. This assimilationist French model has often been contrasted with an essentially differential, ethnicist Anglo-American model of management of minorities.

But this claim freezes the two countries in fixed realities that ignore their repeated reversals in the domain of immigration and integration policies. As Joppke points out:

> In particular French authors have been fond of identifying the 'minoritarian' logic of British immigrant integration, juxtaposing it to the norm of Republican assimilation in France (e.g. Schnapper, 1992: 108–13). This is at best a half-truth, for two reasons. First, as Patrick Weil and John Crowley (1994: 112) have seen, there is 'no common British myth, widely shared across the spectrum of political opinion'. Accordingly, integration policy has been more driven by pragmatism than by principle, and its direction has at times been severely contested. Secondly, the stress on group particularism ignores the countervailing citizenship universalism that has also been at work in Britain. (Joppke, 1999, p. 224)

More convincing are works that emphasize institutional and political differences which, while durably entrenched, are also linked to clearly delimited periods, or policy cycles, resulting from specific conditions and determined in time. One such analysis that must be put forward is that Britain tended, on the whole, to depart from an 'assimilationist' attitude towards a more 'pluralist' style from the mid-1960s onwards (Castles, 1995). Goulbourne proposes the notion of 'new pluralism' to characterize 1980s and 1990s Britain (Goulbourne, 1991, 1998). The 1960s 'liberal hour' saw an ideological shift from this benign neglect approach to a formulation in terms of 'relations between communities', policies against racial discrimination and multiculturalist educational policies.

This new official policy line was institutionalized from 1965 in important and well-implemented anti-discriminatory legislation, with the Race Relations Acts of 1965, 1968 and 1976, and official recommendations for the furthering of 'harmonious relations between communities' at the local level. This was inspired notably by black and Asian pressure groups such as CARD (Campaign Against Racial Discrimination), which were themselves influenced by the American civil rights movement (Bleich, 2003; for a detailed presentation of the Race Relations Act, see Goulbourne, 1998, ch. 5, pp. 100–22). This legislation was also facilitated by the influence of academic works which approached the issue of immigration as an issue of racism and racial disadvantage (notably Rose et al., 1969; Rex and Moore, 1967; Rex and Tomlinson, 1979).

France also passed a law against racial discrimination in 1972, but with less emphasis on discrimination against extra-European immigrants, and, indeed, it has had a very limited impact up to now. It also proved virtually impossible to implement because it made racial discrimination a criminal offence, where the task of establishing proof of the crime lies with the prosecution. Arguably, this lack of enthusiasm for strongly enforced anti-discrimination laws on the part of French elites derived from the fact that those most concerned with the issue were pressure groups related to the Communist Party. They construed racism as principally an anti-Semitic crime of Nazi inspiration, and they shunned any American influence, in contrast to the aforementioned British groups (Bleich, 1997, 2003). Furthermore, in France, the individualistic assimilationist ideology that serves as the guideline for all policies was seldom challenged in the 1980s and 1990s, except during a multiculturalist stint in several policy areas by the moderate right-wing governments of the mid-1970s, when Portuguese and Arabic classes for children of immigrants were tentatively introduced in some schools (Weil, 1995a, pp. 384–90).

These differences explain why Soysal placed France and Britain in different categories in her typology: she regarded France as a 'statist' model, while she construed Britain, together with Switzerland, as typically 'liberal'. France was 'statist' because it had a centralized organization focused on the state, and Britain was 'liberal' because it was considered to have a decentralized organization focused on society (Soysal, 1994, p. 37). This classification highlights the fact that there has been an emphasis on voluntary organizations as ways of aggregating immigrants' interests. Indeed, quantitative data lend some credence to this by showing that British ethnic minorities frequently formulate claims in terms that are induced by the British legal and institutional structure of opportunity, in terms of religious/cultural specificities and local group recognition (Koopmans and Statham, 2000b).

In France, the volatile issue in France of nationality and immigration law is by definition dealt with at the national level. Likewise, the French state, often in cooperation with French business interests, closely planned and controlled migratory flows into France from the outset, encouraging or restricting flows according to economic circumstances (Freeman, 1979).

The late 1990s seemed to mark the end of this policy cycle that had seen the two national frameworks drift away from each other, and the beginning of a new cycle, which can be interpreted as a new convergence. Clear signs of a return to a more assimilationist perspective appeared in the early 2000s in Britain in the policies of Home Secretary David Blunkett. The 'Cantle Report', which he commissioned after severe riots in the summer of 2001 in the Asian areas of Bradford, Oldham and Burnley, stigmatized the 'parallel' and 'polarized' lives led by people of different ethnic origins.[29] It called for a strong concept of citizenship. Later, Blunkett called for an oath of allegiance proving loyalty to 'British values' for newly naturalized citizens. In 2004, the Commission for Racial Equality (CRE), which has long embodied Britain's proactive race policies, was to be merged with other bodies that work against discrimination to form a new institution less directly focused on race issues.

Symmetrically, France seemed to edge towards a new-found interest in the recognition and institutionalization of minority religions, which it had avoided until then, with the creation in 2002 of the Conseil Français du Culte Musulman (CFCM, French Council of the Muslim Faith). The CFCM is intended to work as the official voice of the Muslim community in France. Its members are elected by local Muslim clerics and are representative of the main trends in French Islam, in particular Algerian, Moroccan and Turkish. In the field of anti-discrimination, change seemed to be coming too in 2004, with the creation of a new body with more extensive powers in that domain, the Haute Autorité de Lutte contre les Discriminations et l'Exclusion (HALDE, High Authority for Combating Discrimination and Exclusion). It took its inspiration from the British CRE, which seemed about to disappear in Britain.

But all these remarks concern the election of councillors indirectly only. Soysal and Goulbourne are concerned with, respectively, the rules of membership for migrants in western European welfare states, and the relation between nationality and ethnicity in Britain. All of these are related to patterns of political struggles of immigrant groups in local political systems, but only partially. The main point of both these authors is that a pluralist model recognizes and institutionalizes minorities, through specific social and educational policies, and through anti-discrimination policies, even if not in an official, corporatist manner. But this is not enough to account for faster empowerment in that type of model than in an assimilationist model. In addition, beyond the differences in timing and levels of representation, the differences between the paths of access to elected office also need more explanatory elements in order to be properly accounted for.

Two things are lacking. First, the consequences of these elements are often more far reaching than a rapid analysis reveals. It is not enough to know that the French nationality code has kept disenfranchised most first-generation migrants, or that the main policy guideline in matters of 'integration' has been universalistic assimilation; it is also crucial to understand the multiple repercussions this has had in framing and defining political debates, on elite and popular perceptions of migrants, on the divisions it has entailed among migrant and ethnic minority activists, and on their political agendas. In addition, the political debates surrounding immigration policy, as well as nationality policy, have a strong impact on 'integration' policies. The way immigrants are defined and discussed in immigration and nationality politics orients and limits integration policies. More profoundly yet, they shape the very understanding that all actors have of the legitimate place of minorities in society and in political institutions.

Second, the two most important aspects of the British–French contrast need to be highlighted: (1) the eminently party-political character of the problem, as also noted by Koopmans and Statham (2000a, introduction), and (2) its local dimension. The latter is also made necessary by the important intra-city variations observed earlier. Even when it is limited to protest, or even violence, ethnic minority participation in cities is often directed towards affecting institutionalized arenas of power. As such, it is more or less directly subjected to the rules of conventional politics in cities; it is part and parcel of locally defined political struggles, and must therefore be studied as a sub-field of local politics. In this perspective, the differences in timing can be more clearly and forcefully explained, as well as the variations between cities.

Research that reflects this understanding of the subject exists on both sides of the Channel.[30] What is generally lacking in these works is a comparative approach, both international and between cities (with the exception of Favell, 1998). Most French and British research has been nationally bounded, not least because each has been rooted in its nationally defined normative underpinnings: first 'race relations', then 'ethnic diversity' and multiculturalism in Britain, and the 'integration' of immigrants and the post-industrial disintegration of 'social links' in France.

To remedy this lack of research focused on the political, local and comparative aspects of migrant participation, this book builds on a strand of research that has sought to bring new institutionalist approaches to the study of the politics of immigration, ethnicity and citizenship, and has recently started focusing on the local aspect of the question (Bousetta, 1997, 2001; Ireland, 1994; Jones-Correa, 2001). In a nutshell, this type of approach consists in proposing institutional variables as explanatory factors for cross-national variations in patterns of ethnic minority politics. The book applies this framework to a comparison of selected case studies in the two countries in order to account for cross-city differences and to highlight the local political processes at work that fully account for differing levels of representation. The comparison addresses these differences in the two countries with the contrasting cases of Birmingham and Lille. But it also seeks to nuance the conclusion derived from the French case by including a second French city, Roubaix, where local factors have played out differently and have allowed for a burgeoning trend of minority inclusion on the city council.

This approach is elaborated in chapter 1. The chapter begins by transposing to the study of urban politics approaches derived from the politics of ethnically divided countries that argue that the elites of these countries have been able to use institutional arrangements to maintain the stability of their political systems. I suggest that patterns of minority participation in the three cities under discussion are largely shaped by the strategies of local elites, co-optation or absence of co-optation. I also ground the comparison in historical-institutionalist theory. I devise a framework for the explanation of variations between these strategies that consists of three variables: (1) national politics of immigration and centre–periphery relations; (2) local parties and party systems; and (3) styles of local government. I then introduce the selected cases for comparison and explain in detail how the national variables are applied to these case studies in the rest of the book.

1

Historical Institutionalism and the Comparison of Local Cases

Strategies of Management of Ethnic Conflict and Historical Institutionalism

Ireland (1994) and Bousetta (1997, 2001) constructed institutionalist narratives to account for variations in styles of political organization and participation of minorities between countries and cities, arguing that elements such as citizenship frameworks, legal frameworks for community organization or ideology of party in power form structures of opportunity that shape styles of participation. Ireland called it 'institutional channelling' (1994, p. 8), while Bousetta talks of 'citizenship framework' (1997, p. 216). Some approaches to ethnic politics in American cities, for instance that of Jones-Correa, also emphasize institutional environments as causal factors for patterns of cooperation and conflict among ethnic groups (Jones-Correa, 2001).

Like these authors, I turn towards institutions as powerful constraints on patterns of minority politics, with however, three innovations. I move away from their 'bottom-up' approaches, which construe the styles of mobilization of minorities as their dependent variables, and prefer a 'top-down' approach, focusing on the strategies of the local elites in managing both immigrant mobilizations and xenophobic mobilization against immigrants. This enables a more direct focus on the party-political dimension of ethnic minority politics, giving more prominence to the dynamics of the interplay between minority activists and community leaders, on one side, and local politicians and party organizations, on the other. I draw more heavily on historical-institutionalist theory, following the lead of a growing body of research on immigration and citizenship that is also based on historical-institutionalist hypotheses (such as Guiraudon, 2000; Favell, 1998; Hansen, 2000; Bleich, 2003). This aims in particular at exploring in greater depth the effect of institutions on outcomes, in particular their role in framing issues and actors' goals, and not just as constraining their strategies. Finally, my institutional framework is limited to a number of selected institutional variables at the local level, in an attempt to create a parsimonious explanation of variations.

Strategies of management of ethnic conflict

I derive the focus on the attitudes of city elites from the institutional approaches of ethnic conflict explored by Nordlinger (1972), Esman (1973) and Horowitz (1985) to the study of the politics of ethnic minorities in French and British cities. The main thrust of these authors' arguments is that the elites of states that are faced with cross-cutting ethnic conflicts are able to maintain the stability of the system by using institutional arrangements as instruments. I seek to transpose this type of model to the urban politics of ethnic minorities, viewing the strategies of elites in dealing with minority-related issues as 'strategies of management of ethnic conflict' (using Esman's terminology; 1973, p. 52).

I consider that the governments of cities in western Europe are broadly autonomous, in that they have interests which are distinct from the interests of other actors, and particularly from those of local groups and local economic interests, on one side, and from those of the central state, on the other. They are considered as independent political actors. Their general interest is to stay in power, and, to this end, to maintain law and order and to sustain continued electoral support for themselves.

The presence of a large ethnic minority population within the territorial boundaries of local government has become a challenge to these objectives, because it creates a new socio-economic cleavage that translates into political conflict. It is in this perspective that ethnic minorities can be defined as populations which share an interest in agendas of struggle against racial discrimination and recognition of cultural and religious difference in various policy areas, in particular education and the construction of custom-built places of worship. The cleavage between these populations and native, 'white' populations is complex and overlaps with other cleavages. Most notably, they are overwhelmingly lower-income households and they have tended to vote principally for left-wing parties, when they vote (Saggar, 1998b; Anwar 1994, 1998, for Britain; and Kelfaoui, 1996; Richard, 1999, for France). The conflict is thus not just an ethnic one but a combination of ethnic and class conflicts. Ethnic minorities of recent immigrant origins also have a very specific relation to space, because they have no claim to sovereignty on a part of the territory of the nation-state in which they live (contrary to native ethnic minorities, as the Basques in Spain or the Corsicans in France), and because for the most part they are concentrated in specific areas of cities.

The presence of these minorities, and the reaction of native populations to this presence, does translate into political conflicts of a specific nature, and this type of conflict entails fundamental and specific challenges for cities. First, it breeds public disorder, both from second-generation immigrants who express frustration at racial discrimination coupled with economic disadvantage, and from violent anti-immigrant movements. Most cities with a high concentration of immigrant populations in both France and Britain have been shaken by riots or low-intensity disorder, with large riots in 1958, 1981 and 1985 in Britain, and in 1981 and 1989 in France. Second, it is often correlated with the development of anti-immigrant political movements which directly undermine electoral support for the mainstream political establishment, such as the Front National in France or the strong anti-immigrant movement that developed in the 1960s and 1970s in Britain around Enoch Powell, then the National Front. Both these movements scored well in local elections, although the Front National much more spectacularly and lastingly so than its British counterpart. In the 1960s, British cities also came under pressure to take anti-immigrant stances from local xenophobic community associations, often connected with the Conservative Party (Hill and Issacharoff, 1971, p. 50). Third, and most important, ethnic groups often mobilize and formulate specific policy demands: recognition of specific cultural needs (typically the construction of mosques, and catering for Muslim pupils' specific requirements in schools), official policy against racial discrimination and representation in political assemblies are often perceived by mainstream politicians, rightly or wrongly, as potentially divisive for their electorate. All of these problems pose a serious threat to the goals of local authorities (and arguably more strongly than to those of the central state [Le Galès, 1995]).

Significant waves of mobilization in local representative politics happened at approximately the same periods of time in France and Britain. In the late 1970s, both 'black' and 'Asian' community leaders and political activists were starting to appear on local scenes. They were from various backgrounds: church-based groups for African-Caribbeans, Muslim leaders from the Pakistani and increasingly the Bangladeshi community, anti-racist activists, and left-wing unionists and party activists, all concerned with local politics. In France, the mass protest movement of the Beurs (second-generation North African immigrants) that started in 1983 led to the emergence of a flurry of associations that were active in local arenas. In the 1990s, individuals of immigrant origins were also very active in local associations and sought to play an active role in municipal politics.

The strategies of management of ethnic conflict are understood as the practices that the local elected governments of cities use to minimize the challenges posed by these mobilizations. They have most of the time been characterized by a dilemma between two conflicting aims: give in to ethnic minorities' demands (recognition of, and accommodation for, cultural difference and implementation of policies against racial discrimination), on the one hand, or, on the other hand, give in to those who express anti-immigrant feelings or refuse to recognize that the issue is a legitimate political issue and seek to keep it off the local political agenda. The strategies of cities have varied considerably within each of our two countries between those two extremes in the 1980s and 1990s. They have ranged between: (1) explicit anti-immigrant attitudes (for instance Leicester City Council during the Ugandan-Asian crisis of 1973, or Birmingham in the late 1950s, for Britain; and the Communist Parisian suburb of Vitry in the late 1970s, for France [Schain, 1993]); (2) 'benign neglect', or the refusal to acknowledge that there is a conflict with a need for ad hoc policies and increased representation, as is the case for most French cities, and in some British cities controlled by the Conservatives; and (3) explicitly 'pro-ethnic minority' stands, chiefly characterized by the establishment of various kinds of political and electoral alliances with ethnic minority groups, as in many British cities since the 1980s.

In the latter cases, where elites give in to minority demands, this often takes the place of facilitation of election through the formation of a governing coalition. This can take several forms and lead to varying degrees and styles of incorporation. Examples from black and Latino incorporation in American cities are classified by Browning, Marshall and Tabb (1984, p. 47) into the following typology: (1) biracial electoral alliance; (2) co-optation; (3) protest and exclusion; (4) weak minority mobilization.

In a biracial electoral alliance, 'a liberal electoral coalition with strong minority participation is formed prior to the period of peak minority demand–protest and results in strong incorporation'; co-optation consists of an 'electoral coalition led by whites with minorities in subordinate roles', and the result is 'partial incorporation'; protest and exclusion defines a situation 'where strong demand–protest is met by a tenacious, resistant dominant coalition' and leads to 'exclusion for some time'; and weak minority mobilization is when there is 'little or no concerted demand–protest activity and fragmented electoral effort is met by a resistant dominant coalition', leading to failure to achieve 'incorporation' (Brown, Marshall and Tabb, 1984, p. 47).

An attempt to apply this typology to British cities would come close to the second type of incorporation, co-optation, because minority activists who made it into city councils were mostly chosen individually in the context of grassroots politics. Yet it is difficult to rule out the first type, 'biracial electoral alliance', because, as mentioned earlier, the presence of these individuals was also the electoral expression of coordinated movements within parties supporting anti-discrimination and pro-diversity agendas. One can characterize Manchester (Ben-Tovim et al., 1986) Birmingham, Wolverhampton, Coventry (Joly and Candappa, 1994), Bradford, Leicester and many Labour-held boroughs of London (Joppke, 1999, p. 244) as mixing elements of co-optation and biracial electoral alliance.

Meanwhile, there has been no such shift in France in the 1980s and 1990s, but rather a stalemate, in which original hostility has endured or turned into indifference, with most cities avoiding dealing with the issue and ignoring demands for recognition and participation on the part of minorities. Those French city elites who in some instances were enticed to engage in co-optation activities of their own in the 1980s usually did so in very limited ways and abandoned them quite rapidly, because of limited strategic use or because of outright failure (Wihtol de Wenden, 1988, p. 282). For instance, a challenge to the Socialist council of Grenoble by moderate right-winger Alain Carignon led him to take on board one symbolic North African councillor for the 1989 election; and an experiment in consultation with community leaders in the same city has also failed (*Libération*, 2/05/00). Similarly, Socialist leaders in the Lyon suburbs frequently sought to appeal to their North African electorate in the 1980s by taking one North African candidate on their lists, but with short-lived and limited results (Geisser, 1997, pp. 136f.).

When ethnic minorities finally appeared in local councils in 2001, the strategy of party officials drawing up the lists can be described, more firmly than in Britain, as much closer to co-optation than to a biracial electoral alliance. These candidates were in many cases not representing ethnic constituencies, or agendas explicitly related to ethnic disadvantage, but were chosen from within the local community by party list-makers at the time of the election. When they were members of parties, they were in many cases not associated with specific agendas as part of their activities in the party. Their presence on a list was frequently intended in many cases as a broad political statement, simply indicating recognition of the changing make-up of French society. This recognition was noted guardedly in the media, and usually interpreted as an overdue correction of past exclusion.

There were some attempts at articulating issues pertaining to ethnic disadvantage as part of a left-wing coalition, but with little success. The most important one was in the large southwestern city of Toulouse, where the alternative left 'Motivé-e-s' list[1] had a large number of immigrants and others from disadvantaged backgrounds, and campaigned on the theme of a deep social divide in the city: wealthy, white, city-centre dwellers vs. economically unstable, ethnically mixed suburbanites. The list reached a significant score of around 10 per cent in the first round, and became a central partner in the Socialist-led coalition in the second round. But the coalition was defeated by the centre-right list that was its main opponent[2] (*Libération*, 19/03/01; Moore in Kraal et al., 2004).

Historical institutionalism

Historical institutionalism (or HI) is one of three strands of institutionalist approaches that sought to rejuvenate political science's longstanding interest in political institutions in the 1990s, with rational choice institutionalism and sociological institutionalism mostly being presented as the two other main strands.[3] What all three have in common that distinguishes them from old institutionalism is that they do not just study institutions per se, they also analyse the causal role that these have on political change. In this, they all build on the main teaching of behavioural approaches applied to the social sciences that construes individual behavior as the impetus for change; but they maintain an interest in institutions because the latter help to explain the behaviour of individuals (March and Olsen, 1989, introduction). In rational choice institutionalism, institutions are 'rules of the game', such as laws that constrain the strategies pursued by rational and utility-maximizing actors to pursue their objectives. In sociological institutionalism, they are given a wider definition to encompass norms, conventions and routines, and they impact on individuals' behaviours profoundly, compelling them to conformism. In this light, institutional change can be interpreted as institutional isomorphism, the result of processes of imitation and adaptation of institutions at the macro level (Koelbe, 1995, p. 235)

An influential definition of institutions among historical-institutionalist writers presents them as 'formal rules, compliance procedures, and standard operating practices that structure the relationship between individuals and various units of the polity and economy' (Hall, 1986).[4] Unlike rational choice institutionalism, it does not just consider institutions as constraints and incentives for actors' strategies, which implies that the formation of actors' preferences is factored out, but on the contrary seeks to show how institutions not only determine these strategies, but also, beyond this, how they also shape the formation of the actors' goals (Steinmo, Thelen and Longstreth, 1992, p. 7; Hall, 1986, p. 19). Unlike sociological institutionalism, it is unambiguous with regards to political culture, clearly excluding it; and HI also perceives the actor as a rational agent whose strategic decisions, while informed by institutional settings, do have a degree of autonomy. This makes it possible to devote attention to logics of competition and alliance between actors while not losing sight of the defining and framing power of institutions.

Institutions are often construed by historical institutionalists as expressions of previous political and sociological patterns; through them, past political situations, as they are encapsulated and transmitted over time in institutions, act as forces that shape and define the interests and goals of present actors (Hall, 1986, p. 19). Therefore, their utilization as explanatory variables makes possible a contribution to the discussion of national models rooted in history, and their impact on contemporary developments. But HI also leaves some room for an understanding of rapid change, in a more evident way than sociological institutionalism. HI studies have shown how social or economic evolutions increase or decrease the importance of institutions, giving them new 'roles' when strategic actors, whose fortunes and aspirations change, come to react to the influence of old institutional settings in new ways (Koelble, 1995, p. 238).

HI focuses on meso-level institutions, typically established patterns of interest representation, party politics or state organization (for instance Skocpol, 1979; Hall, 1986), as opposed to macro institutions, such as class conflicts or capitalism, which often explain general cross-national similarities. Hence, HI is heuristic for the study of variations between patterns of ethnic politics in western European countries because these are characterized by a broad resemblance, but a closer focus reveals differences. Working-class, post-colonial immigrants form a part of the 'underclass' of western industrialized democracies (Castles and Kozack, 1973). These communities are generally excluded from their institutions of power, but differences occur between the specific modalities of this pattern: more obvious, and permanent, political exclusion, in some cases rather than others, and varying paths toward inclusion, when the latter does take place.

HI is therefore well suited to nuancing and renewing debates on national models of participation and reactions of nation-states to the arrival of immigrants, as well as the processes of participation of immigrants in pre-existing structures. Nuancing deterministic accounts of national models of immigration politics such as Brubaker's and Schnapper's, which posit a rather monolithic link between fixed historical legacies and models of incorporation, the institutionalist literature on immigration and citizenship seeks to highlight the conditions in which various sub-elements of state structures may hinder, trigger and shape permanence and changes in styles of participation and inclusion.

Central and local factors

Rather than being shaped just by local factors, local politics are shaped at the same time by both national and local forces. Both types superimpose themselves on localities, and the study of local cases invariably reveals complex relations between them. I nonetheless operate an analytical distinction between the two, resulting in the construction of two types of variables: 'national frameworks' and local frameworks.

'National frameworks': national politics of immigration and central–local relations. National developments have a very strong impact because a large part of what politically defines ethnic minorities in relatively homogeneous nation-states such as Britain and France is their extra-national origin. While I have noted that the local level is pertinent to the discussion of minority-related issues, it would be difficult to ignore national-level developments in the national politics of organization of immigration flows, restriction of migration and discussion of status given to foreigners or newcomers. In both countries, the main institutional determinants of these developments are citizenship laws, ideological trends and policy guidelines, structures of party systems, organization of national bureaucracies and organization of central–local relations in each country. The latter, in particular, is emphasized, because it shapes the ways in which national developments impact on the grassroots. These constitute what I call 'national frameworks'.

The national frameworks have shaped outcomes in ethnic minority incorporation in two ways. They have worked as distinct sets of 'rules of the game' that have constrained actors' access to political resources, thus influencing their strategies. The differences between the citizenship regimes of the two countries must be emphasized here. They have also worked, as this book will seek to show, to frame different perceptions of the legitimate place of ethnic minorities vis-à-vis the political system. In turn, these perceptions have played a strong role in determining the attitude of political elites vis-à-vis ethnic minority mobilizations and would-be councillors. In particular, the book shows how the politics of *immigration* have defined fields of possibilities in the domain of *integration* policies: how debates on migration flows and their legitimacy shape debates on the legitimacy of migrants' and minorities' claim to belong to society and to participate in its institutions.

Many of those national institutions that have an impact on local developments rooted in history and, in many instances, in past developments institutionalized in legal dispositions and administrative statutes, have a path-dependency effect on contemporary developments, as shown by the institutionalist literature on the subject (particularly Hansen, 2000). For this reason, I will analyse national developments as they unfold from the post-war years until the period in which I study the cities, the 1980s and 1990s.

The 'locality' factor: parties and party systems, and styles of local government. There are two types of local variables: those common to all or large numbers of localities, and those that are idiosyncratic to one locality. With respect to the politics of minorities, those common to all or many localities are local electoral systems, the organization of local authorities, patterns of party organization and of internal party politics that are to be found in several or all cities of one country. Variables specific to localities include patterns of internal party politics, patterns of community organization, and patterns of relations between local authorities and local groups. They often find their roots in local history, and, as becomes particularly evident in the French case studies, they play a large role in explaining differences between cities. Most importantly, it is the very localized and specific patterns of combination of all of these factors in each city that shape their specificities.

I operate a distinction between local parties and party systems on the one hand, and local styles of organization of local government on the other. The first variable is a crucial one. All three case studies highlight the high control exercised by parties, cliques and trends within parties, and the relative place of parties to each other in local political competition, on representative politics and, therefore, their importance in shaping patterns of minority participation. First, parties can campaign to increase the electoral participation of minorities. Second, they can co-opt activists and staff of ethnic minority background, who are then able to stand as candidates for the parties and attract ethnic minority votes. Third, they can promote minority-related issues in local political debates because they are often actors with privileged access to media and public exposure. In all these ways, they are often the main springboard for the incorporation of the latter into the political system.

The styles of organization of governments are electoral systems, and the ways in which they combine with residential concentrations and local tradition of management of communities: styles of relations between local authorities and the interests of local communities. Electoral systems consist of electoral districting, which, combined with patterns of segregation of ethnic minorities, give them more or less electoral clout. They also include modes of election, majoritarian or proportional, single candidate or list systems, etc. The first element, the political geography of minority politics, is a structural determinant of minority politics in cities. The latter elements play a secondary role in explaining outcomes, compared to the other variables. In some cases they are important because they can amplify their effects, for instance if they channel the choice of a candidate towards one well-placed decision-maker.

In sum, I focus on three types of variables: (1) national frameworks, consisting of history of immigration politics and central–local relations in each country; (2) local party politics; and (3) styles of local government. These three variables combine in different ways in each British and French city to produce an institutional framework.

Birmingham, Lille and Roubaix, 1980s–2001

Birmingham in Britain, and the Lille–Roubaix–Tourcoing area in France, have been selected for their comparability on the basis of social and economic criteria. Both are among the largest cities of their country. Both are old industrial zones that lie at the heart of large industrial urban areas, the West Midlands and the Nord-Pas-de-Calais. In both cases, post-colonial ethnic minorities (predominantly Pakistanis, Indians and West Indians in Birmingham, and Moroccans and Algerians in the Lille area) make up a significant fraction of the population. They are overwhelmingly working class, with high unemployment rates, especially among the young, with some variations between groups. In both cases they are concentrated in particular areas of the city: the inner-city areas in Birmingham, the southern periphery of Lille, and specific areas within the cities of Roubaix and Tourcoing outside Lille. My analysis of minority politics in the two areas is based on extensive personal interviews with members of local councils, officers in local administrations, community leaders and political activists, previous academic works and newspaper sources (see appendix).

In the time period chosen for the study, from the early 1980s to 2001, there was widespread racial discrimination against minorities in the two urban areas, as well as widespread awareness of this on the part of the minorities. Both cities have suffered from significant disturbances and riots in neighbourhoods with large ethnic minority populations. Finally, both cities have been controlled by the mainstream left for a long time (the Labour Party in Birmingham since 1983, and the Socialist Party in the Communauté Urbaine de Lille, which has functioned as a grouping of the communes of the area since its creation in the 1960s). In a nutshell, Birmingham and the Lille area were both controlled by the moderate left in the period considered, and they have large ratios of immigrant/native populations (following the criteria used by Browning, Marshall and Tabb, 1990, for the comparison of ethnic minority politics between American cities).

A fundamental difference between the two cities is that Birmingham is one large city, while the Lille–Roubaix–Tourcoing urban zone is fragmented. There are zones which are part of the Birmingham urban area and which are governed by other city councils, such as Wolverhampton or Dudley, but the Birmingham City Council itself covers a very large zone at the centre of the area, and is the largest local authority in Britain since the abolition of the Greater London Council (GLC), with close to 1 million inhabitants. By contrast, the Lille–Roubaix–Tourcoing urban area is sprawling and institutionally fragmented into 87 communes, with only the three largest, Lille, Roubaix and Tourcoing, topping or coming close to 100,000 people, with populations of, respectively, 178,000, 97,000 and 93,000. While this reflects the fragmentation that is common to French cities, this represents an extreme case. Each of the 87 communes has an elected *conseil municipal* (municipal council) and each is thus a distinct political arena from its neighbours. The Communauté Urbaine de Lille (Greater Lille Urban Community) plays an important role in local politics and policy-making, but it is elected indirectly, by the members of local elected authorities that are part of its geographical remit. Because it is impossible to study all 87 communes, the book focuses on the largest and most significant.

These two cities form an interesting Franco-French comparative duo in the context of my hypotheses. They are the two most important communes in terms of immigrant population in the area, with nationals of North African countries making up, respectively, 7 per cent and 15 per cent of their total population.[5] Cities in France display a large variety of political configurations, because of the diversity of their local traditions, the greater number of parties that control cities, the diversity of sizes, geographical situations and socio-economic structures of cities that have large minority populations, and the relative positions of French communes to one another in the context of inter-communal structures. Lille and Roubaix offer a series of contrasts which encompass many of these factors and make it possible to use them to some extent as test cases for each other.

The patterns of interaction between cities in the context of these inter-communal structures are often one important institutional factor in shaping the politics of ethnic minorities through their impact on housing policies and regeneration programmes. Roubaix is also often noted as a particularly inter-esting case of successful immigrant incorporation, and as such is a particu-larly welcome test case to Lille, where even after the modest increase in minority representation nationwide in 2001, Lille continued to lag behind. Birmingham has not been matched by a similar test case, because variations between cities tend to be more limited among British cities than among French ones.

What were the strategies for managing ethnic conflict in Birmingham, Lille and Roubaix from the early 1980s to 2001? There was a broadly similar pattern of management in each city, characterized by the type of political dilemma that is common in European cities. All three cities have had to grapple with the pressure to address problems of exclusion, discrimination and urban violence that affect minority communities, as well as their demands for the construction of places of worship, as one factor potentially challeng-ing their political stability; and all three feel that the extent to which they can do this is limited because of the potential negative reactions from the wider electorate. Thus, all three situations are characterized by an unstable and permanently renegotiated *modus vivendi* between the local power and ethnic minority interests.

A fundamental divergence, however, has been emerging over the last 20 years between Birmingham, on the one hand, and Roubaix and especially

Lille, on the other. During that period, the *modus vivendi* of the Birmingham City Council evolved towards a carefully considered yet solid alliance between the dominant Labour group and a group of ethnic minority leaders and activists of African-Caribbean and 'Asian' (predominantly Pakistani) background who were increasingly active in grassroots politics from the late 1970s onward. This alliance can be summarized as the following implicit deal: (1) a relative inclusion of ethnic groups in the political process through co-optation, and (2) significant concessions to their interests, in exchange for electoral support, or absence of electoral challenge, and cooperation in maintaining law and order.

The Labour group won control of the council in 1983, and it has remained in power since then, with a very comfortable majority until the early 2000s. From 1983 it increasingly included ethnic minority councillors, including in posts of major responsibility. In parallel to this, the council continuously defended a proactive policy in defence of specific ethnic minority interests in terms of racial discrimination and recognition of cultural difference. In 1984, the council created a department devoted to the fight against racial discrimination, and programmes and institutions have existed in various guises since then.

In the early 2000s, the Labour/ethnic minority coalition was displaying signs of strain, with former Asian Labour councillors seeking, and winning, election as independent candidates or as members of the rival Liberal Democrat Party. Yet it was too early to announce its demise, as the bulk of ethnic minority councillors remained Labour and some of them continued to occupy significant positions in the leadership of the council.

Overall, Birmingham is representative of many of the large British industrial cities and many London boroughs with large working-class and minority communities, which now all have a strong and lasting presence of minority councillors. There are, however, important nuances: Birmingham came to this situation later than other cities (e.g. London boroughs [Ouseley, 1984] or Liverpool [Ben Tovim et al., 1986]), but has become one where the situation of minorities at the council is particularly strong.

In Lille, on the contrary, there has been no evolution towards any kind of alliance comparable to the one in Birmingham. This was apparent during the two mayoral tenures of 1983–9 and 1989–95. In 1983–9, local offshoots of a national protest movement of second-generation North African immigrants campaigned actively in the city on behalf of various issues related to racial discrimination, social and economic exclusion and cultural recognition. In 1989–95, more bitter and loosely organized groups of disaffected youths were posing a constant preoccupation in terms of law and order, and openly challenging the municipality's insistence on maintaining the political status quo in the city. In response, there has been a continued effort on the part of the municipality to (1) keep the issue out of the spotlight of electoral politics and

(2) divide and weaken, or fund and control, ethnic groups, in order to neutralize potential electoral competition from them when they became impossible to ignore. Neither the ruling Socialist Party headed by Mauroy nor the local mainstream right-wing opposition is keen to push the issue to the forefront of electoral competition. Until 2001 it also put forward a strong republican-assimilationist discourse, purposefully avoiding the recognition of groups that are explicitly 'ethnic' or Muslim.

Lille's strategy can be understood as representative of a large number of medium-range and large French cities, where there is little or no will to co-opt minorities. But in many respects it is an extreme case of immigrant exclusion, because of local institutional specifics (see below). The results of the 2001 municipal election confirm this, with little sign of the significant shift towards inclusion that occurred in many cities nationwide. In this respect, Lille is more indicative of the strategies of many rather well-off cities that are historical and economic centres of urbanized areas. They are able, more than other cities, to ignore ethnic diversity, in spite of significant minority populations, by externalizing the problem on neighbouring towns through housing policies, and because of entrenched political machines.

Finally, the strategy of the municipality of Roubaix falls somewhere in between that of Birmingham or Lille. The leadership has changed frequently over the last 20 years, from Socialist between 1977 and 1983 to centre-right between 1983 and 1997, when it came under Socialist leadership again.[6] Because of this, the strategy of the council has frequently wavered, from giving clear xenophobic hints to encouraging the election of North African councillors. Between 1995 and 2001, there were five North African councillors (9 per cent of the total number of councillors), making Roubaix one of the French cities where ethnic minorities are the most represented. Roubaix therefore stands as an exception among French cities, one where minorities are doing particularly well in the local electoral game, and where ethnicity-specific interests are more than elsewhere taken into account. After 2001, it became less exceptional in terms of levels of representation, but the modes of access to elected office in the city remain distinctive and reflect an original political history.

The Main Propositions and the Outline of the Book

The framing of debates on immigration and integration in national politics:
1945–2001

In Britain (chapter 2), the liberality of the citizenship regime applied to all migrants from former colonies until restrictions were gradually imposed in the 1960s and 1970s. This entailed the incapacity of the British administration to control immigration flows from former colonies until 1962, and has enfranchised the populations of extra-European migrants. The other fundamental element is the early depoliticization of migration issues, in the early 1960s, and the passage by Labour of legislation against racial discrimination in the 1960s encouraged the formation of a lasting Labour/minority alliance. Ulterior spells of repoliticization and xenophobic mobilization never fundamentally challenged these 1960s developments.

The tendency towards inclusion in Britain was particularly strong locally because of the configuration of central–local relations in Britain. The country is characterized by a tight separation of 'low' and 'high' politics, as opposed to a strong inter-penetration of these two levels of government in France (see Webman, 1981). Since the beginning of the migration wave, this has made the local level a stronger focus for ethnic minority mobilization in Britain than in France, because the issues that matter for immigration politics (housing, education, social policies) have all traditionally fallen clearly within the remit of local authorities in Britain, while the distribution of remits is much more complex in France (Webman, 1981; Le Galès, 1993, pp. 34–41; Ashford, 1982). This relative separation of local and national politics in Britain has also facilitated the devolution of the issue to the local level by central elites as part of the 1960s 'liberal consensus' on race and immigration, thereby facilitating the construction of the issue at the local level in terms of 'race relations', adaptation of local public service delivery to specific ethnic minority requirements and anti-discriminatory policies (Layton-Henry, 1992; Saggar, 1991b). This took the focus of public discussions away from migration flows, that is, the desirability of the migrant's presence, and shifted it towards the best way to facilitate the incorporation into society of those who were already settled on British soil. That channelled migrant mobilization towards anti-discrimination policies.

The separation between local and national politics was also reflected in the organization of the Labour Party, and made possible the emergence of the left in the party. More than other groups, the left was open to minorities, and when it won control of large cities in the 1980s, it picked up and radicalized the existing issues of equal opportunities and racial equality at the local level and facilitated the access of minorities to election on councils. The final section of the chapter retraces the emergence of such policies and of Labour/ethnic minority alliances in British cities in the context of this national framework.

In France (chapter 3), the recent history of migration politics has also been characterized by a strong influx of post-colonial, extra-European workers, but with two essential differences from Britain. The bulk of these migrants have not been granted citizenship upon arrival, as has been the case in Britain. And, when minority issues did become inflamed, in the early 1980s, they were persistently agitated by the Front National in the political arena. This inhibited major parties of the left and right alike from taking up minority claims, and encouraged them to adopt a 'universalistic-assimilationist' attitude to immigration and minority issues which further caused a reluctance to promote minority interests.

This has been compounded by the inter-relatedness of the two levels of government in France. This is true both administratively and politically, with the *cumul des mandats* system (several elected positions for one person). The way the issue has been formulated at the local level has emulated the formulation at the national level, that is, in terms of immigrants as passive objects of policy (capacity of the country to 'assimilate' immigrants, discussion of restriction of migration flows) rather than as active participants in politics who pursue their own interests (racial discrimination, participation, cultural and religious recognition). As a result, local authorities have sought either to stay clear of the issue, as is the case in Lille, or in many cases to echo the concerns of the Front National. In all cases, there was little interest in putting forward ethnic minority candidates on party slates.

A turning point was reached in 1997, when the mainstream right approved a moderate reform of nationality law passed by a Socialist government. This, coupled with a temporary weakening of the Front National's capacity to define the debate because of a split, removed inflammatory, anti-migrant rhetorics from political discourse. Nationality law and immigration law reforms, which were a staple ingredient of political discussions until the late 1990s, have since then almost disappeared from public discourse. This created a new political climate favourable to new discussions on the place of ethnic minorities in French society, which in turn encouraged political parties to co-opt minority individuals.

Contrasting local political systems

Chapter 4 shows how the British national framework, presented in chapter 2, inter-played with local parties and local government to produce an outcome of rapid and, to a significant extent, substantial representation on the Birmingham City Council. The two most important characteristics of the party system and of the organization of local government are: (1) the combination of the ward-based, first-past-the-post electoral system of city council elections, and (2) the specific timing and dynamics of left–right competition in the Birmingham Labour Party in the 1980s. The combination of the two facilitated the coalescence of an electorate preoccupied with both ethnic and working-class issues around a rising generation of minority politicians in the Labour Party. Emerging minority leaders have benefited from a situation in which an ethnic vote was appearing in the inner city, and Labour politicians were interested in tapping into this vote to maintain and increase their domination over internal rivals and the Conservative group at the council. Over time, this first generation of ethnic minority councillors was replaced by radical campaigners for racial equality allied with the left of the party. In the late 1990s, Asian councillors disappointed with Labour's management of the inner cities weakened the Labour pluri-ethnic coalition by getting elected without the party's support, as independent or Liberal Democrat candidates.

Chapter 5 discusses how the national factors that make incorporation difficult in France were reinforced by the characteristics of the local institutions of Lille to create the outcome of strong exclusion. First, Lille has benefited from its dominance of the greater Lille area to externalize parts of its ethnic minority population on Roubaix. In addition, the Socialist Party, dominant in the city for the last four decades, has important political resources to control, and keep at bay politically, local groups from civil society, and especially ethnic minority groups. In the 1989 municipal tenure, it fended off attempts by the Beur movement to raise issues of discrimination and lack of effective citizenship for populations of immigrant background.

This was in part due to the nature of the French municipal electoral system, which allows local elites to remain isolated from social movements, at least for some time. The city-wide single constituency dilutes the electoral clout of ethnic minority populations concentrated in some neighbourhoods. The majoritarian system handicapped smaller, leftist bids that were most prone to take minorities on board. In the 1989–95 tenure, Socialist veteran mayor Mauroy built on the traditional networks of his party in the remnants of local working-class communities to construct a machine that perpetuated the status quo in his favour. With this strategy, it was possible to ignore groups of dissenting North African youths from the most disadvantaged areas of the city, or to divide and weaken them when they managed to present a threat. The Socialists were all the more prone to this type of strategy because the Front National, and its anti-immigrant rhetorics, were repeatedly successful in the poorer areas of the city. The discourse on universalism and republican integration that was pervasive both nationally and locally in the 1980s and 1990s worked for the Lille municipality as a tool legitimizing inaction and ignorance of ethnic diversity.

As in the model of the American party machine of the turn of the century, the Lille machine has relied on patronage to perpetuate the domination of the city by one leading individual in the party; but, unlike American machines, it has kept immigrants out, and instead has relied on native French supporters. While both the majoritarian municipal system and some of the urban regeneration programmes integrated by the Socialists into their networks are common to all other French cities, and are at the heart of the process of exclusion of minorities across France, they have combined in a particularly powerful and lasting way in Lille.

Chapter 6, devoted to Roubaix, emphasizes the existence of strong, autonomous community movements at neighbourhood level, and the relative weakness of party politics. This has made both parties and municipality more open to influences from community organizations. Since these are heavily neighbourhood based, and since North Africans reach very high concentrations in some Roubaix neighbourhoods (sometimes up to 80 per cent of the population, among the highest concentrations in France, and equivalent to Birmingham), they act as a training ground and stepping stone for young North African leaders. These leaders are able to bargain their political competence and credibility as serious associative actors to obtain positions on the candidate lists of political parties, as well as to exert some leverage on certain departments and councillors of the council.

This is in spite of the strong influence of the Front National in the city, which has reached very high scores (around 17 per cent of the vote) in the last two municipal elections of 1989 and 1995, and has influenced local parties and mayoral candidates to take occasional anti-immigrant stances. This shows that general features of the French local system, such as the municipal electoral system and the inter-penetration of national and local politics, have a greatly different impact from one locality to another, depending on more localized patterns of community and party organization, which are more localized. While these factors have contributed to the construction of the Socialist machine in Lille, in Roubaix they have worked to encourage a neighbourhood-based process of inclusion that is relatively independent from partisan politics.

2

The British Policy Framework: Liberal Citizenship Regime, Depoliticization and the Race Relationism of British Cities

In both France and Britain, local developments in the politics of ethnic minorities have been framed and constrained by national policy frameworks. These are the result of different combinations of three types of variables: (1) legal frameworks on citizenship and nationhood, and ideas on race and ethnicity; (2) party systems; and (3) the organization of central–local relations.

The interaction of these three variables in Britain from the late 1940s up until 2001 has resulted in several institutional elements. First is the overall depoliticization of immigration in national politics, give or take some periods of repoliticization. Second is the construction of immigration-related issues as issues of relations between racial communities in the 1960s, which resulted in two policy guidelines: that immigration of non-European workers increases racial tensions and should be stopped, and that those members of the black and Asian community who are established in Britain should be protected against racism by specific laws and policies. Third, an emphasis was placed on the local level of government as the main level of management of racial and ethnic issues. These three elements are deeply original in comparison with other European countries, and indeed with France; they constitute what I call the British framework.

This framework has shaped attempts at participation in a way that is specifically British, with in particular three outstanding elements: the formulation of claims that are specific to ethnic minorities, and the legitimation in the political sphere of claims linked to racial and cultural difference and racial discrimination; the emergence of the local level of politics as an important focus for these claims; and the emergence of the Labour Party as the main supporter of these claims in cities (until the early 2000s). These three elements have compounded the liberal citizenship regime to create a favourable context for the emergence of pluri-ethnic alliances in local government and for the development of anti-discrimination policies.

This chapter provides a chronological narrative of the development of the British policy framework from the post-war years until 2001, and of the way in which it has provided a favourable context for the emergence of minority/Labour alliances in cities in the last two decades. The main argument is that the precocity of the political change towards inter-ethnic alliance in British cities in comparison with other European cities is due not just to the precocity of the migration process to Britain, but rather to the combination of this precocity and of the way in which national elites succeeded in depoliticizing immigration and creating an innovative race relations framework in the 1960s. The broad terms of the consensus were never really questioned in later years, despite the short-lived success of Enoch Powell's anti-immigrant campaign in the late 1960s, and despite markedly more illiberal attitudes and policies in the Conservative Party in the 1970s and early 1980s.

The result was that the legitimacy of the settlement of ethnic minorities on British soil, and of their claims to participation, were never seriously questioned (as was often the case in France). This appears clearly in comparison with the success of the French far right in the 1980s and 1990s, in the context of a party system more favourable to the emergence of small parties than in Britain, which made it impossible for French mainstream parties to emulate the British strategy. While the consensus led to the 1962 and 1968 Commonwealth Immigrants Acts, which arguably promoted a restrictive, anti-black conception of Britishness by de facto denying the right of entry onto British soil to extra-European British subjects (Paul, 1997), it also led to the Race Relations Acts and the subsequent efforts to fight racial discrimination and disadvantage. The most notable result of the bipartisan consensus, from a comparative, cross-national perspective, was therefore to shift the terms of the debate on immigration, from a debate on the desirability and management of immigration flows to a debate on whether the government's efforts to integrate those black Britons already established on British territory were ambitious enough.

The 1960s bipartisan consensus also led to the promotion of the local level of government as the main level for the management of racial and ethnic tensions through the creation of 'Race Relations Committees' in cities, the adaptation of local service delivery to racial diversity (Section 11 of the 1967 Local Government Act), and the creation of urban regeneration programmes largely targeted at black and Asian areas. One of my institutional factors, the configuration of central–local relations, plays a specially important role here. In Britain, it is characterized by a tight separation of 'low' and 'high' politics, and this made it politically profitable for national elites to devolve the issue to local councils in order to insulate themselves from its potentially damaging consequences (see Bulpitt, 1986). The devolution of race-related issues was also encouraged by the clear policy remits held by local authorities in areas of social policy that matter particularly for immigrants (as opposed to a strong inter-penetration of the two levels of government and a more complex organization of social and education policies in France).

1948–1958: Pressure on Local Authorities and National Indifference

This first period saw the beginning of the mass migration of extra-European, post-colonial workers to Britain. This migration was in large part uncontrolled, because of the liberality of the British nationality regime codified in the 1948 Nationality Act, and resulted in the establishment of a large African-Caribbean and Asian population. This period of initial settlement had little impact on politics, but it did place strain on local authorities, which led to a build-up of agitation in cities. This eventually propelled immigration into the political sphere in the form of anti-immigrant agitation in local Conservative parties and anti-immigration rioting in 1958.

The beginning of mass migration

Two inter-related events in 1948 mark the beginning of the story of post-colonial immigration into Britain: the British Nationality Act, and the beginning of the post-colonial migration wave. The first British Nationality Act was passed, defining the status of the individual in terms not of citizenship or nationality, as is usually the case in European countries, but of relation to the crown (subjecthood). The large majority of British subjects, whether in Britain itself, in the colonies or in independent countries that are members of the Commonwealth, were to fit into one of two categories: citizens of the United Kingdom and Colonies (CUKCs) or Citizens of the Independent Commonwealth Countries (CICCs). In both cases these citizens retained their status as subjects of the British crown. Subjecthood implied two fundamental rights: the right of unrestricted entry into Britain, and full political rights (Hansen, 2000, pp. 45–52; Crowley, 1992a, p. 74). This did not actually introduce any change: it was simply a formalization of the traditional common law on the status of the individual, which had only been partially formalized before by laws in 1905, 1914 and 1919. The legislation was the object of a consensus between the two main parties: the Conservatives saw in it an important way to preserve Britain's place at the centre of the Commonwealth, and Labour supported it for humanitarian reasons (Hansen, 1998, pp. 23–39). As Hansen shows, this was to have a considerable and varied impact on subsequent developments in immigration politics and constituted the essential building block of what he has called the 'institutional origins of a multicultural nation' (Hansen, 2000). It did this in two main ways. First, it made possible the mass migration to Britain of workers from former colonies. Second, it was to facilitate the political incorporation of immigrants residing in Britain by automatically granting them full political rights upon their arrival on British territory.

This legislation was inherited from a time when colonial populations were not expected to move to Britain. But its passage in Parliament coincided with the second important event of the year, the arrival of the first post-colonial migrants from the West Indies. Because of the principle of freedom of circulation, granted by the British Nationality Act throughout the Commonwealth, and unparalleled in other colonial empires, these migrants were the first wave of a vast migratory movement, soon originating not just from the West Indies but also from India and Pakistan. Between 1955 and 1960 alone, 200,000 migrants from these countries came to Britain (Messina, 1989, p. 22). At the end of the 1960s, the population in Great Britain originating from the New Commonwealth reached around 800,000 people (Joly, 1992), who had come to Britain for mainly economic reasons. The timing of this migration wave is in itself an important difference from France: it started and peaked a decade earlier than it did in France, which received most of its North African immigrants in the 1960s and 1970s (Hargreaves, 1995, p. 11).

The combination of this legal context and this mass migration paved the way for the imminent anti-immigrant movement in British cities. Because of the principle of freedom of entry for British subjects, this movement could not actually be controlled by the British administration, although some plans were drafted by the civil service. This is an essential difference from France:[1] both countries saw in immigration a convenient way to combat the chronic shortage of labour in the post-war years, but France managed to some extent to exert a degree of control over it, adapting it to the fluctuations of its economy, while Britain was less successful in this respect. Second, this population had an automatic right to vote, which of course constituted a strong resource for participation, although it was not to be exercised significantly before the 1970s. This is another fundamental difference from France, where nationality and citizenship are linked, and where post-colonial immigrants are non-nationals and therefore cannot vote, apart from those who apply successfully for naturalization or dual nationality, or those born in Algeria before 1962.

National apathy and local agitation

Until the late 1950s, there had been very little official and public concern about this migration flow on the part of national elites, who essentially treated it with 'benign neglect'. Both the Labour and Conservative parties accepted it because they both considered it an important part of their economic policy to fuel the reconstruction effort (Messina, 1989, p. 22); in each party, there was also a strong feeling that the liberal legislation was essential in maintaining the unity of the Commonwealth. The arrival of migrants seemed to cause little reaction in the British population. In the realm of social policy, the general assumption was that immigrants were citizens among others, and that they would assimilate (culturally, socially, economically) into mainstream British society.

Overall, as Katznelson puts it, the issue was in a 'pre-political age', because there was an unspoken consensus according to which what few problems there were with immigration, if any, would right themselves in the end (Katznelson, 1973, p. 130). Only some isolated Tory backbenchers voiced discontent (Messina, 1989, p. 23). Some attempts were also made at cabinet level to limit the numbers of immigrants, but this was made difficult because it would have meant changing the 1948 Act, a complicated parliamentary task (Hansen, 1998).

However, during the same period, immigration did become an issue in certain local authorities. This difference between the cycles of politicization of the two levels of government anticipates later development. Local politicization was precipitated by two main factors. First, immigrants migrated to specific areas of the country and created highly concentrated populations of immigrants, which then evolved into local ethnic minority communities. Second, the organization of central–local relations in the British political system made the local level a clearer focus for the politicization of immigration-related issues than in the French context.[2]

The vast majority of the migrant population settled in industrialized urban areas, which in Britain meant Greater London and the centre and north of the country. This was the case from the start and has endured until the present day. As Koopmans and Statham noted:

> Greater London accounts for 10.3 per cent of the overall population, but for 44.6 per cent of Britain's minorities, with a fifth of Greater London populations being minorities. A further 36.8 per cent of Britain's minorities live in Northern England, especially congregated in the metropolitan conurbations of Birmingham, Bradford, Leeds, Manchester, and Leicester. In contrast, Southern England which accounts for about a third of the overall British population houses only 15 per cent of the minority population, with

minorities accounting for only 2.7 per cent of the population, compared to 4.8 per cent in the North and 20.2 per cent in Greater London. (2000c, p. 11)

Within this regional concentration, there was also a process of residential concentration in certain areas of cities, namely, certain parts of the inner cities. While residential concentration is also a feature of French immigrant populations, it is more marked in Britain. I argue here that this is due to the dynamics of the housing market in Britain. In France, many aspects of the migration wave were more or less controlled by the central state; in particular, a network of government-controlled centres for the accommodation of migrant workers enabled the central administration to keep some measure of control over minorities. In addition, cheap accommodation, of the kind sought by immigrants, is in France predominantly owned and managed by local bodies which are half private and half managed by local authorities, the Offices des HLM *(habitations à loyers modérés)*. These are understood as performing a public service, and are grouped as part of a nationwide federation that gives some level of coherence to their policy, although they do function autonomously at the local level. In Britain, a large proportion of the low-rent accommodation was managed by local councils in the post-war era, but, in contrast with France, a substantial part of it was owned by private landlords, who rented it directly to tenants. For instance, in 1971, 42 per cent of housing in Birmingham was owner-occupied, 38 per cent was rented from the council and nearly 20 per cent was rented from private landlords; in Bristol, the figures were a comparable 49 per cent, 31 per cent and 20 per cent (Dunleavy, 1981, pp. 256, 304).

Large sections of immigrant populations have rented this type of accommodation since the 1950s. On the basis of the Birmingham case, Rex and Moore have convincingly argued that the dynamics of the housing market facilitated processes of concentration in certain areas of Birmingham, where privately owned, low-rent, low-quality housing was predominant (Rex and Moore, 1967, ch. 1). Immigrants from India and Pakistan favoured this type of accommodation, and as a consequence migrated mainly to areas of the inner city where it was most common, i.e. the southeastern part of the inner city, in the areas of Moseley, Sparkbrook and Sparkhill (where over 40 per cent of the accommodation was rented from private landlords in 1971 [Dunleavy, 1981, p. 256]). This situation snowballed because the populations of white residents in these neighbourhoods tended to leave as the Asians arrived, which brought property prices down and made them even more desirable to immigrants. Hence, the specific fact that a large part of the low-rent housing market is privately owned in Britain was a major factor in making possible high levels of concentration of minorities in British cities, compared to France (Jones, 1967; Rex and Moore, 1967, p. 31).

The policy remits of the national and local levels of elected government are tightly separated, very much in a 'two-layer cake' organization (as opposed to a 'marble cake' organization in France [Webman, 1981]). In addition, the policy remits which are traditionally those of the local level are social services. This is the result of a trend that started in the middle of the nineteenth century whereby central government has tended to delegate more and more prerogatives of the welfare state to localities, while retaining funding, norm-setting and inspecting functions for itself (Johnson, 1990, p. 14). It has also been encouraged by the 'municipal socialism' approach applied to local government by the Labour Party in many industrial cities it has come to control in the twentieth century (Gyford, 1985). This has changed considerably during the last 15 years, which have seen an increasing number of responsibilities transferred to unelected bodies, so-called 'quangos', at both national and local levels (Stoker, 1991, p. 145). But, until the early 1980s, local authorities, which in the case of most large cities was the city council, were in charge of public housing (council housing), social services, which include many health services, and the education system.

These policy sectors are precisely those in which the issue of ethnic minorities is salient. Post-war immigrants are overwhelmingly from a working-class background and, since the 1960s, when family regrouping began, they have often had higher fertility rates and lower average ages than native populations (Modood, Berthoud et al., 1997). They are of concern to ethnic minority populations themselves, first, because a significant proportion have traditionally dwelt in council housing, in spite of the importance of private landlords noted above (in particular, African-Caribbean households have tended to rent council housing more than Asian immigrants). They have long been discriminated against in the system of attribution of housing (Rex and Moore, 1967, ch. 1) and often have certain requirements regarding the school curricula. Second, ethnic minorities are often perceived by local populations as the cause of the deterioration of these services.

In this context, the arrival of hundreds of thousands of immigrants in specific industrial cities (mainly in the London and West Midlands area) within a few years put enormous strain on social services, particularly in inner-city districts, where health, educational and housing problems arose almost overnight. These pressures had two political consequences. First, some local authorities felt that little of their concern was being understood at government level, which elicited growing xenophobia in local party organizations. This led several local authorities, especially those led by Conservative majorities, to attempt to put pressure on central government to start restricting the immigration flow. Second, local agitation encouraged the creation in many cities of voluntary liaison committees (VLCs) by civic-minded white residents of areas of immigration who wanted to help immigrants settle in, often with the aid of the local church or local council (for a complete history of these bodies, see Hill and Issacharoff, 1971). These VLCs were meant to carry out diverse functions centred around the notion of welfare for immigrants: monitoring newcomers and delivering juridical services and social services such as English classes.

VLCs conveyed a largely paternalistic conception of immigrant welfare, primarily aiming at explaining to immigrants how to conform to British society. They can hardly be considered as efficient or politically significant at the time of their creation. Not only was migration into Britain largely unplanned by state authorities, but, in addition, there was confusion as to which department at Whitehall should manage the VLCs: the Colonial Office, the Home Office, Commonwealth governments, voluntary groups or city councils. Situations varied locally, but on the whole the committees were run by volunteers, with limited help from local councils, and in some cases the Colonial Office, although the latter was persistently reluctant to get involved.[3] In the 1940s and 1950s, they were marginal on local political scenes and largely ignored by local councils, who either did not take an interest at all or gave limited bureaucratic help (Hill and Issacharoff, 1971). A Marxist-inspired approach to these bodies by scholars of immigration politics has construed them as instruments of control of minority populations and argued that they insulated local politicians from such populations and thus contributed to the non-politicization of racial or ethnic issues during the period of initial migration (Katznelson, 1973).

While, as noted by Joppke (1999, p. 238), this interpretation can be viewed as a slightly 'conspiratorial' one, it is nonetheless clear that VLCs contributed to some extent to reproducing at the local level the attitude of benign neglect that prevailed nationally. Two crucial points, however, must be made to balance this view. First, these bodies did not contain the increasing xenophobic agitation that was brewing in Conservative circles at the time and that was to spill over dramatically into national politics. Second, they were to have a lasting impact on the way in which central governments dealt with such agitation in the future, by encouraging them to construe the issue as one that had to be dealt with locally, by bodies insulated from national politics (see below). In fact, their very appearance and existence in the late 1940s and 1950s can be understood as having set a strong precedent in British local politics, putting subsequent developments on a racialist and localist path.

1958–1968: The Birth of the British Race Relations Policy Framework

Depoliticization

What eventually jolted the issue away from the relative obscurity of local politics and brought it to the forefront of national politics were riots that occurred in Nottingham and Notting Hill (London) in 1958, and that were widely perceived as racial riots. In the following years, as the issue was becoming increasingly divisive, both main political parties struggled to decide what approach to take. Original attitudes were characterized by a strong polarization, but scholars of British immigration politics have shown how this polarization was to evolve towards a remarkable consensus on the issue in a few years, as both parties sought to minimize the place of immigration-related issues in electoral contests. They did this by taking moderate and eventually almost interchangeable positions on immigration issues. Katznelson (1973), Layton-Henry (1992), Saggar (1991a, b), Hansen (2000) and particularly Messina (1989) give detailed accounts and interpretations of this period that sustain this line of argument.

The evolution took place between 1962 and the 1964 general election, at which point Labour's position evolved towards that of the Conservatives, that is, in favour of the restriction of immigration flows.[4] Several reasons have been proposed for this, including Gaitskell's death in January 1963 (Katznelson, 1973, p. 144; Messina, 1989, p. 31) and his replacement by Harold Wilson, less determined to defend a liberal standpoint on the issue.[5] More important, however, was the electoral interest of the party in the 1964 general election in which it adopted a 'centrist strategy', consisting in trying to capture the middle ground of the electorate, which was then seen as the only way it could again become the majority party. This positioning as a centrist, non-ideological party that had been chosen in 1951 was seen as threatened by a too-liberal stance on immigration (Messina, 1989, pp. 33–34).

Overall, this strategy proved quite successful during the campaign, but a notable local exception to the national pro-Labour swing unexpectedly exacerbated the political tensions on race. In the West Midlands constituency of Smethwick, Labour's shadow Foreign Secretary Patrick Gordon Walker, a prominent opponent to the 1962 Commonwealth Immigrants Act, lost his seat to the Conservative Peter Griffiths, who played strongly on the voters' fear of unrestricted immigration from the Commonwealth by likening immigrants to 'criminals, [the] chronic sick and those who have no intention of working' (Singham, 1965, p. 364). This re-emphasized the danger of too liberal an attitude for Labour, and the need for depoliticization. Wilson's strategy was twofold. First, he reaffirmed the commitment of the party to liberal principles of anti-racism. At the same time, his government quietly maintained a newly embraced restrictionist stance on immigration, renewing the 1962 Act as an interim measure immediately after taking office (Saggar, 1991b, p. 29).

This dual attitude – restrictive immigration policy, but an effort to facilitate the integration (whatever meaning was given to this word) of those immigrants already in Britain – constituted the basis of the whole framework that was to emerge out of the 1960s. In the same period, the Conservatives were gradually deciding that their best interest was to do the same thing as Labour, i.e. accept their opponent's policy, while sticking to their own. As Messina puts it, the two parties engaged in 'conspiracies of silence' (1989, p. 38), gradually trying to minimize the issue altogether to avoid the electoral damage that it might incur. In 1968 the fear that drove this strategy was the vehement, and popular, anti-immigration campaigning of Enoch Powell (Messina, 1989, p. 41).

1965–1968: the first 'race relations' policies

The tacit agreement between the two parties became particularly clear during Labour's tenure in power between 1964 and 1968, during which time they consistently maintained a restrictive immigration policy while enacting a series of ambitious and far-reaching policies of integration. During these four years the Conservatives explicitly approved Labour policies and even participated, as members of parliamentary committees, in drafting the major piece of legislation on the subject (Katznelson, 1973, pp. 140–1). The first piece of liberal legislation passed by Labour was the first Race Relations Act of 1965. Then came the 1965 White Paper, which spelled out in detail how Labour sought to implement its by now widely accepted vision of immigration policy, famously encapsulated by Roy Hattersley (Labour MP for Birmingham Sparkbrook): 'Without integration, limitation is inexcusable; without limitation, integration is impossible'.[6] The White Paper was thus careful to follow the restrictive line on immigration by reducing the number of work vouchers from 20,000 to 8,500 per year, while at the same time promising to 'create positive measures designed to secure for immigrants and their children their rightful place in British society' (Messina, 1989, p. 37). In addition, Labour again reinforced the possibility of immigration control in 1968 in the second Race Relations Act.

The combination of this restrictive policy and the liberal innovations of the Labour Party constitutes the 'institutionalization of consensus', in Katznelson's eloquent formulation. This consisted of a new dominant formulation of policy guidelines for facilitating immigrants' settlement in British society, characterized by two elements: anti-discrimination policies and the idea of 'community relations' at the local level.

The first two Race Relations Acts (1965 and 1968) provided the bases for a comprehensive legislation against racial discrimination. In the early 1965 version, the law prohibited incitement to racial hatred and discrimination on racial grounds in public places, and set up another administrative body, the Race Relations Board, to administer the law. The anti-discrimination provision was extended in the 1968 Commonwealth Immigrants Act to the fields of employment and housing. While these efforts may be viewed as too limited and tokenistic (for instance, Katznelson attacks the 1965 Act as 'declaratory'

[1973, p. 149]), their importance must be stressed. They marked a departure from the 'colour-blind' policy approach that predominated earlier in Britain; they paved the way for the expansion and reinforcement of anti-discrimination policies that occurred later in 1976 and 2000 with the third and fourth Race Relations Acts (see below); and they marked the beginning of Britain's exceptionalism, and perhaps of its status as precursor, in western Europe, where other nations were not to adopt similar policies before decades had passed.

Some sort of anti-discrimination law had been part of Labour's proposals before the 1964 elections, but recent research shows that it attained its importance only through the lobbying of the Committee on Racial Discrimination (CARD), a group close to the left of the Labour Party (Bleich, 2003). The law was also supported by the largest immigrant associations: the Indian Workers' Association, the National Federation of Pakistani Associations, as well as a number of individual white liberals (Rex, 1991, p. 83). The participation of ethnic minority groups in this process constituted an exception to the general low profile of immigrant populations in public life at that time.

The CARD campaign insisted that discrimination should be made a civil offence, as opposed to a criminal one, as originally intended. The result was that the law was made much more effective than if it had made discrimination a criminal offence, because it would then have been much more difficult to prosecute offenders. In France, a 1972 law making racial discrimination a criminal offence has had very little impact. CARD was directly influenced by the American example and was successful because the intellectual climate of British politics in the 1960s was receptive to American ideas (Bleich, 2003). The Act created a quasi-administrative body, the Race Relations Board (RRB), to oversee the implementation of the law.

The other guiding principle in Labour's policy was the conceptualization of immigration as a problem of relations between communities, or between races (race relations, as it came to be commonly known). Because relations between communities take place on a daily basis in a local, urban context, this was closely associated with an emphasis on the local level. This took the form of several policy innovations which placed the issue of migrant minorities, or 'race relations', firmly on the agenda of local authorities. Messina stresses the Britishness of this approach, and notes that the structures that were set up then were specific to Britain, as opposed to France and Germany, which, with their comparable immigrant populations, did not invent an equivalent. The same applies to the United States and the way its black population has been managed in cities (Messina, 1989, p. 53).

Third, and most importantly, the 1965 White Paper as well as the first and second Race Relations Acts institutionalized and centralized the VLCs created locally in the 1940s and 1950s. One of the main tasks of the National Commission on Commonwealth Immigrants (NCCI) created by the White

Paper was to try to give a national and official direction to their national move-ment, the Community Relations Movement. It sought to legitimize it and give it new life as an official body, in particular by funding the permanent post of community relations officer in each of the VLCs, renamed community rela-tions councils (CRCs). The second Race Relations Act of 1968 increased the investment made by the government in these bodies and replaced the NCCI with the Community Relations Commission, reinforcing its status, increasing the capacity for coordination and allowing for increased funding (Messina, 1989, p. 60).

This British exceptionalism can be seen as a result of the combination of two factors. First, although the dominant ideas in the Labour Party when it took office in 1964 leaned towards 'colour-blind' policies (i.e. not making special provision for the recognition of racial differences among the public), this changed in 1966, when Roy Jenkins, well known for his liberalism and interest in issues pertaining to immigration, replaced Frank Soskice as home secretary and introduced a radical change towards the formulation of policies explicitly designed to cater for 'coloured' (as they were then known) populations. In this Jenkins was translating into policy the dominant concep-tualization of the issue in British academic circles in terms of race and com-munity (for instance the influential work at this time of E. J. B. Rose et al. [1969] and John Rex and Roger Moore [1967]).[7]

The emphasis on the local level that is linked to this was also one element of the strategy of depoliticization pursued by the central government. Because the centre had isolated itself from grassroots xenophobic pressures, these pressures were at risk of being exacerbated in local politics. Hence the need to institute non-political bodies that could channel these tensions away from party government, both local and national (Bulpitt, 1986). This type of territorial management fits in well with the structure of the relation between central and local government in Britain as described above: the state's 'race statecraft' has involved using the territorial dimension of political power in Britain as a means of sustaining national depoliticization (Bulpitt, 1986, pp. 17–44). Bulpitt argues that this fits with the practice of 'shire government' rooted in the history of English dominance of the British Isles over the cen-turies. What is certain is that the main structure put in place by Labour gov-ernments from 1965 onwards drew heavily on the way in which the issue had been managed by VLCs in cities in the 1950s,[8] which in turn reflected the 'dual polity' character of British politics in the 1950s and the devolution of welfare issues to local governments by the centre in the first half of the century (Goldsmith, in Lagroye and Wright, 1982, p. 23).

To this must be added in 1968 the launch of an 'urban programme', designed as financial packages awarded to local authorities confronted with urban decline and poverty but which was in effect aimed at the immigration problem. Taking its inspiration from American programmes, this programme sought to finance social and cultural projects funded by local authorities and was to be the first in a long series of urban regeneration programmes that have been developed since then. Although the level of effort to fight disadvantage related to race and ethnicity by these programmes has often been branded as insufficient by British specialists (Beazley and Loftman, 1998; Edwards and Batley, 1978), they remain characterized by a comparatively high emphasis placed on them. In particular, Jenkins' other most important policy innovation with the CRCs was the inclusion of a scheme to attribute extra funds to local authorities which had high percentages of populations of ethnic minority background in an otherwise unrelated piece of legislation on local government (section 11 of the 1966 Local Government Act).

Importantly for later patterns of minority participation, the launching of the urban programmes in Britain also contributed to the development of the new urban left in the 1970s by providing an intellectual guideline for the reassessment of traditional styles of management of cities by the Labour Party in the 1970s and 1980s. One of the themes of the new urban left was the association of ethnic minorities with the management of local programmes, together with similar plans to open up to women's groups, environmental issues and local economic planning (Le Galès, 1990).

Consequences of the race relations framework on later patterns of minority participation

Devolving the issue to the local level had an ambiguous legacy, as is shown below. It is hard to find evidence of their lasting success in addressing racial disadvantage and in defusing racial and ethnic tensions. However, it remains important to note that their institutionalization as an integral part of race relations policies in the 1960s established early on the notion that race or ethnicity was to a large extent a local issue. This has permeated the British debate ever since, and, indeed, local authorities were later compelled to move into their field because of a widely held and well-entrenched view that cities were a prime arena for race relations.

The other aspects of the 1960s combination of depoliticization, immigration restriction and race relations policies were also to have a lasting impact on later developments. They encouraged the move away from a conceptualization of immigrants in terms of objects of policies towards their formulation as actors of politics and consumers of policies. This had already been facilitated by the liberality of the citizenship regime institutionalized by the 1948 Act. In this context, immigrants and their children stopped being labelled immigrants (which they have remained until very recently in France) and became racial minorities, then, with the arrival of multiculturalist discourses and policies in the 1980s, ethnic minorities.

This has legitimized their participation in British politics. It made both electoral participation and pressure group politics easier. It also meant that when immigrants started participating in politics in the 1970s, they did not spend their energies obtaining voting rights but moved on directly to issues of racial discrimination, religious recognition and cultural diversity, as opposed to the situation in Germany or France where much of the debates focus on conditions of access to nationality or voting rights (as shown by the quantitative study on claims by migrant groups conducted by Koopmans and Statham, 2000b). While the 'race relations' framework was contested in the 1980s for making it difficult for Asian minorities to define themselves in terms of their religious, Muslim, affiliation, it did constitute the essential breaking point from colour-blind policy guidelines that had prevailed before. 'Race relations' also reflected a political definition of blackness, originating in Marxist academic debates, whereby all minorities, African-Caribbean and Asian, were treated together as victims of racial, cultural and post-colonial domination. As such it provided the main ideological fuel for the birth of minority political consciousness and mobilization, before being challenged by multiculturalists in the 1980s. Furthermore, multiculturalism never replaced race relations, but rather was superimposed on it in discourses and practices, so that through the 1980s and 1990s the latter has remained a powerful tool of legitimation of race- and ethnicity-conscious policies.

The 1970s and 1980s: The Legacy of the 1960s Settlement

The 1970s marked a period of renewed agitation around immigration and race relations. In the long run, however, and in spite of this period of repoliticization, the two tenets of the previous period – the notions that immigrants may have legitimate claims and should be considered as recipients of social policies and that the local level is an important one for participation – remained in place, and in fact became solidly anchored in the British polity. Hansen notes that in the late 1990s, in spite of several attempts by some Conservatives in the 1980s to make political capital out of Labour's 'laxity' on immigration, the bipartisan approach of the 1960s to immigration, race and ethnicity remained largely intact (Hansen, 2000, p. 128).

The polarization of the 1970s

After the culmination of the bipartisan consensus with the passage of the 1968 Race Relations Act, the two main parties started moving away from each other on immigration-related issues. Messina argues convincingly that this was due to the conjugation of renewed internal tensions within the two major parties on the issue (1989, p. 127). The Conservatives took an increasingly restrictive stance on immigration flows, while Labour's policy leaned towards more liberal positions.

On the Conservative side, Enoch Powell's campaign of denunciation of extra-European immigrants as a threat to British stability sent the first ripples through the still waters of the 1960s consensus. However, the real impact of extremists on the Conservatives' attitude was modest. The moderate Conservative leadership of Edward Heath was quick to distance itself from Powellite rhetoric, and therefore avoided disrupting the 'conspiracy of silence' carefully maintained in tacit collaboration with the Labour Party (Messina, 1989, ch. 2).

More importantly, the party political debate clearly radicalized after 1975. This was largely the result of the replacement of Edward Heath by Margaret Thatcher as leader of the Conservative Party. She brought to the party her radical and polarizing agenda, and the deliberate will to exploit illiberal sentiment amongst voters (Hansen, 2000, pp. 263–4). She was encouraged in this by the growing influence of the anti-immigrant National Front, which came to replace Powell as the far-right agitator on the issue. The National Front's electoral influence was significant, but was undermined by Thatcher's success in wooing illiberal voters away from it and towards the Tories (Layton-Henry, 1986, p. 75). Her first government in 1979 adopted a tougher stance than ever on immigration and drastically restricted the definition of British citizenship with the 1981 British Nationality Act (Layton-Henry, 1986, pp. 73–99). In the subsequent decade, Conservative politicians such as Norman Tebbit or Kenneth Baker sought to prop up the issue with anti-ethnic minority statements or criticism of Labour's liberalism on immigration (Hansen, 2000, p. 128).

The Labour Party also moved towards a strengthening of its race relations legislation in the mid-1970s. The most tangible policy result of this attitude was the third Race Relations Act of 1976. This act sought to build on the race relations policies of the 1960s (Young, 1990, p. 26). It established a new agency, the Commission for Racial Equality (CRE), which combined the functions of the old Race Relations Board and the Community Relations Commission. It considerably extended the field of application of the law by extending it to cases of 'indirect discrimination'. It made local authorities officially responsible for 'equality of opportunity' and 'good relations between people of different races',[9] and in this way further influenced the impact of the 1960s legislation on local developments.

The Labour Party as the minorities' party – until 2001?

Most importantly, repoliticization encouraged, and was reinforced by, the increasing identification of emerging ethnic minority interests with the Labour Party. Both black and Asian electorates and ethnic minority activists

Table 2.1 Level of Labour and Conservative support among ethnic minorities in general elections

	1974[a]	*1979*	*1983*[b]	*1987*	*1992*[b]	*1997*[b]
Labour	81	86	83	72	81	78
Conservative	9	8	7	18	10	17

[a] Figures are for the October 1974 general election.
[b] Figures represent recalculated average of Asian and African-Caribbean support levels.
Source: Saggar, 1998b, p. 26.

became closely allied with the party at that time. This alliance was to prove a lasting one through the 1970s, 1980s and 1990s. Anti-racist movements, which gained temporary prominence in these years largely in reaction to the National Front and the radicalization of the right, acted in collaboration with grassroots Labour networks to mount anti-racist campaigns. In this, the Labour Party functioned fully as an umbrella organization of the British left.[10] These movements included a collection of local self-help ethnic minority movements, which were starting to organize around the country as immigrant populations became increasingly settled and structured.

In addition, immigrant participation in politics also increasingly took the form of electoral participation. This was mostly a new phenomenon, although there must have been some level of immigrant participation in the electoral process before the mid-1970s. But it became significant in the 1970s because the major political parties became clearly aware of the potential leverage of that electorate, in particular under the influence of a report by the Race Relations Board on the 1974 general elections. This report suggested that Labour owed its victory to the support of ethnic minority electorates in certain electorally marginal areas (Community Relations Commission, 1975). Although these propositions appeared later to have been based on uncertain methodological premises, they carried considerable weight at the time and helped to shape the perception that minority electorates might need to be considered as such by party strategists (Saggar, 1998b, p. 25).

The black and Asian electorate has been characterized by one remarkable feature: its support for the Labour Party has been overwhelming since the mid-1970s (Layton-Henry and Studlar, 1985; Saggar, 1998a, introduction). This continued unchanged through the 1980s and 1990s, despite recurrent predictions that some segments of the Asian community might shift in significant numbers towards the Conservative Party (Crewe, 1983; Saggar, 1998a, introduction).

As far as this support for the Labour Party is concerned, ethnic minority voters have behaved in the last decades as a roughly coherent voting block.

Messina argues that this is due to the fact that Labour is understood by minorities to address the most effectively a set of concerns which they all have in common, and which white voters do not share. According to Messina, this is due to the higher preoccupation of minorities than whites with issues of race relations legislation and immigration rules. In turn, so Messina's argument goes, the Labour Party is 'structurally' the best-placed party in Britain to address these issues because it has consistently claimed paternity of the British race relations framework and spent the 1980s taking liberal postures on race and ethnicity issues, such as proposing yet another Race Relations Act or repealing the 1981 British Nationality Act (passed by the first Thatcher government to restrict access to nationality for immigrants) (Messina in Saggar, 1998a, pp. 60ff.). This is not to deny that the support of ethnic minorities for the party also stems from their support for general Labour themes such as the defence of working-class interests: these two factors work in conjunction.

Following this line, the Labour Party emerged from the period of repoliticization of the 1970s with a new, faithful and growing group of political allies and electoral supporters. It won this support to a large extent because it, and it alone, reaped the benefits of the 1960s bipartisan relations policies, while its active role in the restrictive immigration rules that were passed at the same time was not held against it.

At least until the early 2000s, Labour has come over the years to consider that ethnic minorities are a safe electorate, and indeed some commentators have stressed that its attitude towards them can be understood as arrogant or neglectful (Fitzgerald, 1988). Indeed, a potential downfall of minorities' unflinching allegiance to the party has been that they are its captive electorate and are unable to bargain their support to other parties. At the same time, when either Labour or other parties have sought to woo ethnic minority voters, they have done so on the premise that they were primarily concerned with issues specific to their non-white character, stressing issues of racial discrimination. This has at least enabled ethnic minorities to secure many policy advances from the Labour Party when it was in power, from the third Race Relations Act in 1976 to pro-minority policies in Labour-controlled local councils. Tony Blair's first government also further broadened the field of application of anti-discrimination legislation with the Race Relations (Amendment) Act of 2000.

This state of affairs may start to change with the feeling of disenchantment with New Labour which is clearly perceptible in the British Asian population in the early 2000s. Some by-elections in 2004, in the wake of the war in Iraq, displayed signs of an evolution, in particular with an Asian Liberal Democrat candidate easily beating Labour in a Leicester constituency with a large proportion of Asian voters.[11] Many Muslim organizations were also drifting away from Labour in the early 2000s, turning to the Liberal Democrats or even the Conservatives. This was the case, for instance, of the web-based pressure group Muslim Public Affairs Committee (MPAC), which campaigned for the Tory candidate in the Leicester by-election.[12]

The 1980s onwards: local Labour activism

In the 1980s and 1990s, the radicalism of the early and mid-1970s is absent. Although contentious, the issue remained so in a conventional way, as opposed to France where it became monopolized by the far right, which imposed the terms of the debate on other parties. Indeed, in the context of a comparison with France, what stands out is that after 1979, extreme forces of the right have either been neutralized or become components of the mainstream Conservative Party. The latter's xenophobic lapses were not enough to challenge the 1960s consensus. They did not inhibit the formulation of race- and ethnicity-related claims in party politics, as they did in France in the 1980s. In the end, the bipartisan nature of the British party system has contained tendencies towards the polarization of the debate. In this context, ethnic minority interests came to be represented in the political sphere by Labour, and opposed by the Conservatives.

Even with regard to the fundamental policy developments of the 1970s, it can be argued that the legacy of the 1960s consensus was maintained; in particular, neither Labour nor the Conservatives made much effort to repeal legislation passed by their opponents once they got back into power. This comes as a sharp contrast to their attitudes on other issues, particularly socio-economic issues, for which this period is usually described as one of increasing polarization. Labour made no effort to repeal the 1971 Immigration Act when it took office in 1974. Symmetrically, the third Race Relations Act of 1976 was a moderate bill that was passed without meaningful opposition from the Conservatives, in spite of much posturing in that direction. In addition, upon taking office in 1979, the Conservatives did nothing to pass new restrictive measures or to abolish the Commission for Racial Equality and existing race relations legislation, in spite of pressures in that direction within the party. During the passage of the British Nationality Act of 1981, the Labour opposition limited itself to ritualistic attacks in the Commons, because it had itself previously been committed to a revision of British nationality laws and because the Conservative proposals owed much to the Green Paper of the previous Labour government (Layton-Henry, 1986, p. 84). Once it passed the 1981 British Nationality Act, the Conservative government limited its policy on immigration to vociferous criticism of Labour proposals and local policies (Bulpitt, 1986, pp. 38–9). Layton-Henry notes that by the start of the second Thatcher government in 1983, the Conservative leadership seemed to have decided to play down the issue and to avoid allowing it to remain a prominent area of conflict and policy-making (1986, p. 73). This attitude persisted throughout the 1990s. Saggar notes that the notion that the 'race card' may have been played to some effect in the 1992 general election by the Conservatives is unconvincing (Saggar, 1998c, pp. 1–21). The electoral victory of Labour in 1997 was also achieved in the context of a campaign where immigration and race played a minor role (ibid.).

This was made possible from the early 1980s by the second important point: the fact that the territorial dimension of British politics continued to be a major factor in shaping the issue. The cleavage between the two parties coincided with the local–central distinction, with the Labour Party increasingly entrenched locally and using cities to further a radical local agenda, among other things on race issues, which local Conservative parties fiercely opposed. In this way, the real front had been displaced from national debates on immigration to local debates on the advancement of the position of ethnic minority populations in British society.

Not only did Labour control major cities, there were also developments within the Labour Party in the 1970s and 1980s which deserve our attention here. The party was the theatre of intense conflict between two broad groups or trends, usually designated for convenience's sake as 'the left' and 'the right'.[13] The left was a diverse movement of grassroots activists who sought to rejuvenate the party with new, radical ideas, and who openly and violently challenged the more traditional and established elements of the party, the 'right', which included the majority of Members of Parliament, and had the support of the trade unions affiliated to the party. The struggle between the two took the form of ideological challenges, the left campaigning on environmental issues, international disarmament and new forms of poverty, as opposed to the traditional working-class politics of the right. It also took the form of a struggle of the party base against the establishment, with the left pushing for more 'democracy' within the party, that is, greater influence of active party members at the constituency level over the selection of party candidates. The left also actively encouraged the defence of women's rights and ethnic minorities, and campaigned for the inclusion of the categories of the population in the party. Crucially for us here, the grassroots nature of the movement, coupled with the retreat of Labour in cities in the 1980s, meant that these activities took place largely at the local level. A constellation of Labour left leaders who became successfully involved in city council politics throughout the country became known as the 'new urban left' (Seyd, 1987, ch. 3). The new urban left viewed city councils as a platform from which to publicize their issues of concern, and sought new forms of public action by restructuring local bureaucracies.

With regard to such postmodern issues as racial and ethnic disadvantage, Labour city councils were successful. As is well known, the Conservative central governments sought to reduce the autonomy of local government.

The onslaught was efficient in the areas of housing, welfare, education and economic development policies (see Le Galès, 1988). But, in those areas that pertain most directly to minorities, it was in fact quite limited and had few consequences.

First, the traditional organization of representative government, in the shape of the distinction between low and high politics, remained largely intact, in spite of the suppression of the county councils and the metropolitan authorities; and, while the distinction between the two levels of government became blurred in terms of policy remit, it remained valid in terms of electoral representation. In contrast with French politics, where local politics serve as power bases for national political careers, the link between the two levels is relatively tenuous. Local politicians have rarely undertaken national careers.[14] In addition, local elections take place every year in Britain. These two elements make local elections a means of expressing a protest vote against the party which is in government by voting for the other major party. This was more than ever the case during the 1979–97 Conservative spell of government. Leftist activists who in many instances were dominant locally thus found themselves granted increasing electoral legitimacy to carry out radical agendas in cities, notoriously Sheffield, Manchester, Leeds, Bradford and the Greater London Authority for the new left, and Lambeth and Liverpool for more traditionalist, Marxist groups in the party.

Conservative governments did not actively combat these agendas, although Thatcher was vocal in her denunciation of the policies of the Greater London Council (GLC), and the Conservative tabloid press took delight in printing headlines scorning the 'loony left' and its multiculturalist inclinations. This attitude of relative passivity on the part of the Conservative government came from the fact that, as mentioned above, it was not particularly keen, on the whole, to step into the field of immigration politics. Another reason is that pro-minority policies did not involve structural aspects of policies such as housing, social services and education mentioned above. Instead, they involved rather limited adjustments within each of these policy areas: changes in procedures in the attribution of housing and social services to combat racial discrimination, minor changes in curricula to address cultural differences. This was not easily contestable by central government, as opposed to housing or social services, which were destroyed by a series of laws that tended to take housing and education away from local authorities and greatly impaired the fiscal and financial autonomy of cities. If anything, the fiscal and financial attacks on local authorities made them more prone to embark on radical multicultural policies, because they reduced the authorities' capacity to implement redistributive agendas in expensive policy areas such as housing, and drove them to seek other policy areas in which to display creativity and innovation.

The 'Race Relationism' of British Cities in the 1980s and 1990s

The history of immigration and race relations politics presented in this chapter has resulted in three superimposed linkages at city level: (1) the linkage between ethnic minorities' interests and local politics, established in 1960s British politics by the creation of the VLCs, then CRCs; (2) the linkage between ethnic minorities and Labour; and (3) the linkage between Labour and local government. The combination of these three linkages created a durable structure of opportunity for the development of Labour–ethnic minority alliances in industrial cities throughout the country. This has taken two inter-related forms: the development of 'race relations' or 'equal opportunities' policies, and the rise of representation of non-whites in city councils. The first section below presents these developments in British cities and shows how they were often linked to the emergence in city politics of new groups in the Labour Party that were interested in new agendas, such as urban regeneration, feminism and ethnic communities. The second section argues that the national structure of opportunity cannot alone explain these developments, if only because important local variations point to the weight of the 'locality' factor in explaining local race relations politics.

Equal opportunities policies, city networks and the election of non-white councillors

There has been an important development of race-related policies in British local authorities since the early 1980s (Saggar, 1991b; Young, 1982; Ouseley, 1981, 1984; Fitzgerald, 1986). Local councils supported a variety of local campaigns usually broadly categorized as 'anti-racist' in the 1980s. The most active local authorities in this area were London boroughs and the GLC, the latter being controlled by left-wing leader Ken Livingstone until its abolition in 1986.[15] In fact, the pioneering boroughs of Haringey and Camden both launched major initiatives in 1978, Lambeth followed suit in 1979, as did Brent, Hackney, Newham and the GLC in 1980 and 1981, while Southwark, Islington and Greenwich joined the fray in 1983 (Ouseley, 1984, p. 133). These boroughs often went to extremes in their anti-racist initiatives. Examples abound of local councils firing headteachers suspected of lack of enthusiasm for anti-racist policies, renaming streets after anti-apartheid activists, or promoting such slogans as 'If you are not part of the solution, you are part of the problem' (Joppke, 1999, p. 243).

Local authorities across the country also created Race Relations and Equal Opportunities Committees and Units, most of the time between 1980 and the late 1980s (for detailed histories of such structures in five British cities, see Joly and Candappa, 1994). This included the formulation of equal opportunities statements, often aiming at increasing the number of ethnic minority individuals employed by local councils; the training of 'race relations officers', and often the creation of whole 'race relations' departments within the councils' structures, to help local bureaucracies implement these changes; and the direct consultation of local immigrant communities (Ball and Solomos, 1990b, pp. 11–16). As in the United States, the employment of minorities by local authorities became a crucial issue, because this was one of the few domains in which local authorities could easily make a difference. Unlike in the United States, however, no quotas were ever set; instead, local authorities set indicative 'targets' of percentages of ethnic minority staff. After the exaltation of the 1980s, most local authorities scaled down such agitation in the 1990s. Equal Opportunities Committees and Units were often scaled down, or turned into sub-committees, or aggregated with other structures dealing with women's and disabled people's rights, in the late 1980s. Likewise, experiments in consultative politics have often ended after a few years, most of the time because of inefficiency and discontent among the community groups they are supposed to represent. But what is important is that the notions that some sort of racial balance should be reached in the composition of local councils' workforce, and that housing and educational policies should be ethnicity-sensitive, have remained unchallenged through the 1990s and the early 2000s.

The legislation created in the wake of Labour's liberal hour in the 1960s and 1970s, namely the section 11 programme and the 1976 Race Relation Act, has acted as a resource for local authorities that were interested in defending the interests of their non-white populations. But it is important to note as well that local authorities that chose to act on this did not do so in isolation, but were helped and encouraged by the examples of other cities, or by the influence of bureaucracies specializing in 'race relations'. Networks of actors concerned with the creation of race relations and equal opportunities programmes in local authorities across Britain appeared at that time. Hence to the national level one must add a level of national networks of like-minded cities that contributed to the rise of these policies.

In addition, the period also saw the take-off of ethnic minority representation in local councils. This had to some extent a causal role in bringing about the equal opportunities policies mentioned above.[16] This trend has generally continued to grow into the 1990s. This was itself the result of the growing participation of minorities, both in a variety of community groups and in the Labour Party. The election of blacks and Asians in growing numbers was also most conspicuous in the London area, with the number of non-white councillors in London boroughs moving from 35 in 1978 to 79 in 1982, and to somewhere between 132 and 179 after 1986 (Adolino, 1998, p.

44). Provincial cities during this period also saw the development of similar Labour-led race relations politics, and had their share of ethnic minority representation. In the early 2000s, the number of ethnic minority councillors in London decreased slightly; there was a movement towards more diversity in their political affiliation, with more Liberal Democrats and more Conservatives, although Labour councillors were still markedly more numerous.[17]

Local variations

Young shows that there was a wide variation among local bureaucracies in their attitudes towards these policies, with some becoming extremely militant, while others remained tepid or in many cases hostile (his threefold typology terms them the pioneers, the learners and the waverers [Young, 1981, pp. 58–9]). Joly and Candappa (1994) corroborate this by showing that the importance and financial strength of Equal Opportunities Units in Britain varied considerably in the 1980s depending on the amount of pressure exerted on local authorities by local community groups.

Similarly, the number of ethnic minority councillors elected in local councils varied greatly from council to council, and, most importantly, the ratio of councillors to the ethnic minority population varied as well. Asian populations in particular are well represented in some cities (for instance Bradford, 13.6 per cent of the total population, 12.2 per cent of the councillors); in others they are over-represented (Nottingham, 4.8 per cent/12.7 per cent); and in yet others they are under-represented (Wolverhampton, 12.3 per cent/5.0 per cent). Similar observations can be made about the black population, although it must be noted that the tendency here is more often toward under-representation (although statistics are more difficult to interpret because the numbers involved are smaller) (see Le Lohé, 1998, p. 89).

Both types of variations, in terms of the sensitivity of bureaucracies to race-related issues and in terms of levels of representation, point to the importance of the 'locality' factor in understanding the local politics of ethnic minorities. While national developments and the emergence of the 'race relations industry' as presented in this chapter have provided a framework for local changes, it is purely local factors that have determined whether changes were to happen or not, when they were to happen, at what speed and to what extent. I argue that institutional factors were instrumental. The key to understanding why Asian participation is higher than African-Caribbean participation also lies essentially in the types of relations between community groups of different ethnic backgrounds and institutional contexts, which are largely local.

Commentators have pointed to differences between 'circumstances, the black electorate, community relations pressure and street uprising' as prompting variations between cities' policies, described as 'sometimes enlightened and innovative, sometimes tokenistic' (Ouseley, 1984, p. 134). What little evidence is available on the influence of local styles of government and local party politics suggests that these variables go a long way towards explaining styles of minority politics. First, patterns of white–black coalitions varied from city to city. Of course, those local authorities that were led by Labour were much more prone to adopt a race-related agenda than others, although some Conservative- and Liberal Democrat-dominated cities with significant minority populations did follow the trend (Saggar, 1991b, ch. 6, shows that the Conservative borough of Barnet was not unreactive to pressures to implement race relations programmes). A survey of local authorities' race relations policies in the early 1980s indicated a discrepancy between Conservative-controlled councils and Labour-controlled councils, with the former markedly less enthusiastic about these policies than the latter (Young, 1981).

But, beyond the Labour vs. Conservative distinction, there are also important distinctions to be made among Labour authorities. In particular the role of the new urban left, which was gaining influence in some Labour areas in the 1980s, was often instrumental in putting minority issues on local agendas and enticing electoral alliances (for a comprehensive review of the new urban left, see Boddy and Fudge, 1984; Seyd, 1987, ch. 3; see also Shukra, 1998b, pp. 119–20). In cities where such groups have thrived, they have often brought to power with them anti-racist activists and expanded the equal opportunities departments of city councils. This was the case for instance in Birmingham (see below), and in the GLC of Ken Livingstone. It was also the case for some strands of the more radical, Marxist-inspired groups that were active at the time. For instance, those Militant groups that gained control of the London borough of Lambeth in 1981 were pioneers in anti-racism and the development of equal opportunities issues.

In other areas, other Militant groups had a tense relationship with minority groups and on the whole acted more as a hindrance than a facilitator for incorporation. This was the case of the Militant groups that dominated the Liverpool council in the early 1980s (argued in detail by Ben Tovim et al., 1986). Their emphasis on Marxism and class struggle made it difficult for them to recognize the legitimacy of cross-class struggles such as race issues. In this, the attitude of the Liverpool Labour Party was related to that of traditional blue-collar Labour parties with strong connections to trade unions. Another typical example was Wolverhampton, where the incorporation of minorities was much delayed in comparison with neighbouring cities, particularly Birmingham, because of the strength of traditionalist groups related to trade unions that dominated the local party there (Joly and

Candappa, 1994). Residential concentration, and the ethnic composition of minority populations, also varied from city to city. These factors combined in different ways with the British local electoral system to put different issues on local agendas, and affected in varying ways the careers of ethnic minority politicians.[18]

Conclusion

The history of the politics of immigration on the British national political scene since the post-war years until the present has followed three main phases: (1) a 'pre-political phase' up to 1958, (2) politicization and depoliticization in the 1960s, and (3) continued depoliticization in the 1980s. The first phase saw the establishment in Britain of a large migrant population under a liberal immigration and citizenship regime. The second phase saw the depoliticization of immigration in national politics, linked with the development of a combined policy of increasing immigration restriction and encouragement of integration for already settled populations. This policy took the form of the creation of the first urban policy programmes, an ambitious legislative framework to combat racial discrimination and the devolution of the management of 'relations between communities' to local councils. In spite of a repoliticization of the issue in the third phase during the 1970s, this framework was maintained in the 1980s. It was a factor for the changes of strategies of management of ethnic conflict of British cities in the 1980s.

It encouraged political change in the direction of inter-ethnic alliances in these cities, by legitimizing the presence of minorities in Britain and their participation in British politics, by constructing local politics as an important arena for race-related conflict, and by encouraging the ethnic minority electorate to support the Labour Party. National developments also framed participation as largely linked with demands to develop policies that addressed racial or ethnic disadvantage, in the language of race relations and with some inspiration from the American civil rights movement. The degree of success of local politicians of ethnic minority background varied from one city to another. Existing evidence suggests that the causes for these variations lie with cross-city variations between patterns of community organization and Labour politics.

In the early 2000s, the pluri-ethnic alliances of the 1980s and 1990s may be weakening, or at least moving toward some degree of reinvention. Disillusion with Blair's social policies in the party's grassroots, and anger against his foreign policy since the terrorist attacks of September 11, 2001, are felt particularly strongly in black and Asian communities. These have played a prominent role in the collapse or decline of Labour's long-standing domination of cities in the 2003 and 2004 local elections. In parliamentary politics as well, the Muslim electorate's revolt against Labour, evident in the 2004 by-elections in Leicester and Birmingham, may accelerate this trend in the future. Yet other sections of the black and Asian community within the Labour Party may on the contrary perpetuate the trend towards representation and incorporation.

3

The French Policy Framework: Planned Migration, Xenophobic Politics and Durable Political Exclusion

In parallel with the argument made about Britain, this chapter argues that the quasi-absence of pro-minority strategies in French local authorities for the last 20 years, apart from limited exceptions such as Roubaix, and in spite of the existence of important pro-ethnic minority local movements, is not just due to the time lag between the two migration waves in the two countries, or to differences between citizenship regimes, but must also be traced to a national framework that has on the whole inhibited both minority mobilization and an elite strategy that would be favourable to it. This framework has shaped modalities of exclusion that are specific to France and has given it its lasting character, while also setting the conditions for the evolution towards a more inclusive situation in the late 1990s and early 2000s. The interplay of three institutional variables is highlighted: (1) the French nationality regime, which has constructed migrants as non-nationals with no voting rights; (2) the bureaucratic management of migration flows which has long given credit to the notion that immigrants and their descendants were not here to stay but were temporary and alien '*immigrés*'; and, from the early 1980s onward, (3) the irruption into French politics of the Front National, which imposed a xenophobic bias on French party politics.

This chapter begins by retracing the evolution of French migration politics from the immediate post-war years until 2000 during which these three elements emerged. First, between 1945 and 1973, the French state laid the legal and organizational bases for an ambitious immigration programme, which included a reappraisal of the country's nationality law. In spite of its ultimate failure, this attempt at planning immigration is a defining moment because it framed many ulterior policy developments by defining the nationality status of migrants and framing the conditions of their stay in France. Second, as Weil (1990) shows, the period from 1973 to 1983 saw immigrant populations unexpectedly turn into an extra-European ethnic minority population, dominated by North African Muslim families, and saw successive governments compelled to readjust policy, gradually redefining the state's standpoint on immigration and thereby providing the bases for their attitude in the face of politicization after 1983. Third, from 1983 onwards, the irruption of the Front National as a major electoral force on the national scene prompted the durable politicization of debates on immigration flows in illiberal terms. This was in spite of a consensual agreement by national party elites from 1984 to attempt to depoliticize the issue along the lines set down in the previous decade. Fourth, the arrival in power of Socialist Prime Minister Lionel Jospin in 1997–8 and his reform of French nationality created a new political situation in which a more liberal consensus emerged, making it possible to discuss the place of minorities in French society in a more serene political climate.

1945–1973: State Planning and Unintended Effects

While the British framework was characterized by a liberal subjecthood regime which made possible the unchecked arrival on British territory of migrants with voting rights, the French citizenship and nationality framework, in which citizenship was dependent upon nationality, made it possible, in theory, to plan the patterns of immigration from foreign countries into France. The organization of the mass migration of foreign workers is precisely what France set out to achieve in the immediate aftermath of the Second World War. The most important characteristic of this endeavour for subsequent developments in city politics is that it was initiated and carried out by central bureaucracies, acting very much according to their own will, with little involvement from politicians and in the complete absence of public debate on the subject. In fact, the measures taken after 1945 until 1973 regarding the management of immigration were solely governmental or administrative decisions and for the most part did not require parliamentary procedures.

The issue of immigration was much debated among policy-makers in this period of national reconstruction. It was formulated in terms of demography and manpower, in the context of an aging population diminished by the two successive World Wars, and at a time when manpower was needed to rebuild the country. These two concerns were opposed, with demographers pushing for long-term settlement of ethnically desirable immigrants to repopulate the country, while economists called for short-term, temporary migration of single, male guestworkers. Particularly influential among demographers were Alfred Sauvy and Georges Mauco; the latter in particular proposed introducing a system of ethnic quotas, with a detailed hierarchy of preferred nationalities and ethnicities. Scandinavians were placed at the top of the scale and blacks and North Africans at the bottom, and it is ironic that the next few decades saw precisely the establishment in France of a large North African population. In addition to being opposed by economists, this position was also fought by a group of humanist lawyers with links to the Second World War Resistance movement, who sought to remove the notions of ethnic quotas from the proposed legislation (Weil, 1995a, ch. 1; 2002, ch. 5, pp. 135–64).

Eventually, the economistic and humanist positions largely prevailed and shaped the two *Ordonnances* of 19 October and 2 November 1945, two ambitious pieces of legislation that created the framework for immigration policy for the next decade (Hollifield, 1991; Weil, 1995a, p. 85). They updated the country's nationality law (*code de la nationalité*) and sought to organize migration flows intro France as well as the modalities of workers' stays in France.

The 1945 framework and the generation gap

The objective of the nationality code was partly to facilitate the integration of migrant workers, and more generally to go back to a liberal, humanistic nationality framework to replace the illiberal one of the Vichy regime. It maintained the French conception of nationality, mixing *jus soli* and *jus sanguini*, that had obtained before the Vichy period. It maintained the principle of attribution of nationality by descent. Automatic acquisition of nationality was made possible for all individuals who were born in France, were residing there at the time of their majority and who had resided there for the preceding five years (Body-Gendrot, D'Hellencourt and Rancoule, 1989).[1] It also accorded French citizenship at birth to children born in France of parents born in France. Finally, the code facilitated the conditions for naturalization in order to encourage the assimilation of immigrants in French society, reflecting the influence of the demographers' 'populationist' school. Applicants qualify for naturalization after a period of five years of residency, but they first need to apply for this. There have been a number of such naturalizations in the extra-European community in recent decades, especially since applicants are not in practice required to renounce their original nationality (Weil, 2002, ch. 9, pp. 247–70). But, on the whole, the number of immigrants who have sought to naturalize has remained rather limited, because the procedure is little advertised and dauntingly complex. In 1999, only 36 per cent of immigrants, defined as persons residing in France and born a foreigner in a foreign country, had acquired French nationality, or in absolute terms 1,560,000 people out of 4,310,000 (Weil, 2002, p. 251).

The *Ordonnances* also created the Office National de l'Immigration (ONI), which was to have a monopoly over the importation of migrant labour, as opposed to letting employers act autonomously. The ONI was to organize immigration according to employers' needs, and supervise all its aspects from the recruitment of workers in their own countries to the management of their stay in France. On this last point, in particular, the *Ordonnance* set up a new system of residence permits of varying lengths, pegged to the obtaining of work permits. The system was not particularly restrictive but it did leave most *immigrés* with different degrees of stability of residence, until a reform of the system in 1984 merged the permits into a single 10-year permit. In the next decades the French state followed through this attempt at organizing migration by setting up a series of similar ad hoc structures intended to supervise populations of migrant workers in France.

The combination of these two texts created a comprehensive framework that was to shape the figure of the *immigré* soon to emerge in French society and politics. The *immigré* was a foreign national settled on French territory for more than three months for an unlimited period. One should also add a socio-economic component to this juridical definition: the presence of the *immigré* in France was usually justified by employment in a large industrial company (Weil, 1995a, p. 89). As we shall see later, the other additional feature of the archetypal *immigré* in the French consciousness was soon to be someone of North African background, or more generally, of post-colonial background: North African or black African. This originated more in the unexpected failings of the French plan than in its intended effects.

The nationality code was to be modified significantly only during the 1980s and 1990s when immigration became politicized, and it has framed the politics of ethnic minorities in France throughout the post-war period. It has shaped the style of mobilization of immigrant communities in France since the 1970s in two fundamental ways. First, immigrants in France are foreigners and hence do not have the vote, and, despite the relaxation of the conditions for naturalization, there has never been any mass movement towards naturalization, as noted above. As a result, immigrants in France have for the most part been alienated from the French political community and have tended not to participate in electoral politics. This in itself has served to inhibit contacts with parties and politicians, who have had little interest in these non-voting populations. This must be qualified by a certain degree of immigrant participation in the Communist Party in the 1970s and in trade unions, who have sought to counterbalance their decline since the 1950s by recruiting foreigners (Miller, 1981, pp. 59–62). But, on the whole, participation of first-generation migrants was confined to the field of industrial action,[2] or to the spectacular rent strike of the late 1970s in the SONACOTRA *foyers* (Verbunt, 1980, pp. 319–21). Importantly, this state of affairs has also had a fundamental consequence on the way in which immigration has been constructed in the French national debate on the issue (Freeman, 1979, ch. 1). This appeared most clearly in the 1980s. Since immigrants were not citizens, they were not seen as entitled to formulate claims in the sphere of conventional politics. In addition, the fact that a large proportion of ethnic minorities are foreigners focused liberal concessions to their interests on the granting of voting rights or on the provision of ad hoc social services for foreigners. More ambitious policies, such as anti-discrimination legislation or multicultural education, of the kind that emerged in Britain, have largely remained hypothetical ambitions despite some timid innovations in the late 1990s.

The second characteristic of the nationality and citizenship regime – the automatic granting of French nationality to children of immigrants born on French territory – has resulted in second- and third-generation North Africans and other extra-Europeans who live in France having the vote. This has had three consequences. First, their existence as a potential electoral force began to be acknowledged by political parties, local politicians and associations in the mid-1980s, albeit in a tentative and partial way (Leveau, 2000; Geisser, 1995; Jazouli, 1986), when they came of age (although many second-generation individuals were already active in associational politics in the late 1970s [Jazouli, 1986; Bouamama, 1994]).[3]

Second, and perhaps most importantly, the automatic granting of voting rights to second-generation immigrants creates a deep division between first-generation immigrants (commonly dubbed *les immigrés* [the immigrants]) and second- and third-generation immigrants (*les Beurs*, or euphemistically *les jeunes* [youths]), adding this juridical division to socio-economic and political divisions: not only do first-generation immigrants care more about domestic political issues and industrial disputes than their children, who are more concerned about unemployment, social disadvantage and racial discrimination, but they are also for the most part voiceless while the latter have the vote. To this one might add that the instability of residence authorization for the first generation also served to deepen the gap between the two generations. This gap lies at the heart of many of the developments in ethnic minority politics in the 1980s and 1990s. The second-generation Beur movement focused on the deepening of citizenship, calling for the recognition of cultural and religious diversity within the community of French citizens. In doing so they were involved in organizational difficulties, one being the lack of skill and support that more mature and experienced first-generation immigrants could have brought to the movement (as first-generation West Indian and Asian immigrants did in campaigns against racial discrimination in Britain).

Third, the fact that second-generation migrants could easily become French through these legal provisions proved to be fertile ground for the mobilization of rightist anti-immigrant sections of public opinion in the 1980s, including by the Front National. The notion of *Français de papiers* ('paper Frenchmen') was freely bandied about by proponents of immigration control in this period to highlight the ease with which the code turned second-generation Algerians into French nationals – French in law but not in fact, according to this ethnicist line of argument.

The unexpected arrival of extra-European immigrants

France had been an immigrant country long before the Second World War, importing engineers, workers and soldiers to remedy declining birth rates. Hence, by 1946, foreigners, mostly from other western European countries, accounted for 4.4 per cent of the population in France (Hargreaves, 1995, p. 8). In the post-war years, the foreign population of the country continued to rise to around 6 per cent in the 1980s and 1990s. This increase was fuelled in part by immigration from western Europe (mainly Spain and Italy, but also Belgium and Poland) until the mid-1960s, then from Portugal in the late 1960s and 1970s, and, as will appear below, of large Maghrebi populations in the 1950s, 1960s and 1970s.

Scholars have noted the failings of the organization of migration flows by the ONI.[4] These failings produced unexpected consequences that changed the profile of the immigrant population in France. Immigration flows in the 1950s and 1960s soon got out of hand, as shown by Freeman (1979, pp. 73ff.). France sought to organize migration through a series of bilateral treaties with countries of origin: Italy in 1946 and 1951, West Germany in 1950, Greece in 1954, Spain in 1961, Morocco, Mali, Mauritania, Tunisia and Portugal in 1963, Senegal in 1964, and Yugoslavia and Turkey in 1965 (Freeman, 1979, p. 74). But the variety of the conditions and numbers among these different accords created confusion. The ONI system also quickly proved inefficient and incapable of processing the large number of individual migrant cases, while employers frequently did their own recruitment of clandestine workers, who were more easily acquired than through the ONI system and made for a more malleable workforce.

Because of this situation, the migration flow to France increasingly included migrants from North African countries (Morocco, Algeria and Tunisia), as well as more limited, though significant, numbers from French overseas territories (300,000), from the 1950s onwards (Freeman, 1979, p. 76). The percentage of foreigners in the total population did not increase dramatically between 1946 (4.12 per cent) and 1990 (6.35 per cent), but the proportion of North Africans among them did. Between 1946 and the 1980s, the percentage of European immigrants in the total population of France rose by just 13 per cent, while that of extra-Europeans, mostly from North Africa, was multiplied by 14 (Schain, 1990, p. 254). By 1990, Maghrebis accounted for around 40 per cent of foreigners, the same proportion as Europeans (the remaining 20 per cent being made up largely of Asians and other Africans [Hargreaves, 1995, p. 11]).

Consequently, the total of extra-European migrants in France was estimated to be 2,150,000 in the 1980s (Schain, 1993). Excluded from this count are individuals of foreign descent but of French nationality who, if counted, would considerably raise the total. The most significant part of this population, politically and demographically, is the Algerian and Moroccan group, although it is important to bear in mind that Europeans form a large population in France as well. These two groups are largely congruent with the Muslim population of the country (with the addition of the smaller Tunisian and Turkish populations), which is impossible to estimate precisely but which was frequently cited as being around 3 or 4 million in the 1990s (Kepel, 1991).

The migration flows from Algeria proved particularly difficult to regulate, and indeed this had been anticipated and feared by the architects of the 1945 *Ordonnances*.[5] This was linked to the colonial status of Algeria, in this respect not entirely dissimilar to the status of New Commonwealth countries in the British case. Since 1946, and until it gained independence in 1962, Algeria had the status of a metropolitan territory and Algerians were therefore free to move into France proper as they wished. Incidentally, this was also, and still is, the case of DOM-TOM territories (*Départements et Territoires d'Outre-Mer*), whose residents have been free to migrate to Metropolitan France without controls. As part of the 1962 independence settlement, France agreed to continue to accept large numbers of Algerian migrants into France (Freeman, 1979, p. 82; Weil, 1995a, pp. 95–8). In 1964 this freedom of movement was restricted by a bilateral agreement, which only partially succeeded in limiting the flow of Algerians.

The management of North African populations by the central state

The French state reacted to the unexpected flow from North Africa in the centralized ad hoc style inaugurated with the ONI. First, it created the Fonds d'Action Sociale (FAS), a governmental fund, to cater for the needs of Algerian immigrants. The FAS was exemplary of the differential treatment meted out by the French state to Algerian migrants, who in Algeria until independence in 1962 were given the status of second-class citizens. As the demographics and national origins of immigrants changed and diversified, the FAS adapted itself and, in 1966, its policy remit was extended to funding all local groups and projects pertaining to the welfare of immigrants in France, not just Algerians. In this way the construction of Algerians as differentiated populations eventually spilled over into the management of all foreigners.

The broad objective of the FAS came to include co-funding housing renovation and health awareness programmes with local authorities, as well as funding well-established charities that provided leisure, cultural and educational activities for ethnic minorities (Schain, 1993). This encouraged the development in France of a large and active network of immigrant community groups. In the same way, a special agency for the housing of immigrant workers, the SONACOTRA, was created and run centrally, independently of local authorities (Kepel, 1991, pp. 126ff.).

The notion that the state should be responsible for the welfare of immigrants stands in sharp contrast with the attitude of the British government. The latter did not organize migration flows because they were uncontrollable, and because the responsibility for the delivery of social services in Britain lies with local authorities (see chapter 2). In this way, the French state assigned the category of '*immigrés*' to immigrant workers of foreign nationality who were to be dealt with separately from others through ad hoc institutions and programmes. This again could not be in sharper contrast with the British situation, where there was in fact never a hint of differential treatment, before the notion of race became dominant and race relations policies were introduced. In fact, as Freeman points out, this type of treatment directed at New Commonwealth immigrants in Britain could have been perceived as discriminatory (1979, p. 171). This contrast is paradoxical, since after the 1960s the British became more prone than the French to emphasizing pluralist values in the field of migration and race relations. But it can be understood by looking back at the status of the colonial subject in the two empires: while British 'subjecthood' was applied without discrimination throughout the British Empire, the French never gave full citizenship to indigenous Muslim populations, always construing them as second-class French citizens.

The French programmes also helped to distance local authorities from preoccupations linked to immigrants living on their territories. Local authorities in France did not appear to governments and immigrants alike as a focus for policy innovation or mobilization, although this must be qualified by developments in the late 1970s in which local authorities played a part.

1974–1983: The Bureaucratic Management of Political Incertitude

From migrants to minorities

After the student rebellion and the general strike of 1968, the authorities tried to restrict immigration; but it was not before the oil shock of 1973 and the rise of unemployment that the immigration of all guestworkers was brought to a complete halt in July 1974. The decision was taken in the context of high uncertainty by the *secrétaire d'état aux travailleurs immigrés* (secretary of state for immigrant workers), a newly created ministerial post intended to coordinate the action of various ministries on the issue of immigration. In this, France was following the example of Germany, which had suspended its own migration in November 1973 for similar reasons. Six months after the suspension of immigration, in 1975, family reunification was again authorized. These steps marked the first ostensible realization by the French government that the population of immigrant background settled in France was to pose a series of new problems throughout the following decades.

The emergence of immigrant populations as a policy problem was also prompted at the time by the ongoing process of transformation from a population of temporary workers into a large ethnic minority group, with all the salient characteristics of an ethnic minority: a new and foreign religion, Islam, and waves of racial hatred directed against minorities among the native population. A growing population of second-generation immigrants, young French nationals born in France of foreign parents, was developing.

The main policy response to this situation was a social policy with some attempts towards multiculturalism. This was undertaken primarily by the *secrétaire d'état aux travailleurs immigrés*, Paul Dijoud. The control of the Paris mosque was handed over to the Algerian government, in an attempt to create some sort of representative institution of Islam in France. Foreign language classes, especially Arabic classes, were started in schools (Weil, 1990, p. 9). Finally, the rising issue of Islam in France in the mid-1970s was dealt with in the same way. The authorities sought to cater for the religious needs of North African workers by discreetly encouraging the construction of prayer rooms in factories, workers' *foyers* and public housing (Kepel, 1991, p. 62). Here again, as with the creation of the FAS the authorities were trying to extend their centralized style of management of immigrants. This time, however, what they were trying to monitor was no longer a migratory wave but a multicultural element in French society.

Struggling to define immigration policy

While the 1970s was a period of renewed concern about immigration on the part of administrative and bureaucratic elites, it did not yet elicit a debate in the political arena. Rather, the elites sought to anticipate and prevent fully fledged social disorder and the political damage this could entail by continuing to monitor ethnic minority populations (Weil, 1990). As in the previous period, immigration was a state affair and was debated between various interest groups and personalities behind closed doors. As Freeman argues, there was neither enough public agitation nor interest for the main parties to get involved in debates on immigration:

> None of the major Left parties have had a great deal to say about immigrants until relatively recently [the author is writing in 1979]. In general, they have limited their activity to rhetorical attacks on government policy, protestations of solidarity with migrants, and condemnations of racism. The reasons for this should by now be clear – migrants pose difficult problems and they do not necessarily or easily fit into traditional categories of analysis. Furthermore, they have lacked the essential political privileges that would have allowed them to be recruited and organized by parties for electoral or agitational purposes. Besides, many migrants are apolitical or petit-bourgeois in their orientation. Given the essential election strategy of the PS–PCF [Socialist–Communist] coalition, a strong defence of the rights of immigrants might have reduced its support among the working class. All of these facts have led the established parties to tread lightly in this area and forfeit the immigration issue to the revolutionary Left and counter-revolutionary Right. (Freeman, 1979, pp. 244–5)

However, unlike in 1945, the governmental elite were reacting to the unintended consequences of the previous period. The governments of the moderate right-wing UDF president Valéry Giscard d'Estaing tried a series of different, often contradictory, approaches. On the whole, the basic thinking was that immigration was now a problem because it represented an unwanted workforce in the context of rising unemployment. But proposed solutions ranged between extremes. Weil (1990) shows how between 1977 and 1983 governments took various policy initiatives oscillating between, first, an attempt to repatriate large numbers of North African workers in 1979 and, second, bold openings towards ethnic minority groups on the part of the new Socialist government between 1981 and 1983.

An important turning point came in 1977 in the direction of forced returns. The deteriorating economic situation triggered xenophobia among an unemployment-weary electorate, in the perception of the government, and encouraged it to take increasingly illiberal measures. Family unification was slowed, voluntary return was encouraged, and in 1978 the government, closely supported by President Giscard d'Estaing, decided to organize mass returns of populations that had been established in France for a long time. The original aim was to 'ship back' 500,000 people over a five-year period, mostly to the Maghreb, and especially Algeria, because of their particular visibility for the xenophobic section of the public (Weil, 1990, p. 9). This operation was to combine two aspects: an external one, the negotiation with the Algerian government over the repatriation of its citizens, and an internal one, to extend the French state's possibilities of expulsion to other categories of foreigners and increase the possibilities for control of work permits by departmental authorities.

Weil shows how the plan encountered principled opposition from the Conseil d'État and from certain segments of the government's majority in Parliament, all acting in the name of 'Republican values of tolerance and respect of human rights'. Elements in Parliament manoeuvred so as to deprive the government of vital resources in its negotiations with Algeria. Ultimately, the final negotiation with Algiers in 1980 made possible only voluntary returns (Weil, 1990, p. 10), and the original plan of repatriation failed. It had been the most extreme illiberal position taken by a government in this period, and its failure marked the limit of the field of possibilities in that direction.

The victory of François Mitterrand in the 1981 presidential election one year later provided the opportunity for the government to experiment with opposite possibilities, in the direction of liberal policies. Mitterrand's first government[6] set out to implement the '110 propositions' of the Mitterrand presidential campaign, which in the area of immigration consisted of a series of measures aimed at facilitating the incorporation of ethnic minorities within the population. This included the reversal of the illiberal measures taken in 1977: family reunification was again authorized and encouragement to return was stopped. The job market could no longer justify the non-renewal of a work permit. Most importantly, the government legalized the situation of 130,000 illegal immigrants who had arrived before 1 January 1981. However, the Socialists rapidly discovered the limits of liberal policies, especially when confronted with strong resistance to one of their pro-immigrant proposals, the establishment of voting rights for immigrants in local elections. The idea raised constitutional difficulties and put the Socialists on a collision course with a hostile public opinion. At the end of 1982, immigrant strikes in the car industry, and the politicization of immigration in the 1983 municipal elections, put an end to the liberal phase of the Socialist governments (Weil, 1990, p. 10).

1983–1997: National and Local Politicization of Immigration in Xenophobic Terms

In contrast with previous developments, immigration became politicized in the 1980s and 1990s. From 1983 onwards, it became an almost constant preoccupation of political parties, overshadowing electoral contests, if not figuring at the forefront of debates. It was politicized both because of a national protest movement by second-generation North Africans (Beurs) and, most importantly, because of the rise of a strong far-right party, the Front National (FN). What I argue here is that overall, and in contrast with Britain, the specific terms under which the issue was politicized played out against attempts to participate by minorities. Hence, the marginality of immigrants in French public life, caused to a large extent by the French citizenship regime and the bureaucratic organization of the migration wave in the previous period, was continued in the early 1980s because of the general climate of intolerance towards issues pertaining to minorities stirred up by the Front National. Their marginality was due in this period to the internal politics of the Socialist Party, which weakened migrants' movements. More generally, it is due to the reaction of French party elites to the Front National, since they failed to argue effectively for liberal values against those of the FN, which in turn further pushed issues of ethnic minority representation away from the political agenda.

In the first section below, I argue that the attitude of the Socialist Party was central in bringing about the failure of the Beur protest movements of 1981–4 as well as the failure of their offshoots that were still active later in the decade. Much of the support for the movement came from factions within the party elite that sought only short-term benefit from their association, and withdrew support when circumstances changed. The overall result is that the Socialist Party did not play the role of solid, long-term ally, as the Labour Party did for anti-racist and black liberation movements in 1970s and 1980s Britain.

The second section shows that the evolution of the party system in the 1980s was marked by the emergence of the FN and by the convergence towards the centre of the two mainstream blocks, led on the left by the Socialists, and on the right by the UDF/RPR.[7] This mainstream political establishment was held hostage to the FN's relentless instrumentalization of migration issues throughout the 1980s and 1990s. The political elite on both sides responded with an uneasy mix of attitudes. They sought to promote the notion that there was no immigration into France, which was dubious, if only because of illegal immigration. At the same time, in a clear contradiction, election after election saw the multiplication on both sides of promises to restrict immigration flows, in an attempt to take on board the FN's agenda. The dominant discourse on both sides of the political divide came to rest on the defence of a rigid interpretation of an idealized French republican model of citizenship against the perceived threat of multiculturalism. The result was the imposition on French politics of a vision of immigrants either as an issue not to be mentioned or as undesirable foreigners.

The Socialist Party and the failure of the Beur movement

By 1980, and throughout the following two decades, immigrants were a diverse and numerous population, of both European and North African and African origins. European migrants represented around half of the migrant population, with in particular a large Portuguese community (764,860 or 21 per cent of the foreign population), other populations being Italians and

Spaniards (9 per cent each). The North African population was made up predominantly of Algerians (785,920/22 per cent), Moroccans (431,120/11 per cent) and Tunisians (189,400/5 per cent). Roughly the same proportions held for 1990, apart from a rise among Moroccans and Turks, who moved respectively to 16 per cent and 5 per cent.[8]

While European migrants, dominated by Portuguese and Spaniards, did not attract attention, the extra-European was confronted with classic issues of racial discrimination and racial violence. The period between 1978 and 1981 saw a large increase of racist violence against anti-second-generation North African youths, typically police brutality or racist murders. This climate of violence sparked a nationwide series of sometimes violent youth protests, which had two main consequences.

First, it encouraged the Socialist government, already well disposed towards migrants, and in some respects building on the social policies experimented with under Giscard d'Estaing's presidency, to expand policies aimed at migrants. This took the form of the relaunch and expansion of French urban regeneration programmes by the central state (which had already started in 1977). Like their British equivalents, these programmes were on the whole colour-blind and targeted areas rather than groups, relying on the notion that the crisis was to be understood primarily as an urban crisis rather than one affecting a particular social or ethnic/nationality group. For this reason they included regeneration programmes that were mostly non-ethnically discriminant, such as the funding of cultural associations, support for local branches of job-seeking agencies or the renovation of housing blocks. They were to be periodically renewed and extended in the next two decades, often in line with five-year funding programmes allocated by the state to regional authorities (Donzelot and Estebe, 1994).

There were caveats to this general indifference towards specific ethnic subgroups of the population. The central preoccupation of these programmes – violent behaviour on the part of disaffected youths of recent migrant background – appeared implicitly in some of their central measures: the organization of holidays for youths from housing projects to avoid summertime agitation (*opérations anti-étés chauds*) (Dubet, Jazouli and Lapeyronnie, 1985), and the creation of 'zones of priority education' (*zones d'éducation prioritaire*, ZEPs), one of the criteria for which was the percentage of foreigners in particular areas (Bachman and Le Guennec, 1996; Dubet, Jazouli and Lapeyronnie, 1985). Indeed, the main policy guideline of the early 1980s was *insertion*, designating a pragmatic approach to integration problems that encompassed various social policy measures such as the ones mentioned above, and which to some extent recognized that immigrants and minorities were to be dealt with differently from other recipients of social services (Lorreyte, 1989; Ministère des Affaires Sociales et de la Solidarité Nationale, 1986; Commissariat Général au Plan, 1988). However, *insertion* came to be replaced in the second half of the 1980s by *intégration*, a vision with more assimilationist leanings which left little or no place for the recognition of ethnic diversity.

The resources and powers of the FAS, the large fund for immigrant and minority groups created in the 1960s, were also much expanded, its budget doubling between 1980 and 1986 and the number of associations it funded increasing fourfold (Schain, 1996, p. 22). In the course of this process, it became the major organizer of immigrant and minority politics in France, and made possible the emergence of a lively scene of minority cultural and social associations, cstimatcd at around 4,600 in 1983 (Schain, 1996).

The second consequence of the wave of violence was to spark a large protest movement among second-generation North Africans. It developed on an unprecedented scale and was directed against the authority of the state. In doing so, it emulated other protest movements in France and reflected the structure of opportunity offered by the French state, whose centralized organization and preponderant role in initiating social change encouraged such movements (Duyvendak, 1995). The movement was also largely shaped by the French nationality framework mentioned above. It coalesced around the fact that there was a generational, institutional and social gap between first-generation immigrants, mostly non-French nationals, who stayed out of the movement, and their children, a large number of whom were born in France and therefore had French nationality, and who felt that they had a strong claim to effective citizenship and recognition. Hence, the demands of the new associations that emerged focused on anti-racism, recognition of the equality of all before the law, regardless of cultural or racial difference, and the acceptance by French society of these differences: what the Beurs called 'real citizenship' as opposed to formal citizenship. This was in essence a claim pertaining to ethnic difference. By the nature of its institutional and legal origins it was condemned to weakness from the start, because its youthful actors were inexperienced and cut off from older and more experienced first-generation movements which, as noted earlier, had mostly kept to industrial disputes in their few attempts at participation.

The movement culminated in the summer of 1981 in a series of sit-ins, hunger strikes and demonstrations in various suburbs and housing projects, mostly in Paris and Lyon, which were widely portrayed by the media as racial riots (Poinsot, 1994, p. 80). This spontaneous and uncoordinated movement became popularized by the national media as the 'Beur movement'; Beur then went on to become a byword for second-generation North African youths, although many later rejected the term as a simplifying label. It crystallized initially in the *Marche contre le Racisme et pour l'Égalité des Droits* (March against Racism and for Equal Rights) in the autumn of 1983, then in the 'Convergence 84' movement the following year. The 1983 march began as a local initiative in Lyon led by a coalition of young North African leaders, Christian movements, both Catholic (led by the charismatic figure of Father Delorme) and Protestant (with the human rights group Cimade), as well as radical Trotskyite and other far-left activists. A handful of marchers started out from Marseille, with the aim of reaching Paris after a series of stops in towns with a North African population. What began as an obscure and tentative enterprise slowly gathered pace and started attracting media attention; the arrival in Paris was nothing short of triumphal, with a crowd of 100,000 coming to greet the marchers (for the history of the movement see Jazouli, 1986; Lapeyronnie, 1987; Negrouche, 1992; Bouamama, 1994).

In spite of this success, the movement was unable to organize itself into durable structures and failed to obtain noticeable policy concessions. Convergence 84 met with limited success the following year. By that time the movement had edged closer to the Socialist Party, which encouraged the creation of associations that would tie it in with the movement and its supporters with public opinion, and attract sympathetic voters to the party. Two such associations were SOS Racisme and France Plus. SOS Racisme, the first and most successful of these associations, was supported by the group within the Socialist Party that was closest to Mitterrand, in particular the young *député* Julien Dray, but also senior figures such as Laurent Fabius, then prime minister, and Jack Lang (Bouamama, 1994, p. 122). It sought to build on the sympathy inspired by the movement among French youths in general, and on the sensitivity of the public to human rights issues. It therefore stressed the relevance of the Beur issue to other ethnic minorities, Caribbeans and Asians, as the 'right to be different' (*droit à la différence*). It also challenged a broader progressive public, appealing to notions of an all-embracing, tolerant and enlightened France. SOS Racisme was from the outset a highly centralized organization, run by a charismatic figure of African-Caribbean descent, Harlem Désir, who focused on media campaigns. Its heyday was between 1984 and 1987, with its popularity reaching a peak during its successful campaign against Prime Minister Chirac's proposal to restrict the conditions of access to nationality (see below).

In contrast, France Plus, created in 1985 by other groups within the party who were supporters of Lionel Jospin, the future prime minister, and Louis Mermaz (Bouamama, 1994, p. 126), chose the alternative strategy of narrowing their focus on the specific problem of the Beurs themselves and their participation in conventional politics. It sought to address the Beurs' defining problem – formal citizenship, but actual economic and social exclusion – by encouraging their electoral participation through three stages: campaigning to encourage electoral registration, encouraging higher turnout at elections, and using this voting power to negotiate the selection of ethnic minority councillors by parties (France Plus, 1989). The Socialist Party was a prime target, but all other parties apart from the Front National were approached as well, with some success. This was the closest attempt to encourage the participation of North Africans in electoral politics, with the aim of enhancing their visibility in French institutions and their ability to influence policy. It succeeded to some extent in getting around 200 councillors of North African origin elected in town halls in 1989 (Geisser, 1995, 1997).

However, after the heyday of the early 1980s, and mid-1980s for SOS Racisme and France Plus, media attention and grassroots mobilization subsided in the later years of the decade and the movement entered a phase of terminal decline. First came several ideological conflicts, centring on the amount of emphasis to be given to multiculturalism, as well as groups focusing on issues of citizenship, which exacerbated the rifts. The movement also split into complex divisions, mainly between Christian and left-wing activists on the one hand, and young North Africans themselves on the other, with the latter accusing the former of seeking to 'reclaim' the movement for political purposes.

The decline was also largely due to the diminishing support of the Socialist Party. Competing groups within the party who had provided essential support to both associations, but whose interest was only in short-term strategies aimed at seducing progressive public opinion, withdrew their help when other issues arose (see Bouamama, 1994, ch. 4, pp. 113–53).

The rise of the Front National and the contradictory reactions of party elites

An attempt at bipartisan depoliticization. Although the Beur movement was a highly publicized major social movement of the 1980s, it was rising electoral xenophobia that actually pushed immigration into the French election arena. The Front National, hitherto a marginal party of the far right, rocketed to electoral success on a populist, anti-establishment and anti-immigrant platform. This phenomenon can be dated precisely to the municipal elections of 1983, in which the FN fielded candidates in a handful of cities and in some cases won 11 per cent of the vote, and to the European elections of 1984, in which it also gained 11 per cent of the vote, a stunning result in a nationwide election for what had been until then a marginal party (Perrineau, 1997, pp. 32–4). This radically altered the climate of political debate in subsequent decades and goes a long way towards explaining why the Mauroy government, formed in March 1983, reneged on its liberal promises and reverted to illiberal policies, encouraging voluntary repatriation, reinforcing controls along borders with Maghreb states, restricting family immigration and intensifying the state's fight against illegal immigration.

Following the left's U-turn, French political elites consensually reached a common policy guideline on immigration, not altogether different from that reached by Labour and the Conservatives in 1960s Britain. This was partly a reaction to the FN phenomenon, and partly the culmination of a process of defining a coherent immigration policy through trial and error that had begun in earlier times (Weil, 1990).

Parliament passed a bill on 17 July 1984 that instituted a 10-year residence and work permit stabilizing the situation of a large number of immigrant workers in France. This fostered a consensus on the main features of an immigration policy acceptable to the parties on the basis of the various policy attempts of previous years. The main features of this consensual policy closely resembled those of the British consensus: temporary suspension of migration flows to France, on the basis that immigration to France was no longer desirable; and, at the same time, official acknowledgement that those already settled in France should be allowed to stay, with the inauguration of a more liberal system of residence permits. In an alternative formulation, there was a consensual focus on two tasks perceived as complementary: (1) the control of borders and the consequent repression of illegal aliens, and (2) the 'integration' of those already settled (Viet, 2004, pp. 259–60).

The reasons for these specific modalities are also strikingly similar to those that shaped the British consensus on race and immigration 20 years before: political party elites realized that continuing to experiment with policies that were either too illiberal (such as the repatriation of 500,000 Algerians in 1979 by the moderate right-wing government) or, on the contrary, too liberal (such as the granting of local voting rights by the Socialists after 1981) might contravene the basic values of the national polity, essentially liberty, equality and 'public order' (Weil, 1990, p. 16), on which their legitimacy as leaders rested.

There were, however, two crucial differences from the British consensus of the 1960s. First, the French consensus was markedly less liberal than the British one. The difference between the two countries is rooted in the political and administrative history of migration. While in Britain the liberal citizenship regime inherited from the colonial subjecthood regime had made it impossible from the outset to deport immigrants, and hence focused the debate on the twin policy areas of restricting flows and seriously attempting to combat racial discrimination, in France there was no such check on repatriation possibilities; indeed, repatriation was even contemplated in 1978 (although ultimately not adopted). In addition, Britain alone in Europe was influenced by the ideology of community relations and the US black liberation movement. While Labour and the Conservatives had linked immigration restriction with anti-discrimination policies and attempts to monitor the well-being of ethnic minority populations at the local level, in France the Socialists and the moderate right coupled their immigration restriction with only a tacit acceptance of the idea that those who were already settled in France should be allowed to stay. 'Integration' policies in France never reached the degree of innovation and explicitness of British policies. French integration policy, with the *politique de la ville* as its centrepiece, did not depart from the mostly colour-blind approach set by the Socialists after 1981. It achieved only limited or even negative effects, as retrospective assessments recognized later (Donzelot, 2003).

The Front National: a pervasive and durable force in immigration and minority politics. The situation in 1980s France differs fundamentally from that of 1960s Britain in one more respect. While depoliticization was successful in Britain, in the sense that it effectively resulted in the marginalization of radical illiberal voices, including those of Enoch Powell and then the National Front in the 1970s, it failed spectacularly in France. From the 1983 municipal elections and the 1984 European elections, and all throughout the 1980s and 1990s, the Front National went from strength to strength, always using anti-immigrant feelings as its trademark. The party did particularly well in the first round of the presidential election of 1988, when it polled 14.4 per cent, and in the presidential election of 1995, when it polled 15.1 per cent of the vote. In the first round of the 1997 legislative election, it was polling 14.9 per cent of the vote (Perrineau, 1997). Even after a split in 1998, it still polled a record 16 per cent of the votes in the first round of the 2001 presidential election, beating the Socialist candidate Lionel Jospin to second place behind centre-right candidate Jacques Chirac, losing against the latter only in the second round.

The rise of the FN was concomitant with the emergence of right-wing populism in several western European countries in the 1980s, but it was starker than elsewhere. The explanations for its successes are diverse, but it is clear that it managed to aggregate a variety of grievances: unemployment, immigration, insecurity, revolt against the political establishment. In 1984, it attracted mainly voters from the right, but later it attracted large numbers of abstainers and disappointed voters from the left, particularly former Communists (Schain, 2000, p. 3). Its comparative strength was encouraged by two institutional features of the French political system. First, the emphasis placed in the French system on the presidential election, which stresses candidates' qualities of charisma and leadership, favoured Le Pen. The heavily proportional system used in the 1986 legislative elections, which helped smaller parties, also favoured the emergence of the FN at the beginning of its rise in 1986.

Second, the weak cohesion of the two electoral blocs in French politics made it more difficult for party elites to operationalize strategies of depoliticization. In particular, Mitterrand's policies did much to divide his own side on minority-related issues. His invitation of a delegation of Beur marchers in 1983 to an official meeting at the Elysée Palace angered some among the Socialists. Symmetrically, on the right, the national line on ignoring the FN's agenda was often disregarded in regional politics, where some moderate right-wing leaders chose to govern local assemblies in coalition with the FN. This happened as early as 1983 in Dreux, and it always occurred with the implicit blessing of large sections of the national leadership.

The weak cohesion of the two electoral blocs was also in part linked to the presidential aspect of the system, which encourages individuals to divide their own sides in order to eliminate potential opponents. It has often been argued that the introduction of a proportional element into the electoral system in 1986 was engineered by Mitterrand to favour the FN and thus weaken the right. He also seemed to resuscitate the proposal to grant local voting rights to foreigners before each election in order to mobilize the left-wing electorate, as well as to weaken the moderate right in its struggle to retain voters attracted by the Front National (Weil, 1991, pp. 95–6). Certainly, the proportional system used in the 1986 legislative election was introduced by Mitterrand and had the direct effect of bolstering the FN's results. The latter polled 10 per cent of the vote and obtained 35 *députés* in the National Assembly (Perrineau, 1997, p. 41).

The strength of the FN effectively brought the issue of immigration to the forefront of the electoral debate and kept it there, in spite of constant efforts on the part of the Socialist Party and the RPR/UDF to keep a low profile on the issue. Because these parties on the whole clung to the consensual policy outlined above throughout this period, they effectively cleared the way for the Front National to run the debate. The FN easily succeeded in portraying itself as the only party that did not adhere to the status quo on immigration inaugurated in 1984 (Viet, 2004, pp. 262–3). It powerfully shaped the construction of immigrants and their children in the French political debate, in terms of a xenophobic denunciation of North Africans. The latter were portrayed as a numerous population that constituted a threat to French identity and to law and order; they were therefore to be stopped from entering the country, or repatriated for those who were already settled on French soil. This of course did not ease discussions on deepening the citizenship rights of French nationals of North African origin, racial discrimination, foreigners' rights, and the participation of immigrants and minorities in French politics.

The other parties were intimidated by the FN's capacity to steal voters just by mentioning immigration. Consequently, they sought to avoid the issue. Yet, in many instances, they caved in to the temptation to try to outflank Le Pen's party by developing anti-migrant (and anti-minority) rhetoric of their own. On several occasions, the FN's electoral successes encouraged mainstream parties to take on board its xenophobic agenda (Schain, 2002, p. 237). Socialist Prime Minister Laurent Fabius was noted for declaring in 1986 that the Front National asked 'real questions', although it offered 'false answers'.[9]

Most notably, elements of both the liberal UDF right and the Gaullist right were repeatedly tempted to conclude local alliances with FN leaders in the context of regional politics in the late 1980s and 1990s. The FN's popularity also convinced the right-wing governments of 1986 (Prime Minister Chirac) and 1993 (Prime Minister Juppé, Minister of the Interior Charles Pasqua) to propose restrictive reforms of the nationality code. In the first instance, the attempt was repealed by the mass protest of left-wing students, monitored by SOS Racisme and by President Mitterrand.[10] In the second instance, the proposed reform was accompanied by a proposal to tighten immigration legislation, in a departure from the 1984 consensus, and to further restrict conditions of acquiring French nationality. In particular, French nationality was no longer automatically granted to children born on French territory to foreign parents, as had been the case since 1945 (and before that since the end of the nineteenth century), but was made dependent on a 'declaration of intention' between the ages of 16 and 21 (see Weil, 2002, pp. 175–82). This provoked an outraged reaction from the liberal segment of public opinion, represented by a variety of humanitarian and migrant-help organizations. It also did nothing to bring back FN voters to the moderate right, as the party's high score in the 1995 presidential election demonstrated.

The twin myths of zero immigration and republican 'integration'. In spite of these nationality law crises and the nationality reform laws of 1986 and 1993, consensual agreement over immigration was on the whole maintained and included a set of assumptions about immigration and minorities. Prominent among these was the official stance that immigration had now been halted, and that all attempts at suggesting that there might in fact be a problem linked to immigration in France were misleading. It was hoped that this type of discourse would defuse public emotions about immigration, but in fact it brought them to a head. While the statement was true enough of legal immigration, it did not account for the continuing and significant flow of illegal immigrants in the 1980s. Hence FN voters who did witness new arrivals of immigrants in their areas were comforted in their impression that the establishment was lying (a point made by Weil, 1995b, 2001).

In addition, the consensus crystallized in the 1980s and 1990s around a longstanding tradition of republican 'integration' of migrants. While there were several strands of policy guidelines directed at ethnic minorities in this period, such as *insertion* or *intégration*, which were more tolerant of ethnic diversity than mere assimilationism, the vision of minority inclusion conveyed by these guidelines was nonetheless largely 'colour-blind' in comparison to British policies. Steeped in the values of the French Revolution and promoted by centre-left governments during the first decades of the Third Republic, this popular understanding of French identity holds that the French nation is a 'political' nation, i.e. that it is primarily the adherence of its members to a single, indivisible political community that makes them nationals; hence, all nationals automatically share full citizenship rights on an equal footing, and no distinctions are to be made between nationals, in order to preserve equality between all and the unity of the nation. This approach to nationality and citizenship has some legal foundations. The stress on equality of treatment regardless of sex, colour or creed is grounded in French public law (Lochak, 1989).

The transposition of this approach to the context of the late 1980s and 1990s eclipsed possible alternatives until 1997, and led to a radical and intransigent reconstruction. In this version, ethnically conscious policies were to be avoided, because they reified ethnic difference and led to the formation of ethnic conflict and the creation of ghettos. As peasants were assimilated into French society under the Third Republic by the action of institutions such as schools and the army, so it was felt that North Africans should simply melt into French society. Here, liberal premises led to the rejection of mechanisms that might defend the implementation of individuals' rights, if the recognition of racial diversity were necessary to defend those rights. The precedent of Italian and Polish workers who blended into French society in the first half of the century through participation in trade unions and the Communist Party (see Noiriel, 1986) seemed to confirm the viability of this model for the 1980s and 1990s.

The specifically French nature of this model was stressed by the often used phrase '*le modèle français d'intégration*' ('the French model of integration'). It was opposed to an Anglo-Saxon or German model, often presented as organized around the interests of ethnic groups, which encouraged the formation of ghettos and created ethnic conflict (see Ireland, 1994, p. 96; Hollifield, 1994; Guiraudon, 1996; Favell, 1998, chs 3, 5; De Rudder, Poiret and Vour'ch, 2000). Some academic works also served at the time to reinforce the influence of the republican assimilationist perspective among the public (prominent among which were Schnapper, 1991, and Todd, 1994; Crowley, 1992b, offers a review of other characteristic works). Originally advocated by the left, this vision of nationality and citizenship was gradually accepted by the moderate right as well, which became evident in the 1980s and 1990s (until 1997), when its dominance on the political scene became overwhelming. The much publicized 'headscarf affair' of 1989[11] revealed the passionate commitment of much of the country's elite and public opinion to this vision (Feldblum, 1993). Support for the reconstructed doctrine of republican assimilationism has been so vehement that its inconsistency with previous or ongoing policy lines, such as the multiculturalist stints of the *Secrétariat d'État aux Immigrés* in the late 1970s, immigrant-specific policies such as the *zones d'éducation prioritaire* (ZEPs) in the early 1980s, or the growing role of the FAS in institutionalizing minority associations in the 1980s, has been little noted in France until the late 1990s (Ireland, 1994, p. 96).

Discourse putting forward republican integration was dominant because it functioned particularly well as an apparatus for legitimating the defensive status quo maintained by the principal parties. Republican integration side-lined the idea that voting rights in local elections should be extended to foreigners, since citizenship was granted only to nationals, and thus this embarrassing issue was conveniently excluded from discussion. This was useful for the right, which sought to avoid exposing its indecision in the face of tough competition from the Front National. It also worked to the Socialists' advantage, since, apart from Mitterrand, they were notable for their lack of sustained support for the issue (Oriol, 2003, pp. 71–4).

The situation provided no ideological or policy ground for a lasting alliance with minority interests such as those articulated by the Beur movement, even if the latter had been able to carry on after its initial emergence. It made it difficult to justify a place for an equal opportunities policy or the recognition of cultural or religious difference, or anything for that matter that would depart from the general precept that all 'citizens must be treated equally'. It inhibited the realization by political parties that the second-generation immigrant vote remained, in strategic terms, largely untapped, and it prevented those within parties who were tempted to seek that vote from making any visible and reasonably ambitious attempts to do so.

The exclusion of ethnic minorities in the 1989 and 1995 municipal elections. The negative impact of this national framework inhibited the participation of minorities in city politics from the 1980s up until 1997. Two features of central–local relations in France contributed to this outcome. The inter-penetration of central and local politics has caused the issue to be constructed locally in the same way that it has been constructed nationally (see Grémion, 1976; also Hoffman-Martinot in Gabriel and Hoffman-Martinot, 1999). In particular, the fact that cities with large minority populations are controlled by a variety of parties, all of which have a stake in national politics, makes it impossible for a British-style situation to occur, where minorities' interests have come to be entrenched locally in industrial cities dominated by Labour. In addition, the FN's influence in national politics is also felt in local politics. In fact, the FN obtained high scores in local politics, just as it did in national elections, as soon as it became capable of fielding candidates across all large cities, in the 1989 municipal elections (an average score of 8.95 per cent of the votes in cities of more than 100,000 inhabitants, with peaks above 15 or even 20 per cent [Gabriel and Hoffman-Martinot, 1999, p. 116]). In the 1995 municipal elections, it increased its average score in these cities to 11.95 per cent (ibid.).

National-level factors have impacted differently across localities. In particular, republicanism has been most influential in local politics by enabling those actors who perceived it to be in their own interests to reject attempts by minority interests to gain leverage and representation. The

Lille–Roubaix comparison in chapters 5 and 6 serves as an illustration of this.

The modalities of that exclusion were shaped not just by national politics, but also by the characteristics of French local politics. The electoral system, with its majoritarian city-wide emphasis, discourages the participation of small outsider groups that propose candidates for election without the support of mainstream parties. To have a reasonable chance of getting elected, candidates must be on lists that are assured a minimum of votes (5 per cent) in order to be allowed to compete in the second round. The presence of ethnic minority candidates therefore depends on the decisions of senior local party leaders who compile the lists of candidates. These leaders take all the decisions with little internal opposition, for the whole of their party's list in one city. In a context in which ethnic minorities are seen as desirable, as became the case in the 2001 municipal elections, this is actually a facilitating factor because local leaders can easily choose the candidates they want. But if ethnic minorities are seen as a liability, as was the case in the 1980s and 1990s, the reverse is true: ethnic minorities have little possibility of exerting pressure on the list-makers (see chapter 5 on Lille for an illustration of this situation in 1989 and 1995).

An important exception to the repeated absence of minorities in representative politics were the 1989 municipal elections, when an unprecedented – and unrepeated – number of North African candidates were elected. On this occasion, these candidates surfed the wave of publicity for the North African population created by the Beur movement in preceding years to negotiate places on parties' lists. In a large number of cases (varying from 90 per cent to just 25 per cent, depending on estimations), they benefited from the institutional support of France Plus, who organized negotiations with the parties and acted as a 'community placement agency' (Geisser, 1995, p. 27). As a result, between 100 and 200 councillors of North African background were elected in cities across France in 1989. This result remained limited, and the predominant feeling among those elected was that of marginalization within the council; many resigned or were not re-elected in 1995.

As in Britain but even more forcefully, a strong 'locality' factor was in operation. Arguably, this is difficult to observe because in most cases there was little participation to speak of. But there were various degrees and types of exclusion, and, in the case of the 1989 municipal elections, the process of candidacy and election of North African councillors followed a great variety of paths. They were taken on board by diverse parties, although the Socialist Party was by far the most frequent with 83 per cent of the elected councillors, followed by 15 per cent for parties of the moderate right (and 2 per cent for other parties) (Geisser, 1995, p. 26). The variety of paths was most pronounced with regard to the candidates' relation to the party that chose to put them on their lists: 40 per cent were 'personalities', i.e. individuals who were desirable because of their socio-economic background (e.g. doctors or professors), while 19 per cent were leaders of local associations.

The configurations of the two local institutional variables under discussion – local party politics and local styles of government – combine into a greater variety of situations than in Britain, thus accounting for the more pronounced variations between cities. The complexity of local political systems means that cities with large minority populations can be either large communes in the centre of urban areas, such as Marseille, Lille, Strasbourg, Nice and Paris, or in many cases small suburban towns at the periphery of these areas with high-rise housing projects. In the latter case, the percentage of minority populations in the commune can reach high levels, while in the central communes the percentage is usually lower. In addition, the dynamics of cooperation and competition between these cities within the structures of local groupings of urban communes add to the complexity of the system (as illustrated by the Lille–Roubaix comparison; see chapters 5 and 6). Some are controlled by the moderate right, some by the Socialists and some by the Communists (particularly in the 'red belt' around Paris but also in other traditionally industrialized areas such as the Marseille area, the Rhône-Alpes region and the Lille–Roubaix–Tourcoing area). Finally, in spite of the growing influence of political parties on local politics (Dion, 1986), the persistent institutional and political weight of the mayor in the French municipal system makes the individual personality and career trajectory of the mayor a prominent element of local politics, in contrast with the limited and temporary hold exercised by council leaders on their group in British cities. The personal approach taken by mayors on particular issues may therefore vary greatly and reflect their personal approaches and strategies rather than partisan ideologies (as was the case in Roubaix under Diligent's terms as mayor; see chapter 6).

The Construction of Consensus after 1997

Only after 1997 did mainstream political parties break away from the xenophobic subtext of the 1993 nationality reform and the crackdown on undocumented migrants. Three inter-related elements participated in this shift.

Socialist policy innovations

First and foremost was the return to power of a Socialist government led by Lionel Jospin, after the two centre-right governments led by Prime Ministers Edouard Balladur (1993–5) and Alain Juppé (1995–7). One of the new government's first moves was to undo the illiberal changes made by the right to the nationality regime in 1993, while not entirely returning to the previous legislation. In particular, the declaration of intention to become French for youngsters born in France of foreign parents was abrogated and replaced by automatic accession to French nationality, except for those who wished to remain foreigners. The aim was to guarantee the right to choose one's nationality in a more effective way than before the 1993 reform (Weil, 2002, pp. 178–81). This reform had far-reaching effects because it was largely accepted by the right, and therefore took the sting out of the debate on nationality and immigration. In the years that followed, immigration and nationality essentially stopped being discussed in the political arena, for the first time in 15 years. In an interview given to *Le Monde* a year and a half after the reform, former Prime Minister Alain Juppé (RPR) declared: 'I hope the time for consensus has arrived. Certainly, when I was in power, I didn't always contribute to the consensus, but the left also has to take some of the responsibility. Today, the climate is more favourable for the definition of a policy that can have the support of the great majority of French people. [. . .] I admit that it has, in a way, released the tension surrounding immigration issues by taking its inspiration from the Weil report's proposals [which directly inspired the Socialist reform]' (*Le Monde*, 01/10/99).[12]

At the same time, in January 1998, the Front National went through the most severe internal crisis of its history, with Bruno Mégret, a former associate of Jean-Marie Le Pen, leaving the party along with some of its activist base and creating a new, competing far-right party, the Mouvement National Républicain (MNR). While it became evident in the 2001 municipal elections and the 2002 presidential elections that the FN had not at all been weakened by this split, but had on the contrary continued to improve its scores (Mayer, 2003), the immediate perception among public opinion and political parties in 1998 was that the FN had been dealt a severe blow. With its charismatic leader aging, the party's heyday seemed a thing of the past.

The Socialist reform of the nationality law, coupled with the FN's troubles and a renewed economic dynamism, fuelled a new confidence in the future. It ushered in a new political context which encouraged changes in policies of 'integration'. It encouraged intellectual and political elites to operate a moderate shift away from the hardline interpretation of republicanism that had dominated since the mid-1980s. An influential report by the Haut Conseil à l'Intégration (High Council for Integration) recommended following the example of British policies and creating a French version of the Commission for Racial Equality, recognizing de facto that racial discrimination was indeed a policy problem in France (Haut Conseil à l'Intégration, 1998). The Socialist government launched modest initiatives in that direction, most notably with the creation of a national hotline to report acts of racial discrimination (Body-Gendrot and Wihtol de Wenden, 2003). Minister of the Interior Jean-

Pierre Chevènement took the initiative of instituting local forums, known as CODACs (Commissions Départementales d'Accès à la Citoyenneté [Commissions of access to citizenship]), for discussing discrimination issues at the *département* level (Bleich, 2003, p. 199).

These innovations showed that republican assimilationism was not after all incompatible with ethnically conscious policies, but that the latter might on the contrary serve to preserve and consolidate the values of the republic. Indeed, some of the crucial actors in the post-1997 changes were leading proponents of *l'intégration à la française*, for instance Jean-Pierre Chevènement, a veteran defender of left-wing nationalism steeped in the idealistic and universalistic values of the French Revolution. The Haut Conseil à l'Intégration noted as much, pointedly entitling its report: 'Combating Discrimination: Implementing the Principles of Equality'[13] (Haut Conseil à l'Intégration, 1998).

Parties across the political spectrum gave some positions on their lists to ethnic minority candidates during national elections that were considered to be less important, i.e. regional and European elections. During these elections, both the number of minority candidates and elected representatives were on the increase in the 1990s. Between 42 and 59 regional councillors in the 2004 regional elections were estimated to be of extra-European background, which remained a modest number but was up sharply from the previous European elections.[14] The European Parliament was also the opportunity for several to gain seats, again for all parties. Then came the municipal elections of 2001, which, as noted above, produced a significant number of ethnic minority councillors of ethnic minority background, at least for a time. As in Britain, most of these were candidates on left-wing lists (Geisser and Oriol, 2001, 2002).

Yet these innovations remained limited. Anti-discrimination policies have been criticized for their piecemeal and limited character (see Hargreaves, 2000). Instead of a French version of the British Commission for Racial Equality, what was created was a modest advisory board, the Groupe d'Études et de Lutte contre les Discriminations (GELD; Group for Studying and Combating Discrimination [see Geddes and Guiraudon, 2002]), which did not succeed in having a lasting influence on policy-makers. In hindsight, the failure of the Beur movement in the 1980s appeared to many in the early 2000s as a historic failure to articulate problems linked to ethnic diversity in the French polity. Increasingly voiceless and frustrated segments of the North African population, concentrated in disadvantaged estates on the peripheries of cities, seemed to be withdrawing from attempts at participation in mainstream institutions, turning instead in many cases to political apathy or to fundamentalist brands of Islam.

What remains striking is that, in spite of this belated spate of anti-discrimination policy activism, it is the idea of republican assimilationism that has the most profoundly coloured French thought and action. While not as stringent and hegemonic as in the 1990s, negative assumptions on the desirability of ethnic categories and recognition of diversity in the public sphere still underpinned French policies and inhibited the development of more ambitious policies. The decision to pass a law banning the Islamic headscarf in public schools in 2004 is motivated by a different rationale. It may be cautiously interpreted as a manifestation of lingering assimilationist feelings, but it must also be understood as a specific reaction to the ostensible radicalization of some Muslim groups encouraging girls to move towards increasingly stringent interpretations of Islam (in particular the Union des Organisations Islamiques de France [UOIF; Union of Islamic Organizations in France], which is the largest and most influential of the traditionalist and fundamentalist Muslim groups in France). Some members of the Stasi commission (which proposed the ban on headscarves in public schools) have adamantly defended their decision to recommend the ban, but these are also the same people who pushed for anti-discrimination policies after 1997.

The 2001 local elections

The emergence of a new consensus favourable to ethnic minorities impacted heavily on the 2001 local elections. The very same features of the French political system – the inter-relatedness of the local and national levels of government – that had contributed to delegitimizing ethnic minorities in local arenas now encouraged local party organizations to consider them in a more positive light. In a national context of discussion about creating anti-discrimination policies, it became almost fashionable to feature French men and women of extra-European background on electoral party lists. Correlated with the new context was the belated realization by national partisan headquarters of the electoral potential of French people of immigrant descent (*Le Monde*, 08/03/01). In addition, as noted earlier, the characteristics of the local electoral system that had previously served to keep ethnic minorities out of party lists now conspired to facilitate their inclusion. With large powers of selection of candidates concentrated in the hands of the leadership of local parties, the shift from undesirable to desirable was followed by clear effects.

Many minority councillors, however, were elected only by a narrow margin because they were placed lower on their party's lists, often in barely electable positions (see *Libération*, 02/03/01). Accession to elected positions rarely meant accession to symbolic and powerful positions, such as the meaningful post of adjunct or mayor in medium or large cities. The election of city councillors of ethnic minority background was not correlated with any substantial change or innovation in cities' attitudes towards their disadvantaged areas and populations, or even simply recognition of the scale of the problems faced by urban ethnic minorities. As noted above, efforts to implement anti-discrimination policies remained largely discursive and tentative in 2001, and this was reflected in the attitude of local assemblies and bureaucracies (Ghemmaz, 2002). Finally, there was still no *député* (Member of Parliament) of North African background in the National Assembly after the 2002 general election, although two women of North African background were elected to the Senate in the 2004 senatorial election (one Green and one Socialist).

What characterized these elections compared to Britain is the lack of an engrained vision of racial or ethnic disadvantage as a political issue that had legitimacy in the sphere of urban politics. This in turn can be traced to the long marginality of municipalities in managing migrant populations, and to the superficiality of the Socialists' interest in minorities. The failure of the Beur movement was still felt in 2001 because it deprived the Socialists of a large, committed and politically mature pool of minority activists, which the new urban left brought to the Labour Party as early as the late 1970s. If the trend towards increasing inclusion continues in the next municipal elections in 2006, it will probably remain patchy, devoid of hard policy effects, or in forms that are difficult to foresee.

Conclusion

By depriving a large section of the ethnic minority population of voting rights, the French nationality framework created from the outset a structure of opportunity that discouraged immigrant participation in conventional politics. This was compounded by the quasi-monopoly exercised over immigration affairs by specialized state institutions, many of which, like the FAS and the SONACOTRA, had their origins in the special treatment accorded Algerian migrants before decolonization. This policy framework contributed to keeping issues related to immigration out of the spotlight of public debate.

When politicization did occur in the 1980s, its terms were set by the anti-immigrant Front National, in spite of the temporary success of the Beur movement. This inhibited the change towards pro-minority strategies on the part of local councils. Mainstream parties were never able to make liberal measures in favour of immigrants a part of their consensual policy, as they were in Britain. Their main response to the Front National's repeated electoral successes was to defend a republican assimilationist policy line which devoted little attention to issues of symbolic recognition and empowerment, including ethnic minority participation in city councils.

Because of the inter-relatedness of local and national competition, the issue of minorities in city politics has been formulated in the same way as the issue of immigrant politics at the national level, that is, in terms of the country's capacity to assimilate immigrants and their desirability (Schain, 1993, 1995; Crowley, 1993). This has meshed with the characteristics of French local institutions to exclude immigrants from politics, with the limited parenthesis of the 1989 municipal elections. The importance of mayors and their grassroots support has created a greater diversity of situations than in Britain. This is reflected in the large differences between the two case studies described in chapters 5 (Lille) and 6 (Roubaix).

The moderate reform of nationality law and immigration law made by the Socialists in 1998 has not since been challenged. This phase of political appeasement coincided with the temporary weakening of the Front National to shift the terms of the political debate towards the issue that has lingered since the Beur movement, that of the economic, social and political inclusion of minorities. A period of economic growth, the coming of age of a large number of ethnic minority voters and the Socialists' introduction of a 50 per cent quota of women on all lists of candidates for elections coincided with this political context to produce the outcome of burgeoning inclusion in the 2001 elections. The cases of Lille and Roubaix serve to remind us, however, that the impact of this change was far from uniform, with cities perpetuating patterns of exclusion and others moving towards inclusion.

16

4

gham, 1980s–2001: Inner-city ~~Labour~~ Politics and Pluri-ethnic Government

After the break-up of the Greater London Council (GLC) in 1986, Birmingham became the largest local authority in Britain (with a population of around 1 million). It has a large and diverse ethnic minority population, and it also retains an essentially English 'provincial' aspect that makes it typical of many other British cities. The authors of a landmark study on the politics of immigration and race in 1960s and 1970s Birmingham made this very point 25 years ago about the Handsworth inner-city area:

> It is a symbol of areas of black, and particularly West Indian, settlement in Birmingham and possibly of black immigrant settlement in Britain as a whole. Obviously there are some areas of greater immigrant concentration in London, such as Brixton, Ealing or Willesden, but arguably, since these are part of the main metropolitan area of Great Britain, they are subject to some special circumstances which make them atypical. While Handsworth and Birmingham are provincial, on the other hand, it is hard to conceive of a scenario in the development of race relations in Britain in which they do not figure importantly. Certainly one could say that outside London, Handsworth is one of Britain's race relations capitals. (Rex and Tomlinson, 1979, p. 70)

This could probably still be said of the whole city today. The city has undergone all the metamorphoses typical of large industrial British cities, having been hit hard by the demise of Fordist styles of production in the 1970s and slowly converting to new technologies and services since then. It has also moved from being the symbol of British anti-immigrant politics to one of the symbols of new, multicultural Britain.

In the 1950s and 1960s, Birmingham acquired a reputation as a hotbed of urban racial conflict and xenophobic agitation. This image reached its peak when right-wing leader Enoch Powell gave his anti-immigrant 'rivers of blood' speech in 1968 in a Birmingham hotel. Spectacular changes have occurred since then, the city becoming a national and international centre for Muslim life and displaying signs of a rather advanced process of inclusion of minorities in the economic and political fabric of the city, in spite of racial riots in 1985. In 2001, an Asian candidate, Khalid Mahmood of Pakistani-Kashmiri background, was elected for the Perry Barr constituency in the north-west of the city, becoming one of the 12 Members of Parliament of ethnic minority background in Birmingham.

The city council has found itself at the heart of these changes, moving from indifference to minority-related issues in the 1950s, 1960s and 1970s to an avowedly pro-minority strategy of government in the 1980s and 1990s, with new, proactive policy-making in race equality and with multiracial coalition government in the 1980s and 1990s. Most notably, minority activists, especially of Pakistani, Bangladeshi and African-Caribbean descent, have become involved in grassroots Labour Party politics, fuelling the emergence of a black and Asian elected elite on the Labour benches of the council.

It is important to note that some localities with different institutional configurations have offered fewer opportunities for participation. This is the case, for instance, in Wolverhampton, just outside Birmingham, where ethnic minority councillors are less well represented on council benches in the early 2000s than their Birmingham counterparts. Nevertheless, Birmingham is broadly representative of a clear nationwide trend.

This chapter analyses how the Labour elites of the city co-opted ethnic minority politicians in their networks in the 1980s and 1990s, in effect building a multi-ethnic coalition and thereby encouraging a process of incorporation of minorities in the political system. The argument is based on a qualitative survey made in the city between the autumn of 1997 and 2000, based on personal interviews with city councillors (mostly of ethnic minority background), council officers, leaders of local community groups and charities with local press sources,[1] and a variety of local government documents. I also build on work produced on the politics of immigration, race and ethnic minorities in Birmingham by Rex and Moore (1967), Rex and Tomlinson (1979) and, most importantly, by John Solomos and Les Back (1995). Solomos and Back's study provides an in-depth portrait of racial politics in the city in the 1980s and early 1990s as well as many illuminating insights into local political developments of that period.

In keeping with the general thrust of this book, I argue that the institutional structures that frame and constrain the conduct of local elites have played a central role in explaining this phenomenon, opening up the networks of the grassroots Labour Party. Acceptance in these networks then opened an avenue toward representation and influence on the city council because the Labour Party has enjoyed unprecedented dominance of the politics of the city. In the three cities under discussion, as most probably in the whole of western Europe, ethnic minorities who wish to participate in conventional politics have experienced difficulties doing so because they cannot access the organizations that exercise a strong control on candidacies to elections: political parties.

The usual reason for this in western Europe is that parties are always to some extent organizations that favour insiders, and, in the case of minorities of recent, extra-European background, this problem is compounded by the prejudice almost always displayed by grassroots party members towards foreigners who wish to join (regardless of the party's position on the political spectrum). There is clear evidence that the Labour Party in Birmingham used to be no exception, until a new configuration of local institutions appeared. This institutional configuration was a particularly important factor, compared to both other factors in Birmingham and the configuration in Lille and Roubaix, which made minority leaders lean towards the Labour Party; crucially, this configuration also made it difficult for them to be ignored by the various components of the party.

As in the cases of Lille and Roubaix, the institutional variables that are considered here are the local party organizations, as well as the organization of local government, mainly electoral systems. In particular, a comparative back-and-forth look at the three cases points insistently to two aspects of the organization of local government, and two institutional features of the local Labour Party. The first two are the fragmentation of the electoral territory of the Birmingham City Council into wards and the plurality (first-past-the-post) electoral system in use for local elections in the city. The other two features are the relative autonomy of branch organizations for candidate selection and the structure of intra-party competition within the local Labour Party.

These elements combined to provide an open political opportunity structure for ethnic minority leaders and activists in the city who were coming of age in the late 1970s and 1980s. They were of varied ethnic background, but had in common an ideological proximity with the Labour Party coupled with an involvement with local community work. The combination of closeness to Labour and rising electoral leverage of the communities that they were in effect leading made them valuable allies for more established, native British leaders and groups in the party. Solomos and Back (1995) showed that, in addition to this, there was an internal struggle then taking place between the left and the right of the party, and that both sides sought the support of these activists in one way or another. These activists were able to play on the afore-mentioned institutional resources to establish themselves as important members of the party in the inner-city wards, to get elected as Labour coun-cillors, and to encourage the council to introduce race and ethnicity as a pre-occupation in the conception of its policies.

In the first section below, the shift from indifference to minorities in the 1950s, 1960s and 1970s to a lasting alliance of the newly dominant Labour leadership with ethnic minority activists in the 1980s is retraced. The second section begins by presenting the groups of left-wing, community-oriented ethnic minority activists in the city, and then moves on to describe the favourable opportunity structure offered by the institutions of the Birming-ham polity. In the third section, I examine the processes by which they ascended the party ladder. This occurred over the last 20 years in the context of annual local elections in the 10 or so inner-city wards that have large ethnic minority populations (out of 39 wards in total). In all wards and throughout the period, rising representation was based on the bargaining of electoral resources by minorities in the context of left–right divisions in the party. But they have differed in terms of choice of allies, left or right, and in terms of the relative importance of the electoral bargaining and ideological proximity with activists. I distinguish between three overlapping models: the patronage model, the activist model and the ethnic community model.

From Indifference to Multi-ethnic Coalition: The Birth of Ethnic Politics in Birmingham

This section begins by drawing a profile of the city's institutional landscape and its minority population, both of which constitute the essential context for understanding ethnic minority politics in the city. It then retraces the process by which the council moved from indifference to pro-minority, multi-ethnic government.

Birmingham government: polycentric and partisan

The city of Birmingham lies in the middle of the metropolitan area of the West Midlands.[2] The total population of the West Midlands was 2,551,700 in 1991, making it the third largest urban area by its population in Britain after Outer London and Inner London (about 110 miles to the south). Alto-gether these local authorities constitute a largely urbanized and industrialized area that sprawls around Birmingham itself, and includes several other large cities such as Coventry and Wolverhampton, each with a population of about 250,000.

The region has been at the centre of the British metal and engineering industry since the industrial revolution. Indeed, the development of the city of Birmingham and its rise to the position of the first provincial British town occurred rapidly during the nineteenth century and are closely linked to the development of industry (see Briggs, 1952). Birmingham's traditional areas of specialization are the manufacture of motor vehicles and the processing of non-ferrous metals; it also used to be known for small arms, jewellery and small metal products (Joly and Candappa, 1994). Today, it remains a major industrial centre and is recovering from the economic crisis that blighted industrial Britain in the 1970s and 1980s. In the 1990s, the city council tried to diversify the industrial base of the city by developing new, high-value activities such as telecommunications, pharmaceuticals and computer software/hardware services (Economic Development Programme 1997/1998, Birmingham City Council). It has also worked on transforming the city's image by renovating the city centre and rebuilding the Bull Ring shopping centre, originally constructed in the 1960s, which had become a byword for urban decay in Britain.

Birmingham was officially granted the title of 'city' in 1897 by Queen Victoria. But the bases of its present organization date back to 1974, when the current borders of the city were established. There has been little change since then, apart from the abolition of the West Midlands county in 1986 by the Thatcher government, which made Birmingham City Council the largest local authority in Britain with around 1 million people (961,041, 1991 census, table 4.1[3]). Like all British local councils, it traditionally played a central role in the delivery of local services, particularly housing, social services and management of primary education. Since the 1980s, large parts of these remits, especially housing and education, have been taken away from city councils in the wake of successive Conservative reforms.

The city's political system is characterized by territorial and institutional fragmentation. The city is divided into 39 wards, each ward electing a councillor every year in a plurality 'first-past-the-post' (simple majority) system (see map 7, p. xvii). In Birmingham, there is no election every four years; hence, at any given moment, each ward is represented by three councillors on the city council, making a total of 117 councillors.

Until 2000, in addition to meeting in plenary sessions, these councillors carried out most of their work in 18 committees, divided into sub-committees. Among the most important were community affairs, economic development, education, equalities, general purposes, housing, National Exhibition Centre/International Convention Centre (NEC/ICC),[4] personnel, planning, social services and urban renewal. As was increasingly the case in British cities, decision-making procedures in the committees were dominated by political parties (see Stoker, 1991, p. 57). Important political decisions were voted by committees, and the control of the committee went to the party that had the overall majority on the council. Following the Westminster parliamentary model, the leader of the largest group was also the leader of the council and centralized much of the decision-making power, usually seconded by a small circle of influential councillors. What is important to note is that this system made the leader a markedly less powerful figure than a mayor, and the comparison with French cities is a case in point. Much in this system depended on the internal debates and conflicts within the largest group, with the leadership sometimes having to take into account 'rebellions' by the 'backbenchers', in other words, policy demands made by groups of rank-and-file councillors. More frequently, the ruling party group could scrutinize and regulate the leadership's activities, and 'at the very least senior councillors and officers must be careful not to offend the core political values and commitments of back-benchers' (Stoker, 1991, p. 98).

In 2000, the Labour council leader Albert Bore initiated a reform of the council's structure which replaced the committee system with two innovations: the introduction of a cabinet of 10 members, each of whom acts as head of a council department, and the creation of scrutiny committees, which have the power to examine and challenge the council's decisions. In conformity with nationwide reform trends, these changes were meant to open the way for the institution of the post of mayor, which was to be decided later by the local electorate in a referendum.

A large, diverse and disadvantaged ethnic minority population

The history of migration of ethnic minority populations and their socioeconomic characteristics determine to an important extent the issues that are of interest to them and which they are likely to translate into political mobilization.

History of migration and ethnic groups. Post-war migration into Birmingham is in many ways typical of national British patterns: it started in the late 1940s, earlier than in many other European countries, and consists mainly of two groups, West Indians and Asians, the latter comprising Pakistanis, Indians, and later Bangladeshis. In addition, there are a variety of much smaller communities, including Yemeni, Chinese and Irish. In the late 1990s a new wave of immigrants appeared, largely asylum seekers from a variety of countries, in particular ex-Yugoslavia and East Africa. What distinguishes the city from many others is the numerical importance of the ethnic minority population, around 200,000 people in the 1991 census, for a total population of just under

1 million, making Birmingham both the largest city in Britain and the largest ethnic minority community in the country. In relative terms, around a fifth of Birmingham's population was of post-war, New Commonwealth immigrant background in the 1990s, making it highly visible and relevant to all aspects of urban life. A strong increase continued through the 1990s: in the 2001 census, close to 300,000 people, or nearly 30 per cent of the city, described themselves in the new census category as either 'mixed', 'Asian or Asian British', 'Black or Black British' or 'Chinese or other ethnic group'. The same trends were also at work in the urbanized areas of the West Midlands lying just outside the city, which had the second highest concentration of ethnic minorities in the country after Greater London.

Unlike industrial ports such as Liverpool or Cardiff, however, which had black African populations as far back as the eighteenth century, Birmingham did not witness any significant immigration movement prior to the post-war, post-colonial wave. There is one important exception, the Irish community, which already made up 4 per cent of the city's population in the 1960s (Woods, 1979), and under 3 per cent in 2001. The economic boom of the 1950s, fuelled by the reconstruction effort, resulted in a shortage of labour in industries and foundries around Birmingham, and prompted the first phase of the migration, consisting of young, single men who came to work in industries in and around the city. This was facilitated by the liberalism of British legislation on nationality and immigration, compared to other post-colonial European states. Increasingly restrictive legislation with the 1962 and 1968 Commonwealth Immigration Acts prompted many immigrants to have their families join them in Britain while it was still possible, thus initiating the diversification of the country's immigrant population and the emergence of full-blown communities. The West Indian community started arriving first, in the early 1950s, while immigrants from South Asia came mostly during the 1960s. In 1971, a third Act effectively halted all immigration from New Commonwealth countries, except for family reunification. The 'myth of return' (Anwar, 1979) faded away in the 1970s as it became increasingly clear that this population was going to settle permanently and that the social and economic diversification of the community was continuing. Since then, a second generation has emerged, born in Britain of parents of New Commonwealth origins.

This migration pattern triggered a spectacular increase in the ethnic minority population over the years. In 1951, the population of people born in the New Commonwealth was under 1 per cent (1951 census); by 1961, it reached 2.65 per cent of the population with around 30,000, and it more than doubled in the following decade to reach 6.73 per cent (around 68,000) in 1971. The 1981 census, showing a category of 'population living in a household where the head of household is from the New Commonwealth or

Table 4.1 Ethnic group of residents in Birmingham, 1991

Ethnic group	Number	Percentage
White	754,274	78.5
Black	56,376	5.9
Black Caribbean	44,770	4.7
Black African	2,803	0.3
Black Other	8,803	0.9
Asian	129,899	13.5
Indian	51,075	5.3
Pakistani	66,085	6.9
Bangladeshi	12,739	1.3
Chinese and Others	20,492	2.1
Chinese	3,315	0.3
Other Asian	5,653	0.3
Other Other	11,524	1.2
Total	961,041	100

Source: Birmingham City Council, 1991 census.

Pakistan', showed yet a stronger increase in the rate of ethnic minority population growth, with 15 per cent in the city belonging to that category, more than doubling the 1971 population of migrants.

Swelled by second then third generations, the ethnic minority population of the city kept increasing to reach its 1991 and 2001 levels. In 1991 the two main groups were 'black' and 'Asian'[5] (1991 census, table 4.1). There were more than twice as many 'Asians' compared to 'blacks', and Pakistanis formed the largest single ethnic/national minority group. In 2001, the black or 'black British' population had maintained itself at a broadly similar level (approximately 60,000), but the Asian population had increased strongly, totalling around 190,000 people. The main cause for this was a near doubling of the Bangladeshi and Pakistani populations, the latter in particular moving from 66,085 to an impressive 104,017. It is important to bear these figures in mind in the context of the discussion below on the increasing assertiveness of politicians of Pakistani background in the city in the late 1990s and early 2000s.

Residential concentration and socio-economic disadvantage. In 1991, ethnic minority populations in Birmingham were heavily concentrated in inner-city areas (see

Table 4.2   Percentage of black and other ethnic minority groups in the total population by alphabetical order of wards[a]

Ward	%	Ward	%	Ward	%
Acocks Green	10.3	King's Norton	4.8	Shard End	3.6
Aston	**54.7**	Kingsbury	4.8	Sheldon	3.4
Bartley Green	5.3	Kingstanding	6.7	**Small Heath**	**59.7**
Billesley	6.8	**Ladywood**	**41.9**	**Soho**	**66.8**
Bournville	5.9	Longbridge	3.9	**Sparkbrook**	**66.6**
Brandwood	0.8	Moseley	25.3	**Sparkhill**	**62.3**
Edgbaston	24.2	**Nechells**	**48.9**	Stockland Green	17.0
Erdington	7.8	Northfield	3.0	Sutton Four Oaks	2.5
Fox Hollies	14.5	Oscott	5.2	Sutton New Hall	2.8
Hall Green	13.3	Perry Barr	10.9	Sutton Vesey	3.7
Handsworth	**69.3**	Quinton	7.7	Washwood Heath	37.9
Harborne	7.4	**Sandwell**	**56.5**	Weoley	5.5
Hodge Hill	6.1	Selly Oak	11.7	Yardley	8.2

[a] Wards in bold have more than 40 per cent ethnic minorities; Birmingham average = 21.5.
Source: Birmingham City Council, 1991 census.

map 2, p. xvii), and the 2001 figures show that the concentration was slowly increasing through the 1990s. The inner-city area covers approximately two parliamentary constituencies: the Ladywood constituency in the north-west, comprising the wards of Soho, Aston, Ladywood and Nechells, and the Sparkbrook and Small Heath constituency in the south-east, comprising the wards of Sparkbrook, Small Heath, Sparkhill and Fox Hollies. To these wards must be added the Sandwell and Handsworth wards, also with large minority populations, which are part of the Perry Barr constituency but neighbour the Soho and Aston wards, and Washwood Heath, which is part of the Hodge Hill constituency but touches on the Small Heath ward and has a large South Asian population. In 1991, Handsworth, Soho, Sparkbrook, Sparkhill, Small Heath and Sandwell wards had more than 55 per cent of their population composed of people from black and ethnic minority backgrounds. Aston had more than 54 per cent in 1991 (table 4.2).

In 1991, 57.3 per cent of Birmingham's ethnic minority population were to be found in seven of these wards: Handsworth, Soho, Sparkbrook, Sparkhill, Small Heath, Sandwell and Aston, discussed below. More than half of the population in each of these wards was composed of people from ethnic minority backgrounds, usually a combination of the various ethnicities. Within this, there were marked differences between the various groups. In a nutshell, African-Caribbeans tended to be concentrated in the northwestern inner city (nearly half of that population lived in six wards: Handsworth,

Table 4.3 Age structure of Birmingham's population
(percentages), 1991

Age range	White	Ethnic minorities	Total
0–17	64.6	35.4	100
18–24	73.7	26.3	100
25–39	77.4	22.6	100
40–59	84.2	15.8	100
60+	93.2	6.8	100

Source: Ethnic Groups in Birmingham, 1991 Census Topic Reports,
Birmingham City Council, 1991 census, p. 22.

Soho, Aston, Ladywood, Sandwell and Sparkbrook), while South Asians, and
particularly Pakistanis, were more heavily concentrated in the Sparkbrook and
Small Heath constituency, particularly in the Small Heath, Sparkhill
and Sparkbrook wards, where their concentration was particularly high, the
highest in the city for any group. Indians had their high concentrations in
Sandwell, Soho and Handsworth, and the highest proportion of Bangladeshis
was in Aston and Sparkbrook.

This being said, there is a certain degree of residential mix of these different groups in all these wards, with all groups present everywhere. The
important exception to this is the Pakistani areas of Small Heath, Sparkhill
and Sparkbrook, where in 2001 the Pakistani population alone accounted for
a very high 40 to more than 50 per cent of the total population, while other
ethnic minority groups reached lows of 3 to 5 per cent (see map 3, p. xix). In
those wards, the population self-described as white British was around 20 per
cent.

The ethnic minority population was younger than average in 1991 (see
table 4.3). The lower the age group, the higher the proportion of ethnic
minority representation within that age range; conversely, the higher the age
bracket, the higher the proportionate representation by the 'white' category.
There were, however, substantial differences in age structure between specific
ethnic minority groups. While nearly a fifth (20.7 per cent) of the white population was aged between 0–17, almost one third (32 per cent) of the black
and 44.2 per cent of the Asian populations fell within that age range.

On the whole, ethnic minorities have been upwardly mobile in Britain since
the early 1980s, with an increase of the proportion of those occupying positions of top-category employees – though it must be noted that this concerned
some ethnic groups much more than others, Caribbeans and Indians bene-
fiting most from this mobility, and Pakistanis and Bangladeshis much less so.[6]
However, the fundamental point to note here is that ethnic minority

Table 4.4   Unemployment by ethnic group (percentage), 1991

Ethnic group	Males (16+)	Females (16+)
White	14.9	8.2
Black Caribbean	27.2	15.9
Black African	27.7	19.7
Black Other	32.2	21.3
Indian	18.3	16.6
Pakistani	35.3	44.8
Bangladeshi	41.5	44.0
Chinese	15.5	14.3
Other Asian	29.4	27.2
Other Other	27.6	22.2
Total	17.3	10.4

Source: Birmingham City Council, 1991 census.

populations of inner-city areas as a whole remained chiefly characterized by economic disadvantage in the 1990s.

In 1991, ethnic minority residents were spectacularly more affected by unemployment than white residents: the rate of unemployment amongst black and Asian men was nearly double that of white men (14.9 per cent) (table 4.4). In particular, the highest rates of unemployment were amongst Pakistanis and Bangladeshis: 35 per cent of Pakistani men and 45 per cent of Pakistani women, and 41.5 per cent of Bangladeshi men and 44 per cent of Bangladeshi women were unemployed. Unemployment among black and Chinese women was almost twice as high, and, among Asian women, it was more than three times as high as the rate for white women. In 2001, the wards with the highest ethnic minority residential concentrations still presented clearly higher unemployment rates than other wards: for instance, 10.58 per cent in Aston, 8.90 per cent in Handsworth and 9.58 per cent in Sparkbrook, while other wards usually revolved around 5 or 6 per cent.

In sum, the ethnic minorities of Birmingham present the outward characteristics of the working-class population of Birmingham, of which they can be considered to be a sub-group. This is the first element in explaining the high level of support for the Labour Party among them. This situation is compounded by the spatial concentration noted above, because the inner-city wards have traditionally been Labour strongholds. The high level of minority residential concentration in these wards is also important because it has

combined with other factors presented in this chapter to give minority electorates a high level of electoral leverage.

The youth of the population and its high level of unemployment suggests
a high level of interaction with the school system and with social services, two
areas in which the council plays a large role. These two factors are also relevant in explaining the salience of certain issues among minorities, particularly relations between the police and young people (in general in Britain,
Solomos, 1998; in Birmingham in the late 1970s, Rex and Tomlinson, 1979,
pp. 223–4). African-Caribbean youths were often associated by the media with
negative images of street violence after the 1985 disturbances in the north-
west part of the inner city (see Gaffney, 1987, on the interpretation of these
disturbances by the press), and by the early 2000s Asian youths were also
increasingly described as violent (e.g., 'Leaders warn Asian gangs are getting
guns, organized crimes are increasing', *Birmingham Post*, 3/1/03).

From indifference and hostility to pluri-ethnic government: 50 years of ethnic politics

Because of the precocity and size of the wave of immigration, Birmingham
has had a long post-war history of immigrant politics. Looking back at the
last 50 years, the most striking feature is a radical and lasting change that
occurred in the early 1980s: from a general attitude of indifference to minority-related issues, laced with occasional displays of hostility towards them, the
council then started placing issues of race, cultural diversity and racial discrimination in a prominent position on its agenda. These types of policies
were then pursued consistently throughout the 1980s and 1990s. They took
two main forms: a fully fledged commitment to race relations and equal
opportunities policies on the part of council services and, most importantly,
an increase in the number of ethnic minority councillors from close to none
in the late 1970s to around 20 in the 1990s.

In a first phase of general immobility (1948–81), Labour and the Conservatives succeeded each other in power, with neither paying much attention to
immigrant populations and issues related to them. The Conservatives had no
policy on immigrant-related matters, other than displaying complacency
towards occasional xenophobic outbursts that came from their own ranks. As
for Labour, they took only limited steps to create some awareness of ethnic
minority issues, and did so only when prompted by the local church or by
concerned councillors from their own bench. In a second phase, from 1981
onwards, a new Labour majority managed to seize long-term control of the
council, permanently marginalizing the Conservatives, implementing a fully
fledged race relations policy and co-opting ethnic minority councillors into a
governing coalition.

1948–1981: alternating between benign neglect and anti-immigrant rhetorics. Anti-immigrant agitation became manifest in the city as early as the late 1940s, in the form of sporadic and limited anti-Indian protests.[7] From the late 1950s onwards, it grew in the hands of groups related to the Conservative Party. It rode the tide of increasing anti-immigrant feeling among the local population: a local opinion poll in 1956 showed that nearly 74 per cent of those questioned considered that there was a colour bar in Birmingham, over 98 per cent said they would be unwilling to take a coloured lodger and over 80 per cent wanted Commonwealth immigration to be restricted.[8] When the Conservatives were in the majority, for instance in the late 1950s, they passed a resolution asking the government to restrict immigration flows; when in minority, they continued to argue in favour of restrictions. They were encouraged in this attitude by several xenophobic campaigns initiated by grassroots Conservative members during that period; most prominent among these were the Nationalist Association in 1965, the Birmingham Citizen Association in 1956 and the Birmingham Immigration Control Association in 1960, all of which demanded immigration restrictions and were led by the same Conservative councillor, Charles Collett (Hill and Issacharoff, 1971, pp. 49–50).[9]

Support for these groups was considerable among local public opinion, as shown by the amount of letters to the editors on the issue received by Birmingham daily newspapers at that time.[10] In 1965, this support encouraged the minority Conservative group on the council to draft plans aiming to show the feasibility of a local ban on immigration. These developments took place in the context of the general election of 1964, when a Conservative, Peter Griffith, won the traditionally Labour constituency of Smethwick (just outside Birmingham) by campaigning energetically in favour of immigration restrictions, in the face of a general swing for Labour (Hartley-Brewer, 1965). This anti-immigrant period in the Conservative Party culminated in the summer of 1968, when, having just regained the majority in the local elections, they were encouraged by the conjunction of grassroots pressures and Enoch Powell's popularity. Powell's influence was then at its height and whipped up anti-immigrant fear and resentment among large and diverse sections of the British electorate (Hill and Issacharoff, 1971, p. 50; Hansen, 2000, p. 190). In the 1970s, the xenophobic agenda was picked up by the National Front, which managed to prop up some agitation (Newton, 1976, pp. 208ff.; Rex and Tomlinson, 1979, pp. 272–4), but without a lasting impact.

Pro-immigrant pressures in this period did exist, though they were discreet and limited. Most attempts by liberal-minded councillors to raise awareness about minorities met little success (Sutcliffe and Smith, 1974), and when the party did react, it was with limited humanitarian policies. From the 1950s onwards, there was a consultative body in charge of the welfare of immigrants, which had been set up on the initiative of the local bishop and which changed names several times over the years. At best, the Labour group on the council's education committee opened a Centre for Coloured People at the Clifton Institute, Balsall Heath, in 1951; a Labour alderman was also appointed as liaison officer for coloured people in 1954 (Sutcliffe and Smith, 1974, p. 368). In this, Birmingham was echoing nationwide policies documented in chapter 2.

In the 1970s, indifference to minorities was reflected among councillors of all affiliations: 53 per cent of councillors surveyed by Newton were unable to name an organization that was active in immigrant matters, while figures for educational and housing organizations, which were also studied in the survey, were lower, at 31 per cent and 35 per cent respectively (Newton, 1976, p. 215).

The Labour pro-minority regime from 1984. This situation started to change in the mid-1980s and led to a completely new outlook. The traditional alternation between moderate Conservative and moderate Labour leaders gave way to an unprecedented domination of the council by the Labour Party that was to last until the early 2000s. Labour briefly gained control of the council from the Conservatives in 1981, lost it in 1982, then regained it for good in 1984 (*Birmingham Post*, 4/5/84, 14/5/84). After this, it kept improving its majority, reaching the very comfortable level of around 80 councillors out of 117 in the late 1990s. The once-powerful Conservatives were reduced to a marginal opposition group, and even at times struggled with the Liberal Democrats for second place on the council (in particular briefly losing that position in 1996). In this, Birmingham was typical of many large cities in Britain which became the bastions of the Labour Party in the face of the Conservative domination of national politics in the 1980s and 1990s. After the election of a Labour government in 1997, the Labour group fell back to around 65 councillors, and its majority was slowly eroding until 2003, when it lost the absolute majority on the council by a narrow margin (57 seats, 59 needed to obtain the majority) and was forced to share power with the Conservatives. The Liberal Democrats had also become a potent political force by that time with 20 to 30 seats in the early 2000s.

In this period, the Labour group implemented a largely uncontroversial agenda of urban renovation and economic development which did not really contrast with previous policies (Loftman and Nevan, 1992). But, with regard to ethnic minorities, it departed from the city council's consensual style of politics and ventured into more controversial territory. It accelerated a burgeoning race relations policy, embracing as it did so the politics of left-wing London boroughs (albeit belatedly and somewhat tentatively), and co-opted a large number of ethnic minority councillors on the council, where there had been close to none before.

Proactive race relations policies. The Labour leadership of the council had a long-lived agenda of economic regeneration, involving in particular an ambitious project of renovation and renewal of the city centre.[11] This agenda went largely unchallenged by the Conservative opposition, who had initiated it before losing to Labour. The strong commitment of the council to these policies has generally been thought to reflect the pre-existing tradition of public partnership in the city. It also involved collaboration with local business interests, which is a local tradition that is consensually embraced by both parties, even when the Labour left took over the leadership in the 1990s. Indeed, it spontaneously embraced the American-inspired 'privatist' style of urban regeneration, based on partnership with the private sector, that the Conservative government was then seeking to impose on reluctant Labour cities such as Glasgow and Manchester (see Keating, 1988; Keating et al., 1989). This essentially economicist approach to urban regeneration (Loftman and Nevan, 1992) is based on the perception that the most pressing issue for cities is to facilitate the transition from an industrial to a post-industrial economy, rather than to tackle directly the problems of unemployment and social exclusion that increasingly affect the impoverished residents of these cities (Barnekov, Boyle and Rich, 1989, p. 12).

Where Labour did depart from the traditional mode of government and dominant creeds on urban policy is in its evolution from indifference to de facto alliance with a burgeoning black and Asian elite. In the case of cities such as Birmingham, the residents who are most directly hit by the crisis are the unemployed working-class inhabitants of the inner cities, many of whom are of ethnic minority background. In this respect, the strategy of Birmingham City Council did start moving towards addressing these issues as well: in parallel with urban regeneration projects, the council's most radical initiative in the 1980s was the adoption of a series of policies aimed specifically at increasing the welfare of ethnic minority populations.

The first such policies were brought in by the Conservative-led council in the first years of the 1980s: the declaration of commitment to an education policy for a 'multicultural society' (Joly, 1995, p. 192) and the adoption of formalized goals in the field of equality of employment within the council's workforce. In the early 1980s, the national context encouraged local authorities in this direction, in particular with the provisions of the 1976 Race Relations Act asking local authorities to implement race relations policies. But Labour clearly brought these policies to new levels of commitment when it gained control of the council for good in 1984. Targets for the employment of ethnic minorities by the council were maintained then extended. In the 1990s, a general target was that 20 per cent of the council's workforce should be of ethnic minority background (*Birmingham Post*, 31/10/00). In 1984, the new Labour Party created a race relations and equal opportunities committee, which was to sit alongside the 11 existing traditional committees of the council, and along with it a Race Relations Unit, a new structure that was the responsibility of the newly created committee. The unit was designed to promote good race relations in the affairs of the city and to monitor racial discrimination in the activities of the council's service delivery departments (mainly housing, social services and education). From its inception, it was placed at the heart of the council's administrative apparatus and reported directly to the chief executive. It became involved in a variety of education and regeneration programmes targeted at ethnic minority populations, and participated in impressing the need for ethnically conscious social policies on the council at large. In 1988, the council officially recognized over 300 ethnic minority community organizations by making them members of nine sub-umbrella groups, themselves part of a larger umbrella group, the Standing Consultative Forum (SCF). This decision was partly motivated in reaction to sporadic urban unrest in areas of the city,[12] in an attempt to cool tensions in the area by giving formal recognition to local community leaders from ethnic minority groups. The body was to function as an arena for discussion and a means for representatives of these organizations to voice their concerns to the city council. It was part of a broader policy of recognition of minorities' cultural difference and included, for instance, the recognition by the council of Pakistani and Indian national independence days, with large celebrations for each held in public parks.

Whether or not these policies were at least partially successful is hard to assess; what is certain is that, beyond the politically motivated criticism that was levelled at them (presented and analysed below), they were also unfavourably reviewed by many of their supporters. The SCF came quite rapidly to be viewed as a failure, mostly because of inefficiency due to internal bickering, lack of representativity and incompetence; there were also accusations of patronage and favouritism, and competition between representatives of different ethnic groups (Smith et al., 1999). The structure was disbanded in 1999. The Race Relations Unit was also replaced in 1997 by a new Equalities Unit which deals with women's rights and issues affecting people with disabilities, as well as discrimination against ethnic groups.

In March 2001, a commission set up by the council to review these policies concluded that the overwhelming perception among the ethnic minority community was that they were not working (*Evening Mail*, 22/03/01). The continuing under-representation of ethnic minorities in the council's qualified workforce was of particular concern, as well as the poor treatment including discrimination of those who were employees of the council.[13] Indeed, in 2000, figures emanating from the city council showed that Pakistanis made up 6.9 per cent of the city's population but only 2 percent of the council's workforce (*Birmingham Post*, 31/10/00). The 2001 commission talked of 'institutional racism' to characterize the situation, a phrase which had become widespread in Britain after the McPherson report of 1999.[14] A few months later, the council's Labour cabinet itself recognized that the policies of the last two decades were a failure.

What is important to note is that in spite of such challenges, these policies did in fact continue to be supported in different guises by the Labour leadership. At the same time that the Labour cabinet admitted failure in 2001, its proposed solution was simply to continue and expand the existing policies, with new, more ambitious targets for ethnic minority recruitment, and to challenge major employers in the private sector in the city to emulate them (*Evening Mail*, 12/07/01). The policies of recognizing cultural difference were still continued, and expanded in the early 2000s with, for instance, a new plan to rename part of the inner city 'Apna Town', which means 'our town' in Punjabi. The city council was to erect several signs proclaiming 'welcome to Apna Town' along the main roads in the area (*Evening Mail*, 3/11/00).

White-black and Asian liberal alliance. In 1979, there were just two ethnic minority councillors out of a total of 117; their number kept on increasing steadily throughout the 1980s and 1990s, to 14 in 1986, 18 in 1989, 19 in 1991 and 21 in 1993. Since then, their numbers have hovered around 20, making 21.5 per cent of the population of Birmingham only slightly under-represented. Throughout this period, most of these councillors sat on the Labour benches; significant exceptions in the persons of independent Liberal Democrats started appearing in the late 1990s. These ethnic minority councillors have been from both African-Caribbean and Asian background, with roughly twice as many Asians as African-Caribbeans. This made Asians particularly well represented on the council, with 13.7 per cent of the councillors in 1991 for 13.5 per cent of the total population of the city, while the black population was still under-represented with 3.4 per cent of the councillors for 5.9 per cent of the population (Le Lohé, 1998, p. 89). Among Asians, Pakistanis, who have the largest population in the city, are overwhelmingly dominant on the council. Asian councillors other than Pakistani have included people of Indian Sikh, Bangladeshi and Yemeni background.

From the beginning, a small proportion of ethnic minority councillors obtained positions of responsibility in the Labour group, in the form of chairing committees or acting as advisers to the leadership. In addition, several councillors have been comparatively well integrated into the decision-making circles of the group. In 1998, two had been elected chairs of committees (transportation and the important personnel and general purposes committee), and four were committee vice-chairs (commercial services, equalities, personnel and urban renewal). Before this, several had served as chairs of the equalities committee. Several were long-serving members of the council who had gained prominence through their expertise and dedication.

Government through multi-ethnic coalition can be understood as a major policy concession from the Labour leadership to ethnic minority interests, first, because recognition within the traditional political system is often perceived in itself as a major goal for ethnic minorities, and second, these councillors acted collectively as an incentive for the leadership to accept, facilitate or encourage the racially conscious policies presented above. Solomos and Back give contradictory evidence on this point, arguing that many ethnic minority councillors feel that they have little or no influence on the council (Solomos and Back, 1995, p. 200). Indeed, many of those I interviewed complained of being often sidelined, and that their preoccupations seldom appeared to be placed at the forefront of the Labour group's agenda. However, Solomos and Back also note that the increase in black personnel, both elected and non-elected, has encouraged the city council to become more proactive in tackling racial discrimination in a range of its policies (Solomos and Back, 1995, p. 201). This is consistent with research on Britain as a whole that shows that ethnic minority councillors tend to think that the political system is responsive to their claims related to ethnic disadvantage (Adolino, 1998, pp. 100–1).[15]

In their comprehensive study of racial politics in American cities, Browning et al. underline that the political configurations most likely to have a positive impact on the efficiency of race relations policies (such as employment of ethnic minority individuals by local authorities, relations with the police, anti-discrimination policies) are those that fulfil two conditions: (1) the existence of an inter-racial coalition and (2) the inclusion in this coalition of a white liberal party (1990, p. 278; see also Judd and Swanstrom, 1998). In Birmingham, both conditions were met from the mid-1980s to the late 1990s. Evidence tends to confirm that black and Asian councillors have played a role in bringing about policy change. They did this through informal networking with native British councillors, which encouraged the latter to take race-related preoccupations into account. As the former leader Theresa Stewart puts it, 'having them at the council with us made us think in new ways' (interview 8/1/99). Councillor Alton Burnett notes that when Theresa Stewart became leader, access to the leadership for ethnic minority activists became easier and this made it more sensitive to the racial and ethnic dimension of social policy problems. In particular, one local figure in the Muslim community, councillor Afzal, had a strong influence in the local party for a long time. Others rose to positions of influence within the Labour group, or wielded significant power over certain policy areas by getting elected as chairs of committees. In an important symbolic decision, a black female councillor, Sybil Spence, was chosen by her Labour peers in 1996 to become the city's first black lord mayor[16] in 1997 (*Birmingham Post*, 4/12/96).

At the same time, black and Asian councillors have periodically resorted to confrontational tactics against those very same Labour councillors with whom they routinely cooperate, when they felt that their cooperative attitude no longer worked. For instance, in December 1997, black and Asian councillors walked out of an official council meeting in protest at the suspension of an Asian worker employed by the council's economic development department. The suspicion was that he had been suspended because of his role as a union steward (for Unison, a union which is outspoken on race equality issues), and because of racist bias against him. Black councillors resorted to protest because council leader Theresa Stewart had refused to reinstate him, and because in their view this was symptomatic of a persistent failure to tackle the council's discriminatory employment policies effectively. One of these councillors declared to the press: 'If Luqman [the employee in question] is not reinstated by Saturday, there will be problems for Theresa. It could be that black councillors will refuse to attend council meetings' (*Birmingham Post*, 4/12/97).

The electoral dynamics of the white–black and Asian alliance. This steady increase in numbers and influence was closely correlated with the increase of Labour domination over the council. Ethnic minority councillors started entering the council in 1983 and 1984, just before and during Labour's take-over from the Conservatives. The Conservatives moved down from 55 councillors in 1983 to 42 in 1984, and stayed at that level until 1992, before reaching new lows in 1995 and 1996 with just 13 councillors). In the same period, the Labour group grew from 60 in 1983 to 61 in the following two years, increasing in steps to the 70 mark. This pattern of progression appears also in the second half of the 1990s, when the Labour group reached the considerable size of 80 councillors, crushing all opposition, Conservative and Liberal Democrat, and with Labour ethnic minorities averaging 20.

The rise of minorities was not directly caused by Labour's progression, because this progression was largely the result of Labour's inroads into previously Tory wards, and these gains were mostly made by white Labour candidates. The Conservative losses were not surprising, since they represented to a significant extent a vote of sanction against the Conservative government then in power; British local elections are traditionally used by disgruntled voters to pronounce judgment on the party in power at Westminster. In 1986, Labour seized seven seats from the Conservatives (*Birmingham Post*, 9/5/86). In 1995, another year of spectacular progress fuelled by popular dissatisfaction with the central Conservative government, Labour seized 12 of its 13 new seats from the Conservatives (*Birmingham Post*, 5/5/95). All these shifts from Conservative to Labour occurred in outer-city, white, middle-class wards.[17]

But the growing number of minority councillors did help, however, in the sense that it enabled Labour to perpetuate its traditional control of the inner city. The party was able to channel the growing political clout of minority communities and their leaders and to translate it into lasting electoral success, at least until the late 1990s. What made the election of minorities possible in the Labour wards was an ethnic shift within the inner city, with a replacement of white Labour councillors by black and Asian Labour councillors in those wards. There was a sudden rise in 1986 in particular in the number of blacks and Asians contesting local elections, the large majority of them for Labour, and in the inner city (*Evening Mail*, 22/4/86). There was a two-way relationship between minority councillors and continued Labour domination of the inner-city area during this period: the presence of these councillors in the group helped the party to keep control of the inner city, while the party made it possible for minorities to get elected by giving them its support.

The late 1990s seemed to announce the beginning of the end of this pattern. Labour domination was eroded by the arrival of New Labour in government, which reversed the direction of the anti-government local protest vote that until then had benefited Labour: from a high of 85 councillors in 1996–7, the number went down to 77 in 2000–1. At the same time, a growing number of Pakistani candidates stood successfully against Labour candidates as members of small, independent parties such as the Justice Party. In the early 2000s, some disaffected Labour councillors left the party to stand as Liberal Democrat candidates. In spite of this erosion, the Labour–black and Asian alliance in the inner-city wards remained the key to minority politics in the city in the early 2000s.

By contrast, the Conservatives and Liberal Democrats have usually had limited relations with local ethnic minority figures, and have rarely sponsored ethnic minority candidates. The Conservatives have sometimes fielded ethnic minority candidates in both parliamentary and local elections in the city, but most often with very modest scores, and without any success. For instance, an estate agent of Asian background, Paul Nischal, became a member of the party in 1965 and fought the parliamentary elections of 1983 and 1987 in the Small Heath constituency. His membership of the party was especially valued for his strong influence in the Asian business community of Birmingham.[18] In local elections too, the Conservatives have fielded their own ethnic minority candidates, albeit in much more limited numbers than Labour: for instance, three in the 1986 election, when Labour was fielding 10 (*Evening Mail*, 22/4/86), and six in 1992, a year when Labour was doing poorly. On that occasion they managed to cut the Labour majority to around 500 votes, including the leader of the council's majority.[19] The Conservatives were concerned about their disadvantage compared to Labour in this respect in the 1990s (Solomos and Back, 1995, p. 92), but had no realistic prospect of reaching Labour's level of success. Finally, as noted above, Liberal Democrats seemed to be just starting to dent Labour's quasi-monopoly on minority politics in the late 1990s, building on the resentment of some Labour defectors.

Why did the Labour majority co-opt these ethnic minority councillors within its ranks in such numbers for so long, and why did these minority activists choose and, in most cases, continue to commit themselves to the party? In the 1980s and 1990s, Labour was identified by ethnic minorities nationwide as their party, or at least the party that best represented their interests. As noted in chapter 2, support for the party by ethnic minorities never wavered, even though Labour was experiencing a prolonged series of electoral defeats in parliamentary elections. Between 1974 and 1997, support among ethnic minorities for Labour oscillated between 81 per cent and 78 per cent, while their support for the Conservatives increased from 9 per cent in 1974 to 17 per cent in 1997 (Saggar, 1998b, p. 26). As discussed at greater length in chapter 2, this was a reaction to the fact that Labour was the party that passed all three Race Relations Acts (1965, 1968 and 1976) and was generally associated with liberal policies for ethnic minorities; it is also due to the fact that minorities predominantly vote to defend their perceived interests as members of the working class, and also that there may be an 'environmental effect' on their party affiliation because they mainly live in inner-city wards where Labour is traditionally strong (Fitzgerald in Anwar and Werbner, 1991, p. 21).

That Labour enjoys the support of ethnic minority voters, however, does not necessarily imply that it needs to govern in a coalition with them in city politics. On the contrary, it may suggest that the party can rest on the assumption that this support is relatively safe and does not require policy concessions. In Birmingham this tension appears all the more clearly because race-related policies, and the presence of minority councillors, have a clear political cost. Both are a frequent political embarrassment to the leadership, which is routinely faced with hostile coverage of its race relations policy by the two large local papers, the *Evening Mail* and the *Birmingham Post*, which both have a Conservative editorial line. In just one example in November 1998, large headlines in the *Evening Mail* poured scorn on the council's controversial recruitment policies, because they included numerical targets that were explicitly ethnic (specifically, they encouraged Pakistani and Bangladeshi applications over those from Indians and Sikhs) (*Evening Mail*, 20/11/98). In the same period, this paper routinely argued against voluntaristic equalities policies and in favour of liberal, 'colour-blind' policies, as used to be advocated before the 1960s turn to race relations (and incidentally echoing dominant arguments in the French Socialist Party in 1980s and 1990s Lille).

Two examples among several are 'Boxed in by ridiculous race questions', a column by Ed Doolan, 'Voice of Sanity' (*Evening Mail*, date unspecified), which denounces racially conscious housing policies, and the column 'No harmony without equal whites' (*Evening Mail*, 16/10/98). The latter column concludes: 'They won't need pushing. Their excellence will ensure their progress. It took the Irish immigrants who fled their homeland during the great famine almost a century to get a favourite son in the White House, didn't it? All Birmingham needs is time and newcomers who show themselves worthy of trust. There is no place for lectures, quota surveys and bossy wagging fingers.' Another argument made by opponents of Labour policies was that they favoured inner-city ethnic minority wards, while members of the 'white underclass', many of whom lived in outer-city estates, were being neglected.[20] The same point has also been made, in a less emotional way, by some managers of the council's regeneration policies, who have argued for a more accurate allocation of funds to disadvantaged communities all around the city, including outer-city, predominantly white housing estates (interview with officer of economic development department, 5/5/99).

Labour has also met opposition from the Conservative group on the council. Criticisms of its policies are often combined with attacks on the alleged radicalism of its 'Socialist' policies: neighbourhood councils, participatory programmes or sex education in local schools are frequently targeted. For instance, councillor Neville Bosworth, leader of the Conservative group in 1986, lumped together multicultural education and issues related to the place of homosexuality in sex education in a single denunciation (*Evening Mail*, 6/5/86). Interviewed in June 1999, the secretary of the Conservative group at the time explained that, in his view, the Labour Party had a totally wrong approach to race relations issues, and that ethnic minority councillors had too much influence in the Labour group.[21] When the council decided to rename a predominantly Asian neighbourhood with a Punjabi name in 2000, a Conservative councillor criticized the decision in the press in the following terms: 'I think it is a great pity. It is a step on the way to removing the Britishness from Birmingham and especially its inner city. The city is a multi-racial society in which everybody is accepted as part of our British culture. To revert to individual components or tribes is not progressive' (*Evening Mail*, 3/11/00). Another Conservative councillor was quoted in a sympathetic article in the same newspaper as criticizing the city council's monitoring of its employees' ethnicity in a way that was unfavourable to the English. The council recognized such groups as Rastafarian, Creole, Pushtu, Urdu, Irish and even much smaller groups such as Kurds, Afghanis, Iranians, Kosovans and Somalis (to make allowance for asylum seekers arriving in the early 2000s, predominantly from these groups). The councillor complained: 'I am English and I don't get a mention. Not being Irish, I can only qualify on this list as British and white.[22] We English are being discriminated against by the city council. It's about time we waved the flag of St George' (*Evening Mail*, 28/02/03).

These kinds of attacks were particularly feared by the moderate Labour leadership of Dick Knowles in the 1980s, as it was thought that the party could lose white voters as a direct consequence (see Joly and Candappa, 1994). Hence, the leadership made several hesitant attempts to scale back race relations policies as soon as they appeared to impinge on Labour's electoral fortunes. In fact, the Race Relations Unit and the race relations personnel committee have over the years come to be used by the Labour leadership as an indicator and a deflector of rising tension over race. In 1987, in reaction to Labour's poor performance in that year's local election,[23] the presumed threat of an even more severe electoral backlash in the coming years was brandished as a reason to clamp down on the left of the party. This included removing all left-wingers from chairs of committees, abolishing the women's committee, and lowering the profile of race relations policies by merging the race relations committee (then called the race relations and equal opportunities committee) with the traditional personnel committee and calling the new entity the personnel and equal opportunities committee (interview with city councillor, 10/11/98; 'Desperate Labour acts to stem electoral tide', *Birmingham Post*, 9/5/87).[24]

In more recent years, the left-wing Labour leadership has continued to exercise caution in race policy issues. In particular, it has come to use the figure of the head of equalities as a kind of public relations specialist whose job seems to be to manage the media over the council's race policies. The person occupying this position in the early 1990s lost his job because of his failure to handle rivalries between different community organizations, which often took the form of rivalries between African-Caribbean and Asian groups.[25] His replacement, Haroon Saad, a young, articulate, media-friendly outsider who had previously worked in London and Bristol, clearly reflected the leadership's view that in addition to being a skilled bureaucrat, the head of equalities should also be able to sell the council's policies to the press and to public opinion and to deflect criticism in times of crisis.

The white–black and Asian alliance is also far from being an example of cohesion, and has often displayed significant internal tensions, although it is only since 1999 that it has given signs, not of breaking, but of losing some of its Asian members (see below, pp. 00–0). Until then tensions were more limited, although they were more of a concern because they attracted media attention to racial politics within the Labour group. This was the case in 1997, when several black and Asian councillors walked out of a council meeting in protest over a case of discrimination against an Asian council employee ('Labour team split as black councillors stage walk-out', *Birmingham Post*, 4/12/97). Controversies that occurred over the suspension of some inner-city constituencies in 1994 also exposed Labour divisions and provided a more serious source of concern, encouraging the independent candidacies for seats on the council that have subsequently proliferated.

The rationale for the alliance. Given these conditions – little obvious need for meaningful political concessions to non-whites, combined with anti-minority pressure from the press and the Conservatives – what were the benefits for the Labour leadership of maintaining such an alliance? First, it is worth mentioning again here the rapid and large increase of the city's ethnic minority population. Already in 1976, Ken Newton noted that, with 1 out of 10 of the population from an ethnic minority background, race relations constituted a potentially important issue in the city (Newton, 1976, p. 194). Twenty years later, this proportion had more than doubled to between one fifth and one quarter of the population, which is large by any standards. It would seem surprising if this situation, coupled with the increase in electoral participation of these populations first noted by the CRE in 1974 (Saggar, 1998b, p. 25), failed to turn them into an increasingly potent force, or at least an important concern, in the 1980s and 1990s. But, at the same time, evidence from other British cities shows that there is no clear link between the proportion of ethnic minorities in the total population and their representation on city councils, with cases of both over- and under-representation for all ethnic groups (see chapter 2 on Britain, pp. 00–0). In addition, we still need to know why minorities have been so successful over such a prolonged period of time, and why their success has taken the form of a coalition with Labour.

The answer lies in the political configuration of inner-city Birmingham, which has been characterized for the last 20 years by a game of mutual dependency between minority communities and the Labour leadership. Each needs the other to obtain its objectives, the former seeking representation and influence, the latter seeking continued control of the city council. While minorities have until recently needed to move through the party's structure and to obtain the party's support to win local elections, Labour has needed them to stand in its name in most inner-city wards in order to keep on winning there. The ingredients of this situation are, first, an important and active ethnic minority electorate; second, the existence of minority candidates; and, third, the preference of this ethnic minority electorate for a Labour candidate who hails from their own community, over both white Labour candidates and ethnic minority candidates who are not Labour members.

How did these elements come together in the inner city of Birmingham in the 1980s? Until then, the first ingredient, an ethnic minority vote for Labour, already existed in Britain, as noted above and as shown by electoral studies since the 1970s (Anwar, 1980, 1986, 1990, 1998; Saggar, 1998b). What happened is that both the second and third ingredients came together at that time: individuals appeared who were at the same time interested in standing for the Labour Party, attractive to minority voters and, crucially, accepted by the party's established activists and higher ranks.

The crucial element, then, is not a change in voter preference but a change in the choice of candidates on offer on the electoral market of inner-city wards. This in turn is a function of the choice of the Labour ward organizations, and behind them the Labour city and regional-level hierarchy, to start fielding ethnic minority candidates. In other words, the explanation for the change can be sought in a 'demand' factor rather than a 'supply' factor (Norris and Lovenduski, 1995, p. 15), because it is the choices made by candidate selectors that have changed. In the next section, this change in the preferences of Labour decision-makers is explained with reference to the new institutionalist framework outlined earlier. I argue that the institutional structure of the Birmingham polity has impacted on the strategies of local political actors, particularly ethnic minority activists and community leaders, as well as established Labour Party activists, in such a way as to open Labour networks to ethnic minority activists. It has done this by simultaneously providing political resources to those minority activists who were interested in working with the Labour Party and forcing Labour decision-makers to accept their collaboration, in spite of a long-enduring reluctance.

Institutions and Activists: How Ethnic Minorities Penetrated the Labour Party

Until the early 1970s, minorities were all but excluded from the party. As Newton noted in 1976, this may be attributable to the dominance of the class cleavage in British politics, which, according to him, prevented the emergence of issues cutting across class, such as race relations: 'It is only to be expected that party structures which have been built around age-old class divisions now find it difficult to accommodate new issues and new social cleavages, but the result, as far as coloured people are concerned, is a set of closed if not barred doors which make the parties difficult to approach, and, some would argue, not even worth the effort of trying' (Newton, 1976, p. 216). Whether or not the pervasiveness of the class cleavage in Britain is a direct cause, it is clear that the party in Birmingham was indeed impenetrable to minorities until the late 1970s and early 1980s. One sure cause of this was linked to classic problems confronting not just immigrants but generally all newcomers to a political system: lack of adequate socialization and resistance from closely integrated networks of insiders, often organized around family ties. Scholars have noted the existence of a Labour establishment, often based on dynastic and kinship ties, and that many Labour MPs are the sons and daughters, nieces or stepsons of trade union officials and Labour Party politicians (Fitzgerald in Goulbourne, 1990, p. 18).

In the case of ethnic minorities, this was compounded by the racism generally displayed against extra-European minorities seeking to join British organizations. In this section, I explain how the Labour networks, until then closed to issues relating to minorities and to minority individuals, started to display more sensitivity to these issues and how they also started recruiting blacks and Asians, who moved from the status of outsiders to that of insiders. This was linked to the emergence at that time of a generation of activists who presented all the necessary conditions for such an opening. In this, Birmingham is typical of nationwide trends: in 1992, there were three times as many non-whites in the Labour Party as in the Conservative Party nationwide (Seyd and Whiteley, 1992, p. 37). Whether of black or Asian background, religious or secular, local activists had a proximity with the left and were involved in local community leadership that was increasingly entrenched in local organizations. Their presence and growing prominence in the inner city made them fit to benefit from the dynamics of the left–right competition that characterized Birmingham politics at the time.

The first section below gives a brief description of the modes of political socialization and organization of the main types of activists and community leaders who made political careers in the party. I then outline the features of the institutional framework of the Birmingham polity that encouraged their rise up the Labour ladder. Finally, I retrace three models of incorporation in the city council through co-optation as Labour councillors.

Styles of community organization

As in French cities, in Birmingham ethnic minority individuals involved in community activities are overwhelmingly from working-class or modest backgrounds and are mainly involved in left-wing politics, broadly defined. This is a fundamental point because, as such, they have been amenable to participation in the politics of Labour rather than in the politics of the Conservatives, or even of the Liberal Democrats (although this was beginning to change in the early 2000s). Beyond this, however, their styles of mobilization have differed for decades from those of their French counterparts. First, it is important to recall here that many first-generation migrants from the New Commonwealth automatically obtained voting rights upon arrival in Britain, because this encouraged and facilitated their participation in public life, broadly defined. This helps greatly to understand why a British city such as Birmingham has been able to produce minority activists and leaders with political experience and the maturity necessary to succeed in public life. In contrast, many activists in Lille and Roubaix (tellingly, often called 'youths' in France) are children of first-generation migrants who have been sidelined because of their inexperience. Their parents have not benefited from voting rights in most cases and have often participated little in public life, or in benign ways which do not lead to party politics.

Beyond these general elements, there are more specific styles of mobilization that vary between ethnic groups and within ethnic groups. This needs to be dealt with briefly because these specificities have 'fit' the institutional structure described above in specific ways, and therefore they are necessary for understanding the ways in which that structure has acted as a political resource for leaders and activists. In particular, as will be shown in greater detail, it is arguably the case that the Pakistani population tends to present patterns of sociability, as well as religious practice, that shape the ways in which it interacts with local electoral systems and party politics. In at least this case, it is these patterns combined with the patterns of organization of Labour local organizations that have produced the high level of representation of Pakistanis on the city council.

Styles of community involvement of minorities in Birmingham can be classified in either ideological or ethnic terms. Here, I follow a mainly ethnic guideline, observing a broad distinction between African-Caribbeans and Asians (focusing among the latter on Pakistanis) because of the differences between the levels and styles of participation of these two groups.

Some differences between the two were noted in the 1970s. By and large the political behaviour of activists of West Indian background was more fashioned by preoccupations with local neighbourhood issues, particularly housing and relations between youths and the police. Asian activists oscillated between negotiation with local authorities over educational and religious issues, on one side, and classic working-class politics, on the other. In particular, this involvement in class politics was reflected in the existence of large and active left-wing Asian unions, the Indian Workers' Union and the Asian Workers' Union.[26]

However, I focus below on styles of organization of each community as they appeared in the 1980s, when the penetration of Labour networks took place. In the 1980s and 1990s, some styles of involvement that were marginal in the 1970s, such as radical black activism, had gained prominence and produced an experienced personnel. African-Caribbean community political personnel on the council originated from two political traditions: Marxist and black liberation militantism, and Christian activism. Those politicians who came to politics through the former tradition now bear many similarities with Asian left-wingers: like them, they are ideologically close to the Labour left wing, and, like them, they participate in left-wing politics in the Labour Party. The Pakistani community, like the Bangladeshi community, was still characterized in the 1980s by a tension between community politics and working-class politics, as in the late 1970s, and both styles have been fertile sources of involvement with Labour.

The African-Caribbean community: Marxism and churches. Both radical black movements and black-led churches have functioned as training grounds for activists and local leaders, in the case of black-led churches by participating in successive urban regeneration programmes that have targeted British inner cities, mostly in collaboration with Labour-controlled local authorities.[27] While a significant proportion of the African-Caribbean population is often actively Christian, its religious practice is often different from that of the native British populations, to a large extent because of denominational differences (they are more often Methodists or Pentecostalists), but also because of the general context of isolation from the rest of society in which the black populations of the inner cities lived, at least until the 1970s (see Cross and Entzinger, 1988). The churches have made it possible for young African-Caribbeans to move out of isolation and develop leadership skills, and they have provided a platform for further public involvement (Johnston, 1991).

This is important in the context of British cities, where churches have been associated with the management of local welfare since the birth of local government in the late 1800s. Birmingham is a case in point, because the path chosen towards modern local government by Joseph Chamberlain in the 1860s included partnership with business and churches. The role played by churches in developing urban regeneration programmes in the 1960s and 1970s is a testimony to this tradition. Black-led churches offered to play a similar role in predominantly black areas, where they were increasingly influential. Birmingham is a typical example; Rex and Tomlinson noted in 1979 the existence of several black churches in Handsworth (in the north-west of the inner city, where the bulk of the African-Caribbean population is located). In the 1980s and 1990s, there were around 20 such churches in the city, headed by a 'council of black-led churches'.[28] They have proved to be an important source of black councillors. Sybil Spence, the city's first black lord mayor, migrated to Birmingham from Jamaica in 1961 and is described as a 'leading figure in Birmingham's black-church movement' by the Birmingham Post (4/12/96).

The Pakistani community: between left-wing unionism and community interests. The Pakistani community is still characterized as in the 1970s by a tension between communitarian concerns, such as provision for religious education in schools, and identification with wider left-wing concerns for social justice. Pakistanis have a long tradition of involvement with left-wing politics in Britain through their participation in trade unionism, particularly specific Indian and Pakistani trade unions.[29] From there, many Pakistanis moved to activities as shop stewards in a union at their workplace, which in turn has shaped their approach to politics, with activism in the Labour Party an almost natural step for many. Several are preoccupied with both unionism and the politics of the Labour Party and the concerns of their local Pakistani, Muslim, neighbourhood-based communities.

Beyond this, however, the Pakistani community of Birmingham has sociopolitical characteristics that make it even more prone than African-Caribbeans or Sikhs to benefit from the resources offered by the institutional structure. Not only do Pakistani councillors come from a left-wing and active community, but they have also benefited from a combination of kinship ties and religious structures, both focused on the local, neighbourhood level, that give them additional resources to exploit openings in the Labour local organization. The notion of kinship is a translation of the term *biraderi*, or extended patrilineal family, but it is also used here to refer to a broader set of social relationships, such as village of origin, caste or Islam, which are all to varying degrees factors of allegiance among Birmingham's Pakistanis (see Joly, 1995, p. 59).

These bonds are activated in the Pakistani community in the context of heavy residential concentration. As noted earlier, the Pakistani population is mostly concentrated in the Sparkbrook and Small Heath constituency in the south-east of the inner city, reaching up to 70 per cent of the population in some wards there. This population originates for the most part from one particular rural district of Azad Kashmir, Mirpur. Sub-groups came from particular villages, which were destroyed in the 1960s for the construction of a dam in the area. In several instances, the populations of these villages migrated together to Britain and sought to re-establish their communities in the neighbourhoods of Sparkbrook and Small Heath. Family and kinship networks have therefore been able to continue having a prominent role in the community, whether through new formal associations or in their traditional form.

The spectacular development of Muslim groups and mosques also plays a part in the structuring of the territorial community, to the extent that Birmingham Pakistanis provide a case of identification between ethnic or religious bonds on one side, and territorial, neighbourhood-based communities, on the other (which is a frequent feature of immigrant communities in European cities [Body-Gendrot and Martiniello, 2000, pp. 1–10; on Asian communities in Britain from an anthropological perspective, see also Werbner, 1991, and Vertovec, 1994]). In particular many families of Kashmiri background have over the years shown the need to continue living in the same localized areas of the inner city in order to be close to mosques and halal butchers. This became apparent in the 1980s because many Asian families refused offers of council houses because they were located in outer-city areas far from these services. The problem was so severe that it was claimed that offering such houses amounted to indirect discrimination (*Birmingham Post*, 'Housing policy is "unfair" ', 2003).

Religious structures appear to many British Pakistanis as a line against the westernization of the community, and, very importantly, as a means of passing on religious and cultural values to younger generations. Indeed, the most important point about these organizations is that they have provided formalized structures in which kinship and family ties have been able to perpetuate themselves and evolve in an urban British environment, in spite of their brutal transposition from a rural Kashmiri environment. Mosques started appearing in a hostile context in the 1970s in the face of strong opposition from both the press and the city council (Hodgins, 1985), which have become more favourable since the 1980s. As Joly observed, there was a pressing demand in the community in the early 1980s for more mosques to be built so as to accommodate people living in their vicinity. Indeed, their numbers multiplied in the early 1980s: when Joly carried out her survey in the 1980s, 40 per cent of the existing mosques had been created before the 1970s, 32 per cent in the 1970s, and 27 per cent in a five-year period between 1980 and 1984. At that time she counted 55 in the city (Joly, 1995, p. 26). That figure was rising rapidly and is expected to be even higher in the early 2000s. Several, such as the Central Mosque in Highgate or the Golden Hillock Road in Small Heath, were purpose-built and featured a large white dome and minaret. Since that period, mosques and Muslim organizations have been able to articulate the demands of their religious followers in the local arena because the local council has responsibility over many issues of interest to them (notably to do with education) and has been willing to engage in negotiations. In 1983, a Muslim liaison committee composed of local Muslim leaders secured a declaration of principles from the council on the provision of services for Muslim pupils in local schools (Nielsen, 1995, pp. 58–9).

Beyond purely recreating and perpetuating the traditional bonds of their homeland, Pakistanis have built a new style of community by adapting these bonds to the forms of organization of local communities in Britain: charities, support groups dealing with administrative problems, job centres adapted to the specific needs of the Pakistani population. There has been a genuine flourishing of organizations of all types (227 in the Standing Consultative Forum's Pakistani sub-umbrella group in 1988).[30] Many of them are concerned with the welfare of the Pakistani community and issues connected with their daily life in Britain, very often from a religious perspective. They include burial organizations, which organize the repatriation of bodies to Pakistan (about a third were repatriated in this way in 1987 [Rex and Samad, 1996]), welfare organizations and religious groups. All of them are now increasingly integrated within the institutional fabric of mainstream institutions in Birmingham, through the Standing Consultative Forum or through various types of grants. Community organizations have increasingly participated in different urban partnership programmes that have been operating since the 1970s, and the main associations have taken the initiative to obtain representation on police liaison committees. At the same time, traditional social networks have found support and a framework in these associations, and Joly notes that the patron–client relationship that existed within kinship relations has often been reproduced in these associations (1995, p. 49).

The political institutions of the inner city

Two local institutions play a strong role in shaping opportunities for the participation of minorities: first, the organization of local government and, second, the local party system and party organizations. The organization of local government presents two features of particular importance: (1) the fragmentation of the electoral territory of Birmingham City Council and (2) the plurality (first-past-the-post) electoral system in use for local elections in the city. Of particular relevance in local partisan politics are the structure of intra-party competition in the Labour Party and the relatively high level of codification of rules governing local branch activities such as candidate selection.

The fragmentation of the electoral territory into wards (of around 30,000 people each) has ensured that populations that are concentrated in certain specific areas of the city can exercise a strong electoral leverage. This electoral strength is compounded by the first-past-the-post system, which ensures that groups of voters that mobilize in such a way as to constitute the majority in their particular electoral constituency can exercise substantial control over the representation of that constituency on the local council. Both these elements have favoured ethnic minority candidates in Birmingham politics[31] because of the high residential concentration of minority populations in the inner-city wards noted earlier, to the extent that in many instances they constitute the absolute majority of the population. This situation has provided a strong bargaining resource for minority activists seeking to stand as candidates for elections, because it quickly became apparent that they were able to attract the ethnic minority vote.

The presence of the Labour left in Birmingham in the 1980s is in itself an important factor, because it has campaigned within the framework of the Labour Party in favour of black and Asian representation and empowerment, while far-left movements in France have been marginal groups evolving outside, and in opposition to, both the Socialist and Communist parties. This was true in British cities in general (see chapter 2; also Geddes, 1993, p. 46; Shukra, 1998b, pp. 119–20). While in Birmingham the left was less precocious and less influential than in other cities (see chapter 2), it is crucial to point again to the prolonged internal struggle it led against the right from the late 1970s to the 1990s, which consisted in a competition over votes and over control of the party's organization (both constituencies and 'branches', the party's ward-level organizations). In the context of this struggle, both sides have been keen to enrol ethnic minority activists as supporters, in different ways, but which both had the consequence of making it easier for minority activists to gain a foothold in local Labour organization (see Solomos and Back, 1995, ch. 4). It might even be suggested that if the left had gained dominance more easily, opportunities for progress for minority activities would have been more restricted. The role of ethnic minorities as allies of both sides at different times and in different circumstances, in the context of sharp competition, increased their importance in the party.

The organization of grassroots Labour structures and the structure of intra-party competition have complemented the electoral resources outlined above by providing yet more political resources to black and Asian activists, in the following way. First, the style of selection of candidates gives much of the decision-making power to the ward-level organizations of the party, or branches (noted by Le Lohé, 1998, p. 75). This is crucial in inner-city politics, because there has been a strong level of voter identification with the party, and because the turnout is low. Available statistics showed that average turnout in local elections in metropolitan counties averaged 39 per cent, compared with a turnout of around 76 per cent in general (parliamentary) elections since 1951 (Stoker, 1991, p. 51). In France, local election turnout is usually high, around 70 per cent (Stoker, 1991, p. 51; see chapter 5). The result is that a British local election is often played out as much in the selection process of the dominant party as in the election itself. The combination of the ward system, ethnic segregation, low turnout among voters and ward-level selection of candidates tends to encourage, if not ethnic minority representation, at least some sort of racialization of politics. This combination creates a political environment in which the best strategy, or the least costly one, for party bosses or dominant interests is to recognize and negotiate political influence with those social and community groups that are the most organized and capable of mobilizing their networks.

Even in cases where ethnic minority interests have not gained dominance in selection processes, the simple fact that the latter are to some extent codified gives minorities opportunities to appeal, campaign and publicize their cause in ways that are unseen in French parties, with the possible exception of the Greens. The organization of the Labour Party and, beyond that, its historical roots in the trade union movement of the late nineteenth century have acted not just as an institutional resource in candidate selection procedures, but also as a mode of legitimation of activists' powers. The Labour Party is a highly organized party, where diverse sectoral interests have been historically prominent, in particular trade unions (Minkin, 1991). This means that the concept of the representation of a plurality of groups in the party has always been present. Other 'minority' groups gained similar recognition, and power, in the 1980s, such as women, who obtained the creation of a specific shortlist of female candidates for general elections in 1989 (Norris and Lovenduski, 1995, p. 59). It also encouraged the formulation of claims related to ethnic and racial difference.

In addition, the constitution of the party from its origins insisted on internal democracy and membership rights. This has always guaranteed a minimum of leverage for the lower echelons of the party, although trade unions have wielded strong influence on the leadership and have often confiscated much of the decision-making, as Seyd and Whiteley explain:

> In practice, for much of the party's history, power has been a subtle and complex process in which the parliamentary leadership has been sustained by the block vote of a small number of trade unions. Thus the party leadership has been able to use the rhetoric of member sovereignty knowing full well that its point of view should prevail within the deliberative process. Nevertheless, the fact that the constitution legitimizes the authority of the membership means that the party leadership has been forced to argue and defend its position, and to mobilize majorities, in the day-to-day running of the party. (Seyd and Whiteley, 1992, p. 20)

In the 1970s and 1980s, the left of the party was effectively playing on a 'fundamentalist' note, referring back to the participatory foundations of the party's constitution in order to take the leadership at its word and to increase its influence. It is important to stress that these efforts solely concerned the party's *activist* base, as opposed to *individual* party members who did not participate intensively in day-to-day party activities. The new left focused its efforts on obtaining recognition for this group essentially because that is where its strength lay; increasing ordinary members' rights would on the contrary have meant weakening its influence by empowering less politicized and less radical members. Indeed, the rights of individual members were constantly promoted by the leadership precisely in order to counter the left (Seyd and Whiteley, 1992, p. 21). Radicals' efforts to promote the role of activists as a means of gaining ascendancy over more conservative interests essentially gave meaning to the notion of 'activist democracy' that was at the centre of much controversy in the 1970s and 1980s (Seyd and Whiteley, 1992, p. 21). In the late 1990s, the decline of the Labour left as a force of contestation and as a challenging factor to the leadership deprived some sections of the black activist milieu their main allies in the city. As noted above, this decline was correlated with the more general decline of the Labour Party in the city.

In contrast with all these elements, the city-wide electoral districts of Lille and Roubaix have diluted potential ethnic minority electoral power (which is already weaker than in Britain because fewer ethnic minority individuals have the vote), and the list-system for municipal elections has reinforced the importance of the city-wide leadership of the party as a gateway to the candidacy. This constitutes an obstacle to minorities because both the modes of candidate selection – consensual, brokered by groups defending the interests of city-wide and region-wide leaders – and the structure of internal competition – frequently the preserve of heavyweight politicians, often with regional or national stature, with grassroots activists playing only a limited role – work against them. Hence, incorporation in French cities either has not taken place or has done so in different ways, for instance through neighbourhood-based community activity in cities where parties have an unusually weak grip over local politics, as in Roubaix.

Three styles of co-optation in Labour ward-level politics: from vote brokerage to independent councillors

This section retraces the processes by which leaders and activists from these organizations managed to emerge in Labour politics in the 1980s thanks to the favourable institutional structure mentioned above. Since the Birmingham political system is fragmented into small electoral territories, the wards, it is difficult to speak of a single, unified political system, as is the case in Lille or Roubaix; rather, there are as many sub-systems as there are wards. Out of the 39 wards in the city, 10 can be characterized as 'inner city' with high levels of unemployment and large ethnic minority populations. Beyond these common features, these wards have highly diverse social and ethnic mixes, economic situations and political problems. The fact that an election takes place every three years in four in each ward also ensures that political situations evolve quickly, with support for one party or another increasing or waning in accordance with the political developments of the year, in contrast with the French municipal elections, which take place only every six years. Because of this, there is no single model to describe the penetration of networks characterizing the whole city. Rather, the characteristics of the institutional framework presented above play out in distinct ways in different wards, creating a complex mosaic of different, sometimes contrasting, situations, at times converging, and at other times remaining on different paths. Because of this, the four institutional variables outlined above have not combined in a unique way in the city, but rather have been more or less relevant according to ward-specific situations.

To capture the diversity of ways in which these variables have combined, I distinguish between three types of career paths, each one reflecting a different institutional configuration: the 'patronage' model, the 'radical activist' model and the 'ethnic community' model. In each of these, the four institutional variables (electoral territories, plurality electoral system, styles of candidate selection and structure of intra-party competition) combine in different ways to shape patterns of inclusion in the party and, from there, within the city council. Although the models overlap in time, with at least two, if not all three, operating simultaneously in different wards, they do to some extent characterize three phases in the city-wide process of growing access to representation. In fact, one can note a progression in time from the first model through to the second and third, in terms of degree of political independence and/or assertiveness of minority politicians in relation to dominant interests in the party.

The patronage model: late 1970s and 1980s. In this model, the influence of minority activists on black and Asian electorates, compounded by their ability to bring new recruits to the party, turned them into desirable political allies for right-wing leaders in the context of their struggle against the left, because they could help fight electoral decline and fend off attempts by the left to seize control of the branches.[32] The function of vote brokers that befell minority activists in this model was enough to give them an important role in branch politics and, at best, to bring them seats on the city council, but it was not enough to give them real influence, since they remained dependent on their white patrons in numerous ways. This model existed in all areas of the inner city, in both the north-west and the south-east, mostly at the beginning of the process of incorporation, from the late 1970s and early 1980s onwards. From the early 1980s it coexisted for some time with the second model, before the latter eclipsed it in the 1990s. An institutionalist perspective on this situation suggests the combination of three of the institutional variables under discussion: (1) the local electoral system, which gives strong electoral leverage to ethnic minority community leaders; (2) the importance of the grassroots level for the selection of candidates in the party; and (3) the structure of internal competition within the party, specifically here attempts by moderate right-wing Labour leaders to defend their turf against rising left-wing influence.

The two levels of electoral competition in the city – ward-level competition for positions on the council and constituency-level competition for seats in Parliament – are separate arenas with limited interaction. However, MPs do exert a power of patronage over local politics because they can render services to local communities and because they wield influence in the local Labour machinery; conversely, councillors and community leaders contribute to securing the popularity of their party in their wards, thereby reinforcing the position of MPs. It is this type of relation between ethnic minority councillors and MPs that provided the first opening for ethnic minorities in ward-level politics in the late 1970s and early 1980s in the context of the domination of the party by moderate, right-wing leaders and MPs. This happened in all three inner-city constituencies of Birmingham, each of which had right-wing MPs: Roy Hattersley in Sparkbrook, Brian Walden in Ladywood and Denis Howell in Small Heath, who all sought the support of black and Asian community leaders (Solomos and Back, 1995, p. 68).[33] Roy Hattersley, for instance, was well known among minorities as a solid ally (interview with city councillor, 26/05/99). These MPs were relatively uninterested in the radical ethnic minority agenda (anti-discrimination and anti-racist campaigns); rather, they adhered to a liberal, 'colour-blind' view on matters related to race and immigration. Hattersley in particular is known for his position of simultaneous sympathy for minorities and persistent refusal to take on board the radical agenda of anti-discrimination struggle, not to mention the idea of black sections (see below). In his political memoirs, he notes that he always felt at odds with Roy Jenkins' proactive policies against racial discrimination, and that he was alienated from his Muslim constituents over the Salman Rushdie affair, because he stuck to a liberal attitude. For instance, he explicitly argued that Rushdie's *Satanic Verses* should not banned, in the name of freedom of speech, and in opposition to demands by influential Muslim groups (Hattersley, 1995, pp. 301–2).

Independently of their views on minorities, the political situation in which they found themselves at that time led these MPs to encourage a process of growing representation of ethnic minority leaders in ward-level politics. This was shown in detail by Solomos and Back, who pointed to the conjunction of three problems: the increasing volatility of the working-class vote, a crisis in the recruitment of grassroots activists and the rising challenge of left-wing networks in the local party. They needed dedicated supporters to counter the influence of these networks within the party machinery and felt a need to elicit continued support among the ethnic minority electorate, which had supported them without intermediaries in the 1970s.[34] Indeed, studies of Labour Party membership at the time show a general trend of decline since the 1950s (Seyd and Whiteley, 1992, p. 16), especially in the inner-city areas, where the party had transformed itself from a 'centre of social life' to a 'rusty and seldom activated election machine'.[35]

It is worthwhile remembering the social and political background of the ethnic minority community and activist milieu in Birmingham outlined above. These characteristics explain why many of the local community leaders and activists of minority background in Birmingham revealed themselves to be valuable allies in this context, particularly African-Caribbeans involved in local charities, or Asians active in their communities. This type of individual presented two qualities for right-wing leaders. They were building up some sort of leadership in their community principally on the basis of local community work, typically centred on practical help and/or religious leadership, in the case of the Muslim and Sikh communities. At the same time, they were broadly speaking sympathetic to the Labour Party, at least to its commitment to working-class interests, although for the most part they did not have more precise ideological commitments. Solomos and Back (1995, p. 136) note that of the 23 councillors they interviewed, 11 came to the party in the hope that it would help them solve problems of daily life in their community, and that this took place in the context of the right-wing's recruitment drive (while in contrast, only four joined out of a commitment to the Labour Party as such, and six out of an involvement in radical left-wing politics).

The political and strategic needs of right-wing leaders as they are characterized by Solomos and Back could be accommodated by this type of personnel. They accepted the general directions of Labour politics without really seeking to change it from the inside, which made them docile allies, at least for a while. At the same time, their commitment to local welfare ensured that they were influential in the black and Asian electorate in the way that mattered most, i.e., the territorial, ward-based way. Their involvement with the party reinforced these trends, giving them greater resources to play the role of social service deliverer and intermediary between their ethnic community and the wider social and political system. Hence, in sharp contrast with developments in Lille in the same period, burgeoning ethnic minority organization was not perceived as a threat by dominant political interests, but on the contrary as helpful for the continued control of inner-city wards, and therefore ethnic minorities were co-opted as members and councillors.

In all cases their electoral capital as well as their capacity to attract new members to the party were sought, with one or the other being more or less important. The capacity to attract new members appears important in the case of Asian and African-Caribbean activists alike.[36] Solomos and Back report many such cases. For instance, a 'senior official in the Labour movement' is quoted as follows: 'When the party was going through its changes in the 1970s and the Left was emerging as a political force, some of the Right-wing chose to recruit people from the ethnic community as a way of sustaining their position. I think if you were a moderate councillor in 1977 in a ward like Soho what you would do is talk to a couple of community leaders and say that you were under threat and the community leader would recruit thirty people from within the community' (1995, p. 69). And a 'white activist' reports on the effects of the left vs. right competition: 'In the late 1970s a handful of militants got control of the Handsworth CLP [Constituency Labour Party] and managed to replace all the black delegates on the general Management Committee. The result was that a white member organized a Centre-Right take-over and sacked all the militants. This involved mass-recruiting through a couple of black party-members' (1995, p. 70).

In other instances, quite clearly in the case of African-Caribbean leaders, but also with Asians, it is the capacity to mobilize voters that made them desirable. Among the first to be elected in 1983 in this way was one supporter of Brian Walden (MP for Ladywood in the early 1980s), James Hunt. Hunt was a charismatic figure in the African-Caribbean community in Handsworth, known for a variety of charity enterprises, who had started trading votes for services with the party since the late 1970s (Rex and Tomlinson, 1979, pp. 263–4; also Solomos and Back, 1995, p. 69). One of the most prominent councillors of the early 1980s, Muhammad Afzal, first elected in the Aston ward in 1982, was typical of this style of patronage politics, at least at the start (interview with city councillors, 9/11/98), before going on to a long career that ended in the late 1990s. Pakistani activists were also encouraged to become councillors, such as Amir Khan, who later went on to serve for a lengthy period as councillor in the Small Heath ward (interview with city councillor, 26/05/99).

In all cases, the ward system for local elections appears as a constraint for these MPs, limiting their ability to contain micro-level socio-political change such as declining membership or left-wing challenge, and forcing them to find ways to respond. In the Lille city-wide electoral territory, the mayor has managed to remain isolated from similar changes for the last 20 years, although at the neighbourhood level individual North Africans have proved capable of securing positions in the neighbourhood councils. The larger the electoral territory, the more diluted the electoral and networking clout of communities with high levels of residential concentration.

MPs would typically propose services for the community in return, such as help with immigration papers or dealings with council social services (Solomos and Back, 1995, pp. 73, 106). In particular, MPs could provide otherwise unattainable access to the Home Office departments in charge of immigration-related issues. This was an important concern in the context of the 1970s and 1980s, when black and particularly Asian communities were isolated linguistically from mainstream society and were often subjected to a series of problems linked to their vulnerability: threats of denunciation of undocumented immigrants to the police, or various types of swindling.

In this model, ethnic minority members of the party did not gain access to decision-making processes within the party. Only a limited number emerged to become city councillors, and most of these behaved as disciplined backbenchers of the Labour group (interview with Stewart, 8/1/99, and head of equalities committee, 8/10/98). This can be linked to two factors. First, these ethnic minority councillors were not necessarily the most competent to deal with the workings of a large political body such as the Birmingham City Council. Second, their relation of dependence with their patrons, and their position as newcomers in the party, meant that they had difficulties in making their voice heard.[37]

Yet the existence of patronage is crucial because a retrospective analysis shows that it paved the way to greater representation. It started a dynamic of inclusion by giving ethnic minority leaders a first taste of participation, encouraging them to eventually contest the leadership of the right with the support of the left (Solomos and Back, 1995, pp. 80, 85). In this way it prefigured the second model of 'radical activists' which is considered below. While the left and its associate black and Asian activists may have fared worse than in other British cities (see chapter 2), this is not the case compared with French cities, where it is precisely the absence of serious political allies operating from within a major political party that has contributed to keeping minorities out of politics. Beyond this, the very existence, or absence, of a dynamic and open race for the control of power in the representative system is a central element of the Birmingham/Lille/Roubaix comparison. In Birmingham, the existence of such a race, and its role as facilitator of minority incorporation, is manifest in the quest for ethnic minority allies by traditionalist MPs struggling against leftist challengers, and it is equally true when the opposite side finds itself turning to the very same allies.

Radical activists: 1980s and 1990s. In the second, radical model, the main institutional variable at work is again the structure of internal competition within the party, but there are two differences from the patronage model.

First, ethnic minority councillors make their way in the party with the support of left-wing activists. Personal interviews conducted with senior white, black and Asian councillors in 1997 and 1998 show convincingly that those first elected in the mid-1980s went on to long and successful careers in the council, to a large extent because of their symbiotic relation with the left. Left-wing minority councillors were not as numerous as those elected with the support of more moderate elements of the party, but they left their mark on the city.[38]

The second characteristic of the 'radical activist' model is that these councillors benefited from the relatively high level of codification of party rules to impose themselves on local branches as activists, with more autonomy from established figures and less reliance on their capacity to mobilize voters or party members in their community. A series of controversies over the conformity to party rules of some memberships and candidate selection processes provided an opportunity to formulate and publicize opposition to the patronage system. This is crucial because it is what made it possible to legitimize higher ambitions for blacks and Asians.

When Labour came to power in 1984, it was dominated by moderate, traditionalist leaders, who sought to portray the Birmingham party as markedly consensual and noted that they were so moderate that 'even the Left of our party would be scorned by the Liverpool lot' (Daily Telegraph, 14/5/84). The 'Liverpool lot' in question was the group of far-left Labour activists who gained control of Liverpool City Council in the early 1980s and opposed Thatcherite policies of reduction of local social services. They became iconic of the Labour left in the 1980s, although in fact they differed from most other radical elements, in particular by never embracing the cause of ethnic minority representation, which they perceived as subsidiary to the class struggle. In this, Birmingham leaders were in keeping with the tradition of moderate progressivism inaugurated by Joseph Chamberlain, the city's most influential politician a century earlier.

The leader of the council, Sir Richard Knowles, embodied this moderate party. But the left, described as 'intellectuals' and 'professionals' because several were from academic or white-collar backgrounds as opposed to 'hourly paid' traditional activists of working-class and trade union background, were presenting a growing challenge to Knowles' leadership in the mid-1980s. Among them were Clare Short (who, although not directly involved in city government, intervened heavily in the politics of her inner-city constituency of Ladywood, where she was elected as MP in 1983), Albert Bore (councillor for Ladywood ward) and Theresa Stewart (councillor for Billesley ward). During his leadership, Knowles consistently led a policy of containment of these elements, by surrounding them with right-wingers in committees or by orchestrating votes in the Labour group against their proposals. Stewart was particularly targeted because she was emerging as the leading member of the left, and managed to get the chair of social services.[39]

From the early 1990s onwards they did start taking over the group, and with them the first left-wing ethnic minority councillors, particularly Philip Murphy. They were sympathetic to the radical black politics that were then emerging in the national party, and were instrumental in the careers of several prominent black and Asian councillors who were first elected or gained political weight at the time. These included some who had already participated in Labour Party politics before, such as Muhammad Afzal and Amir Khan, but also newcomers with little or no previous history of association with moderate politicians, such as Murphy (Sandwell ward, first elected in 1984). Less prominent activists also sought to work with ethnic minorities, such as, for instance, Kevin Scally (of Irish descent), and were very active in the south-eastern wards in the mid-1980s (Roy Hattersley's constituency of Sparkbrook at the time), coming to play an important role in controversies linked to racial politics in the 1980s.

Some minority activists participated in the rise of the left because they were coming to political maturity in that period and were often ideologically influenced by the politics of black emancipation in the United States, or trained in black and Asian trade unions or student unions. They commonly couched the struggle to represent their communities and address issues of racial disadvantage in a progressive language that often translated into the idiom of British class politics commonly heard in the Labour Party. In one characteristic example, two councillors of Asian background from the Handsworth ward were adamant that they worked hard for the ethnic communities from which they stemmed, fighting to raise money to build community centres for them (interview 7/06/99), but that they also sought to represent working-class communities as a whole.

Many found legitimacy and support in the party by articulating not just minority-specific claims but the more usual concerns of the Labour electorate: social services, housing, frequent discontent with the government's political orientation. A clear illustration is Alton Burnett (of African-Caribbean background). His selection, and subsequent election, as a councillor in 1996 took place in the Selly Oak ward, which has a largely white population. The main issues on which he campaigned had therefore little to do with ethnic diversity and more to do with classic problems of housing and education, in this case the inadequacy of existing provisions given the growing populations of students and elderly people in the area (interview with city councillor, 10/11/98). In addition, his election owed much to a long history of activism for the party, during which he failed several times to be selected in the 1980s and early 1990s before being successful. This of course did not prevent him from being heavily engaged in black activism in the city in addition to his work as representative of the Selly Oak ward. He migrated to Britain as a student and went into politics through student unionism (with the West Indian Students' Association) and subsequently in the Black Workers' Union.

Burnett is an extreme case of election in which ethnic electoral or organizational backing played little or no role, but his career embodies trends that have been at work in other careers as well. Among Asians, particularly Pakistanis, many have come to the Labour Party through trade union activism. Asian councillors active in the late 1990s such as Mohammed Kazi (Handsworth), Mahmood Hussain (Handsworth), Gurdev Manku (Sandwell), Fazal Ellahi (Sparkhill) and Shaman Lal (Soho) were all involved in unions prior to coming to Labour politics.[40]

Exceptions to the importance of trade unions and student unions are personalities who have risen from black-led churches, such as Sybil Spence and Dorothy Wallace, who were both first elected in the 1980s in Soho, and who have become well-established party figures since then. After their work in these churches, they went on to take an active part in the Labour group, beyond pure community politics. In 1993, Sybil Spence was chief whip of the Labour group, and Dorothy Wallace was vice-chair of contract services. Spence had previously been vice-chair of the urban renewal committee, then vice-chair of the social services committee.

Blacks and Asians, as well as the left of the party generally, have found resources in the organization of local branches to advance within the party. In the 1980s and 1990s, applicant candidates for city council elections were interviewed by the party's local government committee (which includes the whips of the council group). Selected candidates made up a shortlist, and could then apply to any individual ward to be selected by the members of the branch. Each stage of the process could be subjected to manipulation, particularly the final stage at branch level. This was notoriously the case with branches dominated by Pakistani networks, which in several instances in inner-city Birmingham were suspended by the regional party in the early 1990s because of irregularities, in particular sudden increases in the number of Pakistani members at the time of the selection process (see below on the 'ethnic community' model).[41] But all stages also offer ample possibility for appeal. In French municipal politics, on the other hand, the goal is not to be selected as an individual candidate for a ward but to have one's name on a party list. The drawing up of these lists by parties is not subject to any particular rule and is usually decided by discreet bargaining between various interests within the parties. In the French system there are few if any possibilities for appeal, thus depriving the less powerful interests in the party of a major resource.

It is also worth noting that recourse to anti-racial discrimination legislation is also one way in which proactive policies towards ethnic minorities since the 1960s have helped transform local debates.[42] In Birmingham, there were several examples of minority councillors going to court over claims of racial discrimination in the context of political intra-party disputes over candidate selection in the late 1980s and 1990s. One such case was Raghib Ahsan, a long-standing Labour councillor who, after being deselected, took the party to court over claims of racial discrimination with the support of fellow left-wing councillors from the Sandwell ward, Philip Murphy and John Tyrell (*Birmingham Post*, 28/7/98, 30/06/99). In this way, the national framework outlined in chapter 2, and the anti-discrimination legislation that is one of its chief characteristics, provide a platform for activists to voice claims linked to racial disadvantage in the context of city politics.

Both proximity to the left and the importance of party rules in explaining the arrival and growing representation of minority councillors became particularly apparent during the debates that raged in the party over controversial attempts to create 'black sections' in 1985–6. This episode was a local manifestation of a wider debate that shook the Labour Party nationwide in the 1980s (for details on the black section movement in Britain, see Jeffers, 1991; Shukra, 1990, 1998a). The sections were proposed by members of Marxist and black emancipation groups.

By putting clearly on the local agenda the question of the place of minorities in the party, the black section issue forced all actors concerned to take a definite stand in choosing between two types of positions: either the existing pattern of patronage, or a more radical form of incorporation similar to that existing in London, in which minorities would cease depending on the support of MPs and thus be able to push more radical issues (Solomos and Back, 1995, p. 90). When an attempt was made to create one such section in the Sparkbrook constituency, the debate became heated because this was the constituency of Roy Hattersley, who was particularly bent on defending his established pattern of relations with local Asian leaders and activists. As deputy leader, he was also a prominent figure of the national party at the time.[43]

Hattersley attacked the black section as a 'racist and divisive move', and one of his representatives declared: 'Roy Hattersley wants total unity of all the community into one Labour party' (Evening Mail, 12/12/85). Proponents of black sections countered by insisting on the necessity for blacks to have a single and autonomous voice in the party: 'Hattersley had three of the organizers expelled from the party. One was Amir Khan, a city councillor mentioned above who was later to go on to a long career at the council. The official motive for his expulsion was that he had kept secret the fact that he had stood as a candidate for the Socialist Unity Party in 1978 and generally his "total disregard for the party" constitution' (The Voice, 7/12/85). Another party activist, Kevin Scally, was accused by Hattersley of having 'brought the party into disrepute'[44] and of having accused Hattersley of encouraging false applications for membership in the local party ahead of an internal election for his reselection as party candidate for his seat as MP. A third councillor, Mohammed Rafique, was also expelled for the same reason (Guardian, 12/12/85).[45] In response, the three councillors mounted a vigorous campaign to have the expulsions overturned, mobilizing existing black sections across the country, organizing petitions and talking extensively to the media.

This controversy made plain the importance of the left in supporting black radicals against the right. One of the two joint chairs of the 'campaign for the reinstatement of Amir Khan and Kevin Scally' was Clare Short, the MP for Ladywood. The campaign against the expulsions was one of many against alleged 'purges' of radical activists in Liverpool, London and elsewhere, which were all consequences of the left's push to gain influence in the party.[46] The sections also had the support of prominent radicals such as Tony Benn and Ken Livingstone,[47] who were primarily active in London politics.

Regardless of the veracity of the accusations made by either side in the dispute, they referred extensively to the party's constitution, its rules and various modes of appeal, and the presentation of resolutions to party meetings. This was particularly so for Khan, Scally and Rafique, who sought to use leverage available in the party's structures. Paul Sharma, the organizer of the black sections for the Midlands, said in their defence: 'It is Mr Hattersley who is behind the expulsion of Mr Khan. Having lost the argument against the black sections, they are trying to silence us by kicking us out of the party. But I pledge that the full might of the Labour party black sections will fight, fight, and fight again for the reinstatement of Mr Khan. We will take it to the national conference and we are confident we will win' (*The Voice*, 7/12/85).

To be taken to the conference, the issue had to be presented in a resolution supported by at least 12 constituency organizations. If the resolution was adopted, it would be binding for the National Executive Committee (NEC), which would then have to reinstate the expelled councillors. A nationwide campaign was mounted to support the resolution. The very terms of the debate, about the best way to organize grassroots groups and the legitimacy of distinct black groups, are characteristic of a party whose organization allows for the cooperation of diverse and sometimes opposed groups, as noted earlier. The conflict ended with the reinstatement of the expelled councillors and the creation of a Birmingham-wide black section. It was to disappear under the pressure of the right wing of the party (interview with city councillor, 26/6/99), but it had a long-term impact.

In the following decade, persistent left-wing influence on ethnic minority politics in the city fuelled an increase in the number of black and Asian councillors, rising from six to nine between 1985–6 and 1986–7, from nine to 14 between 1987–8 and 1988–9, and from 15 to 20 between 1991–2 and 1992–3. Both this rise and the growth of the influence of the left in the Labour group at the council were correlated with the Labour group's size, reaching unprecedented averages of 80 to 85 councillors in the mid-1990s. This situation created a more favourable opportunity structure for black activism and made possible the deepest form of minority empowerment yet in the mid-1990s, beyond the first push of 1986–7. Individuals such as Philip Murphy became close political friends and allies of council leader Theresa Stewart throughout the 1990s (interview with city councillor 9/11/98), and significant numbers of minority councillors, both blacks and Asians, were given the chair or vice-chair of council committees.[48]

The presence of ethnic minority politicians at the core of the Labour group persisted even after the late 1990s, even though the party's standing among ethnic minority communities was being seriously challenged by a spate of independent and Liberal Democrat candidates. This is related to the general decline of black organizations in the party nationwide, a phenomenon which in turn is linked to the decline of the left in the 1990s as the successive leaderships of Neil Kinnock, John Smith and Tony Blair gradually managed to steer the party towards the centre and to marginalize more radical elements (see Shukra, 1998a, p. 120). In Birmingham, the weakening of the pluri-ethnic alliance was also connected with grievances specific to the inner city there and to rising disappointment with the Labour Party in Asian communities.

The ethnic community model: Pakistani/Labour politics in 1990s Sparkbrook and Small Heath. The third, ethnic community, model is characterized by the combination of the three following institutional factors: (1) the local electoral system, (2) the organization of Labour branches and (3) the gradual weakening of the Labour left, and of the Labour Party in general, in the late 1990s. In this model, as in the activist model, the patronage of white politicians is no longer part of the equation, but neither is an ideological alliance with the left wing; instead, councillors of Asian background, mostly Pakistani, operate independently of any other group in the party, building their careers solely on resources drawn from ethnic minority communities. They benefit from the emphasis placed by candidate selection rules on grassroots-based processes in the inner-city wards, where they are the most likely to benefit from the electoral support of voters from their communities. In this configuration, Asian councillors often campaign on issues that are of relevance to their local/ethnic communities. They use the Labour Party structure as a simple platform to legitimize and publicize their candidacy. This model applies mainly to the Pakistani communities of the southeastern part of the inner city (mainly the wards of the Sparkbrook and Small Heath constituency), where they reach their highest residential concentrations.

The party's support for candidates in this model is not essential, and in fact it became contested in many instances; from the late 1990s onwards, a new phenomenon of independent Pakistani councillors appeared, followed by some transfers from Labour to the Liberal Democrats. On the whole, the various forms of ethnic politics stemming from the Pakistani community in the city signalled the first difficulties with the pluri-ethnic alliance in power in the 1990s. The Labour Party does maintain a function in the emergence of this type of political career in the sense that these independent candidacies emerged against it, coming from people who had obtained their political training within Labour ranks. Both the patronage and the radical styles of election as Labour councillors worked as preliminary steps for this form of ethnic minority politics. The patronage system had shown minorities their potential power in the party, and radical politics demonstrated that this power could be used to further agendas beyond interests of a moderate leadership. With the ethnic community model, minorities sought to articulate the needs of a community constructed with reference to ethnicity, a ward- and neighbourhood-based sense of belonging, and a feeling of alienation from Labour.

This evolution can be understood as an example of 'institutional learning', as modes of recruitment and control of supporters clearly inherited from the patronage model are reproduced within the ethnic minority communities. In this sense, some aspects of Asian politics which I characterize as being part of this model, such as the recruitment of ethnic minority activists by other minority activists for strategic purposes, may not be the novel product of British Asian politics but an older mode of functioning that existed within the white communities which have been settled in the inner city of Birmingham for much longer (Solomos and Back, 1995, p. 104). This would suggest a remarkable continuity of forms of Birmingham politics, surviving deep social and ethnic change. This continuity may be attributed to the electoral system and the organization of the party. Yet controversies linked to this political model in the 1990s and those councillors who subsequently got elected on the sole basis of support from their ethnic community overwhelmingly pertain to the Asian communities of the city. It is therefore difficult to rule out some type of hybridization of Asian and native British political practices.

First signs of this model appeared in the mid-1980s, largely as an additional consequence of the black section controversy. Some Asian politicians took note of their growing autonomy and of the reluctance of the right wing to accept it, and decided to create their own breakaway parties. The dominant institutional resource here is the ward-based, first-past-the-post system in the wards that have the highest concentrations of minority population. In these wards, it became possible for minority politicians to envision a political future for themselves which did not include membership or alliance with Labour, whether ideological or purely strategic.

When Rafique was expelled from the party in 1985, he declared, 'I am well known in the Asian community and my expulsion will be very costly to the Labour party' (*Guardian*, 12/12/85). In the same period, Paul Sharma, the Midlands black section organizer, declared: 'Roy Hattersley, representing the leadership, will have no credibility when he asks black people to join or vote for the Labour party while at the same time our community's representatives are being expelled' (*Guardian*, 12/12/85). Many proponents of black sections threatened to join the ranks of a Democratic Party, which was created by councillor Mohammad Queshri who had left Labour in protest against its 'milking of the ethnic vote' (*Birmingham Post*, 19/2/86). The black section's official line was to carefully dissociate itself from the new party, while at the same time showing sympathy and understanding: 'We fear that unless Labour grants its black members the legitimate right to organize in black sections, the Democratic Party will grow beyond its 300 members and beyond Birmingham. The Labour Party must stop the rot and it must do it now' ('Labour risks exodus from blacks frustrated by section issue', *The Times*, 19/2/86). The Democratic Party was able to field seven candidates in inner-city wards in 1986, with but with no success.

The real electoral take-off of such enterprises came in the late 1990s, because of the combination of growing organizational and electoral clout and dissatisfaction with the party. Because of the tightness of their local social networks, Pakistani groups have frequently been able to control the processes of candidate selection, both in the north-west and in the south-east of the inner city. In the mid-1980s, the Sparkbrook branch had 600 Pakistani members out of 800; similarly, the Handsworth branch had around 800 members, 95 per cent of whom were Pakistani (interview with city councillor 7/06/99). There are accounts of inner-city branch organizations being controlled by Pakistani networks. By the mid-1980s, ethnic minority activists, especially South Asians in the south-west of the inner city (what is now the Sparkbrook and Small Heath constituency), had been so successful in incorporating the party machinery that they in fact controlled several, to the extent that many ward organizations and general management committees of inner-city constituencies came to elect Asian chairs and secretaries where formerly these positions had been dominated by white activists. In several instances the situation went so far as to lead to the marginalization of white members; an Asian councillor for Handsworth noted that he felt compelled to campaign particularly hard among white voters because they all too often considered that the party only represented non-white populations (interview with city councillor 7/06/99).

Asian dominance over wards has often been linked to tampering with the party rules, in particular bringing friends and relatives who are not members of Labour to selection meetings. Such allegations must be dealt with cautiously because the stereotype of Asian cronyism and corruption is widespread in political discourse and in the media; while comparable actions by white activists may receive little attention, they tend to be viewed with suspicion when they are carried out by blacks or Asians (see Shukra, 1998a, p. 128; Solomos and Back, 1995, p. 101).

It is certain that such was often the perception of regional and national party hierarchies. In 1994, the regional party launched an investigation when 500 people suddenly applied for membership just months ahead of a crucial internal vote for the selection of the party's candidate for the upcoming parliamentary elections in the constituency of Sparkbrook and Small Heath.[49] Most of these new members were of Asian background and had applied for membership in the Sparkbrook and Sparkhill wards, where the concentration of Pakistani populations was the highest. Party officials were reportedly 'amazed to find that a huge proportion of the applicants came to England from one Pakistani town, Mirpur, in Azad Kashmir' (*Evening Mail*, 17/12/94). The dispute also reached the other inner-city constituencies, Ladywood and Perry Barr, after further allegations about 'bogus membership and intimidation' (*Birmingham Post*, 28/7/96). In total a considerable number of Labour activists, more than 4,000, were affected (*Birmingham Post*, 28/7/96). Time was taken during the suspension to scrutinize the new memberships to see if they were genuine, and the capacity to choose candidates was in the meantime removed from the constituency organizations concerned. Finally, the party excluded around 1,000 new members from the party and fully reinstated the constituency and ward organizations in 1996. This allowed both sides to claim victory, with grassroots Pakistani activists emphasizing that they had gained the right to select the candidate before the parliamentary election of 1997.

This affair remained a major event in the life of the party in the 1990s. It revealed, perhaps more clearly than previous episodes, the extent of a racial cleavage within the party, running between large groups of Pakistani activists of the inner city (particularly the southeastern inner city) on one side, and the upper echelons of the party predominantly consisting of native Britons on the other. The racial conflict was therefore to some extent one between local democracy exercised at the grassroots level and the national party, viewed by the base as distant, arrogant, manipulative and, of course, racist: 'Some members have claimed that the suspensions were being kept in place to prevent local members choosing their own candidate and possibly selecting a black or Asian candidate' (*Birmingham Post*, 28/7/96).[50] Raghib Ahsan, who was the Sandwell ward Labour Party chairman in 2000, proposed the following explanation for the disaffection: 'The undemocratic interference of party officials in the running of inner-city parties, the long periods of suspensions, and the continued refusal to allow local members to select their own candidates have fatally weakened Labour's links with the communities in these areas' (*Birmingham Post*, 23/5/00). This superposition of racial tension and a dispute over the legitimacy of the party organization is important because it marks the first step in the break-up of the Asian–Labour alliance. In contrast with the black section episode, there were no white allies supporting the dissenters; they were on their own. In fact, in the early 1990s, former left-wingers had left the city or become established figures in the party, and more often than not were viewed with scepticism by some minority councillors. The party had moved from being a tool of empowerment to being an obstacle.

Incensed by the suspension of branches, some Pakistani members increasingly decided to stand as independent councillors. They successfully challenged Labour candidates of white, Pakistani or other background in local elections in various areas of the inner city, but particularly in the Sparkbrook and Small Heath area. This area is where the concentration of the Pakistani population was the highest in the 1980s: in 1991, 70 per cent of Pakistanis in the city lived in four southeastern inner-city wards: Small Heath, Sparkbrook, Sparkhill and Nechells. These are the wards where most of the Pakistani councillors are elected, although some do get elected in multi-ethnic wards (such as, for instance, councillor Kazi in the northwestern inner-city ward of Handsworth, which had mostly Indian, white, African-Caribbean and Pakistani populations in the late 1990s). In the southeastern wards mentioned above, the Pakistani community benefited from the highest level of organizational and electoral resources.

However, the suspension of wards was not the only cause for the shift of votes towards independents. Other factors include issues linked with the politics of independence movements in Kashmir, and frustration with service delivery and attribution of urban regeneration funds by the city council in inner-city wards.

Labour was frequently blamed for inaction over the cases of Riyaz and Qayum, and 'forgetting about our issues and our problems between elections'.[51] Riyaz and Qayum were two activists who attempted to murder an Indian diplomat visiting the UK in the 1980s in the context of the Pakistani/Indian conflict over Kashmir. Demands for their release from prison became a major concern of the local Pakistani population, in which feelings over the Kashmir conflict ran high. In 1998, Labour lost one of its seats in the Small Heath ward by a large 400-vote majority, to Allah Ditta, a campaigner for the independent 'Free Riyaz and Qayum Campaign'. In other wards of the heavily Pakistani south-west of the city, Washwood Heath, Sparkbrook, Sparkhill and Ladywood, the same campaign lost to Labour candidates, mostly Pakistani, but still managed to poll between 28 and 38 per cent of the votes cast, or 6,500 votes (*Birmingham Post*, 9/5/98). This constituted a significant challenge to Labour's supremacy, unprecedented on that scale and at that time in the inner-city wards. Small Heath, lost to Ditta, had been held exclusively by Labour for 30 to 35 years (*Birmingham Post*, 9/5/98).

In addition to concern with the fate of Riyaz and Qayum, Ditta's victory was clearly the result of continued anger on the part of many Pakistani Labour activists after the deselection episode of 1994. Revealingly, Ditta's victory was scored against sitting Labour councillor Gulbahar Kahn, one of the chief aides of the constituency's MP Roger Godsiff, the very MP whose selection as party candidate had triggered the mobilization of Pakistani networks against him and brought on the deselection dispute.

Independent candidates such as Ditta also articulated bitter complaints about the perceived neglect of inner-city communities by the Labour council. After his election he insisted on denouncing the millions of pounds that had been spent by the Heartland Development Corporation on urban regeneration programmes for an area that bordered his ward of Small Heath but did not include it. In his own words, 'They built shopping centres, hotels, and dual carriageways but we didn't see a penny. It is not just Small Heath but other inner-city areas where there is low wealth, high unemployment and poor conditions. We don't want special treatment, just equal rights with other communities' (*Birmingham Post*, 20/5/98). He sought to attribute his electoral victory directly to discontent about these problems in the Muslim community: 'They [i.e. the Muslim voters] always used to vote Labour but I don't think they will anymore because of the way this area has been neglected' (*Birmingham Post*, 20/5/98).

Here again, councillor Amir Khan's career, already mentioned in connection with the 1985–6 black section controversy, is particularly illustrative. After 16 years' service as a Labour councillor, he left the party in 2000 for the Justice for Kashmir Party, a new, local, independent party, in protest over the party's decision not to reselect him to defend his seat in the 2000 local election. At the time of his departure, he was quoted as accusing the party of 'excluding ethnic minority councillors from major decision-making' and declared: 'It is not the party I joined twenty years ago and have believed in all these years. They have turned their backs on the inner city wards where people are living in appalling conditions' ('Councillor brands Labour as "racist"', *Birmingham Post*, 21/12/99). While expressed here with reference to local issues, this dimension of the ethnic community model also echoes the disenchantment felt by many among the traditional supporters of Old Labour in the face of the direction taken by the national party leadership.

These episodes were far from isolated but, on the contrary, marked the beginning of a series of setbacks for Labour. Just after Ditta's 1998 victory, council leader Theresa Stewart and the Labour MP from the neighbouring Hall Green constituency were openly displaying their alarm and calling for a change in the party's inner-city policy. What struck them in particular was that the seats lost were considered to be safe, and they were lost while other wards, in south Birmingham, which were considered more vulnerable, actually remained Labour (*Evening Mail*, 7/5/99). In the 2000 local elections, the Labour majority on the council fell sharply from 35 to 15, with the party losing 11 of its 78 seats, down to 67. The Justice for Kashmir group was a major opponent from the start, and already held four seats on the council. Like Khan, the other candidates of the party were concerned with Kashmir but also played on dissatisfaction with the management of local ethnic communities by Labour. When the party burst onto the local scene, it vowed to be 'fighting poverty and deprivation, unemployment in the local communities and raising the standards of education achievement. [. . .] We need to regenerate these areas and target funds from the Government. For example, centrally millions of pounds have been set aside to help Longbridge in the wake of developments at Rover.[52] Why hasn't this money been used to help inner-city areas?' ('Smallest party pledges havoc and looks at war on poverty', *Birmingham Post*, 21/4/00).

In the early 2000s, the movement away from Labour and towards other parties continued, not just to the Justice for Kashmir Party but also to the Liberal Democrats. The latter had long been broadly supportive of the anti-discrimination agenda. In addition, its political fortunes were rising in the city as the Labour Party came to be the target of the discontent levelled against government policies after 1997. Continuing conflict between some Labour Asian councillors and the Labour Party's leadership on the council and against the West Midlands party organization pushed these councillors to switch parties. This was the case for councillor Tariq Khan of the Nechells ward, who defected to the Liberal Democrats in 2001, accusing the regional, district and city-level parties of being run in a dictatorial manner and neglecting grassroots members for the benefit of a small 'clique' of influential members (*Birmingham Post*, 12/1/01). In this, he was following in the footsteps of a few others, for instance Mohammed Masoom. The latter was also a representative of the Nechells ward and had been elected the previous year by a very narrow four-vote margin against Abdul Malik, a Labour candidate (*Birmingham Post*, 12/1/01). This showed that the Liberal Democrats could be a real force in inner-city Pakistani politics and beat Labour at its own game. It also demonstrated how easily some Asian candidates could dispense with Labour's support and transfer their electoral base to an opposing party.

In 2003, the Liberal Democrats became even more attractive to Asians because they were the only major British party that unambiguously opposed the war in Iraq. 'Muslim leaders' were quoted as attributing Labour's loss of some inner-city seats to the Liberal Democrats to a 'Baghdad backlash' (*Birmingham Post*, 3/5/03). Yet the actual effects of September 11, 2001 and of the Iraq war remained hard to assess at that early stage. What is important to note is that in spite of clear signs of weakening, Labour's multi-ethnic alliance was still holding on in the early 2000s. While some segments of the Asian population might be disgruntled and looking for political representation elsewhere than with Labour, others remain a pillar of Labour's system of control of the city. In 2000, after the structure of the council switched from a committee system to a cabinet system, two of the 10 members of the cabinet were Asian Labour councillors, Tahir Ali as head of local and neighbourhood development, and Muhammad Afzal as head of personnel and equality (*Birmingham Post*, 9/05/00). This proportion of ethnic minority councillors in important positions was comparable to their situation in the early 1990s.

After losing 11 councillors in 2003, the Labour group on the council was down from 66 to 57, in other words, two short of an absolute majority (59 out of a total of 117 councillors). As a result it was forced to broker a deal with other groups to continue governing, which it did after much hesitation with the Conservative group, the second largest group with 35 members, just ahead of the Liberal Democrats with 23, and far ahead of the Justice for Kashmir Party. The Liberal Democrats and the Justice Party were almost entirely left out of the agreement, which gave control of the cabinet, and the council's departments, to Labour (*Evening Mail*, 3/06/03).

Conclusion

This chapter has shown how the institutional framework of Birmingham politics facilitated the emergence of a pro-minority, pluri-ethnic Labour-led local government in the 1980s and 1990s. In particular, four institutions of the local polity combined to create a favourable political opportunity structure for minorities: the ward as the district for local elections, the plurality system, the style of organization of the local Labour Party and the structure of internal party competition.

This institutional configuration has functioned in various ways in all the wards of the inner-city area of Birmingham since the beginning of the 1980s. It has constituted the basis for three models of incorporation in the context of ward-level Labour politics: the patronage model, the activist model and the ethnic community model. The patronage model was mostly at work in the early 1980s and consisted in a bargaining process of the minorities' electoral and networking resources against the support of white right-wing party members. The activist model that came to supplant it in many cases in the mid- and late 1980s was an alliance between left-wing activists and ethnic minority leaders concerned with racial equality and/or disgruntled with previous patronage arrangements. This model presided over the election of councillors in the late 1980s and early 1990s who went on to occupy influential roles in the networks of the left-wing leadership of Theresa Stewart. Indeed, their rise was closely linked to that of the left wing in the party, which itself was correlated to the culmination of Labour's success in the city, with the group reaching the unprecedented size of 80 councillors. Finally, from the late 1990s onwards, cracks in the white–black and Asian alliance become increasingly apparent, with the emergence of an 'ethnic' model of politics, in which the Pakistani community used Labour structures as a platform to obtain representation. Growing discontent led to a rising number of successful independent candidacies, in which Asian candidates stood against Labour with the support of the Liberal Democrats or as independent candidates.

There is a progression in time between these three models, but whether this is matched by a progression in the level of recognition and influence on decisions at the city council is harder to assess. Certainly the second, 'activist' model describes the attempt by blacks and Asians to move beyond the limited role assigned to them in the patronage model and to gain political autonomy and real leverage on public affairs. It was successful in the sense that the question of the representation and empowerment of minorities in the city was clearly posed through their action, and that some became influential members of the council leadership in the 1990s. While the plague of racial discrimination and disadvantage persisted in the city, and while many ethnic minority activists pointed to persistent marginalization and sidelining at the council, these developments nonetheless constituted a breakthrough for ethnic minority representatives, and a healthy success for Birmingham's democracy.

But the weakening of Labour's hold on Birmingham's city council in the late 1990s and early 2000s, concomitant with the onset of disaffection among its black and Asian inner-city base, could be interpreted as showing that minority incorporation might not be a permanent achievement but, on the contrary, merely a parenthesis, caused by the belated and short-lived successes of the Labour left in the 1980s and 1990s. Tony Blair's unpopularity and the rapidly evolving position of Muslim communities in British society and politics may accelerate the weakening of Birmingham's pluri-ethnic coalition. Yet that conclusion seems premature since Asians and blacks are still in significant positions in the council's cabinet.

5

Lille, 1980s–2001: Machine Politics and Exclusion of Minorities in the French Municipal System

Introduction

The Lille–Roubaix comparison

French local government is extremely fragmented: with its 36,000 or so communes, France has as many cities as the rest of western Europe. Urban areas in particular are divided into a multiplicity of small, independent communes, which have their own elected councils and their own bureaucracies, the municipalities, attached. This fragmentation underpins many differences between the politics of minorities in France and Britain, with the possible exception of London boroughs. It means that a variety of sometimes contrasting political situations may coexist within one area, and, most importantly, that relations between municipalities often play a major role in shaping situations within these areas.

This is compounded by the decentralization policies of the early 1980s, which introduced a complex system of multi-level local governance that superimposed the Conseil Général (elected on a departmental scale), Conseil Régional (elected on a regional scale) and various types of Communautés Urbaines (indirectly elected groupings of communes that form an urban area).[1] Large, central communes can usually use their dominant positions within these bodies to encourage housing policies and other large-scale strategic policies that serve their goals in the area of transport or environment. In

the area of minority politics, these policies often result, intentional
erwise, in communes located in the centre of urban areas having a larg
portion of white, middle-class inhabitants, while suburbs are more freque
poorer and ethnically mixed.[2] In French cities, therefore, there is usually
rather clear social and ethnic differentiation between central communes in
urban areas and their suburbs (*banlieues*), with social/ethnic cleavage running
through both the internal politics of the *banlieue* communes and between
central and peripheral communes. This stands in contrast with the situation
in Birmingham, where the proportion of ethnic minorities in the city is similar
to that of its neighbours (Wolverhampton, for instance), and the distribution
of populations in Birmingham is very much an issue of inner city vs. outer
city within the city boundaries.

For these two reasons – high differentiation between the social profiles
and politics of neighbouring communes within one area and interlinkages
between them – it is particularly appropriate to study not just one French city
but, rather, one French city together with one of its neighbours. One additional reason is that French cities have on the whole offered a wider range of
strategies of management of ethnic conflict than British cities, largely because
of political parties' weaker grip on local council politics, which creates greater
possibilities for diverse types of alliances and more personal styles of government by mayors. A Franco-French comparison within the British–French
comparison can therefore help nuance conclusions otherwise excessively influenced by the idiosyncrasies of a French case. The Lille–Roubaix comparison
was deemed particularly appropriate because these two cities present two contrasted and complementary strategies: in Lille, persistent political exclusion,
and, in Roubaix, increasing inclusion within the city council. In addition,
the relation between the two is a clear illustration of the type of linkages
mentioned above, with Lille seeking, with some success, to externalize its
social problems by moving them to its suburbs, among which Roubaix figures
prominently.[3]

A strategy of avoidance and denial

Lille has been controlled for the last four decades by the Socialist Party. It was
previously a Gaullist bastion,[4] and the conservative electorate of the 'bourgeois' city centre remains a powerful force to this day. It swung to a Socialist
mayor, Augustin Laurent, in the 1960s, who then promoted the election of
Pierre Mauroy as his successor in 1974. Mauroy, then a promising young
Socialist leader, went on to a brilliant career in both national and city politics. He was the first prime minister of newly elected President Mitterrand
between 1981 and 1983, and later became first secretary of the Socialist
Party. He remained mayor of Lille throughout, becoming the embodiment

...nsensual *notable* frequent in French cities, before
...artine Aubry, another prominent Socialist with gov-
...served as his first adjunct from 1994 to just before
...2001, when she was re-elected, albeit with a lower

...nent as mayor was to turn the city from a declining
...juvenated economy, increasingly driven by services
...ng number of white-collar professionals (Cole and
John, 1997; Giblin-Delvallet, 1990). This involved the departure of some of
the population of workers and unemployed, of both native French and recent
immigrant background, to neighbouring towns. In spite of this, the city still
retained a significant population of workers, unemployed and families on
modest incomes in the 1980s and 1990s. Hence, it remained characterized
by an internal social conflict, which was largely congruent with an ethnic
conflict, because the remaining disadvantaged and unemployed population
included a large proportion of ethnic minorities. This chapter focuses on the
attitude of the municipality towards this conflict during Mauroy's time in
power (1974–2001), and particularly the 1983–9 and 1989–95 tenures. It seeks
to explain why the municipality remained largely unresponsive to issues pertaining to minority disadvantage, and failed to display any interest in striking
political or electoral deals with minority representatives. This strategy stands
in sharp contrast to what happened in Birmingham, and to a lesser extent in
Roubaix, and may come to change in the future as it seems increasingly inefficient. However, there was little sign of change by the 2001 elections.

I seek to explain this attitude primarily with reference to the two elements
of the institutional framework under discussion: local modes of government
and local party politics. These take the form of two striking features in Lille.
They are (1) the combination of a well-established local elite and a majoritarian electoral system for municipal elections, which insulates elites from
social demands, and (2) the emergence since the 1970s of a powerful Socialist Party 'machine', loosely adapting this concept from its American context.
These elements, singly or combined, inhibited the two main attempts at participation by minorities in municipal politics both in the 1980s (local offshoots
of the nationwide Beur protest movement) and the 1990s (small neighbourhood-based groups). The result was very limited representation on the city
council, in both the 1989 and 1995 elections.

The first section documents the municipality's persistent attitude of indifference, or hostility when provoked, towards minorities, and shows how it can
be ultimately linked to the weaknesses and failings of minorities' political
organization and mobilization in the city. The next section begins by
presenting in detail the two institutions outlined above – municipal political
institutions and the machine in Lille. It then moves on to show how the first
element led to the marginalization of the Beur movement in the city in the

1980s, and how the combination of both elements then helped the municipality to fend off hostile mobilization by disaffected North African youths in
the aftermath of this movement in the 1990s.

Lille's Double Strategy of Externalization and Political Exclusion

This section begins by retracing the emergence of a North African minority
in the Lille area. It then shows that the Socialists' strategy of economic regeneration and gentrification of the city in the context of competition with neighbouring cities enabled social and ethnic problems to be externalized to some
extent onto neighbouring cities. In spite of this, such problems remain intense
in Lille. Finally, I discuss the ways in which this persistent problem has fared
in the politics in the city, and argue that the municipality's strategy of avoidance of minority issues and 'one size fits all' republican universalism has
largely been encouraged by two elements: the relative strength of the Front
National, and the repeated incapacity of ethnic minority groups and voters
to aggregate their interests.

The emergence of a North African minority[5]

The Lille metropolitan area lies in the *département* of the Nord, of which Lille
is the *préfecture*, and in the region of the Nord-Pas-de-Calais,[6] of which Lille
is the capital city. It is one of the largest urban areas in France, with around
1,200,000 inhabitants, which makes it comparable to Lyon and Marseille but
leaves it far behind Paris. It contains around 80 cities, the three largest being
Lille, Roubaix and Tourcoing, with populations of, respectively, 178,300,
97,700 and 93,500. The other communes range from long-urbanized and
traditionally poor towns integrated within the urban fabric of the area to villages that lie just outside. In contrast to Birmingham, Lille was an important
urban centre long before the industrial revolution of the nineteenth century.
In the Middle Ages, it was a major commercial city of Flanders. Later, it
became an important French military post and benefited commercially and
demographically from that status. The largest expansion of both the city and
its metropolitan area, however, dates back to the period from the 1850s to the
first decades of the twentieth century (Giblin-Delvallet, 1987) and was due to
the rapid growth of heavy industry in the region. The development of coal
mining in the region south of the city, on the border between the *départements*
of the Nord and the Pas-de-Calais (an area known ever since as the *bassin
minier*), triggered a rapid expansion of metal industries in and around the
city. At the same time, the textile industry also developed very rapidly in the

area. Lille specialized in cotton processing, while Roubaix, and to a lesser extent Tourcoing, became international centres of the wool industry. Both expanded particularly quickly, with factories and housing blocks for workers' families (called *courées*, because they were built around square yards or *cours*) becoming the staple trademarks of the industrialized and urbanized north of France. They peaked at populations of about 125,000 each at around the turn of the twentieth century, since declining to around 100,000 each.[7] During this period Lille also developed rapidly, maintaining its dominance as a regional capital and reaching a population of more than 200,000, about its current size.[8]

Because of this rapid growth, and because of the traditional resistance of French municipalities to structural reorganization, a multitude of small communes, mostly rural villages surrounding Lille and Roubaix, grew to form one continuous industrial urban area, while each retained its own administrative and political structure as an independent commune. For this reason the area is particularly fragmented, even by French standards. Populations range from 1,000 for the smallest commune to 178,000 for Lille. Lille, Roubaix and Tourcoing comprise only 40 per cent of the total population.

As in the other large immigration areas of France (Lyon, Paris, the industrial areas of Lorraine and Franche-Comté, and Marseille), and as in Britain, immigrant workers came to participate in the post-war reconstruction effort by providing cheap labour for industries. Unlike in Britain, however, the migration movement was organized by the French government, in cooperation with the foreign governments concerned as well as the industries themselves (see chapter 3). In the case of the Nord *département*, the local mining, textile and other industries already had a long tradition of importing foreign workers: Belgians from as early as the 1850s and throughout the nineteenth century, then Poles and Italians between the two world wars. Indeed, important Polish and Italian communities still exist in the area, especially in Roubaix where there is a Polish-language radio station. Lille also has significant populations of Italians, Spaniards and Portuguese, who are now socially assimilated with the rest of the population, although they are still concentrated in old working-class areas. From the early 1950s onwards other sources of labour were needed, and employers turned massively to North African and, to a lesser extent, Portuguese immigration.

It is mainly the North African population which has been the locus of ethnic conflict in France (with the issue of Islam, decolonization, racial discrimination, xenophobic vote and demands for recognition of cultural diversity during the Beur movement). Although the Portuguese population is also important in the region, it has never been a social or political issue. In this chapter I will therefore focus on the profile of Algerians and Moroccans.

Algerians started settling in the area between the two world wars as retired French army servicemen and as workers. Their numbers were thus the first

Table 5.1   Foreign population in the Lille area in 1990

City	Total population	Foreigners (nationality other than French)	% of foreigners in total population
Lille	178,000	16,645	9.6
Roubaix	97,700	23,156	23.7
Tourcoing	93,806	10,865	11.6
Unité Urbaine de Lille	959,516	71,808	7.5
Nord (*département*)	2,560,421	187,536	7.3

Source: Compiled from INSEE data, 1990.

to increase in the late 1940s, from 5,200 in 1939, 9,600 in 1948, 16,270 in 1949 to 18,300 in 1954 (Poinsot, 1994, p. 568). They still constitute a larger community in the Lille urban area than Moroccans.[9] Algerians were employed in the wool industries of Roubaix and Tourcoing in the 1950s, often working in night shifts where they contributed to the survival of fragile businesses (Giblin-Delvallet, 1990, pp. 68, 236). From the late 1960s and 1970s their economic situation started to deteriorate with the arrival of the economic crisis and the final decline of the textile industry. This came at a time when wives and children were joining workers in large numbers, because of the 1974 suspension of immigration imposed by the French government. This accounts for the rapid deterioration of the economic situation of this population since then.

Moroccans came to work as coal miners in the mining region south of Lille, as well as to work in other industries and run small businesses in the Lille area. The Moroccan population has since caught up with the Algerian population because of late family unification and a very high birth rate (Correau, 1995, p. 36). For Moroccans too, the situation in terms of level of employment deteriorated rapidly because the mining industry was just starting its decline at the time of their arrival in the early 1970s (Poinsot, 1994, p. 576). Finally, a substantial student population came from Morocco in the 1970s to study at the University of Lille.

The proportion of foreigners in the total population of the Nord *département* (7.3 per cent), as well as in the Lille urban area (7.5 per cent), was slightly lower than the national average (8 per cent) in 1990. But the proportion in the three main cities of the Lille metropolitan area (Lille, Roubaix and Tourcoing) was higher (see table 5.1) and was one of the highest in any urban area of this size in France, together with the Paris area, the Lyon suburbs and Marseille. This must be particularly noted for Lille, whose 9.6 per cent, although lower than the percentages of Roubaix and Tourcoing, was still high,

Table 5.2 Breakdown of foreigners in Lille by nationality in 1990 (main groups)

Nationality	%
Moroccan	57.6
Algerian	24.6
Portuguese	6.3
Italian	3.1
Tunisian	2.4
Turkish	1.9
Spanish	1.1
Other	3.0

Source: INSEE data, 1990.

especially for a French regional and departmental capital. It was enough to
speak of a consequent ethnic minority population in the city.

The municipality's policy of gentrification

Mauroy's overriding preoccupation on taking office was to save the city from
the scourges of deindustrialization, growing unemployment and pauperiza-
tion (Mauroy, 1994). His overall strategy consisted in working with large businesses in the area to create qualified tertiary jobs and attract middle-class
populations, with the inevitable consequence of reducing the working-class
population of the city by encouraging the construction of social housing in
neighbouring towns (see Lojkine, Delacroix, and Mahieu, 1978; Bleitrach
et al., 1981; Giblin-Delvallet, 1990).

  This strategy was made possible in large part by the institutional features
of the French local system, particularly the interlinkages between different
levels of local government. The mayor's personal network of political allies
embraced all the key actors of these institutions and gave him firm control
over them. In particular, the city of Lille is dominant in the Communauté
Urbaine de Lille (CUDL) owing to the support of right-wing mayors in
smaller cities brokered by Mauroy. On leaving his mayoral seat in Lille in
2001, Mauroy managed to get elected president of the CUDL, giving him
even greater influence in the area than when he was mayor. The CUDL
groups 87 communes in the area and is run by an assembly made up of elected
representatives from the city councils of its constituent communes (see CUDL,
1990; Sueur, 1971). It deals mostly with infrastructure, planning and economic development and exerts an increasing influence over the politics of the

area, because it has a large budget, a strong bureaucracy (3,000 employees), and is seen by many as the most relevant scale of government for policy-making in greater Lille, destined progressively to sideline the communes (Cole and John, 1997). It has a growing influence on the area's long-term development and is thus the focus of much political competition between the mayors of its constituent cities.

During Mauroy's tenure as mayor, Lille had the largest number of representatives on the CUDL because of its status as the largest commune, and it also commanded a solid coalition of Socialist representatives from other cities. It used its dominant position to form alliances with groups of small neighbouring communes to turn the CUDL into an instrument of its policy of gentrification and economic expansion (Giblin-Delvallet, 1990, ch. 12). In particular, it used its position to obtain the creation of a new university and technology complex on its fringe (Villeneuve d'Asq) in the 1970s, and a Eurostar train station (on the Paris–London line), together with a large shopping complex on the same site, and, finally, a major convention centre which firmly established it as the undisputed regional capital. Hand in hand with this economic policy went the need to provide accommodation for new, more upwardly mobile families, and therefore to upgrade old accommodation, most of which was owned by local social housing schemes (HLMs), which are partly controlled by municipalities. The consequent rent rises had the long-term effect of driving poorer families out of the city, among which were North African families (Bleitrach et al., 1981, pp. 159–84; Bruyelle, 1993, p. 14). There are strong indications that the low-income populations evicted from Lille often migrated to the Roubaix–Tourcoing area, which, between 1975 and 1982, attracted 20 per cent more migrants from the Lille area, most of them very low-income families, than it sent to that zone (Bruyelle, 1993, p. 19). This inevitably included a large proportion of North African households. In fact, as Bruyelle notes, 'The policy of eliminating inadequate housing is also an indirect means of regulating the immigrant problem' (Bruyelle, 1993, p. 34, my translation).

Most renovated neighbourhoods in Lille formerly contained large North African populations (10 to 16 per cent of foreigners in certain parts of Wazemmes-Esquermes in 1982, 16–18 per cent in parts of Vieux Lille in 1982), but these percentages became negligible in the 1990s (Bruyelle, 1993, p. 33). In Roubaix, by contrast, as much as 20 per cent of the population was of foreign nationality in the 1980s, 23 per cent in 1990, rising to 25 to 35 per cent in certain neighbourhoods.[10] Indeed, Roubaix's dilapidated housing stock, composed essentially of individual houses for workers' families, was very attractive to poor North African families, often with large numbers of children. Roubaix politicians and inhabitants alike bitterly complained about Lille's attitude, accusing it of 'dumping' its undesirable populations onto their territory (Verfaillie, 1996, p. 108; Giblin-Delvallet, 1990, ch. 10).

More recently, Lille has also benefited from legislation encouraging the merger of communes with their suburbs, which around Lille are traditionally the stronghold of the left. In 1999 Lille absorbed the adjacent town of Lomme, with the agreement of its municipal council. This was meant to be a political coup for the Socialists because 65 per cent of Lomme's voters regularly voted for the left, and it was supposed to have garnered 6,000 or 7,000 new votes in the 2001 municipal elections (*Le Figaro*, 20/2/01).[11]

The persistence of a social and ethnic 'problem' in Lille

The trend towards the strategy of gentrification has been both a cause of the social crisis of the southern neighbourhoods and a way of limiting the latter's potentially damaging effects for the municipality. It has caused it because those low-income populations that remained in Lille were the most disadvantaged groups, with high proportions of unemployed and ethnic minorities. It has helped to prevent the crisis from being translated into political conflict simply by reducing the proportion of dissatisfied voters and by increasing the number of more prosperous families, who are more likely to vote for Socialist-led centre-left lists.

However, the gentrification strategy has not meant that all low-income and ethnic minority populations left the city, and, in fact, a large number remained, forming a significant component of the city's population. As noted above, in Lille in 1990, the foreign population represented 9.6 per cent of the total (see table 5.1). A small proportion of these were Italians, Spanish and Portuguese. The North African population, comprising both Moroccans and Algerians but with a Moroccan dominance, represented around three quarters of the foreign population, or around 7 per cent of the total population (see table 5.2). Of course these statistics suggest a significant number of French nationals of foreign origins, in particular North African, in the city.

Migrant populations of European background in the Lille area are socially, culturally and politically assimilated into mainstream French society and have not been an issue in recent decades. The North African population of Lille, on the other hand, had features that made it a highly disadvantaged population, comparable to the ethnic minority populations of Birmingham and Roubaix. This is particularly true in terms of residential concentration, age structure and levels of unemployment. Thus there are three coterminous cleavages in Lille: one opposing the centre of the town against the other neighbourhoods, particularly those in the south of the city; a second one opposing the reasonably well-off employed against the unemployed or low-income families; and finally, one opposing populations from native and old migration background against the North African populations. This produced cumulative disadvantage for minorities. In this respect, Lille presents strong similarities with Birmingham.

The levels of residential concentration in 1990s Lille did not reach those of Birmingham, where concentrations sometimes reached 60 per cent of a ward, but they nonetheless remained significant. Ethnic minorities were almost entirely absent in the north and centre of the city, which is the business centre and the relatively well-off area. They were concentrated in a crescent-shaped zone spanning from west to the east, through to the south of the city, which comprises the neighbourhoods of Wazemmes, Lille-Sud (which includes two sub-neighourhoods, Lille-Sud Nouveau and Lille-Sud Ancien), Faubourg de Béthune, Fives, Moulins and Bois-Blanc. These neighbourhoods are traditionally inhabited by populations of workers and their families and comprise a mix of traditional low-rise, red-brick accommodation, high-rise building built in the 1950s and 1960s, and factories and workshops.

In the gentrified neighbourhoods of the north and centre of the city, such as Vauban, Saint-Maurice and Centre, the percentage of the foreign population ranged from 3 to 5.5 per cent.[12] In Fives, Bois-Blanc and Moulins, that percentage was much higher: from 8 to 14 per cent, which hints at much higher percentages of ethnic minority populations (see map 4, p. xx). This population was usually highly mixed with native French populations, which translated into a relatively low visibility (especially in Fives). By contrast, the percentage of the foreign population was at its highest in Lille-Sud and Faubourg de Béthune (around 19 per cent). As Lille-Sud is by far the largest neighbourhood of the city with around 25,000 people, it has the city's largest North African population. Within that neighbourhood, the North African population was concentrated in Lille-Sud Nouveau, where it reached a maximum of 30 to 35 per cent of the population. In 1991, 34 per cent of the population in Lille-Sud Nouveau was of foreign origin, and 32 per cent was of North African origin (data from Duprez, Leclerc-Olive and Pinet, 1996). Within certain sub-neighbourhoods in Lille-Sud, such as a group of high-rise buildings, North Africans sometimes constituted the majority of residents. Finally, Wazemmes is a special case: it had around 9 per cent North Africans, but they were concentrated in the centre of the neighbourhood where there were many Moroccan small businesses and Lille's largest traditional market, which is largely North African.

Throughout the 1980s and 1990s, the southern belt of the city was dominated by a population of low-paid workers or unemployed (*La Voix du Nord*, 24/11/92). The temporary slight improvement in the French economic situation between 1988 and 1991 was followed by a new surge in the unemployment figures; as always, the Lille area was badly affected because of its high percentage of unskilled and young inhabitants. In the 1990s, all indications pointed to a high level of poverty in the city, in particular a record 40 per

Table 5.3 Unemployment according to ethnic minority background in Lille-Sud Nouveau (%)[a]

Level of qualification	North Africans	Non-North Africans
CAP-BEPC level (leaving school around age 15):		
Unemployed	52.2	34.0
Employed	47.8	66.0
Total	100	100
Bac level (equivalent to A level) and above:		
Unemployed	58.8	10.0
Active	41.2	90.0
Total	100	100

[a] Male and female combined, population of working age only; schoolchildren, students, retired population and those not seeking work are excluded.
Source: Duprez, 1997.

cent of the population living in HLMs (the French equivalent of council housing), and six out of ten neighbourhoods having unemployment rates above 20 per cent.[13] The city of Lille presented a contrast, with a prosperous centre and a highly disadvantaged population on its southern periphery. This was understood among local public opinion, and one local entrepreneur was quoted as saying: 'Lille is both Harlem and Fifth Avenue: after Paris, it's the city with the highest number of people paying wealth tax, but it's also where the percentage of RMIstes is the highest in France'.[14]

Most of the southern working-class belt, in particular Faubourg de Béthune, Moulins and Lille-Sud, witnessed economic decline, high unemployment, endemic law and order problems and an increase in drug dealing. Among these districts Lille-Sud stands out because it is the largest and the most deprived. The neighbourhood's unemployment rate was 27.5 per cent, against 16 per cent for Lille.[15] In the 1990s, the police force had persistent difficulties patrolling or intervening in the area, and in the same period the neighbourhood witnessed the appearance of an emerging private militia formed by members of the local boxing club.[16] There was a general loss of faith among the population in the ability of public authorities to implement law and order.

Rare statistical evidence in terms of ethnic background available on Lille-Sud (table 5.3) shows that not only were unqualified North African workers doing significantly less well in the job market than non-North Africans from the same neighbourhood, but that this was also true, and to a far greater extent, of the few qualified North Africans. In total, the concentration of minority population, their youth and evidence of a high level of disadvantage on the job market are all reminiscent of Birmingham's inner cities.

Social discontent in the political arena: Front National, republican universalism and minority disorganization

Consensual government challenged by the Front National and by abstention. Mauroy's strength lay in the fact that he was able to obtain the support of various key interests in the city: he repeatedly won over many right-wing voters in the traditionally bourgeois centre of town, and gained the long-term support of local business interests. Christian Decocq, the Gaullist candidate in the 2001 municipal election, noted that: 'A proportion of the city's affluent middle class has always voted Mauroy because he knows how to organize consensus. [. . .] The same thing goes for business interests' (quoted in *Le Figaro*, 20/02/01, my translation). To this extent Mauroy's period in office could probably be characterized as an urban regime, with a lasting, broadly based coalition of interests consensually maintaining the same policy line over years (following the criteria proposed by Dowding et al., 1999).

In spite of this support, and in conjunction with the persistence of social and ethnic disadvantage in the city noted above, discontent against the Socialist-led majority persisted in the 1980s and 1990s. This discontent was voiced forcefully in the party political arena. In line with developments in the rest of the country, it took the form of the rise of the Front National (FN),[17] in particular in the 1990s in the poorer areas of the city, and of a rising level of abstention. The FN's scores in general council and regional council elections increased regularly during the 1989–95 period in the city in general, and in the south of the city in particular (Etchebarne, 1996). In all types of elections, both national (European, legislative, presidential) and local (regional, general, municipal), the FN grew from a position of insignificance in the early 1980s to become one of the city's well-established parties. In some elections, it achieved a comparable fraction of the vote to that of the RPR (Gaullists) or UDF (centrists), with around 17 per cent.[18]

The FN became an important force in the city, but later in the 1980s than in Roubaix or Tourcoing, and not to the same extent by far, remaining at a moderate 10 per cent city-wide, whereas it reached huge levels of around 30 per cent in the other two towns (see chapter 6). In 1983 and 1984, the FN vote in Lille emerged not in disadvantaged areas but in the predominantly conservative areas of the city (city centre). It was then very much a manifestation of 'bourgeois exasperation with the perceived inadequacy of the conventional Right' (Etchebarne, 1996, p. 296). It was only from 1986 onwards that the FN started to meet electoral success in the disadvantaged south, when a solid block of polling stations gave it 15 per cent or more of the vote in most elections on a regular basis (Etchebarne, 1996, p. 296).

Focusing on municipal elections, in 1989 and 1995 (the party did not field any candidate in the 1983 election), the FN's score was not particularly high, and was in fact slightly lower than the national average; but there were wide discrepancies between neighbourhoods, and while the wealthy centre returned low scores, the south of the city was at double the average. In the 1989 municipal elections, the far-right candidate Pierre Ceyrac polled 8.66 per cent in Lille-Sud, with peaks of 13 per cent in some polling stations. In the 1995 municipal elections, the FN's candidate Carl Lang polled 11.64 per cent city-wide. Building on this success, Lang went on to contest the second round with Alex Turk, the Gaullist candidate, and Mauroy, in a triangular contest. Lang's presence in the second round helped Mauroy fend off Turk's challenge.

In the poor southern belt, where the FN reached scores as high as 14.6 per cent, it was taking not just right-wing votes but also, and most importantly, a large number of voters away from the Socialists. In some polling stations in Fives, Moulins, Lille-Sud and Faubourg de Béthune, the FN's share of the vote frequently hovered between 15 and 25 per cent.[19]

In 1999, party activists in charge of canvassing the area identified the shift of voters from the Socialists to the Front National as their major challenge, together with abstention (interview with Socialist activist, 6/4/99). This was a major and increasing source of concern to Mauroy's team in the late 1980s and 1990s, because the south was their traditional stronghold. They came to rely on it more and more in the 1990s, when prominent Gaullist leaders started challenging them in the city (Alex Turk, who scored well against Mauroy in 1989 and 1995,[20] and Colette Codaccioni, who was briefly a minister in Alain Juppé's 1995–7 government).

Hence, the effects of the FN's rise have been contradictory: on the one hand, it directly served Mauroy by splitting the right, but, on the other, it also drew the support of disgruntled Socialist voters in the south of the city, thereby threatening its strongholds, along with abstention. In the late 1990s, the party's Comité de Ville (the committee in charge of defining the party line on municipal affairs) had nominated a policy sub-committee on 'how to combat the Front National'.

The municipality's response: urban regeneration and avoidance of ethnicity-related issues. It is important to note that the municipality's unflinching attitude has been to consider the FN as an evil to be fought through economic regeneration and general social policies. In line with dominant national attitudes in the 1980s and 1990s (see chapter 3), it frantically ducked issues that were specifically ethnic. In particular, the municipality relied primarily on one device, the use of urban regeneration funds provided by the jointly administered four-year funding plans of the state and the Nord region, to inject money into the neighbourhood in the form of housing renovation, job-seeking assistance, subsidies to cultural associations, and leisure and educational activities. In this it was typical of many other cities in the *département* of the Nord, which was considered as particularly in need of government-funded regeneration programmes.[21]

This policy response acknowledged that there was a class-based and territory-based disadvantage, but it consistently ignored problems and demands formulated specifically by the large ethnic minority population of the area (19.6 per cent of foreigners in Lille-Sud, most of them Moroccans, to which must be added French nationals of Moroccan background). This was despite the fact that the situation of economic crisis and disorder clearly increased the salience of ethnic disadvantage in the southern belt. City-wide, the unemployment rate for foreigners was twice as high as the unemployment rate for French nationals (Ville de Lille, 1999, p. 7). In Lille-Sud Nouveau, unemployment among young North Africans with a high school degree was 58.8 per cent, against 10 per cent for non-North Africans with similar qualifications (Duprez, 1997; see table 5.3). Access to housing in the 1990s was also a much greater preoccupation for Algerians and Moroccans than for French nationals or other foreigners because of a lower average income and a much greater number of children (Ville de Lille, 1999, p. 7). Most importantly, this negative situation was clearly perceived as such by the North African population. Participation in local community organizations, sports clubs and both drug dealing and anti-drug activity was largely the preserve of these unemployed North African youngsters (*La Voix du Nord*, 24/11/92). All held a cynical view of French society and institutions (interviews with youths involved with associations and sports clubs, Lille-Sud, 29/9/98, and in Faubourg de Béthune, 30/9/98).

In the 1990s, the construction of one custom-built mosque was reluctantly accepted by the municipality, but three other proposals for the construction of similar mosques were originally turned down. In the late 1990s mosques were just about tolerated, because of a perceived risk of ethnic, communitarian separatism on the part of the North African groups concerned. 'Why should all the mosques be here? If we condone that, the area is going to become a ghetto', confided the council officer in charge of the regeneration programme for Lille-Sud (interview with urban regeneration manager, 6/4/99). He went on to explain that he had been brought into the neighbourhood by the municipality in the mid-1990s to 'crack down on wasteful associations that were sucking up the municipality's money for irrelevant projects', which served to accelerate the process of 'ethnic regrouping' (*repli ethnique*) among young North African men in particular. As will be seen later on, this explicit, even adamant, rejection of ethnic or religious groups did not preclude various forms and degrees of implicit, de facto recognition of the very same leaders who were formally rejected. However, issues of racial discrimination, in all areas of daily life but especially on the job market, were completely ignored. This reflected the lack of anti-discrimination policies nationwide at the time,[22] but contrasted with Roubaix's attitude, which sought to address the problem.

Finally, one aspect of this attitude of indifference to minorities was the lack of co-optation of ethnic minority councillors in the municipal majority, although there was no lack of contenders. Exceptions were two councillors in 1989 and two in 1995. All four lacked prominence and were disappointed by their term in office, in a pattern typical of minority politics in French cities so far.[23]

This strategy of avoidance of ethnic minority claims was due to the pervasive influence of the national political climate in Lille in the 1980s and 1990s. 'Republican consensus' on a universalistic and assimilationist approach to immigrant incorporation (labelled *'intégration' des immigrés*) struck a powerful chord among the city's traditional Socialist personnel, more so than in other local towns, in particular Roubaix, which had long been governed by centre-right mayors of Catholic inspiration. Municipal officials, elected or not, rarely mentioned ethnicity of their own accord. When encouraged to do so, they produced a defensive discourse, essentially denying the existence of a problem, or arguing that policies related to ethnicity would only make things worse because they would serve to institutionalize racial difference. This appeared most clearly in a personal interview with the *conseiller municipal délégué à l'intégration* (councillor delegated to 'integration' matters), who argued forcefully that there should be no policy in Lille explicitly directed at groups selected on an ethnic or religious basis, because it would breach republican principles and lead to the creation of ghettos.[24] This had the direct effect not only of inhibiting the adoption of policies such as anti-discrimination programmes, but also of removing from the limelight the issue of minority political representation.

The absence of ethnic minority interest aggregation in the city. In addition there was a strong local factor, namely an unbalanced tension between FN voters and the interests of the North African population. On one side was a xenophobic group, the Front National, whose potency lay in the fact that it could control the national climate on the issue and, as shown above, turn a large fraction of the voters away from the party in local elections; on the other side was a group characterized by both limited electoral leverage and weak pressure groups.

North African voters in the 1980s and 1990s were considered by the municipality as an electorate to be wooed by specific means at election time, but only to a limited extent and in a piecemeal and short-term way. One adjunct in 1995 brought up the old proposal for foreigners' voting rights in municipal elections (interview with association leader, 29/9/98). In 1999, in advance preparation for the 2001 local elections, the Fédération Nord-Pas-de-Calais of the Socialist Party distributed leaflets with guidelines on the legal procedure to be followed in case of racial discrimination at the workplace. Throughout the 1980s and 1990s the Socialists in fact behaved as though it was not necessary to make particular efforts to woo the North African vote because its support was more or less acquired by default. Minority voters in Lille often seemed reluctantly to identify the Socialists as their most likely electoral choice, for want of a better alternative, even though they felt neglected by them. This was because the other parties available locally, the moderate right UDF and RPR, were often suspected by North Africans of racism, in addition to being viewed as unsupportive of modest-income families (interview with association leader, 29/9/98).

The French Municipal System, Machine Politics and Minority Exclusion in Lille

The absence of electoral leverage and representation was compounded by a lack of organizational resources that could have enabled the minority population to aggregate and articulate its claims. In turn, this could have mobilized many young North Africans who had voting rights but did not use them. In contrast with both Birmingham and Roubaix, what was missing was a situation where the concentration of voters in certain districts met the existence of ethnic minority leaders with well-connected white allies, which would enable the emergence of an ethnic minority elite.

The comparison with Birmingham highlights the lack of a competent and experienced personnel of community activists who might come to achieve some form of inclusion in political institutions. In turn, this is clearly due in Lille, as in other French cities, to the sharp generational gap that separates young second-generation North Africans, who have repeatedly attempted to participate, from their parents' generation, who have been remarkable for their discretion, even withdrawal, from French politics. The full effects of the French citizenship regime come into play here, as well as the political culture and recent history of Algeria, which has kept first-generation Algerian migrants away from native French political organizations. In the Lille area, hundreds of Algerians were killed in internal struggles during the war of independence (Genty, 1999).

The contrast with Birmingham is pointed, since the Asian and black city councillors there were born in their country of origin and were middle-aged in the 1990s. The repeated failures of movements and groups run by second-generation migrants in Lille should be analysed to some degree as the result of their lack of experience, lack of training in pre-existing structures and lack of older, more experienced leadership.

Beyond the generational gap, however, I emphasize here institutional factors to account for the failures of participatory attempts. These failures are so systematic and severe that they cannot be attributed only to the generational isolation of North African 'youths', who in the 1990s were in many cases no longer young but middle-aged.[25] The organizational weakness was at the same time the cause and consequence of the national context's pressure on the municipality: this context encouraged the town hall to follow the trend and to marginalize minority groups; equally, the weakness of minority groups made them less able to counter the opposite pressures of the republican assimilationist discourse. In addition, the institutional factors that are characteristic of French local politics, and to some extent of the idiosyncrasies of Lille politics, are emphasized here as constraints that limited the possibilities for the aggregation of minority interests in the city.

There were several occasions when minority organization was built up, which can be grouped into two periods. First, in the early 1980s, a national climate more favourable to the formulation of ethnic claims encouraged the emergence of a vast protest movement on the part of second-generation North Africans demanding the 'right to be different' ('*droit à la différence*'). This movement culminated in 1989 with several hundred North Africans standing for municipal elections throughout the country. But those elected were relatively few and were quickly marginalized (Geisser, 1993, 1997). Second, in the 1990s, more isolated and diverse groups were still attempting to voice protest about disadvantage in municipal arenas, with contrasting levels of success: very limited in Lille, and more successful in Roubaix.

This section shows how local political institutions combined to close the political opportunity structure of Lille to minority movements in both these periods. These institutions are first presented in detail. They are, as in Birmingham, local parties and party systems, and the local structures of local authorities and electoral systems. In Lille, they combined in different ways in each of the two periods outlined above. In the following section I argue that, in the first period, it was mainly the general characteristics of French municipal institutions that had an impact, particularly the electoral system, and the insulation of local elites from societal demands that result from that system. Hence the failure of the Beur movement in the city can be understood as an example of its failure in most French cities. This section also shows that, in the second period, it was the combination of these general characteristics with Lille-specific features that had an impact. These specific features were a particular configuration of party, community (*société civile*) and municipality that facilitated the emergence of a powerful party machine.

Municipal institutions in Lille

The French municipal system. First, the institutional and electoral system that is common to all French cities has worked as an instrument of containment of societal demands in the hands of the political elite, which in the French local political system is an integrated local/national and political/bureaucratic elite. It has insulated these elites from challenges from outsider groups and immigrant communities in particular, because a large fraction of them are disenfranchised. While other levels of local government were created in their present-day form by the decentralization laws passed by the Socialists in the early 1980s, the commune that comes under them is one of the very few political structures, together with the *département*, that has survived all the radical changes that affected the French political system throughout modern history, including the French Revolution, virtually intact.

The central element of the communes, the mayors, are considered as the representatives of the locality in the national political arena, that is, in Paris.[26] This is compounded by the fact that, in the case of large urban communes such as Lille, they frequently have personal connections in ministries and elected assemblies in Paris. This is made possible by the ability afforded French politicians to accumulate several elected positions, informally called the *cumul des mandats* system (accumulation of elected positions). Two types of position often accumulated are those of mayor and deputy in the National Assembly, not least because the position of mayor provides an important source of patronage and influence that can be used as a power base for a parliamentary election campaign (on the *cumul des mandats* system, see Hoffman-Martinot in Gabriel and Hoffman-Martinot, 1999, p. 101; on the inter-relation of local and national political careers, see Garraud, 1989). Hence, in the French case, it would almost be more accurate to speak of one interlinked system that is both national and local, rather than of two levels of government.

The integration of the mayor in the wider political system confers popular legitimacy on the system. Municipalities acquire their legitimacy from the fact that populations identify them as their primary political arena and source of authority, while other local authorities are often considered as remote and less significant. The mayor benefits from a high level of identification by his constituents, who see him as the embodiment of the commune and often look to him as a protective, sometimes paternalistic figure. The mayor obtains his legitimacy through a highly majoritarian electoral system, with elections occurring only once every six years, which insulates him, together with the rest of the political system, from his constituents. Keating summarizes this perfectly from the perspective of a comparison with American cities:

In France, municipal councils (except in the three largest cities [Paris, Lyon and Marseille]) are elected at-large on a list system. There are two ballots, and, until 1982, the list winning a majority at the first ballot or a plurality at the second took all the seats. While in principle the council chose the mayor from among its members, in practice it was the mayoral candidate who selected the list. Once installed, the mayor retained office for the full six-year term. While this was intended partly to contain the Left, the effect was to encourage partisanship on both sides while insulating political leaders from social pressures and neighbourhood demands. By the 1970s, it served to exaggerate Left-wing success at municipal elections, and the Socialists were wary of changing it. In the 1982 reforms, they instituted a modest degree of pluralism. Lists can now be merged between two ballots, so allowing for coalition formation and the co-optation of smaller political movements, and the opposition is now represented at the council. While the winning list still takes a majority of the seats, the rest is distributed proportionately among all the lists gaining more than 5 per cent of the votes. The effect of this has been a containment of social demands and insulation of French political elites – though not, as in the USA, a corresponding rise in business influence. Rather, it protects the interests of the integrated national–local political elite. Containment in France is further aided by the disenfranchisement of most of the immigrant underclass. (Keating, 1991, pp. 45–6)

The system plays out against those ethnic minorities who do have the vote, because in most cases they are a small population when considered on a city-wide basis, while they would be a sizeable minority or sometimes a majority on a neighbourhood basis (provided, of course, that they voted together on common issues). Other classic features of French local politics also play out against the participation of ethnic minorities, particularly the distinction between representative politics and associational activity, and the confinement of minorities to the latter (Crowley, 1991; Cordeiro, 1996, 2001).

The Socialist machine. The increasing ethnic diversity of large French cities and the rise in abstention may constitute long-term trends which could weaken the grip of mayors over cities, as noted by Hoffman-Martinot (Gabriel and Hoffman-Martinot, 1999, p. 102). What happened in Lille is that the features of French local institutions combined to particularly great effect, making it possible for the dominant circles within the party around Pierre Mauroy to remain in control of community organizations over the period, and to keep potentially dissenting interests at bay. While the social and economic trends noted above were eroding the Socialist hold over the city, as the increasingly narrow municipal election results show, there were still enough resources to be found in Lille politics for the Socialists to continue to govern, and to do so without significantly altering their policies and discourses. This was especially evident in the way the agendas of young North Africans in Lille-Sud were marginalized in the 1990s.

First, of course, the mayor's policy of gentrification of the city served to minimize any problems related to traditionally working-class neighbourhoods. Most importantly, the leadership around Mauroy benefited from the particular characteristics of community, party and local authority in Lille. Specifically, it was able to control the remaining population of workers by building a strong municipal party machine. The term 'machine' is used here in its familiar American sense, that is, a party organization used by an individual or a clique to uphold his or their dominant position in an urban political system (Judd and Swanstrom, 1998, p. 53). Hence, to the classic institutional insulation from social demands it has added an extra cushion, more reminiscent of turn-of-the-century American urban politics than of usual French politics, although this is probably the case of many other large French cities where one group has been in power for a long time.[27] It achieved this by combining diverse elements of the city's institutional environment to its advantage. First, the place of associations in the municipal landscape makes them particularly prone to instrumentalization by municipalities. Building on this, the mayor was able to keep a strong grip on the local branches of the Socialist Party, because these branches maintained a high level of inter-penetration with local associations, including old, traditional groups that bear witness to the Socialist Party's history of representation of working-class populations. Mauroy has also been sufficiently adept at riding general trends in local French politics since the 1970s to consolidate his grip over these networks. In the late 1970s, he used the popularity of leftist demands for local community self-government and direct democracy to introduce the decentralization of the municipal council. Whether his scheme resulted in increased control for the population over the council is uncertain, but it clearly increased the control of the Socialist-dominated neighbourhood councils over local associations. The municipality also benefited from the introduction of urban regeneration programmes from the early 1980s onwards to reinforce its control of the allocation of regeneration funds to those same local associations. In fact, the municipality was able to use the decentralized councils to territorialize the allocation of funds on a neighbourhood basis, thereby creating a tight grid of party officials and friendly associations that contain potential political changes.

In spite of basic resemblances to the American machine, the overall outcome with regard to minorities differed sharply in Lille, because American machines usually served to incorporate immigrants, whereas in Lille it served mostly to exclude them. It is also important to note that, taken on its own, the first of my factors – local French institutions and the electoral system – does not necessarily produce an outcome of exclusion. The case of Roubaix serves to show that with the same system, but with a different local configuration of community, party and local authority, things work differently. Finally, the exclusionary effect of the machine may not be everlasting. The very strength that enables it to exclude is also the factor that can enable it to include. This may happen in the future if demographic and social conditions continue to change and to erode the Socialists' electoral potential; however, there was no sign of this in the 2001 elections.

The 1980s: municipal politics and the failure of the Beur movement

Lille was left out of the wave of racial riots that hit most major French cities in 1981 (for details on the riots, see Bachman and Le Guennec, 1996, pp. 341–68). The only plausible hypothesis regarding this apathy is that the transformations of the municipal organization described above succeeded in maintaining the population within a web of paramunicipal community organizations (Poinsot, 1994). However, important movements demanding civil rights and anti-discrimination policies emerged all over France in the wake of these riots in the early 1980s, and these movements did have a large impact on the young North African population of Lille, emulating the creation of numerous grassroots associations (for accounts of the Beur movements see Jazouli, 1986; Lapeyronnie, 1987; Bouamama, 1994; Juhem, 1998). The trend caught on around 1983 in the neighbourhoods of Wazemmes and Lille-Sud, initiated by the Marches des Beurs of 1982 and by a similar event that took place a year later (Convergence 84). Committees were created in various city neighbourhoods to organize the visitors' reception and publicity around them (*La Voix Du Nord*, 16/5/82). Once the agitation subsided, some structures that had been created for the occasion remained active (described in detail by Poinsot, 1993).

Two associations of significance emerged in the wake of the Beur movement in Lille in the early 1980s, Texture and Les Craignos. The emergence of such groups has been studied in detail by Poinsot (1991, 1993, 1994). The analysis presented here is largely informed by this work. Starting from the same general premise of trying to address the issues of racial discrimination and social, economic and political exclusion of North Africans in France, the associations devised two diverging strategies, which both failed in different ways, but for reasons which I argue are in both cases linked to the characteristics of the municipal system outlined in the previous section. Specifically, their main problem, which eventually proved fatal, was the lack of a strong, well-established ally who would be interested in supporting them without absorbing them. Both the left and the right of the Labour Party played this role at various times in Birmingham, but the Socialist Party did not do so in Lille.

This can be linked to a number of characteristics of the party, particularly the fact that it had firm control over local communities (argued by Poinsot, 1994), and all the more so in the next decade with the emergence of a full-blown party machine. What I insist on here is that the most direct factor for the failure of both Texture and Les Craignos was the municipal majoritarian system. This made the Socialists overwhelmingly dominant in the city, distorting in their favour the fact that they were the largest single electoral bloc, ahead of the right and the Greens. Hence, unlike the Labour Party in inner-city wards, the Socialist Party did not need minor groups to support it, but needed only to make sure other large groups could support it (in Lille the Greens, and to a lesser extent the Communists), or were divided (which was the case throughout the 1980s and 1990s of the right, split between the moderate and far-right). This marginalized all smaller left groups, including immigrant groups such as Texture and Les Craignos. The former was marginalized because of its refusal to work with the Socialists, while the latter was absorbed by them.

Texture. Texture was originally a collective of a dozen left-wing activists who had taken part in the early Beur movement at the beginning of the decade and who got together in 1985, following the third and final march for equality through Lille. As was the case of many other local offshoots of the Beur movement,[28] the common denominator of these activists was criticism of SOS Racisme's broad humanistic discourse, its increasing remoteness from the core issues of racial discrimination and social exclusion, and the desire to formulate alternative solutions to the continuing social and political exclusion of North Africans. Like many other local movements of its kind, it was supported at the outset by autonomous left-wing groups, including the local Confédération Française du Travail (CFDT) and Parti Socialiste Unifié (PSU), as well as by other minor left-wing groups in the city, all of which were characteristic of the 'Second Left' (*Deuxième Gauche*, then represented within the Socialist Party by Michel Rocard), a trend that emphasized cultural liberalism and advocated *auto-gestion* (self-management of communities and workplaces). Hence, Texture was characterized by a leftist approach to the issues of immigration and ethnic minorities which attempted to place them within a broader context, transcending national boundaries and what it saw as 'artificial' divisions between generations and categories of immigration. In this respect, it criticized the very idea of a Beur movement exclusively centred around second-generation immigrants as artificially divisive. This made Texture an umbrella organization, supporting a variety of other groups and projects, which could help project its radical vision onto all issues broadly pertaining to ethnic minorities in the Lille area. One major objective was to politicize the masses of youths living in suburbs and housing projects in the south of the city; another was to entice support for related causes: the Palestinian issue, the Algerian troubles in 1988, the national mobilization against the reform of the nationality code in 1986 (Poinsot, 1994, p. 125).

Its main concern, however, as for the whole Beur movement, was the problem of citizenship. In conformity with its left-wing inspiration, Texture proposed a radically alternative conception of citizenship derived from the concept of *auto-gestion*. It made the concept of territorial belonging to a local community the basis for political participation and citizenship. In this way, the two main challenges faced by North Africans in France – the gap between first and second generations, which the Socialists had proposed in 1981 to bridge at least partially by granting voting rights to immigrants at the local level,[29] and the cultural, social and political marginalization of second-generation youths in French society, which France Plus proposed to remedy by stressing participation in conventional politics – would be addressed together and reconciled. Through participation in their local community, first-generation immigrants would be able to participate in public affairs, in spite of their lack of formal citizenship. This, in turn, would strengthen their children's claim to cultural difference by making more evident their belonging to a culturally specific community.[30] Again drawing on their leftist heritage, Texture embarked on a series of spectacular events designed to capture the attention of the media and the public between 1985 and 1990, among them sit-ins against the nationality law reform in 1987, distribution of fake 'identity cards' to demonstrate the arbitrariness of national identity, and other demonstrations of all kinds (Poinsot, 1994, pp. 118–27).

From 1987 onwards, however, the association's level of activity and influence started to decline. First, the debate had become so centralized that even purely local groups such as Texture suffered from the decline of the large national organizations; although it presented itself as a reaction against SOS Racisme and France Plus, it had been free-riding on the publicity it created for the Beur movement as a whole. Once this disappeared, Texture proved unable to sustain media attention and mobilization, because of certain structural weaknesses that were mostly due to an increasing political isolation, starting with isolation from the very population for whom it claimed to speak. In spite of its proclaimed authenticity and faithfulness to the original spirit of 1983 and 1984, it too was in fact a small network of intellectual and activist elites, who had but little ties with the grassroots. While SOS Racisme and France Plus were creations of the Elysée Palace and of the party, Texture was the product of a self-contained local *milieu* of academics and activists.[31] Significantly, a series of attempts to organize events in Lille-Sud in order to attract its large young North African population failed miserably, contributing to giving Texture its image as a group of elite intellectuals cut off from the population. In 1987, Said Bouamama organized a concert followed by a debate on citizenship in Lille-Sud, with the help of a few youths from the neighbourhood whom he had encouraged to form their own association. The event was badly received because it was perceived as vacuous talk disconnected from the 'real issues' that concerned the population (Poinsot, 1994, pp. 118–27; 1993).

In addition, and most importantly with regard to my institutionalist argument, Texture was from the start in the situation of outsider in Lille, because its ideology and choice of alliances alienated it from the Socialist Party. Its radical programme could by definition only be hostile to the municipality, whose legitimacy rested on the conventional, representative and majoritarian system, and which claimed to encourage community life through its *mairies de quartier*, while in fact seeking to exert exclusive control over it. In addition, the attempts by Texture to mobilize North African youths were perceived by the council as disruptive of its quiet patronage relations with this group; for all these reasons, working with the municipality was difficult from the outset, in a political environment where the municipality is a crucial player.

By the time of the 1989 municipal election, Texture was already considerably weakened, but it nonetheless chose to participate in the electoral contest in the hope of using this central element of French local politics as a tribune for its claims. Hence, it decided to support a radical left-wing list, together with other local groups, on the theme of 'citizenship against social exclusion' (*citoyenneté contre la galère*). As a result, and owing to its lack of popularity with the North African population, it obtained a meagre 2.5 per cent of the vote, insufficient to maintain itself into the second round (Poinsot, 1994, pp. 284–8). In this way, the most challenging North African association to the municipality marginalized itself from the municipal electoral scene, conveniently enough from the Socialists' point of view.

Les Craignos. The second association to emerge from the early 1980s agitation as a notable actor on the local scene was Les Craignos. Apart from the fact that it also originated in the Beur movement (although it was created earlier than Texture, in the aftermath of the first march for equality in 1983), it differed radically from the movement in most other respects. It had none of Texture's ideological ambitions, being, on the contrary, a grassroots movement with limited though concrete ambitions that were firmly confined to the boundaries of the neighbourhood of Wazemmes, one of the two largest working-class and North African neighbourhoods in the city along with Lille-Sud. It was founded and managed throughout the 1980s by two young men of North African background, Bouziane Delgrange and Malik Ifri, who had grown up in the neighbourhood. From the start, they were interested in immediate, tangible issues pertaining to the problems of everyday life for North Africans in the area, and conceived of their association as a community self-help association. Their actions focused on organizing health awareness and drug prevention campaigns, as well as educational activities and sports for children in the neighbourhood (Poinsot, 1994, pp. 139–50). As a consequence, one of the association's main functions naturally became dealing with local institutions that might provide backing and financial and organizational support for such campaigns. From the beginning, they had received encouragement from the neighbourhood's *centre social* (a *centre social* is a charity aimed at creating social capital in deprived areas; legally it is an independent institution run by an association founded in 1901). Indeed, both Delgrange and Ifri rapidly went on to take social work degrees and to lead their association as professional social workers (interview with municipal councillor, 24/9/98).

In contrast to its attitude towards Texture, the municipality sought to integrate the young association into its own networks by offering support and funding for its campaigns. Les Craignos came to be associated more and more closely with the municipality and was granted semi-municipal status in order to secure the means for its campaigns. Through this process, it became closer to the Socialist elected officials of the municipality. Thus, at the time of the 1989 municipal elections, it almost naturally claimed a place on the Socialist list. It insisted that it was not to be treated as a 'token' representative, and that it wanted a true decision-making role. The organizer of the Mauroy campaign felt compelled to accept because of the group's influence in the Wazemmes area. What he conceded, however, was just one place, low down on the list, with little chance of being elected; Malik Ifri accepted the offer, and was narrowly elected. Delgrange was offered a similar deal later, in the 1995 election, and was elected then (Poinsot, 1994, pp. 290–5).

In these 1989 municipal elections, Pierre Mauroy was in a relatively weak position compared to his previous elections because of a strong bid from a right-wing (RPR, Gaullist) notable, Alex Turk. Mauroy's list won in the second round because of Socialist mobilization and because Green and Communist leaders were included in his list for the second round, to the dismay of their grassroots activists. Ifri was pushed further down the list to make way for these newcomers, and thus ended up with exactly what he had sought to avoid at the beginning, a token position. Indeed, he was later to walk out of his job in protest over his marginalization at the council. The group's failure came from its attempt to bargain with the Socialists, without sufficient leverage behind it. As in Texture's case, failure was directly due to one main factor, the Socialist Party's domination over all left-wing political forces in the city, which meant that any minority group had therefore to seek an alliance with it.

Both Texture and Les Craignos failed to produce a lasting, established elite that would be able to articulate ethnic minority demands and put them on the municipal agenda. Texture marginalized itself politically because it isolated itself from any possible support from the local population or from potential political allies by insisting on pushing a radical and ideological agenda that found little sympathy. In this respect, its failure is symptomatic of the failure of the Beur movement, whose programme of mass protest at the national level proved incompatible with the national opportunity structure. As for Les Craignos, it became a successful, well-established, paramunicipal welfare organization at the expense of any commitment to controversial issues about ethnic disadvantage it may have originally had. The case of Texture exemplifies the fact that one cannot do without the party, while the experience of Les Craignos shows that too close an alliance leads to absorption.

The 1990s: machine politics and the marginalization of North African dissent

This failure announced and facilitated the next period, the 1990s, which was characterized by apathy and short-term, unstructured mobilization by youths. As Adil Jazouli puts it, the Beurs across France started from the late 1980s onwards to suffer from an 'abandonment syndrome' (*syndrome d'abandonnite*) (quoted in Bachman and Le Guennec, 1996, p. 421). The failure of the Beur movement not only revealed the hostility of the French political opportunity structure, but also was in itself a factor in the continuing failure to raise issues in the next historical period, the 1989–95 municipal term. It did this by stopping the emergence of a potential Beur political elite. This contributed to the growing feeling of youth alienation not just from the Socialist Party (as mentioned in chapter 3) and the political class in general, but from the Beur would-be elite as well. What little organization emerged from North African youths was consequently neighbourhood-based, independent of party influence, and made limited, circumstantial demands, as in many other French cities (Césari, 1993, 1998).

In 1990s Lille, the Socialists were able to maintain the disadvantaged populations of the southern belt in general, and North Africans in particular, in a tight web of subsidies and short-term provision of minor services, which further prevented any trend towards the regrouping of isolated individuals or groups, or towards the formulation of politicized demand, let alone standing for local election or exerting any significant pressure on other candidates. A comparison between the numbers of North Africans on the municipal council and in neighbourhood-based, consultative *conseils de quartier* reveals this. These *conseils* were neighbourhood-based, consultative institutions introduced by Mauroy in 1977 in an attempt to reinforce local democracy. While, as noted earlier, there were only two councillors of North African background out of a total of 56 in 1989 and 1995, there were 21 out of around 150 in the *conseils*. This shows that there were civic-minded individuals of North African background who did take part in associational activities and were interested in getting involved in the *conseils*, but that they were confined to low-level representation that came with no effective power.

Again, this was made possible by the institutional features of the local political system. The electoral system, and the dynamics of coalition-making shaped by that system, still played a role. But, in addition to this, the municipal machine came directly into play to constitute an additional institutional resource that would insulate power from minorities' claims. This section first shows how its various elements came together and made the reproduction of the pro-municipality consensus through patronage a central element of Lille politics. Next, it shows how the machine neutralized or marginalized dissenting voices among the associations of young North African youths in Lille-Sud.

The elements of the municipal machine. The gentrification of the city encouraged by the Socialists had complex feedback effects. In particular, it encouraged changes in the electorate, with new voters often more likely to vote for the Greens, in addition to supporting the Socialists, and thus tended to weaken the Socialists' electoral dominance in the long run. It also de facto made the Socialists the defenders of business and prosperous families, while the status of low-income households as the traditional base of the party tended to fade away. It similarly affected the transformation of the social composition of the party's activist structure, compounding the national trend of transformation from a workers' party to a party of lower-level employees and the lower middle class (see Garraud, 1988, on the gentrification of local Socialist personnel).

One of the main electoral supports, however, remained the shrinking remnants of the working class in the southern belt, which created the following electoral dilemma: continuing to be elected by working-class voters while no longer representing their interests. This made it necessary to ensure that the demands of this electorate could not be appropriated by the party's competitors. To reach this objective in the 1990s, the municipality had to make sure that groups could not organize themselves and 'gridlock' the city. As one anonymous council worker commented in 2000, 'Why have the associations gradually disappeared? Because here, anything that is not under the orders of the *Beffroi* [i.e. the traditional, Flemish-style tower that symbolizes the town hall] is condemned to disappear.'[32]

Since normal channels of expression, elections and even associations have disappeared, the municipality needs another channel to monitor the population's claims. In many ways it has maintained individuals and families in a process of transactions with the town hall for a variety of services, while preventing the emergence of collective demands.[33] In this way it solved the dilemma: filling the gap between the population and the political sphere, without providing an outlet for new demands. This explains to a large extent why few minorities were elected in 1995, and why those who were elected were marginalized.

This section shows how the various elements that constituted the machine combined to both encourage and serve such a strategy. The machine featured both classic features of the French local system and specifically local factors; their configuration is uniquely particular to Lille. It consisted of tight institutional networks, made up of neighbourhood councils, boards of sympathetic welfare groups (which included most of the groups) and urban regeneration teams (*équipes de développement*). The individuals who were part of these networks were themselves linked by strong social networks that were created by a common membership in the local Socialist Party. This dual affiliation – to the party and to the associations – characterized many of the city's association leaders. These networks functioned closely together on a consensual basis. The consensus consisted in the notion that everything the municipality did was acceptable, and rested on the idea that all these groups' demands were satisfied by one fundamental element, the patronage of the municipality. It consisted in protecting the positions acquired by individuals in their associations and *mairies de quartier* as well as their low-ranking positions of responsibility in the party. In this way, the municipality could maintain a high degree of control over the city's associational *milieu*. Finally, these networks were also characterized by the fact that the typical socio-economic profile of party and association members was someone who was employed and economically stable; unemployed individuals or manual workers were rare. Since the 1970s reorganization of the pattern of alliances, class conflict was built into the insider/outsider conflict within each neighbourhood.

In this system there were only two types of groups that did not participate in the dominant consensus. First were the associations that were politically close to the right-wing opposition, which, although scarce, did exist. This was notably the case at the time of the cantonal elections[34] in the late 1990s, when some North African associations in one of the most deprived neighbourhoods with a large ethnic minority population, the Faubourg de Béthune, decided to support Gaullist candidate Colette Codaccioni (interviews with Socialist Party activist, 8/1/99, and association leader, 22/3/00). Second, and most important, were many ethnic minority groups, including all groups of North African youngsters. They were not completely excluded and did benefit from the system, but the benefits were only short term and hindered their longer-term interests. Groups of youngsters in Lille-Sud became fluent in the idiom of bargaining daily social peace against minor services with prominent and powerful city councillors who were informally in charge of their area.

In the next section I show in detail how these elements combined to exclude minorities, starting with the role of associations in local politics, particularly with respect to minorities, then moving on to the hostility of party structures and the organization of state funds to minorities.

The isolation of community politics in France. Ideas of citizen participation and voluntary associations taking part in the political debate are placed at the forefront of political discourse in France. In practice, however, the French political system is highly representative, in the sense that the link between citizens and decision-making processes is mostly the vote and elected representatives. This is especially the case in local politics, where, as we have seen in connection with the electoral failure of Texture and the marginalization of Les Craignos councillors, the majoritarian representative system is closed to small groups, and thus to community associations and independent individuals. Participation in elections is high (around 60 to 70 per cent of those registered in municipal elections), but elections occur only every six years, and there is no control in between. In addition, decisions are made by complex networks of elected officials and technocrats, with only occasional intervention from citizen groups. A tide of participative left-wing politics (see below) failed to reform this situation in the 1970s. On the contrary, the French local political system has succeeded in adapting itself to the transformations of society of the last decades, such as increased demands for a higher-quality environment and local services, by covering new policy areas (owing in part to decentralization) without changing its essentially closed-network style of government; civil society has remained excluded from these transformations. As Mabileau put it, French local politics has achieved 'the integration of those administered without the participation of citizens' (*l'intégration des administrés sans la participation des citoyens*) (Mabileau, 1994, p. 129).

This leads to a disconnection between 'serious' politics and 'amateur' politics. Serious politics is centred on the competition for elected office and is the arena where topics of major importance, pertaining to the common good, party politics and national issues, are discussed; amateur politics is the politics of citizens' associations, where issues relevant to one neighbourhood or to one group within a neighbourhood are expected to be discussed. Associations are also considered as a training ground for serious politics, where an individual goes through some sort of civic education before graduating as a real citizen, i.e. a voter (Cordeiro, 1996, p. 18). This distinction acts as a direct factor in the political marginalization of working-class and unemployed populations in sub-sections of large cities, such as the populations of the southern periphery of Lille. It facilitates and legitimizes the categorization by local politicians of groups as apolitical and focused on service delivery or cultural activities; crucially, this understanding of community organization underpins the urban regeneration programmes that have been implemented in France since the early 1980s and that often put the emphasis on restoring the *lien social* ('social linkages'): areas that suffered from urban crisis and rising Front National votes were in need of more community life, precisely as a means of bridging a gap with representative democracy, in the context of a perceived 'crisis of democracy' (*crise de la démocracie*).

The cleavage between representative democracy and direct community politics is congruent with the national/extra-national cleavage (Cordeiro, 1996, p. 17). Voting rights and eligibility are reserved to nationals, because the political system is understood as representative of the nation; symmetrically, it is commonly accepted that community politics is the natural domain of foreigners, because there is no national interest at stake, only limited local issues. The idea of associational activities as a training ground for serious politics is also congruent with the exclusion of foreigners, because it fits with the idea that the latter may have to undergo training before obtaining possible naturalization, which would then grant them the vote and access to 'serious' politics. As a result, the idea of the participation of ethnic minorities (which include a high percentage of foreigners) in associations has often been encouraged by French authorities as a benign and easy way to give in to participatory demands. In the same vein, a government project of the 1970s aiming to facilitate the incorporation of immigrants proposed setting up paramunicipal bodies made up of foreigners living in a commune and elected by the foreigners of that commune (Wihtol de Wenden, 1988, p. 264; Oriol, 1998). The role of such bodies was only to be consultative, and hence it legitimized the idea that parallel entities deprived of power were acceptable ways of catering for immigrants' demands. Hence, ethnic minorities are doubly confined to associational politics: (1) because they are overwhelmingly concentrated in deprived areas where community life is encouraged as a form of participation, and (2) because a large proportion of them are foreigners.

All of this was made especially relevant for ethnic minorities because one of the central state's main institutions for dealing with immigration and ethnic minority issues in the 1990s was the Fonds d'Action Sociale (FAS), whose sole purpose was to fund ethnic minority associations (see chapter 2 on the origins of the FAS).[35] The fund has undergone a steady expansion since the early 1980s: from 1980 to 1986 its budget doubled, and the number of associations it funded increased fourfold. In 1994 its budget was almost 1.2 billion francs and it employed 219 administrators throughout the country, who worked directly with representatives of immigrant groups as well as with local institutions and political structures to develop programmes to deal with integration and urban problems (Schain, 1996, p. 22). In Lille in the 1990s, the FAS consistently funded hundreds of organizations that provided cultural and educational activities for ethnic minority populations. These were charity-type groups, such as the *centres sociaux*, the Scouts de France or the Foyers Léo Lagrange. This is one additional factor that confined minorities to community politics, superimposing itself on the place of association politics in general.

The subordination of associations to municipalities. There has been a general historical trend over the last 40 years towards financial and political control of associations by municipalities, and towards their consecutive instrumentalization for the purpose of carrying out tasks that fall within municipalities' policy remits (Balme, 1987; Mabileau, 1994, pp. 135–48). As a result, the confinement of foreigners and ethnic minority activists to association politics provided the municipality with significant resources with which to exercise control over them. Again, this was especially the case for immigrant organizations in the Lille area, and most particularly in Lille itself, because of a system of joint FAS/municipality management of the funds. The result was that, in practice, the municipality administration, as well as the councillors within the administration, had de facto control of the allocation of funds.

The FAS Nord-Pas-de-Calais administration attempted to resist the dominant influence of the council, and consequently there were struggles for influence between the two institutions. However, the municipality's views prevailed every time because it had the most direct control over associations. The regional FAS had few political resources because it had to spend all the funds allocated by the ministry, which effectively compelled it to hand them over to those associations selected by the municipality. Hence, funds granted by the Ministry of Social Affairs for the welfare of immigrant populations ended up in the hands of a local authority which had an interest in ensuring that ethnic minorities were confined to innocuous activities. The municipality generally attributed funds to groups that participated in the delivery of services that came within its policy remit (such as providing after-school care for children) or to the communitarian activities of small ethnic minority groups (e.g. the Maison de l'Afrique et des Antilles [House of Africa and the French Caribbean]).

The Socialist Party machine: a closed fortress. As has been shown, one potential means of participating in local affairs, via an association, is in fact a dead end for ethnic minorities. The other plausible channel of access to representation is a political party, in this case the Socialist Party, since it has been in power in Lille for the last 20 years and enjoys a hegemonic position in the local system. However, in Lille, the party has remained largely closed to minorities. To begin with, the Socialist Party functions as a series of tightly knit and interlinked social networks, as emphasized by a landmark study of the party by Frédéric Sawicki (1997). This does not make it particularly adapted to the integration of outsiders. The party's inaccessibility to ethnic minorities is also a symptom of a wider phenomenon, which is its increasing remoteness from lower-income households. The Socialist Party has an increasingly middle-class membership, as the traditional population of workers who created the party and constituted its backbone in the city for a century has shrunk. With the system of municipal patronage that has been growing under the Socialists for the last three decades (see below), the party is staffed largely by association leaders, council workers, or people who are both at the same time.

Those ethnic minority individuals who do attempt to participate are either excluded or marginalized within the party. This stems mainly from the comparative lack of institutionalization and codification of the local party, and appears particularly clearly in the light of a comparison with the Labour Party in Birmingham, where, as I have shown, ethnic minority activists have repeatedly used appeal procedures provided by the party's rule book to raise issues of discrimination within the party.[36] In Lille, the phenomenon of discrimination within the party is as widespread as in Birmingham. However, it is little debated because there is no national legal framework that would enable ethnic minorities to bring a claim against the party. In fact, it is very much a taboo subject, because of the general atmosphere of embarrassment and avoidance that shrouds the issue in France.[37]

In addition, the French Socialist Party is characterized by a loose organizational structure (Ware, 1996, p. 113), in the context of which there are few possibilities for outsiders to gain positions of responsibility. At the local level, the only well-known rule is a motto used as a principle whenever the need arises: *la section est souveraine* (the section is sovereign). This essentially means that the local branch takes all decisions relative to its internal affairs independently of the party's upper tiers (mainly the departmental federation). This is the exact opposite of the Labour Party organization, where all power is devolved down to the branch by the national and regional parties. Decisions within the section are voted by a show of hands, and in practice are taken by the influential leader within the section, who is usually an elected official or an important figure within the federation, or at least secretary of the section. In this system, applicants may be accepted, but once they are members it is difficult for them to gain positions such as secretary of the section in the context of a racist climate, which is common in Lille. There are frequent, though seldom mentioned, cases of North Africans who leave the party after a few weeks of membership because they feel unwelcome (interview with Socialist activist, 22/9/98). In one extreme and rare case, the secretary of the Bois-Blanc section (the western tip of the city's southern district) was forced to expel three of his members for racism in 1997; by that time, the North Africans discriminated against had already left the party. In addition, this organizational structure leads to situations where North African youths may be welcome as temporary helpers, typically for sticking up posters at election time, but are then dismissed, as happened for general council elections in Lille-Sud in the late 1990s (interviews with association leaders, 29/9/98, 30/9/98).

While conflicts between different factions in the Labour Party have acted as a major structural opportunity for penetration by minorities in Birmingham, the absence of such cleavages in Lille has deprived minorities of similar opportunities. This is because there are no significant forces in the party with an interest in challenging the dominance of Mauroy. The only exception to this was the battle for Mauroy's successor in 1995, when Martine Aubry arrived at the council and became first adjunct in place of Bernard Roman. The latter became second adjunct but clung to the possibility of maintaining his status as favoured successor. In the ensuing conflict, the struggle for control of the Socialist stronghold of Lille-Sud might very well have opened up opportunities for minority youths there. But the latter were unable to use the situation to their advantage because by that time they were too marginalized, ideologically inarticulate and lacking in motivation to participate successfully in the Socialist intrigues. A few members of the youth associations in Lille-Sud were elected to the *conseils de quartier* (neighbourhood councils, part of a scheme to promote local democracy; see below), but even they felt that the Aubry–Roman rivalry did not favour them, and in fact worked against them. A North African youth from Lille-Sud who was active in various associations declared: 'Politics? Battles between the Aubry and Roman clans. If you're not part of a clan, you're really on your own. That's what happens to me in the neighbourhood council'.[38]

This was the situation for most youths, although there were exceptions in the 1990s which showed that inclusion in the party could be a possibility. In particular, in the Faubourg de Béthune neighbourhood, most North African youths who acted as leaders in their local community became members of the party in the late 1990s. In 2000, seven members of the 30-strong Socialist section of that neighbourhood were North Africans. The factors that facilitated this integration, and which are absent in Lille-Sud, are the smaller size of the neighbourhood (around 6,000, as opposed to 25,000 in Lille-Sud) and its greater social stability. But issues of discrimination or cultural diversity were no more discussed in the Faubourg de Béthune than in other areas. On the contrary, those youths who became members were kept in their place and wholly adopted the party line that consisted in denying that there was an issue at all.

To summarize, those North Africans who do vote support the Socialists, but they do not participate in the activities of the party, despite the fact that it controls many of the local associations and provides jobs, sports and protection against landlords. This fuels the relations of limited exchanges of services for social peace between the council and ethnic minorities.

The territorial organization of the municipality's political networks. The municipality has been able to exert an especially tight control of the local community through a reconfiguration of networks connected to the party on a territorial basis centred on the neighbourhood. This kind of neighbourhood-based territorialization has been a recurrent pattern in French politics for the last 30 years (Mabileau, 1994; Balme, Faure and Mabileau, 1999). It owed its existence to three factors in 1990s Lille: the decentralized organization of the municipality, the territorial organization of urban regeneration programmes and the FAS funds managed jointly with the municipality. This arrangement forces associations to define themselves in terms of neighbourhood, which limits their capacity to aggregate the demands of comparatively dispersed ethnic minority populations in the city. It also reinforces the cohesion of the activities of the abovementioned organizations behind the leadership of the municipality, and prevents them from becoming potential allies for dissenting ethnic minority associations such as the youngsters of Lille-Sud.

First, Pierre Mauroy exploited the popularity of citizen participation amongst the left-wing electorate by including it in his 1977 municipal election manifesto (he was encouraged to do this by the national context, since these elections were the most politicized of the post-war era in France, with the Socialists fighting alongside the Communists as part of their general alliance, on a leftist platform). Once re-elected, he duly implemented his promise, creating a neighbourhood town hall (*mairie de quartier*) for each of the ten neighbourhoods in the city. Each of these town halls comprised an administrative section, carrying out routine services such as legal paperwork and registering inhabitants for municipal social services, as well as a political section, called a neighbourhood council (*conseil de quartier*), in an explicit attempt to suggest a similarity with the main municipal council. However, unlike the municipal council, neighbourhood councils had little or no political strength, since they were not elected but made up of municipal councillors who combined their official municipal mandate with this additional seat.

This reform displayed the mayor's readiness to play the game of participative democracy and to share power with decentralized groups, and at the same time it reinforced his grip on the neighbourhood-based groups. This was because it did not in any way increase the capacity of the local population to control the municipality, but it did provide the *élus de quartier* with additional organizational resources to control local welfare groups, neighbourhood associations and sports clubs within one territorial area. The president of the *conseil de quartier* in particular was always a close ally of the mayor, controlling the neighbourhood budget in such a way as to play one association off against another within the same territory.

The strategic utility of this territorialized model of municipal management is all the clearer since many other aspects of municipal politics are also territorialized, thus combining to create a very effective municipal machine. First, the urban regeneration programmes that are an important source of funding for the municipality are also organized on a territorial basis. In fact, they were started in reaction to the first wave of urban unrest in the late 1970s and early 1980s (which also sparked the Beur movement), and were inspired by the same capacity-building ideology as the 1977 territorialization reform and, as mentioned above, the new consensual paradigm of social work in the city. The main idea behind these plans was that the crisis was mainly one of urban citizenship, i.e. that social and civic links between citizens had deteriorated in certain areas of cities. Remedies such as the renovation of public services and housing projects, or the funding of local associations, were therefore organized on a neighbourhood basis. This meant that other approaches to urban crises, such as supporting certain groups or boosting the local economy, were on the whole rejected, with a few exceptions,[39] in favour of the territorial angle. In addition, the complex administrative machinery set up to manage the implementation of these programmes in the relevant neighbourhoods consistently gave essential decision-making power to the municipalities, because they were the political entities that had the closest relations with their territories and local groups. In the 1990s, they were not surprisingly managed by administrative teams that were housed in the *mairies de quartier* and worked closely with the presidents of the neighbourhood councils.

The reorganization of the FAS funding schemes mentioned above was also carried out on a neighbourhood basis. The municipality was able to exercise all the more influence over the allocation of funds since local associational activity was already organized along neighbourhood-based lines, and because its personnel in the neighbourhoods was more in touch with the associations than the regional administration of the FAS. As a result, the distinction between *politique de la ville* funds, FAS funds and municipality grants was blurred both in the organization of the application process and in the minds of association leaders who applied for them; the only thing that was clear was that the projects proposed had to be agreeable to the municipality.

Finally, the municipality also closely controlled the Socialist Party, first for historical reasons, but also by using the dynamics of territorialization to increase its grip over the party. At the beginning of the Socialist Party's history in the north of France, in the 1890s, there was a great hope that the electoral conquest of municipalities (including, notably, Lille and Roubaix) would help the party implement its radical reforms at the local level, very much in the manner of British municipal socialism. However, because of the size of the resources held by elected municipal officials in the French political system, the balance of power within the party shifted from the party executive to elected members, and, instead of municipal socialism, there appeared a new model of municipality/party relations, where the municipality was dominant (see on this issue Lefebvre, 1999).

In addition, the party also participated in the trend of territorial reorganization with a reform of its organization in the city in 1992, directly set in motion by the mayor in order to turn it into a more efficient canvassing structure (Mauroy, 1994). In the old system, branches followed the boundaries of parliamentary constituencies, which cut across the city and neighbouring towns; the reform eliminated these and introduced ten branches, one per neighbourhood. This allowed the party to canvass more effectively for municipal elections, which, as has been shown, were a growing concern for the Socialists in the context of the erosion of their electoral base. It also enabled closer control of neighbourhood associations in conjunction with the *conseils de quartier*. Indeed, in most of the city's neighbourhoods, the president of the neighbourhood council is either the secretary of the party's section as well as the leader of a local association, or his/her spouse, or a close friend within the party. This pattern of community/party/council relations stands in sharp contrast to the situations in Birmingham and Roubaix. In Birmingham, the Labour Party has a more balanced relationship with the leadership of the city council, and the party's ward organizations are able to influence the policy process (interview with city councillor, 9/11/98). In Roubaix, parties have little influence over the municipality, which matters less than in Lille because they play a smaller role in the local community. In Lille, the party has a very strong grip on the local associations in the party's southern stronghold, and the municipality has a strong grip on the party. The party thus acts as one additional medium of control of the local community.

In Birmingham, there is a high degree of territorialization of city politics on the basis of the ward. This facilitates the election of ethnic minority councillors, especially Pakistanis, because their ethnic minority electorates are concentrated in certain wards. This is because it is the representative electoral system itself that is territorialized. In Lille, on the other hand, neighbourhood sub-divisions concern only the mechanisms of funding and control of the local community, in contrast with municipal elections which are fought on a city-wide basis.

Relations between municipality and North African groups in the 1990s: patronage and dependence

The first section below discusses how the machine described above impacted on local groups and produced an outcome of division and exclusion. Patterns of patronage were produced even for those groups that sought to evade the machine's influence; ultimately it led to the failure of these groups in the 1995 municipal elections. Most ethnic minority groups in Lille after the Beur movement were cultural or neighbourhood associations, tenant groups or sports clubs for the younger second generation. These groups fell within two broad categories: Muslim and secular. This distinction had a significant impact on modes of relationship with the municipality. Muslim groups were for the most part totally marginalized within the municipal scene, and often had little interest in joining it. The important exception to this was the main mosque, which played a discreet but influential role in the affairs of Lille-Sud in the 1990s, in tacit agreement with the municipality.

The next section describes how secular ethnic groups were wholly controlled by the machine. In some cases they were thriving charities or cultural groups that fully benefited from municipality and other local state funds, provided they did not articulate politicized views. Groups who did voice protest, such as groups of unemployed youths, were caught in a perverse cycle of submission and antagonism with the municipality that rested on trading off law and order against petty benefits. This reflects common patterns of relations between associations of immigrant youths and municipalities across France (as shown for instance in Battegay's survey of such associations in the Lyon area [Battegay, 1990]).

The mosque in Lille-Sud. First, most active Muslim groups were small, highly localized, neighbourhood-based associations or informal groupings whose primary function was to manage a site for collective prayer. Very often these places of worship were a flat or a garage. These groups had absolutely no presence in the local political arena, because of their deep-rooted rejection of French politics and reciprocal hostility or indifference on the part of local institutions. This has long been the case in Lille, where most officials know little about them and are not interested in finding out.[40] When Muslim groups first sought to create a mosque in Lille in the 1970s, the only help they could find was from the Catholic bishop. There are seven large Muslim places of worship in Lille that can be called mosques, although they are not specifically built for that purpose.[41]

An important exception is the large, custom-built mosque in the rue des Marquillies in Lille-Sud. It has two small minarets and accommodates up to 2,000 worshippers, making it the largest in the region. Centrally located in Lille-Sud, it is used by local youths as a daily meeting point, controls several social and cultural associations, and provides tuition in Arabic and in the Muslim religion to the youths of the area. It forms part of a national network of mosques and, most importantly, is run by an ambitious *recteur*, Amar Lasfar, who is prominent both nationally and locally. Under Lasfar's leadership, the mosque has come to exert considerable influence over public affairs in Lille-Sud. It is often rightly perceived as the only true 'institution' in an area where the police were viewed with suspicion throughout the 1990s and where ambulances and fire engines were routinely attacked at night.

This became even more apparent in April 2000 when the neighbourhood, along with parts of Wazemmes, Moulins and some areas of Roubaix, erupted in riots for three consecutive nights, leading to 70 arrests. The riots were caused by the shooting and killing of Riad Hamlaoui, a youth of Moroccan background, by a policeman (*Le Monde*, 18/04/00). In the immediate aftermath of the violence, the only local actor that sought to restore order was Lasfar's mosque. After the first night of rioting, 2,000 protesters, mostly of Moroccan background and including men and women of all ages, rallied in front of the mosque. Their central claim was recognition by the public authorities that their neighbourhood, and particularly young North African males, were treated with undue violence by the police. The father of Riad Hamlaoui stood alongside Lasfar in front of the mosque and read out a statement of thanks to the demonstrators before asking the rioters of the previous evening to refrain from violence (*Le Monde*, 19/04/00). The demonstrators then marched downtown towards the city hall, and again it was the mosque that organized a security service to maintain order. Declarations from town hall officials came later, mostly in the form of a statement by the then first adjunct Martine Aubry, which were limited to general, noncommittal remarks.[42]

Owing to this type of influence in the neighbourhood, Lasfar has amassed a large political capital in the city. However, he has purposefully avoided taking on a visible political role. In the late 1990s, he had little involvement in town hall-sponsored associations and educational projects in the area, as noted sourly by the official in charge of these programmes.[43] The mosque and its activities are entirely self-funded, through personal donations and funding from the Ligue Islamique du Nord.[44] In this way, Lasfar keeps out of the debates that surround municipal politics, building up a strong power base within the North African community.

Secular groups: failure of attempted participation in the 1995 municipal election. In terms of relations with the council, secular groups fall into two categories. First are those which form part of the municipality's machine, i.e. who obtain funds from the SLI (Schéma Local d'Intégration), the municipality's main urban regeneration programme specifically targeted at minorities, cooperate with *mairies de quartier*, and generally avoid making waves. Their activities often consist in implementing policies that fall within the remit of the municipality. The second group are those who refuse to become paramunicipal associations and insist on proposing alternative approaches, which often break the assimilationist consensus to advocate the recognition of the specificity of North Africans' problems (on this distinction between the two groups, see Bousetta, 1997, pp. 227–8). The first group includes a variety of cultural associations, which are entirely apolitical and specialize in the organization of cultural events. The largest, ATACAFA, organizes yearly concerts of African and Asian music. Originally created by a group of young second-generation immigrants in the early 1980s, it was subsequently organized by individuals from various backgrounds. Other major associations include SAFIA (Solidarités des Femmes d'Ici et d'Ailleurs) and Bleu d'Ailleurs (for a complete list see Bousetta, 2001, p. 401). This type of group also includes groups of other immigrant communities such as Sub-Saharan African community groups, e.g. the Association des Maliens de Lille.[45]

The second category comprises groups of second-generation North Africans who were too young to participate in the Beur movement, and which appeared in the vacuum left behind in the late 1980s. This is the population which is most vociferous against racial discrimination; it has extremely high rates of unemployment and crime, and is perceived by the municipality as both a major cause and victim of the crisis in the neighbourhoods. Since the beginning of the 1990s, these associations have revolved around a few permanent structures, the sports clubs in the area: the Gants d'Argent boxing club and football clubs FC Lille-Sud, Étoile de Lille-Sud and Étoile de Ronchin. In addition, several groups appeared and disappeared according to political fortunes throughout the decade. Jeunesse et Avenir emerged in 1990 around the *centre social* of Lille-Sud; it became more autonomous once the latter was burned down in the context of disputes between youths, social workers and councillors in charge (*La Voix du Nord*, 15/3/91). Other groups such as the Mouvement Autonome des Jeunes de Lille-Sud and l'Association des Jeunes de la Croisette also had some influence (interview with association leader, 23/3/99). These types of groups are focused on finding jobs for their members, looking after younger individuals by taking them to sports activities, and practising sports themselves.

In the second half of the 1990s, groups were increasingly less structured and consisted of interpersonal networks based around popular meeting points in the city. Information relating to jobs and events was posted in cafés or at the Lille-Sud mosque, which was situated in front of one popular meeting point. However, these groups were central actors because they were able to reach, directly or indirectly through informal networks, the vast majority of North African youths (mostly but not uniquely male) of Lille-Sud, Faubourg de Béthune and other areas in the south of Lille. In turn, the degree of unrest among these youths was a major determinant of the level of dissatisfaction among the rest of the population for the municipality. Hence, through the adjuncts who were in charge of Lille-Sud and the Faubourg de Béthune,[46] it was anxious to ensure that they were kept at a minimum level of satisfaction.

Both categories of groups share the characteristic of being completely dependent on the council, albeit in different ways. The first are not reluctantly dependent and do not pretend to raise issues that might displease the town hall. As Bousetta notes: 'It would be true to say that participation in local institutional networks has been beneficial in terms of resources for those organizations involved in social work. But, at the same time, these networks exert considerable control which leads to the depoliticization of disadvantages for ethnic minorities' (1997, p. 228). The latter group accept dependence only because of the absence of other support, and because they are bound by the web of petty services and short-term arrangements sustained by city councillors, which makes them unwitting clients of the municipality and ensures the stability and reproduction of the system. While they take every opportunity to present themselves as victims of the municipality, which they accuse of voluntarily excluding them from its urban regeneration programme, they also expect it to deliver jobs and facilities upon command. Hence their demands for jobs and sports equipment are systematically addressed to the municipality, represented by the councillors who are informally in charge of these neighbourhoods or municipality workers responsible for leisure activities. Councillors frequently offer positions on the municipality or in other local assemblies, notably the Communauté Urbaine, or public services, such as the waste disposal company TRU. In fact, the municipality holds a quasi-monopoly on the provision of jobs and services to these associations. This provides it with considerable leverage against them, because it ensures that their relative and temporary satisfaction on these issues maintains the level of politicized demands at a low level.

This pattern of patronage also has a downside for the municipality: it only caters for bottom-line and short-term demands which must permanently be readdressed. As a result, the municipality is caught in a perverse cycle whereby it elicits client groups' demands which can only be addressed by giving more. Council attempts to decrease funds in the 1990s were usually met with local youths burning down sports facilities and social workers' offices; this happened three times, in 1991, 1993 and 2000, and is precisely the opposite of what was intended. In spite of this situation, there has been some scaling down of funds allocated since the beginning of the decade, with significant apprehension of possible violent reactions (interview with urban regeneration manager, 6/4/99).

This mode of relations with youths also provides the municipality with an asset to divide and rule over attempts by these groups to oppose the council. This is the principal way in which North African youths were marginalized in the 1995 local election, in addition to the electoral system, which again worked against minorities, as it had done in 1989. In 1995, the leaders of the youth group Jeunesse et Avenir, disgruntled at obtaining less funding for its associations than previously, decided to join forces with controversial older North African leaders (including former Texture activists), disappointed by the Socialist Party in the 1980s, to form a 100 per cent North African list for the municipal elections.

The municipality perceived this as potentially weakening the mayor's re-election bid, which was being challenged by a candidate from the right, Alex Turk, who seemed to have a serious chance of winning. The Socialists were keen to win as many votes as possible from their base in Lille-Sud. One of the leaders on the list, Farid Sellani, was then offered a place in an electable position on the Socialist list, together with a job at Euralille, the new business centre which was then being built on the site of the new Eurostar station. At the same time, the leader of the Mouvement Autonome, Malek Chagah, was offered a position as *chargé de mission* (council officer) at the municipality, after agreeing to start a new association, Cap 95, with Farid Sellani. The latter had a disappointing career as councillor, rapidly becoming marginalized. Consequently he vowed publicly to break his alliance with the Socialists and encouraged the emergence of independent political forces in Lille-Sud for the 2001 municipal elections.[47] But, by that time, he had already been labelled a traitor by most of his former supporters in Lille-Sud, with whom he had first mounted his own independent list before defecting to form Cap 95.

This is typical of relations between youths and local authorities in France in general, best summarized by Jocelyne Césari: 'There is a widening gap between associations whose members are approached by institutions on one side, and their "social base" for whom they claim to speak and who suspect them of "treason" or compromise, on the other. This explains the perpetual renewal of associations, new ones replacing old, always aspiring to represent their potential clientele better, but quickly suspected of being just another self-serving structure for "token Arabs" or the "beur-geois"' (Césari, 1993, p. 92, my translation). Lille offers a clear example, where this form of politicking is a classic tool for managing local youths by the municipality. As one local association leader argued, 'Racism is a strong influence. They are afraid to give us power. However, they do know how to pick up a youth with a Maghrebi face, show him around the neighbourhood to win votes, then drop him after the elections or control him with a salary'.[48]

Dividing and ruling groups of young North Africans ensures political stability in the short term, but the situation can rapidly deteriorate: on several occasions in the 1990s, violence erupted in the south of the city, notably when two *centres sociaux* were burned down in Lille-Sud and Moulins, and in 1993, during the so-called 'hunt for dealers'. On this occasion, several hundred youths from Lille-Sud, many with close ties to the associations mentioned above, armed themselves with stones and bats and set out to rid the neighbourhood of its heroin dealers by attacking them and destroying their cars, turning the area into a battlefield for two days (*La Voix du Nord*, 25/5/93).

However, after this type of temporary breakdown in the usual *modus vivendi* between the youths and the municipality, the pattern reforms, in the absence of political interests and actors that could come in and trigger lasting change. Even when these groups' only resource, the maintenance of law and order in their area, is used to maximum effect as it was in the 'hunt for dealers', it only prompts the council to give in to occasional demands rather than provoking any substantial change of attitude. The police arrived only at the end of the second day, to take note and appeal for calm. In a rare gesture, the mayor himself came in person to the neighbourhood a few days later for a much publicized guided tour of the area and a series of meetings with local youths. This was a strong indication of how seriously the uprising was considered at the town hall. But Mauroy's attitude remained largely noncommittal. He started by jumping on the bandwagon, stopped short of condoning the violence, and was quoted uttering the following evasive remarks: 'apart from a few excesses, local youngsters have remained within the bounds of acceptable behaviour [. . .] these youths are trying to say enough with the drug market that functions openly in their neighbourhood, and they are sending out a cry for help'.[49] He merely promised more of the usual things: more jobs, reorganization of leisure services in the area and an enhanced drug prevention policy, without making any concrete commitments to support these measures (*La Voix du Nord*, 31/5/93).

A rapid survey of the 2001 municipal elections confirms the steady erosion of the Socialists' hold on the city, with Mauroy's successor Martine Aubry just hanging on to power with a reduced score compared to 1995. The Greens increased their vote and gained the status of major coalition partner for the Socialists, obtaining several senior positions on the council. The election also confirmed the continuance of Mauroy's attitude of neglect with respect to minorities, even after his departure and replacement by Socialist heavyweight Aubry: just two ethnic minority representatives, Dr Wallid Hanna and Latifa Kéchimir, found themselves on the Socialist list and were both narrowly elected. Ifri, who had been elected in 1995 on the Socialist list and had since become bitterly disillusioned, attempted to set up an autonomous 'neighbourhood list' (*'liste des quartiers'*), made up of inhabitants of the south of the city, including around 50 per cent North Africans. The list did not survive internal dissension and lack of credible prospects, and collapsed before the first round. It is also important to note that the far-left list proposed in the city by Lutte Ouvrière (a Trotskyite political party) featured nine candidates of ethnic minority background. The list failed to reach 5 per cent of the vote and could not therefore be present in the second round. The failure of this list was reminiscent of Texture's failure in 1989.

Conclusion

The municipality of Lille did not move from a strategy of indifference to one of co-optation in the 1980s and 1990s, as was the case in Birmingham and, to a lesser extent, in Roubaix. In the context of its general strategy of gentrification of the city, electoral dominance and challenge to the Front National, it has either ignored, absorbed or divided and marginalized attempts by minorities to articulate their claims. This attitude has been shaped and encouraged by the institutional structures of the city. In the 1980s, attempts to voice problems of alternative citizenship, cultural difference and the welfare of minorities in municipal elections were marginalized largely because of the structure of political competition in the municipal electoral system. In the 1990s, the mayor's ability to combine several institutional structures and local organizations enabled him to create a municipal machine. This ensured the persistence of a pro-municipality consensus among most community organizations in the city, and made it markedly difficult for outsider or dissenting groups to reach visibility and influence on the local scene.

In addition to purely local factors, the municipality's strategy of exclusion was also encouraged by the national combination of electoral racism and consensual assimilationist ideology. To a certain extent, the municipal machine translated these pressures at the national level into political exclusion at city level. If these pressures cease to exist nationally, or reduce in intensity, as seemed to be the case after 1997, with national debates creating a more favourable climate to issues of cultural recognition and anti-discrimination policies, then the municipal machine may start communicating these new trends as automatically as it conveyed the former.[50]

Yet the results of the municipal elections of 2001 suggested no clear turn towards more proactive policies and only limited efforts were made to include ethnic minorities in candidate lists. The results also suggest that the Socialists might not necessarily hold on to power much longer. As in other cities nationwide, this erosion is due to the disaffection of the more disadvantaged voters, including ethnic minorities. Thus the Socialists' continued neglect of minorities may eventually contribute to their own downfall.

6

Roubaix, 1980s–2001: Inclusion Thr⟨
Neighbourhood Groups and an Open
Municipal Game

Introduction

The attitude of the Roubaix municipality towards the ethnic minority issue
has followed a distinctive path: neither the immobility laced with hostility of
the Lille municipality, nor the political alliance with Labour ethnic minority
activists of Birmingham. Instead, Roubaix in the 1980s and 1990s was characterized by growing access to representation of ethnic minority activists. This
chapter seeks to explore the specifics of the Roubaix situation and the way
they shaped the municipality's attitude during the two consecutive terms of
centre-right mayor André Diligent, from 1983 to 1995. During this period,
the Beur movement failed to have any impact, as was the case in Lille, but a
younger network of North Africans emerged in its wake, from 1987 onwards
and throughout the 1990s. Again, local party politics and the local style of
local government played a crucial role in producing this outcome. In Roubaix,
they were the product of the French municipal system and a distinctive political history, marked by brutal industrialization and deindustrialization, constant immigration, and the joint management of the city's problems by diverse
and sometimes opposing forces: business interests, the Socialist Party, and
various community and religious groups. This has created a polity characterized by an association with power of an eclectic selection of groups, often
representing various sections of the city's diverse population according to a
territorial, neighbourhood arrangement.

shaped Roubaix politics in two ways. First,
open and subjected to fluctuating patterns
community groups, often organized on a
onally played an unusually important role
ibination of these two factors has enabled
:ome more successful than their Lille coun-
ls incorporation. It has also coincided with
olicies at a time when most other French
e still heavily influenced by the national
oubaix has been consistently ahead of
..... has found itself leading the surge of interest in
anu-discrimination policies and ethnic minority political participation since
1997.

Having noted these exceptional features, it also becomes apparent in
the course of this chapter that this original evolution has remained in some
respects shaped by the national institutions noted in chapter 3. Notably, the
generational divide induced by the French nationality regimes bears heavily
on the politics of the city. Those who have become the most active and had
the most impact on municipal politics are all second-generation immigrants,
while first-generation migrants are absent from public life as they are in Lille.
In addition, the emphasis on spatial identity is frequent in French municipal
politics, although the forms taken in Roubaix are unusual.

Urban Crisis, Migrations and the Political Management of the Crisis

From 'Holy City of the Proletariat'[1] to post-industrial crisis

Originally a large village outside Lille, Roubaix became an industrial boom-
town in the nineteenth century, drawing wool and textile manufacturers
who turned the city into a mono-industrial economy that attracted a large
population of workers. Even neighbouring Tourcoing, which underwent
industrialization at the same period and under the same conditions, did not
experience a similar growth in working-class and immigrant population.
Roubaix became famous for its *courées*, blocks of small houses grouped around
a square yard built by industrialists to house their workers.[2]

It is no surprise, therefore, that Roubaix was particularly badly affected by
the deep economic crisis that hit industrial France in the 1970s. Since then
Roubaix has manifested all the classic elements of post-industrial crisis.[3]
Unemployment has rocketed, up from 6 per cent in 1975 to 24.47 per cent
in 1990, which was twice the national average (see Bataille, 1994, pp. 43ff.).
Recent successes in attracting new businesses to Roubaix have only margin-

ally addressed the problem. In many instances the posts created have been filled by non-inhabitants commuting from outside the city, as the local population is often too poorly qualified for these new jobs.[4] Like Lille-Sud, the city has an exceptionally high level of RMIstes, long-term unemployed and high schools with a large percentage of disadvantaged children.[5] But, unlike in Lille, the crisis has engulfed most of the city's neighbourhoods, the only exception being the Parc Barbieux area, home to a wealthy population of entrepreneurs and executives.

More so than Lille, Roubaix also has a persistent problem with its decaying housing stock. Several extensive slum clearance programmes replaced most of its old housing with rows of modern redbrick houses and blocks, particularly in the central neighbourhood of Alma-Gare, which before it was renovated was little better than a slum.[6] More recently in the 1960s and 1970s, several tower blocks of HLM[7] flats were added. In spite of this, in 1986 there were still 6,000 residences below acceptable standards of hygiene, housing around 25,000 people or 25 per cent of the total population. In the 1990s, more than 50 per cent of the population was still of working-class background, and massively unemployed (Bruyelle, 1993, p. 37). This is reflected in the city's geography. Most of the ten neighbourhoods are characterized by old working-class accommodation and industrial desertification, with the notable exception of the Parc Barbieux area.

Persistent disadvantage is compounded by a vicious circle created by the migration flows between the city and the rest of the area. While poor populations, often of foreign origins, migrate into Roubaix, as noted in the previous chapter, those families who can leave the city because they are from a more qualified background tend to do so, thereby increasing the proportion of the poor.

A large population of Algerian descent

More than in any other city in the area, the mass migration of workers into the city has been quintessential to the development of capitalism since its earliest beginnings in the first decades of the nineteenth century. The first migrants were peasants from the area, then Belgian workers came in large numbers, representing more than half of the population at the turn of the century: 68,000 out of a total population of 122,000 (Florin, 1985, p. 264n. 11). After the Second World War, the largest flows were from Spain and Italy, then from Portugal. These were gradually replaced by large numbers of Algerians, then Moroccans, in the 1960s and 1970s. In 1990, Algerians formed the largest sub-group among the foreign population, ahead of the Portuguese and the Moroccans (see tables 6.1 and 6.2). The proportion of Algerians to Moroccans (roughly two to one) is the opposite of that in Lille. Taken alto-

Table 6.1 Recent history of migration to Roubaix

Year	Total population	Foreign population	Proportion of foreigners in total population
1975	109,230	21,493	19.7
1982	101,852	21,162	20.8
1987[a]	100,000	23,500	23.5
1990[b]	97,793	23,156	23.7

[a] According to the author of these figures, and in view of 1990 INSEE data, figures for 1987 are estimated.
[b] Figures from Ville de Roubaix.
Source: Ireland, 1994, p. 20, based on Ville de Roubaix archives.

Table 6.2 Foreign population of Roubaix by nationality

Nationality	1975	1982	1990
Algerians	44.9	43.0	31.9
Portuguese	21.5	22.5	19.1
Italians	14.4	11.3	8.2
Belgians	4.4	2.8	n.a.
Spaniards	3.5	2.0	1.4
Poles	3.4	2.2	n.a.
Moroccans	2.7	5.7	12.7
Turks	–	0.5	4.8
Others	5.2	10.0	n.a.

Source: Ireland, 1994, p. 23, based on Ville de Roubaix archives.

gether, North African nationals constitute around 45 per cent of the foreigners in Roubaix, and amount to around 11 per cent of the total population of the city.

In total, in 1990, Roubaix had a total population of 97,793, divided between 74,637 French nationals and 23,156 foreigners (23.7 per cent). Taking into account the fact that a large proportion of Roubaix's inhabitants were originally foreigners who recently became French through naturalization, and that a large number are also second- or third-generation children of immigrants who have French nationality because they were born in France, the population of foreign origin of the city is much higher than 23 per cent.

As in Lille, ethnic minority populations are concentrated in the working-class parts of the city, which in Roubaix means just about everywhere, except of course in the rich Barbieux area, where they represent only 4 per cent of the total population.[8] In the rest of the city they represent around 20 per cent of the population, with peaks in the northwestern part (Alma/Fossé aux Chênes, Cul de Four, Hommelet, Pile) and especially in the Fresnoy/ Mackellerie area (36.5 per cent) (see map 5, p. xxi). It is reasonable to suggest that ethnic minorities (individuals of foreign background) may be close to or above the 50 per cent mark in several of these neighbourhoods.

Roubaix identity, Front National vote and pro-minority policies

This situation of severe and prolonged urban crisis has wrought widespread discontent in the city since the early 1980s. This discontent has translated into the political arena in a different way than in Lille, first through the affirmation of a strong Roubaix identity, and second through particularly spectacular successes for anti-immigrant parties in the polls.

Lille's policy of self-transformation into a service-driven economy not only had observable negative effects on Roubaix's population, it was also very much perceived as having these effects by Roubaix public opinion, which developed a victimization complex (Verfaillie, 1996, p. 108). In addition, there was a widely held belief in the city that Lille used its political domination of the Communauté Urbaine de Lille (CUDL), the local authority that groups together the 87 communes of the greater Lille area and of which Lille and Roubaix are, respectively, the first and second most important cities both numerically and politically, in order to impose key planning choices detrimental to Roubaix (in particular the development of a new academic and technological centre, Villeneuve d'Asq, on the outskirts of Lille, and the construction of a subway line there instead of in Roubaix). Discontent is also directed at outsiders because there is still a thriving garment manufacturing industry within the city that only employs highly qualified labour from neighbouring towns, while Roubaix's job-seekers do not benefit from this industry.

The Front National (FN) vote in Roubaix has reached extremely high scores, not just in certain areas of the city, as is the case in Lille, but across the city. The FN's first electoral successes in France date back to the 1983 municipal elections. In Roubaix success came a little later, because the xenophobic vote was monopolized in 1983 by the local racist group Roubaix aux Roubaisiens, which captured an impressive 9.3 per cent of the vote (Etchebarne, 1983). There were then a series of relatively 'secondary' elections which provided the FN with good opportunities of developing its own constituency, which it did with impressive success, reaching 17 per cent of the vote in the 1989 municipal election, and scores higher still in presidential and legislative elections (see table 6.3).

As elsewhere, the FN vote in the city has been concurrently the expression of a protest against the general degradation of the economy and living

Table 6.3 Percentage of votes for the Front National in Roubaix, 1974–89

Year	Election	FN vote (%)
1974	Presidential election	0.8
1979	European election	1.4
1983	Municipal election	9.6
1984	European election	18.3
1985	Cantonal election	19.9
1988	Presidential election	24.3
1988	Legislative election	19.0
1989	Municipal election (first round)	17.6
1989	Municipal election (second round)	17.9
1989	European election	19.3

Source: Ireland, 1994, p. 140.

standards in the city, the perceived alienation of the political elite from the concerns of the population, and the stigmatization of immigration as a main cause for the social and economic crisis. However, in Roubaix, the emphasis on xenophobic campaigning has been particularly strong, especially against the large North African population. Even at the time when the party was beginning its rise, in the early 1980s, Roubaix already had its own anti-immigration association, 'Les Chevaliers de Roubaix' (Knights of Roubaix). FN leaflets were also particularly violent. Its 1989 municipal election leaflet was banned after a complaint from the local section of the French League for Human Rights (Ligue des Droits de l'Homme). It displayed a photograph of a crowd of Muslims praying in the Place de la République in Paris, with the caption 'Roubaix tomorrow?'. It also quoted one Hussein Moussawi, 'Hezbollah Chief of Islamic Amal', as having declared: 'In 20 years, France will definitely be an Islamic Republic'.[9] The effects of this electoral strength on the city's strategy undoubtedly had some impact on Diligent's mayorship, making him cautious towards any minority-related policy, although, as Ireland (1994, p. 140) points out, his attitude always wavered during this period. Diligent's municipality evolved an unstable compromise on the issue whereby it was mostly kept out of the political debate, with some discreet exceptions: 'I believe all men are my brothers. When my brothers come to visit, I try to make them feel at home. But I don't let them run my household', he said in an interview in 1986 (quoted by Ireland, 1994, p. 136). He also refrained from cracking down too visibly on the xenophobic militia Les Chevaliers de Roubaix, then at the height of its popularity, and reduced the scale of activities and the visibility of the Commission Extra Municipale aux Étrangers (CEM), created by the Socialists in 1977. The Socialists in opposition also flirted with anti-immigrant stands at the council (Ireland, 1994, p. 137), without ever expressing openly xenophobic views.

The management of this permanent crisis situation by Diligent's municipality incorporated many classic elements of French management of urban decay. The apparatus of urban regeneration programmes (*politique de la ville*) funded by government and the region has been mobilized since the early 1980s, with the funding of housing upgrades and associational activities. In fact, much of the city was classified as a target for urban regeneration funding as part of the Contrat de Plan État/Region. This was complemented in the mid-1990s by an URBAN programme funded by the European Social Fund (ESF) covering the areas of Roubaix and Tourcoing (Préfecture du Nord, 1998). This comprised ambitious reconstruction of several areas, including parts of the city centre. These efforts were effective in attracting new businesses, in particular a large factory built in 1999 by Kimberly-Clark.

In addition to this relatively conventional strategy of regeneration, which in some ways recalls the strategies of Lille and Birmingham, Roubaix is also characterized by striking peculiarities that differentiate it from other French towns. First, since the crisis was not confined to one part of the city but was so pervasive and persistent that it became quintessential to the city's identity, the very foundation of Diligent's grip on city politics was his ability to manage this crisis, or at least to show the inhabitants of Roubaix that he was eager and able to deal with it. Not only was the municipality a recipient of *politique de la ville* funding, but Diligent was also a major proponent of the development and extension of such policies into national politics, building for himself a reputation of expertise in the issue and chairing a government committee in the late 1980s.

In addition to this policy activism, Diligent made deft political manoeuvres to play on the major issues in the city – resentment towards Lille, unemployment and immigration. Against the outside world in general, and against Lille in particular, he positioned himself as a cross-party mayor who spoke for all Roubaix's inhabitants, carefully cultivating a strong personal charisma to this effect. For instance, many ordinary people in the city prided themselves on knowing Diligent's personal telephone number during his two terms in office. One local official declared: 'Diligent has been for Roubaix what De Gaulle was for France, and that's no exaggeration. He's given us pride and hope, he's devoted himself to the city, and nearly worn himself out in the process' (quoted by Lefebvre, 1997, p. 69, my translation).

In spite of the influence of the racist climate noted above, Diligent's Roubaix distinguished itself from other cities by making unusual moves towards ethnic minorities. The municipality of Roubaix has been a forerunner in France in the field of ethnically conscious policies, especially anti-discrimination policies, with which it has experimented since the early 1990s (the beginning of Diligent's second term). In fact, the city was central in the concerns of the regional administration of the FAS, which was in charge of allocating Social Affairs Ministry funds for ethnic minority-oriented projects in the whole Nord-Pas-de-Calais region in the 1990s. The FAS's regional delegate in the late 1990s was an RPR (Gaullist) councillor in Roubaix, and her predecessor, Michel David, usually more associated with the left, was given a high-ranking executive position at the municipality in 1994. Specifically, he was entrusted with the management of urban regeneration programmes and leisure activities for youth-oriented programmes, which in Roubaix meant dealing with important youth associations.

Under David's supervision, an academic known nationally for his work on racial discrimination at the workplace, Philippe Bataille, became attached to a paramunicipal body, the Agence pour le Développement des Quartiers de Roubaix (ADQR), and wrote a study on the social crisis in the city (Bataille, 1994). The study carefully put forward the notion that racial discrimination, cultural recognition and political under-representation of North Africans were an aspect of the crisis, along with other factors usually mentioned, such as unemployment, at a time – the early 1990s – when this notion was totally absent from the French policy agenda, and indeed was not far from being a taboo in political discussions.[10] Still under David's direct supervision, an association specializing in the study of racial discrimination called D'un Monde à l'Autre (From One World to Another) was established in the late 1990s with funding from all the major local authorities and state agencies in the area, among which were the Conseil Général du Nord and the Conseil Régional du Nord-Pas-de-Calais.

These initiatives remained rather tentative compared to the programmes implemented by British cities. The latter usually involved setting targets for service delivery departments (housing, social services, education) in terms of ethnic composition of the population affected by policies; no such targets were ever set in Roubaix. They nonetheless had an innovative character which earned the municipality the image of a groundbreaking city in this area. This became especially visible after 1997–8, when racial discrimination was placed on the national political agenda by a conjunction of associational mobilization (chiefly involving a redefined and rejuvenated SOS Racisme) and governmental activism (especially on the part of Martine Aubry, Minister for Social Affairs, second-ranking member of the government and first adjunct of the Lille municipality).[11] In March 2000, Bataille was able to declare before an audience of French and British council officers gathered in Roubaix for a seminar on racial discrimination that the city was 'five years ahead of the rest of France'.[12]

At the same time, the municipality was also following developments in ethnic minority activism in the city. It found itself in a position where, without having to face the rise of ethnic minorities within its own ranks as was the case for Labour in Birmingham, it had to take this group into account for the preparation of its lists for the 1989 and especially 1995 municipal elections. Although this did not translate into full representation at the municipality, it did entail the election of four councillors of North African background in 1995, one of whom played a significant political role at the town hall (and was well placed to become head of the Greens' list in the 2001 election). Most importantly, it led to a situation in the late 1990s in which there were a certain number of prominent figures of North African background in the city who were able to bargain high-placed positions on major lists, including the list of the incumbent, in 2001. All in all, and despite the strength of racist senti-ments in the city, the 1990s were a decade of gradual political inclusion for ethnic minorities.

Institutions and generations of activists

This policy activism was connected with the strength of ethnic minorities in the city. The two noticeable waves of immigrant mobilization in Roubaix were the Beur movement in the 1980s, roughly corresponding in time to the first Diligent tenure, and a more localized, neighbourhood-based associational activity after that in the late 1980s and 1990s, roughly corresponding to Dili-gent's second term in office. These two generations of activists corresponded to national trends, what sociologists of immigration have called 'the second and third generations of immigrants' (the first being mainly those involved in industrial action and rent strikes in the 1970s) (see in particular Wihtol de Wenden and Leveau, 2001, on 'la bourgeoisie').

As in Lille, the first-generation Beur movement did not last, and failed to make an impact on municipal politics. In fact, it did not even reach the stage of well-established associations such as Texture and Les Craignos in Lille, although the movement had started well, unsurprisingly given the size of the Maghrebi population. The high point of the movement was the organization of a welcoming committee for the marchers of the *Marche contre le Racisme et pour l'Égalité des Droits* (March against Racism and for Equal Rights) in 1983. This event managed to gain much attention from the Roubaix press, as well as present speakers in schools and obtain support from a variety of local associations (Verfaillie, 1996, p. 34). Among those involved in the organization were Messaoud Bouras, a local youth, Said Bouamama, the founder of Texture in Lille, who was trying to expand his activities into Roubaix, and Slimane Tir, who was later to become a central figure in Roubaix politics.

After arriving in France with his Algerian manual worker parents at the age of 8, Tir became involved in Roubaix community activities and politics through the radical left project Atelier Populaire d'Urbanisme (APU, Popular

Urbanism Workshop), which consisted of setting up a self-management structure for the residents of the Alma-Gare neighbourhood.[13] After the APU, Tir
organized several events aimed at raising awareness around the issue of North
African immigration, among which were a hammam bath, a report for the
municipality on Arab culture, a contribution to a book on the personal stories
of migrants,[14] a publicity operation to encourage Beurs to vote and a debate
on racism. After the Beur movement, Tir remained active in local politics by
becoming a member of the Green Party in Roubaix (see below). In spite of
this original success, the movement was soon to suffer from internal divisions,
both ideological and personal, fuelled according to many by local authorities
which had an interest in weakening the movement: 'rivalries were encouraged
by "local powers"', according to Bouamama, and 'Everyone wanted Said and
Slimane to fight each other', according to Tir.[15] Bouamama subsequently concentrated his attentions on Lille.

But, unlike in Lille, and indeed unlike in most other French cities, the 'third
generation' that came in the late 1980s and early 1990s after the demise of
the Beurs did manage to establish itself as a lasting force in the city. Around
1987, a flurry of new associations appeared in Roubaix similar to those
that emerged in Lille-Sud at the same time. As in Lille-Sud, they had the following characteristics: they were 'youth' organizations, dominated by male
North African membership, often focused on demands regarding local sports
facilities. This stemmed from the importance of sports in the daily life of
these largely unemployed populations and of the difficulty they experienced
in accessing sports fields, which were mostly restricted to members of businesses, schools and other institutions. Behind these demands there always
loomed an urge for social recognition. While the associations in Lille-Sud
were confronted with the monolithic and hostile Socialist machine, their
counterparts in Roubaix found a more open opportunity structure that was
to lead a number of their representatives to local recognition and political
representation.

Roubaix Political History and Immigrant Incorporation in the 1990s

The success of activists of North African background in establishing themselves on the municipal scene is to be understood with reference to a series of
specifically Roubaix institutions. First, the numerical size of ethnic minorities
in the city should be reiterated; as noted earlier, the figure is most certainly
much higher than the approximately 20 per cent of foreigners in the total
population. The difference between the two figures would be the number of
French nationals of ethnic minority background who have the vote. This
group is apparently large enough to exert some political leverage, at least on

certain occasions. The North African electorate's behaviour is difficult to assess. By all accounts it is often apathetic, but it has been known to mobilize strongly when potential North African voters clearly understand that North African candidates are likely to win seats: this appeared to be the case in the second round of the 1995 municipal election, and in some cantonal elections[16] in 1997 (interview with city councillor, 20/4/00). This suggests that what determines the emergence of a North African electoral bloc, or at least the participation of enfranchised North Africans in the political process, is the existence of North African candidates who manage to be co-opted by political groups as candidates.

What has been happening in Roubaix in the last decade is similar to what happened in Birmingham in the last 20 years, with voters, leaders and native established groups coming together to create a situation where ethnic minority participation in municipal politics increases and gains leverage. While in Birmingham this has happened through party politics, in patterns that are roughly reminiscent of Labour politics elsewhere in the country, in Roubaix it has been an exception, and has tended to happen more through the channels of territory-based community politics. The institutional specifics of Roubaix, and the way in which they played out during Diligent's two terms, helped to maintain the traditional vitality of local community and neighbourhood groups, while in the same period the equivalent of these groups became subservient to the municipal machine in Lille. These specifics also helped transform these groups into active and influential elements of municipal politics.

Roubaix's institutions find their roots in a tradition of inclusion of diverse populations on a territorial, municipal basis, owing to the weakness of party cleavages and the high level of influence exercised on municipal politics by organized interest in the city, from business interests to neighbourhood and community organizations of a variety of political affiliations. Because of this exceptionalism, I will start by retracing the aspects of the history of the city that have led to this situation. I will then show how this has encouraged the emergence of politically astute North African activists, who have gradually transferred their ambitions from community politics to city council politics. Finally, I will retrace the emergence of these politicians in parties and municipal electoral contests during the Diligent era, in the context of an open political game, and in spite of the pervasive influence of the Front National.

Cross-party government and inclusion of migrants in the municipal community

As the working-class population grew rapidly in the city through the late nineteenth century, so did the burgeoning Socialist movement. Jules Guesdes, a national party figure, was elected deputy to the National Assembly in the Roubaix constituency, first in 1893, then from 1906 until his death. The politics of the city were then a tale of bitter confrontation between the working class and local business interests, which managed to retain control of the city council until the turn of the century in the face of mounting party influence. When the second Socialist mayor of the city, Jean Lebas, was elected in 1912 (after a brief spell at the municipality by another Socialist leader, Henri Carette, between 1892 and 1901), the city became a live experiment in municipal socialism. This doctrine, a communitarian and locally oriented brand of socialism, was imported by the Belgian workers who streamed into the city in the nineteenth century. In particular, Lebas sought to develop municipal provision of social services for working families, with crèches and meals for schoolchildren. He also developed an ambitious housing policy that led to the construction of a large housing development in the 1920s, Le Nouveau Roubaix.[17]

This politicized, confrontational mode of government changed radically after the Second World War, when a new Socialist mayor, Victor Provo, joined forces with the centre-right Catholic political forces linked to the business interests of the city, in spite of their original antagonism. This new alliance came into being first through cooperation in resistance operations against the Nazi occupation, then as a defensive alliance against the impressive popularity of the Communists in the city during the post-war years. This shifted the determinant cleavage in the city from left versus right to a division between the Communists on one side, and a coalition of the Socialists and the Catholic centre-right on the other (Florin, 1985, p. 257). The centre-right was closely associated to the business interests of the *patronat* (industrial leaders). From the late 1940s onward, this led to the emergence of an original mode of government dubbed 'third way' by local observers, which has largely endured until the present (Lefebvre, 1997). In particular, it was based on the joint management of the city's main problem, slum clearance, by the Socialists and the Catholic centre-right. The issue was depoliticized and delegated by the Socialist municipality to a paritarian (half-public, half-private) body controlled by the *patronat* and the Comité Interprofessionnel du Logement (CIL) (Florin, 1985, p. 257; Giblin-Delvallet, 1990).

This style of government lasted throughout Provo's long reign over the city, until 1977. It created an unusual political situation whereby the mayoral majority on the council was mainly made up of Socialist councillors, but constantly included centre-right councillors. In fact, the centre-right senator, André Diligent, who was to end the Socialists' domination of the city in 1983 by getting elected as mayor, was an adjunct in Socialist mayor Provo's council as early as 1949. Generally, interpersonal links between councillors of different political affiliation were often stronger than party affiliations, and in many cases this has remained so until the present.

This 'third way' collapsed with the 1977 municipal election, which was extremely polarized nationwide (pitting a Communist/Socialist alliance against a centre-right party), and which encouraged the formation in Roubaix of a Communist/Socialist list, while the Christian Democrat UDF was forced back into an alliance with the local Gaullists (the RPR). This new configuration was also precipitated by the personality of the Socialist leader at that time, Pierre Prouvost, who was part of the ideologized left-wing fraction of the local party. Prouvost was elected mayor and steered the municipality towards the left.

In the next election in 1983, however, the Socialists suffered a surprise defeat at the hands of their former ally senator Diligent, in large part because of Prouvost's lack of charisma. Diligent, on the other hand, was to prove a very popular mayor and was re-elected in 1989, before pushing forward his first adjunct, René Vandierendonck, for the 1995 election, which he in turn won. This marked the beginning of the decline of the Socialists, who lost the bulk of their members. They did manage to regain some lost ground in the 1989 and 1995 municipal elections when they mounted strong challenges to Diligent and Vandierendonck, but they failed to recapture the city. In a gesture reminiscent of the old Socialist/centre-right alliance, Vandierendonck switched allegiance and joined the Socialist Party in 1997 (in order to benefit from the Socialists' domination of the Communauté Urbaine, which procured significant rewards for mayors and their cities). But the party never again became the powerful organization that it had been, and Diligent occupied the vacant ground left in the centre of the political space in Roubaix, perpetuating the consensual 'third-way' style of management.

The third way, as shown above, was in itself an alliance between two competing groups, based on the allocation of a specific sphere (housing policy) by one to the other; but other aspects of the city's polity are also characterized by a greater recognition of sub-group identities, especially 'neighbourhood' identities. The unplanned development of the textile industry led to the development in most parts of the city of a mixed habitat: small houses huddled around yards and large factories. This encouraged the emergence of a strong sense of workplace and neighbourhood identity that has endured to this day to form the basis of Roubaix's strong territorial identity (Bataille, 1994, pp. 31–6). Since the nineteenth century, dense networks of cooperatives, associations and housing projects were developed by both *patronat* and Socialist networks with the aim of attracting the support of the city's large and expanding working-class population.[18] This tradition has endured: in 1999, a municipality leaflet boasted 'more than 2,000 associations, or one for every 50 inhabitants, the highest proportion in France'. Indeed, recent research stresses the high level of community activity in the city (Neveu, 1998, p. 26). Community groups cover a wide range of activities, from chess clubs and committees for the organization of neighbourhood celebrations to leftist groups and the far-right militia, Les Chevaliers de Roubaix (Verfaillie, 1996, p. 39).

Both the weakness of usual party political cleavages and the strength of community groups in the city facilitated the emergence, early in the century, of a territory-based style of immigrant incorporation. This became apparent first with the way in which the municipality handled the large Belgian population in the 1920s, which then formed a large proportion of the total population. It was divided into two sub-groups: the *frontaliers*, who commuted daily from Belgium (the Franco-Belgian border runs along the northern side of the city), and those who were established in the city. The former were dealt with considerately and with diligence by the mayor's office, but their status as foreigners, and their resultant exclusion from many French social services, was never questioned.[19] On the contrary, those who resided in the city were in many instances treated as other French nationals in Roubaix, regardless of their legal situation. De Barros notes that this was largely the result of pressure exerted on the mayor by trade unions, related cooperatives and other community groups in the city, who were consistently in favour of the protection of the Belgian population and made constant demands on mayor Jean Lebas to that end. In turn, he used his good personal relations with the prefect to obtain exceptions in administrative procedures to the benefit of Belgian inhabitants of Roubaix.

De Barros (2000, pp. 128ff.) highlights a contrast between this situation and the way foreigners were managed in another industrial commune of the Nord, Ostricourt. There foreigners, who also made up a large proportion of the population in the 1920s (around half), were perceived with hostility by locals and the mayor was constantly pressured by his constituency to crack down on disturbances created by fights between different nationality groups. While in Ostricourt the main line of conflict ran between the city's French inhabitants and its foreigners, in Roubaix it ran between all the city's inhabitants, whether French or foreign (largely Belgian), on one side, and outsiders to the city, regardless of nationality, on the other. In each case the mayor, and, behind him, the local community, played a central role in defining the conflict. In Roubaix, the close relation between Jean Lebas and sympathetic groups in the city, as well as the tacit acceptance of the remaining groups in the city, made this possible.

The high level of community activity and its institutionalization in the 1980s and 1990s acted as a training ground for ethnic minority leaders and activists, and helped to channel them towards electoral politics. The weakness of parties combined with the fluidity of alliances in municipal politics provided allies and places on candidate lists for these emerging elites. In the 1989 municipal election, ethnic minority elites who were starting to emerge did not significantly benefit from this situation because of Front National pressure on moderate parties; in 1995, however, they were more successful.

Young North Africans in local associations There is an active and complex civic milieu in Roubaix made up of activists of various groups, representatives of various kinds of neighbourhood associations and party activists. Patterns of relations between these various groups are unstable and can change considerably from one election to another. Hence, in contrast to the situation in Lille, the municipality has no strong and unilateral control of social and political networks, and as a result there is no established consensus on the municipality's policies. New issues can therefore appear more easily on the municipal agenda, and outsiders can also make their way into networks of influence much more easily than in Lille. Outside electoral periods, associational leadership is a much sought-after position because it provides a privileged outlook on Roubaix public life. This in turn seems to be more desirable than elsewhere, in a city where the only way to escape from unemployment and to 'exist' is often through community involvement (interview with social worker, 7/7/99). The importance of community activity has generally been viewed in a positive light by the municipality as an instrument of social cohesion and of the maintenance of law and order in the city.[20] The current mayor, René Vandierendonck, constantly referred to the 'brave, hardworking social and community-oriented inhabitants of Roubaix' during his 1995 electoral campaign.[21]

This framework has worked for well-established populations as well as for the second-generation North African populations. The type of associations that appeared after 1987 were more suited to Roubaix politics than the Beur movement. While the latter was essentially a nationally led mass movement, the former's community-based style, with its emphasis on the management of local problems,[22] places the emphasis on neighbourhood identities. The youth and immigrant element, being common to all these associations, did not serve to differentiate them from each other in the way that their strong attachment to specific neighbourhoods did. This makes them fit well with the local scene that I have just described, because the main locus for mobilization in French community politics has traditionally been territories,[23] in the form of the neighbourhood. In addition, the numerical importance of the young North African population and their difficulties in leaving it means that they are in the process of becoming 'the' main and most established sub-group of the city's population, as perceptively noted by Bataille. As a result, they tend to increasingly identify with the territory of their neighbourhood and of the city, as previous waves of rural French, then Belgians, Spaniards and Italians did before them (Bataille, 1994). This finds political expression in a pattern of rising involvement in neighbourhood groups. Two organizations in particular have acted as stepping stones towards representation: the Fédération des Associations de Jeunes (Federation of youth associations) and the *comités de quartier*. The former were created by the youths themselves in the late 1980s, while the latter are pre-existing structures which in several neighbourhoods have become multi-ethnic.

The Fédération des Associations de Jeunes. When several sports and leisure associations, run largely by North African youths, became sufficiently numerous (at
a dozen) and active, Diligent's municipality sought to tap into this human
potential and control its potential leverage. Diligent was from the start full of
praise for their role as 'keepers of the social peace' and as 'UN peacekeepers
on the front of unemployment and drug addiction' (quoted by Verfaillie, 1996,
p. 45). They initially sought to create a federation on their own, motivated by
the desire to share skills on filling out grant applications for *politique de la ville*
programmes (Neveu, 1998). Shortly after the creation of the federation, they
were institutionalized by one of Diligent's adjuncts in the form of a Fédération des Associations de Jeunes (FAJ) in 1991. The reasons for this are obscure,
but it seems that this official was keen to rationalize youth and leisure activities in the city, in the context of rivalries between several powerful councillors. The municipality funded the FAJ generously in 1999, providing the
salaries of two or three full-time social workers to help run the organization
and publish the newsletter. Because of this process of institutionalization,
these groups are more than just at the receiving end of a patronage organization, or disgruntled youths that have to be kept under control; they have in
many respects reached sufficient organizational strength to obtain regular
funding from the council while maintaining a degree of autonomy over their
activities (interview with social worker, 7/7/99).

The emergence of these associations before they formed a federation was
facilitated by a favourable configuration of youth groups, the *centres sociaux*[24]
of the neighbourhoods of Roubaix, and the municipality, in a striking contrast with Lille. The *centres sociaux* of the city's ten neighbourhoods have maintained a relatively independent leadership from the municipality,[25] as opposed
to Lille-Sud, where their history since the early 1990s has been a one-sided
tale of increasing control by the municipality, often through the composition
of the *conseils d'administration* (interview with director of federation of *centres
sociaux* in the Nord, 29/5/99; see also chapter 5). In 1993, the Lille municipality decided to regroup all of Lille-Sud's three *centres sociaux* into a single
agency controlled by the municipality, Lille-Sud Développement (LSD) (*La
Voix du Nord*, 12/12/93). Before they were regrouped, they often attracted hostility from groups of young North African men who were supposed to be one
of their main publics (*La Voix du Nord*, 15/3/91); in 1991 in particular, one
centre social was criminally burned down to the ground, apparently by a disgruntled group of youths who disapproved of the centre's activities on their
territory.

Similar patterns of hostility between groups of youths and *centres sociaux*
also existed in 1990s Roubaix; in fact, some of the associations affiliated with
the FAJ were also created as a reaction against perceived indifference on the
part of some *centres sociaux* to the concerns of local youths (availability of sports
equipment, public recognition). For instance, Rachid Bella, the leader of

comités de quartier in the Cul de Four neighbourhood in the late 1990s, originally became involved in associations as a reaction against the *centre social* of the Hommelet neighbourhood; the ACIJ association, in the neighbourhood of Haut-Champs, was also opposed to the *centre social* at the time of its creation. But the striking fact in Roubaix is that many associations were also created with the direct support of some centres, or started later to cooperate with them, as was the case in the Trois-Ponts, Nouveau Roubaix, Epeule and Les Echos neighbourhoods (interviews with urban regeneration managers, 24/3/00).

The institutionalization of the FAJ was one of the main elements that encouraged the emergence of an associative personnel of North African background in the city. In particular, Amar Bouzaoui, former president and now vice-president of the association (interviews with urban regeneration manager, 24/3/00, and social workers, 7/7/99, 12/7/99), entertained friendly relations with the adjuncts in charge of the FAJ, who were Socialist councillors who had crossed over to the Vandierendonck list in 1995. Several associations were politicized, with leaders clearly intent on positioning themselves in municipal politics, notably Christian Zaraoui of Sport et Culture in the Hommelet neighbourhood, and Djamel Kerrouche of the AJG in the Pile neighbourhood. Both are close to the Greens (see below). Several critics of the FAJ, in particular social workers who have been attached to it at various times, have pointed to its passivity, lack of purposeful activities, the waste of money poured into it by the council and the cronyism entertained by its leadership. In spite of these critics, the federation seemed to be difficult to reform, because of the proximity between the adjunct and the federation leader, and because the FAJ was looked upon as an instrument of 'social cohesion' that helped maintain law and order in the city.

The comités de quartier. As mentioned above, neighbourhood community organizations were particularly active in the city and affected electoral politics more than elsewhere. This has been the case especially since 1977, when the political game opened up with the fracture of the traditional Socialist/centre-right alliance. The election coincided with the heyday of the left-wing community movement in the 1970s. Roubaix distinguished itself in that respect as in others, when one of its neighbourhoods, Alma-Gare, became the centre of national attention because a coalition of leftist and Catholic activists was conducting a live experiment in community involvement there, the APU. The enterprise wavered and faltered in the early 1980s, but was to define many subsequent developments in Roubaix politics. First, it was one of the sources of inspiration for the first wave of French urban regeneration programmes that was appearing at that time; Diligent was later to refer repeatedly to it as he became a prominent proponent of urban regeneration. Second, the most prominent politician in Roubaix of North

African descent, Slimane Tir, first became involved in public affairs in Roubaix through his participation in the project. Building on the local recognition that he acquired then, he went on to a political career with the Greens and then became the leader of the Greens' list for the 2001 municipal elections. Finally, and most importantly, the ideological and relational proximity of this movement with the Communist/Socialist alliance which won the 1977 election encouraged the latter to support community activities in other neighbourhoods. This was also consistent with the ideological background of the Socialist revival nationally, which was based on a new left programme open to new social movements, and particularly to urban participation. The party devoted a great deal of attention to these questions in its manifesto for these elections.

The municipality's commitment went so far as to institutionalize community movements in Roubaix neighbourhoods in the form of *comités de quartier* (neighbourhood committees). Twenty years later, these were to act as levers of political incorporation for several young North Africans coming out of the associational movement and creating the core of the emerging North African elite. Originally, the *comités de quartier* were intended as open forums for all inhabitants of the neighbourhood. They were meant to be open assemblies for the inhabitants of each of the city's neighbourhoods and to serve as 'interfaces between the neighbourhood's needs and the municipality' (Verfaillie, 1996, p. 69; interview with social worker, 12/7/99), with regular meetings between them and the municipality. They promoted the notion of inhabitant, as opposed to citizen or voter, as a political actor, and the neighbourhood as a central category of Roubaix politics (Neveu, 1998, p. 105).

The *comités de quartier* evolved very differently from one neighbourhood to another, with some committees coming close to being abolished in the 1980s for lack of grassroots participation, while others maintained some level of activity. They experienced renewed dynamism in the 1990s, in part owing to a municipal charter granted in 1998 which officially recognized their consultative role (interview with social worker). They also provided community leaders in the neighbourhoods with platforms from which to articulate their views and assert their legitimacy in the context of power struggles in local politics, often to gain influence in the Green or Socialist parties, or to win places on municipal lists as 'representatives of civil society' (*représentants de la société civile*).

Although several neighbourhoods were overwhelmingly inhabited by North Africans, and all neighbourhoods had large North African populations, these committees were usually led by native French presidents who had usually acquired considerable experience in activism in leftist organizations and left-wing Catholic organizations such as the Jeunesses Ouvrières Chrétiennes (JOC). Groups of party activists also participated in the *comités de quartier*: until recently, the Trois Ponts committee was run by a group of retired Communist activists, and the committee in Pile had close ties with the local section of the Socialist Party. In the late 1980s/early 1990s, they were viewed by many young North Africans of the FAJ as closed and discriminatory institutions which refused to take them on board.[26] Since then, however, and as young North African activists became older and more mature, the *comités* have started to function as their training ground, in which they have found a way of improving their associational skills and becoming potent political actors. Increasingly in the late 1990s, boards of committees comprised young North Africans, of whom three were elected to the post of president, thus gaining recognition on the local scene. One of these, who first became involved in associational activity through a youth association in the Hommelet neigh-bourhood, became president of the Cul de Four committee (interviews with association leaders, 14/4/99, 7/7/99). The second, who was president of the Association Sportive des Trois Ponts (a member association of the FAJ), was then elected president of the Trois Ponts committee, in a move seen as a putsch against the established leadership of Communist activists. The third was a young woman involved in Muslim activities, who gained the presidency of the Pile committee.

Associational activity as a springboard towards political participation. In parallel with these neighbourhood-based leaders, associations of young Muslims have come to reach new levels of popularity among the North African population of the city. This reflects the very rapid growth of a new European and 'citizen' brand of Islam among French North African youth, branded Islam de France. Roubaix became a national centre of this trend in the 1990s, with the leader Tariq Ramadan, who was increasingly influential in France, coming once a month to give lectures attended by several hundred people. Its main expo-nents in Roubaix included leaders of local religious associations, who were well-known figures within the city neighbourhoods.

It is possible to elaborate the ideal career type of the young, male, North African local association activist in Roubaix, starting with participation in a youth association such as the FAJ, moving on to a position on the board of a *comité de quartier* and thereby gaining experience and visibility on the local scene, and finally, participating in electoral politics by negotiating a place on a list. The next step, getting elected, had been made by only a few in 1989 and 1995, but it was a likely possibility for many.[27] Few individuals mentioned above completely matched this ideal profile, but many did so in part.

These activists are linked by tight social networks. They do not define themselves as activists of ethnic minority issues, but as citizens concerned with Roubaix affairs who happen to be from a particular background (inter-views with president of neighbourhood committee, 14/4/99, and association leaders, 7/7/99, 14/4/99). But, at the same time, they are intent on raising issues of racial discrimination and recognition of cultural and religious difference, and are very militant and vocal in their criticism of the city council and other local authorities. In 1994, some provoked a small media storm in the local press by criticizing a municipal advertising campaign which displayed the faces of blond, blue-eyed children with the caption 'Children of Roubaix'. In 1996, members of the FAJ organized a publicity stunt following the murder of a young Algerian man by a baker in Reims by distributing croissants around the city and proclaiming 'we could be bakers too' to passers-by.

Because of these actions they are often viewed with suspicion by many in the municipality. At the same time, they are part and parcel of the Roubaix civic milieu and are inextricably linked to many of its institutions, because of their multiple and overlapping associative affiliations. The FAJ leaders often worked with the project leaders (*chefs de projet*) of the *politique de la ville* of the Contrat de Plan État/Région filling out funding application forms; one active member of a *comité de quartier* was also a member of the board of D'un Monde à l'Autre, an association promoting a variety of activities such as anti-discrimination policies and multicultural education and supervised by Michel David of the city council. Virtually all have participated at one time or other in the Commissions Départementales d'Accès à la Citoyenneté (CODACs), a series of consultative meetings with relevant local actors on the issue of ethnic minorities set up by the departmental authorities in 1998.

North African activists in an open political game

The defeat of the Socialists at the hands of Diligent in 1983 was to have a lasting impact on the politics of the city, including the politics of ethnic minorities, by opening up the municipal game. First, it led to the immediate and dramatic decline of the Socialist section of Roubaix, which until then had numbered around a thousand members and was the second in the Nord after the section in Lille (Florin, 1985, p. 259). Most of its members left because membership hinged on Socialist control of the municipality and its system of payback of supporters. Until then, the Socialists had been the only local party with any pretence of having any influence on at least some of the local community (right-wing parties in France are more likely to be networks of prominent individuals than mass parties, and Roubaix is no exception); from then on, the influence of parties in the city was extremely limited, leaving the city open to community movements, in particular the *comités de quartier*. Because of this, North African incorporation was not overwhelmingly conditional upon their cooperation or lack of cooperation with the Socialists, as it was in Lille, but depended on their capacity to use other mainstream structures to lead their activist careers, which they did with organizations such as the FAJ and the *comités de quartier*.

The 1983 election also defined the two subsequent municipal elections: although both were won either by Diligent (1989) or by his heir Vandieren-donck (1995), they were closely contested with the Socialists and were very open contests. This meant that the two main lists, the Socialists' and Diligent's centre-right list, were competing for marginal electorates, all the more so because they had shared the same electorate for decades until the 1977 breakup of their alliance. This facilitated the negotiation of places for com-munity activists on the lists of political parties, including North Africans.

The weakness of party cleavages was particularly visible on the issue of immigration in the 1989 elections. Both the Socialists and the centrists and Gaullists displayed a propensity to use anti-minority discourse as a response to the electoral successes of the xenophobic Front National from the early 1980s onwards. As a result, the leaders of youth associations and *comités de quartier*, which were starting to play a significant role, obtained little repre-sentation. The two main lists, Diligent's centre-right bid for re-election and the Socialist list, were faced with the difficult task of having to take account of anti-immigrant feelings running high in the electorate,[28] while including ethnic minority individuals to attract the votes of the minority population. Diligent's centre-right list was tempted to lean towards the far-right electorate, although it was afraid of appearing too radical. As for the Socialists, they were increasingly coming under pressure to take on board the rising North African elite; but they too feared alienating their traditional native French electorate by doing so. The following excerpts from a Front National election leaflet of that period give concrete indications of the pressure exerted by the FN on the two main lists: 'This is the last-chance election. Bernard Carton [leader of the Socialist list] and André Diligent are preparing to do irreversible damage by granting voting rights to immigrants, and, with your money, funding social services for immigrants. [. . .] While Bernard Carton's Socialist Party is the party of foreigners, André Diligent has shown, by including immigrants on his list and by refusing an alliance with the Front National, that he prefers Salem Kacet [a North African-born physician on Diligent's list, see below] to J. P. Gendron [the Front National candidate]. [. . .] They have made their choice, now make yours!' (1989 leaflet, my translation).

Each adopted a different strategy. The Socialist Party commissioned a secret opinion poll on whether it would suffer electorally from the presence of ethnic minorities in its ranks. As the answer was yes, to the point that the party would probably lose the election if it did, it was decided after a heated debate that North Africans would be excluded. As a result, Slimane Tir, the leader of the Greens in Roubaix, who was supposed to participate in the list, chose to run for election on his own on an entirely Green list. The existence of the poll was leaked and exploited by opponents, who highlighted the Socialist Party's alleged cowardice. Because of the public outcry that followed, the Socialist Party decided to readmit Tir and other Greens within its ranks two weeks before the election. Tir was subsequently elected as councillor, but he has remained defiant of the Socialists since this episode.

While the Socialist list was struggling with the issue, the incumbent mayor Diligent managed to turn the problem into an asset. He promoted to number three on his list (a very high and visible position) Dr Salem Kacet, a respected Algerian-born cardiologist from the main regional hospital in Lille who had previously participated in a consultative committee set up by President Chirac on the 1986 reform of nationality law. This enabled the centre-right to claim to be sympathetic to ethnic minorities while avoiding taking on board the more controversial home-grown young leaders. Indeed, Kacet's social and political profile was very different from theirs,[29] since he was an educated professional with right-wing sympathies. With Diligent's victory, the overall result was the election of two ethnic minority councillors, Tir and Kacet.

In the 1995 election, an isolated group of North Africans achieved what some attempted in Lille-Sud, namely, setting up an all-ethnic minority list; however, it obtained no electoral success because of its lack of genuine implantation in communities. More significantly, the network of young North African leaders that had sought to have an impact in the 1989 election again played an important role, this time with much more success than in 1989. After careful consideration, they decided that the best strategy for this particular election was to side with the Socialists (interview with association leader, 14/4/99), who seemed to have decided to play the immigrant card this time and to oppose the bid of Diligent's successor. They managed the acceptance of no fewer than six ethnic minority individuals on the list. This included Tir again, in fifth position, and businessman Haddouche Boualem in sixth position, as well as many of the North African leaders mentioned above. In return, they mobilized the North African population through a systematic scrutiny of the electoral registers (interview with association leaders, 14/4/99). The Socialist list lost by 300 votes in the second round. The narrowness of its defeat was probably to a large extent the result of its successful electoral mobilization. Tir and Haddouche were elected. As for Vandierendonck's victorious list, it had taken on board four activists of North African background. They were all elected but one: Saadi Lougrada, who was another former president of a *comité de quartier*; Mohammed Cherifi, who was a representative of the *Rapatrié* (Harki)[30] community; and Zora Zarouri, a young woman who had worked as a women's rights activist.

Between 1995 and 2001, then, there were five councillors of North African background (three in the majority, two in opposition), which represented less than 10 per cent of the council (53 councillors), for a population estimated at 30 to 40 per cent. But their effective incorporation was in fact greater than these figures suggest. If the Socialist list had obtained 300 more votes, the city would have had ten ethnic minority councillors, twice as many as its current number. In addition, several of those who were elected obtained significant policy remits. Lougrada managed to obtain considerable leverage on decision-making processes by securing the position of adjunct in charge of the Schéma Local d'Intégration (SLI), the municipality's main urban regeneration programme specifically targeted at minorities. Zora Zarouri obtained a delegation to women's rights, but, although her first years were positive,[31] she was later isolated at the council and did not stand for re-election in 2001. In sum, the number of ethnic minority councillors had more than doubled between 1989 and 1995. This progression was to be confirmed in 2001.

The same networks of North African activists who had played an active role in 1995 once again participated actively in the campaign. This time their support went not to the Socialists but to the Greens. This was in large part due to the fact that one of the leading activists of North African background, Slimane Tir, had been a long-serving party member and was chosen by the local party to head its list. Because Tir rallied his North African networks around his leadership, many of those activists who were not affiliated in 1995 and had strategically supported the Socialist Party became members of the Greens in the autumn of 2000 (interview with Tir in *Nord-Éclair*, 17/03/01). In addition, female activists were also co-opted by both the Greens and the outgoing mayor Vandierendonck because of the newly passed *parité* law.[32] The overall result was the election of eight North African councillors, the majority of them women. This continued the ongoing movement of incorporation (two councillors in 1989, five in 1995, eight in 2001) and may mark the beginning of a more lasting alliance between the Greens and some of the North African activist milieu.

Conclusion

Unlike in Lille, where the municipality was able to ignore ethnic minorities, the dominant political actors in Roubaix, i.e. the Socialist Party and the Diligent municipality, were increasingly compelled to consider groups of 'young' North Africans as significant political actors in the 1990s. While, as in Lille, the original Beur movement of the early 1980s quickly lapsed back into obscurity, the subsequent wave of associational activity involving North Africans produced a network of activists who managed to establish themselves as major political actors in the city. During the two mayoral terms of centre-right mayor René Diligent, they were increasingly co-opted by political parties on both sides of the political spectrum, with the exception of the Front National, and managed to obtain significant representation in the 1989 and 1995 elections.

This process of change has taken place in the context of a unique local political history, characterized by an old tradition of immigration and inclusion of outsiders and long periods of cross-party management of the city. The legacy of this history is an unusual vitality of community organizations, particularly youth associations and so-called neighbourhood committees, and the weakness of party organizations and traditional partisan cleavages, which makes community organizations more important in electoral politics than elsewhere. Young North African activists of the late 1980s and early 1990s were able to gain competence and legitimacy as political actors in the community movement and penetrate party politics by using it as a launching platform. This has made Roubaix a precursor of other French cities, with two specific features: an immigrant population that is more incorporated in the representative system, and a particularly strong role for local associations in this process of incorporation.

Conclusion

Strengths and Limitations of Historical Institutionalism in Ethnic Minority Studies

This book has illustrated the relevance of institutional approaches to ethnic minority politics (as noted by Bousetta, 2000). In particular, I have insisted on institutions as not just shaping actors' strategies but also framing the understandings actors have of their situation and the goals they are likely to pursue. For instance, institutions have conditioned possibilities for, and the conditions of, the emergence of ideas and issues (such as the notion of racial discrimination in France and Britain [Bleich, 1997] or dominant conceptions of citizenship and ethnicity in both countries [Favell, 1998]). This has been reflected in this book by the attention given to the way the history of migration politics in the last five decades has shaped the construction of immigrants in political debates; that is, in Britain as legitimate populations who are victims of racial discrimination and who have had a right to participate since the 1960s, and in France as outsiders who are objects rather than subjects of politics, even into the late 1990s when they had already been part and parcel of French society for several decades.

The historical institutionalist approach has also shown how institutions function as past political situations frozen in time which may define the possibilities and modalities of later developments. This appears not just in the British–French comparison but also in the Lille–Roubaix comparison, in which the difference in levels of incorporation is traced back to divergences in social and political histories that appeared in the early stages of industrialization in the region. This has far-reaching consequences for the definition of ethnic identities because it means that they are not just offshoots of the process of self-definition and exclusion of the other that has taken place at the national level, but that they are also shaped by urban histories. If patterns of minority politics continue to diverge in Lille and Roubaix, eventually being a French citizen of North African background in either city will not mean exactly the same thing.

This book has sought to give an account of the dynamics of interaction between various relevant institutions and the ways in which these dynamics produce specific configurations of power. In this way, the importance of the dynamics of city politics for the field of ethnic minority studies has been demonstrated, filling a gap in both Britain and France. As has been shown, the outcome of the black–white alliance, and subsequent political incorporation, is a consequence not just of citizenship rights, electoral systems or left–right competition in the Labour Party, but most importantly of the specific ways in which these elements achieved particular combinations in localized contexts.

The book has sought to support and illustrate Ireland's (1994) contention that political institutions matter more than ethnicity or class as factors that shape patterns of ethnic minority politics. On this point again, however, it has also noted the relevance of ethnic factors as an explanatory variable in explaining why certain groups have responded differently from others to the structure of opportunity offered by institutional framework I have outlined. This is the case in Birmingham, where the coexistence of several large ethnic groups within one political institutional context has made possible inter-ethnic cooperation. The book has shown that while two of my three models of co-optation are common to all ethnic groups, Asian councillors, particularly Pakistanis, have tended in the last decade to specialize in a third, distinctive style of participation in local council politics, based on the instrumentalization of the Labour Party to serve the aims of limited Pakistani groups. Increasingly, the Labour Party's role becomes secondary in these politics, and Pakistanis are elected without the party, or indeed party candidates, including other Pakistanis who have chosen to run for the party. After September 11, 2001 and the start of the war in Iraq, independent candidates have also increasingly been elected as Muslim opponents to Labour and Tony Blair's foreign policy.

This type of incorporation is based on the use of political resources that are specific to the Pakistani community of Birmingham, i.e. the mobilization of kinship and local community ties to advance issues linked to the socio-economic disadvantage of inner-city areas and to home-country politics. The mix of issues that were put forward by Pakistani politicians in the inner city in the late 1990s included a significant share of home-country politics in the form of demands related to the Kashmiri conflict. This points to the importance of ethnicity, but as a caveat to this it should immediately be added that many of the characteristics of these ethnic groups are also the result of the dual process of migration and adaptation to the host country. Hence, even in cases where the causal role of ethnic community organization is the most blatant, it is more the inter-play of host-country institutions and characteristics of ethnic groups that must be taken into account. The kinship ties that bind the Pakistani community in Birmingham are not just the transposition of social links that prevail in rural Pakistan, they are also shaped by the constraints of urban life in Britain. Joly (1987) shows that the charities and associations that blossomed in mid-1980s Birmingham facilitated the perpetuation of traditional modes of social organization in Pakistani populations. These traditions started to combine with the British legal framework at the moment when Pakistani populations began to settle in Britain, and their subsequent evolution in the context of that framework has followed a different route from patterns of social organization that have evolved since then in the context of rural Kashmir.

Yet it would also be excessive to conclude that Pakistani inner-city politics can be understood as merely reproducing the traditional patterns of Labour patronage of working-class communities that existed before post-colonial migrants arrived. In institutionalist terms, this is reminiscent of sociological institutionalist arguments, for instance the concept of isomorphism, in which institutional change is explained by the fact that institutions may import institutional forms from elsewhere in a process of imitation (e.g. DiMaggio and Powell, 1991). This type of argument leaves little place for agency, or for other factors such as ethnicity. But Pakistani inner-city politicians in Birmingham, while indeed showing signs of reproducing old Labour politics by mobilizing communities to exercise control over candidate selection processes, have also shown that they instrumentalize them to some extent in order to raise issues that are specific to them: home-country politics, or more recently opposition to British foreign policy. Their denunciation of racism to mobilize support at the grassroots level against the higher echelons of the party, and the competition between Labour and Liberal Democrat Pakistani candidates, also shows that their politics is not just a repetition of old Labour Party politics but also builds on other repertoires of mobilization.

The End of the Path: Muslim Anger in Britain and the Lingering Burden of Beur Failure in France

Arriving at similar crossroads, Britain and France took different paths. In Britain, the history of the politics of migration and ethnicity of the last 40 years has been characterized by a largely uncontrolled influx of post-colonial immigrants, significant proportions of which obtained voting rights automatically upon entry; by early politicization, rapidly followed by bipartisan national depoliticization; by the emergence of the notion of racial discrimination and race relations as general policy guidelines for government and local government policies; and by the Labour Party becoming the main proponent of these policies. This helped to set the politics of ethnic minorities at the local level on a particular path, characterized by the coalescence of intense immigrant participation in the local political arena, organized around issues of racial discrimination and racial disadvantage, cultural and religious recognition, electoral mobilization and the emergence of an ethnic minority elite within the Labour Party. From these developments emerged a structure of opportunity for the appearance of policies against racism and racial discrimination, and the co-optation of ethnic minority councillors in growing numbers, in particular owing to local electoral systems and the emergence of new groups in the Labour Party that were more favourable to ethnic minorities than other, more established groups. This initially tended to take place in London boroughs controlled by radical elements of the new urban left in the 1980s, then spread into provincial cities.

This interpretation of British immigration politics nuances the focus of the 'racialization' school on the racial, anti-black bias of British immigration policies since the 1950s (Carter, Harris and Joshi, 1987; Paul, 1997). These authors emphasized the continuous use of race as the central criterion of discrimination in granting the right to migration to Britain or access to British nationality in successive immigration acts and nationality acts since the 1960s. This book has, on the contrary, insisted on the fact that, in comparison with France (and with the rest of Europe), the British state is notable for its willingness to fight actively against racial discrimination since the early 1960s and for the extraordinary liberality of its citizenship and nationality regime in the 1940s and 1950s. The fact that immigration policy gradually became restrictive, and arguably racialist (as opposed to intentionally racist), together with the persistence of institutional racism in Britain, does not contradict these basic and essential points, which set Britain's attitude to migrants on a specific path with far-reaching consequences. Following Hansen (2000) on this point, the book has stressed the need to remedy the lack of a comparative perspective among British advocates of the racialization approach. While there is no denying the existence and persistence of pervasive racialist biases in the British state apparatus, it is also noteworthy that British policies have been comparatively responsive to the problems of post-colonial immigrants and their offspring.

In France, the recent history of migration politics has also been characterized by a strong influx of non-European workers, but with two essential differences from Britain. First, the bulk were not granted citizenship, as was the case in Britain, and, second, until the 1970s central state bureaucracy played a predominant role in managing the migration flows of workers and their welfare in France. This tended to keep issues connected to them out of the realm of party politics, both nationally and locally. When those issues did flare up, in the early 1980s, they were persistently agitated by the Front National in the political arena. This inhibited major parties on the left and right alike from taking up minority claims, and encouraged them to adopt a 'universalist assimilationist' attitude to immigration and minority issues which further created reluctance to promote minority interests. This inhibited the co-optation of minority councillors by native elites in the 1980s, and was compounded by the existence of certain features of political institutions in the city: majoritarian electoral systems and the dissolution of a temporary alliance between the Socialist Party and the Beur movement in the 1980s.

The fact that the British political system emerges from this comparison as more open to its minorities than the French system was not entirely predictable. In fact, it may be viewed as paradoxical that British parties actively sought, with greater success than elsewhere, to stop using the 'race card' and to pass liberal measures, because it is in Britain that racial hatred found an early and acrimonious expression. It may also be noted that the anger stirred up among Muslim communities by Tony Blair's enthusiastic participation in the American war on terrorism after 2001 has greatly weakened, or even destroyed, the Labour–minority alliance in parliamentary politics, and possibly also in many local authorities. If the alienation of minorities and Labour proves durable, the 1980s and the 1990s may come to be remembered as a brief period when minorities found their place in the British political system, on the left, in spite of persistent leanings towards the Conservatives by some Asian voters.

But the relative comfort of black and Asian Britons with their status in the British polity, and their relative gratitude to the British state, is evident when British minority organizations condemn other European countries' perceived backwardness in matters of anti-discrimination policies and political representation, and insist, probably rightly, on imposing British-style policies on the European Union. This is despite continuous problems of institutional racism, in particular in the police force. The desire to roll back multiculturalism manifested by New Labour after 2001 seems unlikely to revoke the policies established over the previous 40 years, and the perpetuation of anti-discrimination policies and of ethnic categories in the census seems assured. Similarly, it is difficult to imagine local authorities such as Birmingham totally reneging on 20 years of promotion of racial diversity and pluri-ethnic government. While the chapter on Birmingham has shown that these policies were also contested and dependent on fragile political balances, it also revealed that they constitute a powerful precedent for future policies.

Yet, the story might not be a purely linear one, from exclusion to representation, because the issues at stake have experienced some variations over time, from racial discrimination to multiculturalism in the 1980s, and now the anger of the Muslim electorate against New Labour's foreign policy. A large segment of the ethnic minority electorate may be divorcing itself from its old ally; but that may come precisely at a time when British cities are slipping away from Labour, embracing other parties or pluri-partisan coalitions.

France, by contrast, has spent the last 20 years handling its immigration and post-colonial problem in as disastrous a way as one could imagine; all strategies against the Front National have backfired and have in fact strengthened it; the nationality law reforms of the early 1990s were locked in rear-guard and conservative conceptions of French-ness that only served to delay the inclusion of minorities in the national polity; the Beur movement, which originally created a powerful dynamic of support among liberal public opinion, was dropped and marginalized by a short-sighted Socialist Party. The failure of the Beurs alone is responsible for the lingering crisis of confidence among many second-generation Maghrebis in French institutions, and, to a large extent, for 20 years of political exclusion.

All of this was probably not predictable in the late 1970s. It was possible to imagine that, as immigrants' children gradually came of age and matured in the 1980s and 1990s, some sort of tension or movement demanding greater rights and recognition would arise, as was the case in Britain. But nothing in the French nationality regime or in its policies suggested that the country was headed towards political blockage; more exclusionary models like Germany's would have appeared to be better candidates. In fact, it would have been reasonable to imagine that the left, if and when it gained power, would grant local voting rights to foreigners, as has long been the case in most European countries of immigration. In addition, it would have been difficult to predict the staggering success of the Front National and the ineffectiveness of other parties' responses. All of these events resulted from the specific combination of party politics in the French bipolar system, nationality law and Socialist Party politics that occurred at that time.

It is possible that those 20 years will remain as a parenthesis, a sort of slow-motion crisis of immigration, nationality and integration policy, and that the turnabout initiated in 1997 marks its end. Much hinged on the decision by the Socialists on their return to power to break away from the illiberal attitudes of the 1980s and 1990s with respect to the nationality code and undocumented immigrants. The legislative package proposed put forward a tentatively more liberal vision of nationality law and immigration policy. What was essential was the strong message sent to public opinion that immigrants and their children could not be eternally considered as outsiders, as the right's campaigning and policies had implied. Further initiatives in this direction by a small number of academics linked to the left promoted the adoption of anti-discrimination policies, sometimes directly fashioned after the British example. This further built up the legitimacy of minority groups and individuals in the French public, including in municipal arenas, and in so doing cleared the way for tentative inclusion on city councils in the 2001 elections. Indeed, it is this turnabout that finally seems to have opened the door to inclusion for French ethnic minority councillors, possibly signalling the end of the parenthesis.

Yet the 2001 municipal elections yielded disappointing results for the Socialists, and even more so for the Communist Party, largely because they lost the support of the poorer segments of their electorate concentrated in disadvantaged areas, which means to an important extent ethnic minorities. This occurred despite the fact that this was the election when they began co-opting minority councillors in significant numbers. It suggests that this move-ment of inclusion may be too little, too late to mend the divorce between the left and its old blue-collar base. Thus, in retrospect, it appears that the Beur movement represented a squandered opportunity to perpetuate, for a few more decades perhaps, the alliance between middle and working classes that had been held together by the Socialists since the 1970s.

Ethnic Minorities and the Decline of the European Left

In all three cities, the cleavage between minorities and native populations has largely been congruent with a socio-economic cleavage that runs between the native middle-class and working-class populations. Ethnic minorities are a sub-group of the working-class population in Britain, and of the composite population of retired workers, unemployed or low-paid individuals that make up the disadvantaged areas of cities such as Lille and Roubaix (Lojkine, Delacroix and Mahieux, 1978; Lapeyronnie, 1987). What this book has shown is that institutional configurations distort this correspondence when it is trans-lated into the political arena. Institutional features help to specify whether or not the translation of the socio-economic cleavage in the political sphere features an alliance between representatives of ethnic minority interests and left-wing parties. There is such an alliance in Birmingham, but not in Lille. In Roubaix, the situation is less clear cut, with the Socialists and their Green allies taking immigrants on their lists, and lists on the right doing so as well, though to a lesser extent.

The 1950s witnessed a peak in the importance of the working-class pop-ulation in the local leadership and representation of both the British and the French left. Since then, its relative numerical importance has declined, and it has steadily been replaced by a growing population of employees and other lower-middle-class occupations. But what is important is that this change took place in the 1970s in France, while in Britain it took place in the 1990s. In France, the percentage of manual workers among councillors in a sample of 500 communes fell from 24 per cent in 1945 to 11 per cent in 1983, while the number of teachers and civil servants increased from 20 per cent to 38 per cent (Garraud, 1988). This was particularly the case in the Socialist Party, with teachers accounting for 63 per cent of Socialist mayors in the 1980s. In Britain, in 1985, 35 per cent of Labour councillors had a manual working-class background (Gyford et al., 1989).

At the local level, the Labour Party has tended to be more representative, not just of ethnic minorities but also of the working class, than the Socialist Party. The left-wing mainstream in Britain, in the form of the all-embracing Labour Party, acted as a path to power for minorities in the 1980s and 1990s primarily because Labour controlled large industrial cities. Birmingham in this respect is illustrative of a wider trend that saw cities become the last bastions of the embattled Labour Party against Thatcherite assaults.

The Socialist Party in Lille has been typical of changes in the party across France, moving from completely espousing the city's population of industry workers to promoting the interests of the city's growing population of tertiary employees and middle-class families. In doing so it has reflected the changing place of the party in the party system, moving from an opponent of the Fifth Republic, allied with the Communist Party, in the 1970s to a centrist party of government in the 1980s and 1990s.[1] In this respect, the municipality's exclusionary machine can be understood as a mechanism that amplifies this general trend and gives it a particularly clear expression in Lille. The phenomenon of exclusion of minorities is even more pronounced than that of other low-income groups in the city because it is compounded by factors specific to ethnic minority politics as highlighted in this book. Likewise, the weakening of the native British–black and Asian coalition in late 1990s Birmingham is to some extent a product of the defeat of the Labour left in the trend towards the gentrification of the party that took place in the late 1990s under the stewardship of Tony Blair (on Labour gentrification see Seyd and Whiteley, 2002).

Local Strategies and their Unintended Effects

For all the contrasts that exist between Birmingham and Lille, there is an important common point between the two cities; in both cases there was an established political machine, that run by Mauroy in Lille, and that run by the 'right' in Birmingham in the late 1970s and early 1980s. In the first 'patronage' model in 1980s Birmingham, ethnic minority access to representation was based on the support of the Labour establishment. Since at first minorities were often assigned marginal roles and were meant to function as mere supports, to ensure the perpetuation of the right's dominance of the city in exchange for short-term services to their communities, their situation was not entirely dissimilar to that of the excluded minority youths in Lille, fighting a losing battle against the maverick Socialist machine.

In both cases, the arrival of minorities in local politics was blocked by political institutions that functioned as reproductive tools for the existing political order. In Birmingham, that block crumbled and faded away, and minorities to a large extent won their battle, at least in terms of political representation. In Lille, on the contrary, their exclusion endures. Not only did the Socialists there benefit from a different institutional context, but by building and maintaining their political machine in the 1990s they were also more proactive and astute in steering institutional change in a desired direction, in a clear example of actors engaging in institutional engineering to lock in an acquired political advantage. But the steady erosion of the Socialists' electoral results in the last three municipal elections, culminating with a narrow re-election in 2001, suggests that the Socialists may not necessarily hold on to power much longer. As in other cities nationwide, this erosion is due to the disaffection of the more disadvantaged voters, including ethnic minorities. While the latter are still drastically under-represented on the city council, and are likely to continue to be under-represented if the right succeeds the Socialists, in that eventuality they will at least have contributed, through their abstention or through a possible shift to the right, to defeating the machine that has been crushing them for the last 20 years. If that happens, the machine will have backfired on its designers, by insulating them so well from the pressures of social change that they became oblivious of the inevitable need to adapt, at least to some extent, to their constituents. Until the war in Iraq, the Labour Party in Birmingham taken as a whole appeared, on the contrary, to have successfully adapted to the ethnic changes in the city.

In Roubaix, a traditionally lively and independent milieu of associations provided a fertile training ground for a generation of Algerian community activists, well versed in the vernacular of local politics. This burgeoning minority elite benefited from the lack of dominance by any one party over the Roubaix political scene. In contrast with Lille, it also benefited from the low level of partisanship of municipal politics, and from the high degree of community group participation. As a result of this, it was relatively unaffected by the strong presence of the Front National in the city, and was able to bargain its support to a variety of lists of all inclinations, in spite of the majoritarian electoral system.

Roubaix may appear to be a precursor of growing minority representation on city councils, although the 2001 results were in fact disappointing for some ethnic minority activists, who expected more. In addition, the distinctive historical path towards inclusion in Roubaix sets it durably apart from other cities. The movement of inclusion on city councils in 2001 remained variable from one city to another, and still makes it difficult to conclude with certainty whether French minorities are soon to be as well represented locally as their

British counterparts. Neighbourhood leaders with strong roots in the social and communal fabric of their city are unlikely to attain as much recognition and power in other cities as in Roubaix. But what is certain is that the type of radical, left-wing, pro-minority activism that brought blacks and Asians to power in Britain in the 1980s will not happen in that way in France. Rather, co-optation of apolitical local figures by list-makers at election time seems more likely to become a recurrent pattern; and this low salience of grassroots partisan mobilization is something that Roubaix has prefigured.

The election of ethnic minority councillors in these cities can be interpreted as a Pyrrhic victory. Many of Roubaix's policies are largely dependent on decisions made by the Council of the Greater Lille Area, in which the influence of Lille's mayor is dominant. Likewise, the inclusion of minorities on British city councils came precisely at a time, the mid-1980s, when local authorities were losing much of their tax-raising powers and policy competences to the centralizing onslaught of Margaret Thatcher's successive governments. This onslaught was directed against leftist groups who were the very ones that struck alliances with blacks and Asians. The role of cities as laboratories for social and political change is confirmed, but so is their relative lack of importance in the context of centralized welfare states. The next issue for ethnic minorities is whether they can capture positions in national assemblies. While on this score Britain, with a dozen MPs of minority background, again has a better record than France, where not one member of the National Assembly is of North African background, under-representation is still evident in both countries.

Yet the election and rising influence of ethnic minorities in British cities and in French cities such as Roubaix retains a symbolic and real value that must not be underestimated; as noted at the beginning, it signals an acceptance of newcomers within indigenous political institutions and allows them an albeit modest share of local power, which helps them settle permanently in their host societies. It also signals the capacity of European political systems to adapt to large-scale and rapid social change. The ultimate lesson, once the dust of political protest and racist mobilization settles, may therefore be the resilience, adaptability and capacity for self-reinvention of these systems. The concept of political representation may emerge from these challenges relegitimized and strengthened.

Appendix: Interviews and Sources

Three main types of sources have been used for the local case studies: personal interviews, newspaper articles, and academic works and policy documents. Listed here are all the interviews undertaken, including conversations with academic specialists in the three cities under discussion, as well as the main press sources. Interviews with local actors were semi-directive, using as starting points the family background of interviewees, their education, the tasks carried out as part of their job or elected position, the main problems they faced, the partners, individuals and institutions with which they dealt, their assessment of race relations in the city, and their expectations for the future. Although some of these interviews are not quoted in the book, they are nonetheless important because they helped me gain a sense of city-specific issues.

Birmingham

City councillors: 11
Officers on the city council and regeneration programmes: 10
Representatives or leaders of community organizations: 8
Labour Party official: 1

Lille

City councillors: 4
Officers on the city council and regeneration programmes: 7
Officers in other local institutions (*préfecture*, Greater Lille Urban Community, regional council, departmental council): 6
Representatives or leaders of community organizations: 8
Rank-and-file Socialist Party activists: 4

Roubaix

City councillors: *3*
Officers on the city council and regeneration programmes: 9
Representatives or leaders of community organizations: 5
Total: 76

Main Press Sources

Birmingham Post
Evening Mail
Guardian
La Voix du Nord
Nord-Éclair
Le Monde
Libération

Notes

INTRODUCTION

1 Zollberg, 1981, p. 5, quoted in Joppke, 1999, p. 1.
2 This definition of ethnic minorities is deliberately broad, and encompasses several narrower definitions, in order to permit the comparison of similar political phenomena across countries with populations of recent immigrant descent that are on the whole similar but also present differences. In particular, it subsumes racial minorities, religious minorities and ethnic minorities under the same heading, although it is understood that there are significant differences between them (as shown, for instance, by Parekh, 2001; Modood, 1994, 2000).
3 For instance Castles and Kozack, 1973; Lapeyronnie, 1993; Ireland, 1994; Bousetta, 1997; Body-Gendrot and Martiniello, 2000; Rogers and Tillie, 2001.
4 For instance Glazer and Moynihan, 1963; Katznelson, 1973; Bobo and Gilliam, 1990; Brown, Marshall and Tabb, 1997.
5 Only four Members of Parliament (MPs) were elected in 1987, six in 1992 and nine in 1997, which left ethnic minorities much more under-represented in Parliament than in many local councils (Geddes, 1998).
6 Forbidden since 1872 (see Tribalat interview, *Express*, 04/12/03).
7 Data from www.statistics.gov.uk/. Respondents were asked to choose from a detailed list which featured the following main categories: 'Mixed', 'Asian or Asian British', 'Black or Black British', 'Chinese' and 'Other'.
8 Because it includes those who have acquired French nationality (with the very important caveat that this still excludes the large population of French individuals born of foreign parents, who do not appear on official statistics).

9   On Britain, see Modood, Berthoud et al., 1997, in particular chs 5 and 6, pp. 150–223; on France, Body-Gendrot, 2000, ch. 5, pp. 180–226. Modood, Berthoud et al. also show that economic and educational status varies largely between ethnic groups.

10 The debate has raged in France between competing counts; for a summary of these debates, see Kaltenbach and Tribalat, 2002.

11 In Modood, Berthoud et al.'s survey, 96 per cent of the Pakistani respondents and 95 per cent of the Bangladeshi declared themselves Muslim (p. 298). The rest of the minority religions in Britain were, in decreasing order of numerical importance, Sikh, Jewish, Hindu or Buddhist.

12 Interview given to *L'Express*, 04/12/03.

13 For the French side of the comparison, the municipal tenure of 1983–9 is taken as the starting point, because it corresponds in time to the beginning of minority empowerment on British local councils.

14 The first three figures are quoted by Adolino from Anwar, 1986, p. 109.

15 www.parliament.uk/commons/lib/research/notes/snsg-01156.pdf.

16 France Plus approached all major political parties except the Front National and proposed around 500 candidates of North African background; of these 300 were included on electoral lists by the parties, and around 100 were subsequently elected (Leveau, 2000, p. 273).

17 'Two hundred councillors, 70 per cent of whom were on left-wing lists, thus entered municipal councils. Five years later, they were almost all disillusioned' (Vincent Geisser, CNRS researcher, *Le Monde*, 07/03/01, my translation).

18 The criteria of selection were not specified.

19 In French '*Arabe de service*'.

20 'Intégrés, mais en queue de liste: les enfants d'immigrés sont cantonnés à des candidatures de témoignage', *Libération*, 2/03/01.

21 The estimated net inwards movement of West Indians, Indians and Pakistanis into Britain was 25,900 in 1958, 27,400 in 1959 and 58,050 in 1960, then shot up to 115,150 in 1961. In 1963, the number of work vouchers delivered was 23,969, then around 9,000 in 1964 and 1965, before oscillating between 1,000 and 3,000 for the rest of the 1960s (Freeman, 1979, table 3, p. 23, and table 4, p. 24). The latter figures indicate a higher number of immigrants because many dependents came with the workers. In France, by contrast, the number of foreigners in France of an African nationality (overwhelmingly Algerian, Moroccan or Tunisian) was 428,160 in 1962, 652,096 in 1968, and almost doubled between 1968 and 1975 (moving up to 1,192,300 in 1975), making the 1968–75 period the one with by far the largest number of arrivals. That population then increased to 1,594,772 in 1982 and thereafter its increase was much more limited (Weil, 1995a, appendix VI, p. 559, INSEE census data).

22 Simons, 1974, quoted by Freeman, 1979, p. 21.

23 *Beur* is the French word for Arab pronounced backwards, and designates second-generation North African immigrants in the suburban vernacular French of the 1980s. It has since fallen out of fashion and many second-generation North Africans now resent the word as an artificial and derogatory label.

24 A group of countries which include the main countries of migration to Britain in the West Indies and Asia (see chapter 2).

25　For a history of the British citizenship regime since 1948, see Layton-Henry, 1992; Hansen, 2000.

26　In 1998, the registration rate was 82 per cent for whites, 83 per cent for Pakistanis, but only 74 per cent for African-Caribbeans (Anwar, 1998, p. 11).

27　Though some sections of the 'Asian' electorate (i.e. Indians and Pakistanis for the most part) vote Conservative.

28　With variations depending on the time period when they arrived in France (Tribalat, 1995, pp. 194, 199).

29　*Community Cohesion: A Report of the Independent Review Team, chaired by Ted Cantle,* issued by the Home Office, 2001.

30　On the British side, most notably Katznelson, 1973; Ben Tovim et al., 1986; Saggar, 1991a, 1991b; Rex and Moore, 1967; Rex and Tomlinson, 1979; Messina, 1989; and Eade, 1989, all of whom are concerned more or less directly with the place of ethnic groups in political struggles centred on local electoral politics. More generally, the electoral behaviour of ethnic minorities and their impact on electoral politics has also been well studied on the British side, in part because of the realization, since 1974, of the potential of that electorate, and the interest of British academics in issues connected with racial diversity (Anwar, 1994; Fitzgerald, 1987; Messina, 1989; Saggar, 1998a). In France, Vincent Geisser (1993, 1995, 1997) has analysed the discourse on 'ethnicity', which temporarily gained currency in the 1989 local elections, by conducting a sociological survey of some of the North African councillors who were elected then. Schain has analysed the rise of ethnicity-related themes in the French local system in the 1970s and 1980s, particularly in Communist-dominated areas (for instance Schain, 1993). There are also studies of the patterns of political mobilization of young North Africans during the Beur movement (Jazouli, 1986; Lapeyronnie, 1987). Recently, Olivier Masclet has analysed the complex relations between the Communist Party and North African youths in a Paris suburb (Masclet, 2003).

1　HISTORICAL INSTITUTIONALISM AND THE COMPARISON OF LOCAL CASES

1　Borrowing its name from a popular song by a local band that initially came up with the idea of mounting a multiracial and leftist electoral bid.

2　In an indication of the importance of the ethnic dimension of the electoral contest, the right made thinly veiled anti-minority comments during the campaign; these comments and the disappointment of the left's defeat enticed several hundred youths to burn and loot the town hall square on the night of the second round, once the victory of the right was known. The newly elected mayor, Philippe Douste-Blazy, was surrounded and blocked by demonstrators and looters for several hours in a nearby restaurant, just after the formal announcement of his victory (*Libération*, 19/03/01).

3 For reviews of the three institutionalisms see the two review articles, Koelble, 1995, and Kato, 1996, as well as the discussion of the three new institutionalisms by Hall and Taylor, 1996.
4 For a more detailed presentation of historical institutionalism, Hall and Taylor, 1996, and Steinmo, Thelen and Longstreth, 1992, introduction. See also March and Olsen, 1989, for an approach to institutionalism applied to politics. Much of the discussion in this section is based on these works and the review articles quoted above.
5 Suggesting higher numbers of individuals of North African background but of French nationality, who are not recorded as such in national statistics.
6 Because the new mayor, René Vandierendonck, elected in 1995 on a centre-right list, changed camps two years later to join the Socialists.

2 THE BRITISH POLICY FRAMEWORK: LIBERAL CITIZENSHIP REGIME, DEPOLITICIZATION AND THE RACE RELATIONISM OF BRITISH CITIES

1 It is one of the three essential differences noted by Gary Freeman (1979), the two others being the fact that the British felt threatened by immigration while France did not (the rise of the Front National in French politics happened only in 1983, four years after the publication of Freeman's book), and that the British set up specific political and administrative institutions to deal with the issue, whereas France was for a long time more concerned with the socio-economic aspect of the question.
2 In a similar vein, Joppke, 1998, pp. 237–8 notes two main determinants of British particularities in the field of local integration: demography (spatial concentration) and 'statecraft' (organization of welfare state and provision of welfare).
3 The Colonial Office had played a role in the welfare of some West Indian migrants recruited during the war to work in Britain, but then persistently dismissed requests by local bishops, voluntary groups and city councils to get involved with post-war migrants. When the role of the VLCs was upgraded in 1965 (see further below), the Home Office was put in charge (Hill and Issacharoff, 1971, pp. 4–5).
4 Labour's official election manifesto read: 'the number of immigrants entering the United Kingdom must be limited' (quoted by Messina, 1989, p. 31).
5 After becoming the new party leader Wilson made a declaration to the House of Commons, stating: 'We do not contest the need for immigration control into this country' (H. C. Deb. 702. 27 November 1963, Col. 1254, quoted by Saggar, 1991b, p. 27).
6 Quoted in Saggar, 1991b, p. 31, and Hansen, 2000, p. 26.
7 The influence of academic ideas of race and community on British policy developments has been extensively documented by John Crowley in his doctoral thesis at the Institut d'Études Politiques de Paris (1994).

8   'The significance of the local response to third world immigration in Britain cannot be overstated, for if the shape of the cloth of British race relations has been determined by the outputs of the national political process, its specific patterns and texture have been woven in the cities' (Katznelson, 1973, p. 152).

9   Excerpt from Section 71 of the 1976 Race Relations Act: www.homeoffice. gov.uk/docs/racerel1.html.

10 For reviews of the development of black and anti-racist politics linked to the Labour Party in the 1970s, see Jeffers, 1991; Sewell, 1993, pp. 99–121; Shukra, 1998.

11 For information on these by-elections refer to news.bbc.co.uk/2/hi/uk_news/politics/3899683.stm.

12 See news.bbc.co.uk/2/hi/uk_news/politics/3880231.stm.

13 On the history of the Labour left and its conflict with the 'right', see Seyd, 1987; Seyd and Whiteley, 1992; Stoker, 1991, pp. 43–9.

14 Although this must be nuanced by the fact that Members of Parliament often start by being local councillors (but abandon their local career as soon as they reach the House of Commons), and that the new urban left within the Labour Party in the 1980s has produced a series of politicians of national stature, for instance David Blunkett, former leader of Sheffield City Council and former Home Secretary, and Keith Vaz, involved for a long time in Leicester politics and minister for Europe in the first Blair government. See Seyd, 1987, for detailed studies of the careers of new urban left politicians.

15 On the politics of the abolition of the GLC, see Desmond King, 1989.

16 The extensive literature on racial American cities shows very clearly that policies favourable to minorities are closely related to increasing representation in councils. For an extensive review, see Judd and Swanstrom, 1998, pp. 396–402.

17 See figures on a selection of London boroughs and provincial cities on the Operation Black Vote (OBV) website: http://www.obv.org.uk/blackpolitician/.

18 One of the best analysts of the political participation of ethnic minorities in Britain, Michel le Lohé, argues convincingly that the electoral system, the small size of electoral areas and residential concentration are three main factors in explaining why ethnic minority populations have a chance of being represented by politicians of their ethnic origin in representative institutions (Le Lohé, 1998, p. 77).

3   THE FRENCH POLICY FRAMEWORK: PLANNED MIGRATION, XENOPHOBIC POLITICS AND DURABLE POLITICAL EXCLUSION

1   This rule applies in its general form to foreign parents not born in France, common examples being Moroccan or Portuguese parents; in such cases, the child has the possibility of abandoning French nationality in the six months preceding his/her majority at the age of 18 years. The rule applies differently to children born in France of parents born in Algeria before 1962, because the

latter were born French before becoming Algerian at that time. In such cases, the child has dual nationality and cannot renounce his/her French nationality (Weil, 2002, p. 317n. 8). This is an important point because it has since contributed to making the identity crisis of many Algerian second generations particularly acute, forcing them to accept the nationality of their host country, which in many cases their parents fought to abandon.

2   There were numerous strikes in car plants in the 1970s, particularly Renault in 1975 and 1976 (Wihtol de Wenden, 1988, p. 216), and the strikes in the Talbot factories in the early 1980s mobilized North African workers over issues of prayer facilities at the workplace.

3   They have predominantly leaned towards the left when they have voted, although there is also Beur support for the right and even in some instances for the far right (Leveau, 2000).

4   Wihtol de Wenden (1988, p. 92) calls the situation 'l'échec de l'immigration contrôlée' ('the failure of controlled immigration', and Weil (1995a, p. 91) terms it 'l'échec de la planification des entrées' ('the failure of planned entry flows').

5   As early as 1945 Georges Mauco feared the 'sanitary, social and moral risks' posed by a possible Algerian mass migration. Alfred Sauvy, a noted demographer also closely involved with the drafting of the 1945 legislation, equally foresaw that a rise in Algerian migration could be made possible by the potential granting of freedom of movement (Weil, 1995a, p. 93).

6   Incidentally led by Pierre Mauroy, the mayor of Lille from 1973 to 2001.

7   The Union de Défense de la France (UDF) is a union of small centre-right parties; the Rassemblement pour la République (RPR) is the Gaullist party, led by Jacques Chirac since its creation in the 1970s, which fused with smaller parties in 2000 to become the Union pour la Majorité Présidentielle (UMP).

8   Figures from Weil, 1995a, appendix, based on INSEE data.

9   'L'évolution est renforcée par Laurent Fabius, déclarant que le Front National pose de "vraies questions" mais leur donne "de fausses réponses"' (Bouamama, 1994, p. 155).

10 Who was in this instance fighting his own government, in one of the most confrontational episodes of the first period of cohabitation.

11 A female Muslim high school student refused to remove her Islamic headscarf when entering the school. The headmaster expelled her, arguing that wearing the scarf breached the principle of *laïcité* (loosely translated as secularism, although it indicates a stricter separation of church and state) and created a dangerous precedent. In the ensuing scandal public opinion was divided, but advocates of the headmaster's attitude won the support of the media and the country's academic elite, who argued that no exception should be made to the principle of *laïcité* for Muslims.

12 'Pensez-vous que l'heure du consensus sur l'immigration est arrivée?' 'Je l'espère. Sans doute, lorsque j'étais au gouvernement, n'ai-je pas toujours contribué à ce consensus, mais la gauche y a aussi mis du sien. Aujourd'hui, le climat est plus propice pour que soit définie une politique qui aurait le soutien d'une grande majorité de Français. [. . .] J'admets qu'il a, d'une certaine manière, décrispé les choses en matière d'immigration en s'inspirant des propositions du rapport de Patrick Weil.'

13 *Lutte contre les discriminations: faire respecter les principes d'égalité* (my translation).
14 Depending on the criteria used, as explained by the author of the statistics, posted on the website users.skynet.be/suffrage-universel/fr/frmielre.htm.

4 BIRMINGHAM, 1980S–2001: INNER-CITY LABOUR POLITICS AND PLURI-ETHNIC GOVERNMENT

1 Principally the *Birmingham Post* and the *Evening Mail*, the two daily newspapers in Birmingham, consulted at the Birmingham Central Library or in the personal press files given by some interviewees. These sources have been used with caution because of the partisanship of their coverage of local affairs, largely sensation-alist and generally critical of Labour's management of race relations. My use of the press has mostly been confined to the reproduction of interview excerpts or of hard facts. Analyses or comments have been left aside except when they might themselves be the object of analysis.

2 This area covers the territory of the former West Midlands County Council established in 1974, abolished in 1986, but which remains in use as a basis for statistics.

3 For more on the history of Birmingham, see Briggs, 1952, and Sutcliffe and Smith, 1974.

4 The National Exhibition Centre/International Conference Centre is a major exhibition and conference centre on the periphery of the city.

5 'Black' and 'Asian' are categories which have been commonly used in Britain since the 1960s to refer to ethnic minorities. 'Black' refers to populations origi-nating from the West Indies and Africa, and tends increasingly to be replaced by the terms 'African-Caribbean' or 'Black African'. 'Asian' refers to people from Pakistan, India and Bangladesh.

6 Modood, Berthoud et al. note in the 1997 PSI survey: 'The figure shows that the period 1982 to 1994 was one of structural change and that all groups, though in differing degrees, participated in this change. The main change is an upward occupational shift. In 1982, a fifth of white and Asian male employees who were in work were in the top employment category. In 1994, it was over a quarter, though with whites overtaking the African-Asians. The Caribbeans and Indians, starting from a much lower base, have roughly doubled their representation in the top category of employees, but the mobility of Pakistani employees has been more modest and for Bangladeshis it may even have been proportionately down-wards' (Modood, Berthoud et al., 1997, p. 138).

7 In May 1948, a house where Indians were staying was stoned by a crowd of 200 white men; by that time Indian guests had been banned from certain hotels, and a campaign organized in cooperation with the borough Labour Party had aroused some hostility (Sutcliffe and Smith, 1974, p. 364).

8 From John Darragh, *Colour and Conscience*, 1957, p. 21, quoted by Sutcliffe and Smith, 1974, p. 371.

9 For more details on anti-immigrant organizations at the time, see Foot, 1965.

10   In the autumn of 1960, the *Birmingham Evening Dispatch* attached a note to its correspondence columns stating that 'letters on the racial problem in Birmingham have produced the heaviest mailbag for some considerable time' (*Birmingham Evening Dispatch*, 14/10/60). The letters published by Birmingham papers also accounted for half of the newspaper clippings received by the Institute of Race Relations (IRR) on subjects related to race in October 1960 (Hill and Issacharoff, 1971, p. 50).

11   The overall project was of massive proportions, even by Birmingham's standards, and included turning the area around the old industrial canals in the city centre into pedestrian zones, building a complex of hotels, convention centre and museum around a plaza next to the council house, and tearing down and rebuilding the old Bull Ring shopping centre erected in the 1960s. Construction work lasted throughout the 1990s and was completed in the early 2000s.

12   The Handsworth riots in 1985 (in the northwestern part of the inner city). There was also sporadic urban unrest in Huddersfield in the north of England in the mid-1980s (for details, see Gaffney, 1987).

13   The report noted that more than a quarter of all disciplinary inquiries involved ethnic minority staff.

14   The McPherson report explored the botched enquiry by London's Metropolitan Police into the murder of a young man of African descent, Stephen Lawrence. It concluded that there was persistent and pervasive racism against blacks and Asians at all levels of the police, prompting local authorities across Britain to review their anti-discrimination policies and inspiring the 2000 Race Relations (Amendment) Act.

15   Adolino found that a large majority of the councillors of ethnic minority background that she interviewed considered traditional forms of political participation as highly effective: 74.7 per cent for running for elected office, 77.3 per cent for voting and 74.8 for joining political parties. By contrast, around only 8 to 40 per cent considered non-traditional forms of participation as effective (attending mass demonstrations, joining in boycotts, occupying buildings or factories/sit-ins, joining in wildcat strikes, etc.).

16   A largely honorific role.

17   In fact many of the white, outer-city wards captured from the Conservatives by Labour in the 1980s had only remained Conservative after 1984 because of the Falkland war and the subsequent upsurge of Margaret Thatcher's popularity. These were marginal wards in the 1986 local election that only needed a 0.14 per cent swing to Labour. They were: Brandwood, Perry Barr, Selly Oak and Bournville. The wards of Acocks Green, Erdington, Hodge Hill, Sandwell and Sheldon, mostly outer-city wards with the exception of Sandwell, were also considered marginal in that election (*Birmingham Post*, 24/4/86).

18   But he left the Conservatives to join Labour in February 2000 because of the right-wing drift of William Hague's leadership. His departure further reinforced Labour's domination of the ethnic minority political networks ('Labour joy as Tory defects', *Evening Mail*, 28/2/00).

19   The leader at the time, Dick Knowles (Labour), standing in his Sparkbrook ward, won by only 442 votes against the South Asian Conservative A. U. Hassan (Back and Solomos, 1994, p. 161).

20 'One leading Tory said he was concerned that members of the city's white under-class were being neglected', *Birmingham Post*, 31/12/96.

21 For instance because they encouraged money to be spent on wasteful projects, such as providing email access to local Pakistani women who 'probably have better things to do' (interview with Conservative councillor, 22/6/99).

22 The city council has recognized the Irish category since the mid-1980s, includ-ing it in its staff and population monitoring activities and creating an Irish group within the Standing Consultative Forum (SCF).

23 Labour went down from 70 seats to 65 out of 117, while the Conservatives obtained 45 seats. At the same time, however, the number of ethnic minority councillors was in the middle of its ascending curve, with three new councillors elected that year.

24 This was part of a more general scaling down of all left-wing policies, which also involved abolishing the committee for women's rights and replacing all left-wing heads of committees with more moderate councillors.

25 Indeed, he was accused by several individuals and community leaders inter-viewed of favouring the attribution of council grants to Asian organizations in preference to African-Caribbean organizations (he was himself of Asian back-ground).

26 A complete description of the styles of community organization of the two groups in 1970s Handsworth can be found in Rex and Tomlinson, 1979, ch. 8, pp. 240–74.

27 For detailed analysis of the role of black-led churches in bringing generations of African-Caribbeans to community leadership and political participation in British cities, see Johnston, 1988a, b.

28 *Directory of Black and Ethnic Minority Organizations in Birmingham*, Race Relations Unit, Birmingham City Council, 1995.

29 For a historical perspective on Asian associations, see John King, 1994.

30 The *Directory of Black and Ethnic Minority Organizations in Birmingham* published by the city council also gives a long list of ethnic minority organizations, among which Muslim and Pakistani organizations feature prominently.

31 This also applies to most British cities. Michel le Lohé argues that three main factors explaining why ethnic minority populations have a chance of being rep-resented by politicians of their ethnic origin in representative institutions are the electoral system, the small size of electoral areas, and residential concentration (Le Lohé, 1998, p. 77).

32 This model is based on Solomos and Back's account of developments in the late 1970s and early 1980s (Solomos and Back, 1995, pp. 67–76; on the 1970s see also Rex and Tomlinson, 1979, ch. 8).

33 These three constituencies existed until the 1997 general election, when Spark-brook and Small Heath were grouped together to form the new Sparkbrook and Small Heath constituency.

34 Solomos and Back summarize their analysis of early 1980s developments with two points: (1) MPs' difficulty in defending their position led to an increase in black participation in the party, and (2) an 'instrumental form of politics emerged where MPs secured their position while an elite group of black activists could

influence the distribution of local resources, services and representation to state bureaucracies' (1995, p. 76).

35   S. Goss, *Local Labour and Local Government* (Edinburgh, Edinburgh University Press, 1988), pp. 20–1, 79, quoted by Seyd and Whiteley (1992, p. 16).

36   As recently as 1999, an African-Caribbean councillor is noted by an interviewee as having brought around 100 new black members to his branch (interview with city councillor, 7/06/99).

37   Former activists mention that black and Asian members were systematically confined to the role of spectators during meetings, then told who to vote for at the end (Solomos and Back, 1995, pp. 74–5).

38   Solomos and Back note this trend but they remark that it did not ultimately attain a significant level of influence in the council, and that it was not directly responsible for the increase in the number of black councillors in the mid-1980s. For them, this increase is associated with the relative weakness of the left of the party in the city: it struggled to compete with the right and to become a significant force in the city. In the end, they argue, the controversies initiated by the left sparked off long-term changes, but immediately resulted in defeats, and may even have provided the right with an opportunity to rein in undisciplined supporters (Solomos and Back, 1995, p. 80).

39   Notably, in 1986, a vote was organized in the Labour group to oust Stewart from the group. She was later reinstated (interview with city councillor, 9/11/98 and city council leader, 8/1/99).

40   Respectively through the following unions: UCW (Kazi), TGWU (Hussain), GMB (Manku), GTWU (Ellahi) and EPDU (Lal) (interviews).

41   Information on local selection procedures provided by a Birmingham Labour Party officer, interviewed 14/06/99.

42   However, invoking anti-discrimination legislation against selection procedures remained controversial and was disputed within the party (*Birmingham Post*, 30/06/99).

43   See the detailed account of the episode given by Solomos and Back, 1995, pp. 81–91.

44   He was accused of having formulated his accusations on a Channel 4 TV programme: 'Labour TV film fury, Hattersley denial in "black sections" row', *Evening Mail*, 17/9/85.

45   Another black councillor, Philip Murphy, was expelled from the city council's Labour group by its moderate leadership for attending a meeting favourable to the black section, but he was reinstated shortly afterwards and his case drew less attention (interviews with city councillors 9/11/98, 10/11/98).

46   A tract distributed in the West Midlands Labour Party in 1986 entitled 'Campaign for Labour Party Democracy' listed a series of such purges, in Liverpool and London, and linked them to the party leadership's resistance to the empowerment of minorities and women in the party's structure (biographical and political information of individuals involved from the leaflet 'Campaign for the Reinstatement of Amir Khan and Kevin Scally, Appeal to Secretaries of All Labour Party Organizations').

47   The leaflet entitled 'Campaign for the Reinstatement of Amir Khan and Kevin Scally' also mentioned the following party figures, among others, as supporting

proponents of black sections: Margaret Beckett MP, David Blunkett, Paul Boateng, Tony Benn MP, Ken Livingstone, Peter Hain, Clare Short MP, Keith Vaz.

48 The number of minority councillors with chairs or vice-chairs of council committees culminated at nine in 1994 compared with just four in 1986 or 1987: Saeed Abdi (Handsworth, joint consultative committee), Nam Dev Bagla (Soho, commercial services), Egbert Carliss (Aston, vice-chair of housing), Najma Hafeez (Fox Hollies, chair of social services), Mohammed Kazi (Handsworth, chair of the race relations sub-committee of community affairs, vice-chair of the National Exhibition Centre and International Convention Centre), Khalid Mahmood (Sparkbrook, chair of the race relations sub-committee of community affairs), Abdul Rashid (Small Heath, vice-chair of personnel), Bhagat Sing (chair of joint consultative committee) and Sybil Spence (Soho, vice-chair of social services).

49 The competition for selection was intense because of boundary changes made in the constituencies of Birmingham's inner city after the 1992 elections (Geddes, 1998, p. 164).

50 The Labour constituency of Perry Barr (in the northwestern part of the inner city) did ultimately select an Asian candidate for the 2001 parliamentary election, Khalid Mahmood, who was easily elected and became one of the few Asian MPs in the House of Commons.

51 In the words of Abbas Malik, Birmingham correspondent for the Asian newspaper the *Daily Jang*, quoted by the *Birmingham Post*, 9/5/98.

52 Car manufacturer Rover operates a large plant in this area situated on the southern periphery of the city. The struggle to save the plant from closure included heavy financial support from central government and made the headlines in the national press in 2000.

5 LILLE, 1980S–2001: MACHINE POLITICS AND EXCLUSION OF MINORITIES IN THE FRENCH MUNICIPAL SYSTEM

1 For comprehensive overviews of the French local system, see among others Mény, 1985; Mabileau, 1985a, 1994; Biarez, 1989; and the special issue of *Pouvoirs* on decentralization (1992).

2 A report by the Groupe d'Études et de Lutte contre les Discriminations (GELD, 2001) shows that immigrants in France are systematically victims of various forms of racial discrimination when looking for housing. The report also shows that governments' official policy line since the late 1970s, *mixité sociale* (social mix), which encourages the mixture of populations of varied social – and implicitly ethnic – background in neighbourhoods and housing projects, has had the perverse effect of reinforcing minorities' overall concentration in undesirable areas. See also the special issue of the sociology journal *Sociétés Contemporaines*, 'Immigration et Politique de l'Habitat', 33–4 (January/April 1999), and De Rudder, 1992.

3 Roubaisians would dispute being called a suburb of Lille, but they are quick to denounce Lille's political domination over them.

4 Perhaps partly because Charles de Gaulle was born in Lille.

5 The history presented here is necessarily short and focused on the main points; a more detailed account can be found in Poinsot, 1994, pp. 562–94 (appendix 2: 'Une Monographie Lilloise: Histoire et Situation Socio-économique de l'Immigration').

6 The Nord region is a grouping of the *départements* of the Nord and the Pas-de-Calais.

7 For detailed histories of the area, see Giblin-Delvallet, 1987, 1990, 1992; and Codaccioni et al., 1977.

8 Data from the 1990 INSEE census. Lille had 172,138 inhabitants in 1990, but it absorbed the neighbouring town of Lomme, population around 40,000, in 1999, reaching the figure of 212,000 inhabitants in 2001.

9 In contrast to British statistics, French statistics do not include 'ethnic' categories as such. Instead, the only statistics available are those for nationality. These include all first-generation migrants, who as a rule are not given French citizenship, but exclude those who have been naturalized; most importantly, they exclude second-generation immigrants, who in many cases have French nationality and who now constitute an important part of the ethnic minority population. These figures are used here in the absence of more accurate data, but it must be stressed that the French figures are as a result very largely underestimated compared to British figures.

10 Direction Générale du Développement Urbain (1995).

11 But the move backfired on the Socialists in that election, largely because Socialist voters did not bother to vote in unusually high numbers (*Nord-Éclair*, 19/03/01; Laurent in Dolez and Laurent, 2002, pp. 216–18).

12 Data on residential concentrations of foreigners in this paragraph, unless otherwise stated, are drawn from Ville de Lille, 1998.

13 In addition, the disposable income per capita was the lowest in France for a city of more than 100,000; 10 per cent of children aged 11 had resat a class at least twice, against 3 per cent nationwide (*Le Figaro*, 20/02/01).

14 Quoted in *Le Figaro*, 20/2/01, p. 8, my translation. RMI (*revenu minimum d'insertion*) is a small allocation made by *départements* to individuals who have no other source of income.

15 Statistics from *Les Évolutions Sociales à Lille-Sud, Agence de Développement et d'Urbanisme de Lille Métropole*, report commissioned by the public housing agency Lille-Métropole-habitat, quoted by *Libération* 24/05/00.

16 In the early 1990s, three quarters of the respondents to a survey carried out by a local association in Lille-Sud cited drug dealing as their number one preoccupation and supported the initiative of the local boxing club, Les Gants d'Argent (The Silver Gloves), in undertaking punitive expeditions against dealers. The second most important preoccupation was unemployment ('La drogue et l'emploi en tête de toutes les préoccupations', *La Voix du Nord*, 24/11/92).

17 Protest against the established consensus also existed among the left, but it was less radical and disruptive. The Communist Party suffered a dramatic loss of influence in the city over the last decades and now attracts no more than around 7 per cent of the vote. The Greens are more powerful, reaching averages of 10

to 15 per cent in municipal elections since 1983; they bargain their support in the second round by demanding positions as adjuncts and more environmental and social policies, but so far they have not radically challenged the main policy directions of the municipality.

18 In the first round of the 1988 presidential election, the FN's candidate Jean-Marie Le Pen obtained 16.5 per cent of the vote in Lille, against 17.6 per cent for Raymond Barre and 17.3 per cent for Jacques Chirac, the RPR candidate (Etchebarne, 1996, p. 298).

19 The three polling stations that produced the highest score for the FN were located in the middle of Lille-Sud: booth nos. 608, 609 and 611, at respectively 19.51 per cent, 24.41 per cent and 20.19 per cent (Ville de Lille, 1998).

20 In 1989, Mauroy won in the second round against Turk by 53.86 per cent to 46.14 per cent (Ville de Lille, 1998); in 1995, Mauroy won only because of the FN's participation in the third round, as noted above.

21 The policy line of the *préfecture du Nord* in 1998 was that the youth and poverty of the Nord's population required a continuation and extension in the area of the *politique de la ville* programmes begun in the early 1980s (Département du Nord, 1998).

22 Though this was just starting to change, with Jospin's government taking some initiatives against racial discrimination with a government report published in April 1999 by the *conseiller d'état* (top administrative judge and government counsel) Jean-Michel Bélorgey (*Le Monde*, 7/4/99).

23 There were accordingly few North African candidates in both the 1989 and the 1995 elections. In 1995 there were just five, two on the Socialist list, who were elected, one on the Gaullist list, one on the Green list and one on an independent leftist list.

24 Interviews with elected officials and city council officers, 5/1/99, 6/4/99, 23/3/00, 13/7/99, 30/9/98 and 7/4/99.

25 The term 'youth' is widely used in France to designate young men from disadvantaged backgrounds, generally from public housing blocks (*cités*) and of recent immigrant background. Those who have been involved in community activism and politics since the 1980s, and who were still active in the 1990s and early 2000s, are still often called 'youths' even though they are in many cases reaching their forties.

26 On the importance of the mayor in shaping local political identities in the French political system, see Lefebvre, 1997. Several images have been used to emphasize the centrality and omnipotence of the French mayor in cities: for instance, on French 'municipal monarchism', see Mabileau, 1985b, and on the 'presidentialism' of French mayors, see Mény, 1995.

27 Examples would be Chirac's and Tibéri's Paris, as well as Chaban-Delmas' Bordeaux, for the Gaullists, and Marseille under Gaston Deferre's rule for the Socialists. Repeated corruption scandals in Paris have exposed the interlinking networks erected by Chirac and his allies between RPR activists, the municipal administration, local associations, companies and other local authorities in the area. This is particularly so for Tibéri's fifth arrondissement.

28 For instance the Jeunes Arabes de Lyon et sa Banlieue (JALB), who have long been vocal critics of SOS Racisme and France Plus for not emphasizing enough the ethnic identity of North Africans in France.

29   This was a prominent proposal in candidate Mitterrand's manifesto for the 1981 presidential election and elicited high hopes among immigrant *milieux*; but it was dropped in 1983 amid growing resistance from various quarters (within the party, in public opinion and among the conventional right opposition). The rise of the Front National in subsequent years completely pushed the idea off the political agenda. It was brought forward again briefly in 1999, without success, by a much broader coalition of mainstream political parties and pressure groups which included the UDF (the federation of centre-right parties), the Communist Party, the Socialist Party and minority rights advocates (*Le Monde*, 29/9/99).

30   For a thorough presentation and discussion of this model by their proponents, see Bouamama, 1991, and Bouamama, Cordeiro and Roux, 1992. For a history of the attempts by Texture to launch a national movement along these lines, see Bouamama, 1994.

31   Notably, its leader Said Bouamama was originally a PhD student in economics at the University of Lille. There has been a tradition of North African students, especially from Morocco, coming to complete graduate degrees in Lille; many have been involved in student politics.

32   ' "Pourquoi les associations ont-elles peu à peu disparu? Parce qu'ici, tout ce qui n'est pas aux ordres du Beffroi est condamné à disparaître", dénonce un animateur, salarié municipal qui tient à garder l'anonymat'; interview given in the wake of the April 2000 riots following the fatal shooting of a youth by the police in Lille-Sud, quoted in *Libération*, 24/04/00.

33   There was talk among Socialist activists in the autumn of 1998 of an increasing number of Moroccan families approaching Socialist adjuncts in Lille over accommodation problems.

34   Elections of representatives to the *conseil general*, a *département*-level assembly.

35   In 2001, the FAS changed name and became the FASILD (Fonds d'Action et de Soutien pour l'Intégration et la Lutte contre les Discriminations).

36   However, a comparison with some American cases shows that institutionalization may also work against ethnic minority incorporation, because some party rules can act as resources for insiders who are trying to prevent outsiders from entering the party.

37   Though it must be noted that this climate started to change in 1999 owing to a combination of national factors: economic growth, the popularity of the Jospin government, division and electoral under-performance of the Front National, and the new-found dynamism of SOS Racisme, which now focused on denouncing cases of racial discrimination in the workplace and in public venues.

38   'La politique? Des batailles de clans entre Bernard Roman et Martine Aubry. Si t'adhères pas à un clan, t'es vraiment tout seul. C'est ce qui m'arrive au conseil de quartier', interview with Djebien, *Liberté Hebdo*, 15–21 January 1999.

39   In the early 1980s, some programmes allocated more funds to schools that had a high proportion of immigrant children (Hargreaves, 1995); and Alain Juppé's government set up a programme of tax incentives in 1995 designed to attract businesses to impoverished areas (*zones franches*).

40   Interviews with the councillor in charge of urban regeneration in Lille-Sud in 1999 and with the city councillor in charge of integration matters are represen-

tative in this respect: when asked, they were unable to state the numbers or locations of such groups in the city.

41 In 2000 these were the mosques in rue de Lannoy, rue du Faubourg de Roubaix, rue d'Arras, rue Pierre Loti, rue du Docteur Yersin and rue Paul Lafargue (Bousetta, 2001, p. 409).

42 Aubry asked for decisions to be taken promptly by the judicial system, so that the youths would not lose faith in institutions ('des décisions rapides de la justice pour que les jeunes gardent confiance dans les institutions', *Le Monde*, 17/04/00).

43 This official noted that while theoretically a member of the *mairie de quartier* (a decentralized branch of the city council), Lasfar hardly ever came to meetings; he also said that the mosque's classes and educational programmes never sought to cooperate with those of the city council (interview with urban regeneration manager, 6/4/99).

44 For more details on the Ligue Islamique du Nord, see Bousetta, 2001, p. 306.

45 As in the rest of France, these community organizations are often Black African. Black African communities have the highest rate of association membership among foreigners living in France; 45 per cent are members of an association compared to 42 per cent for French nationals. By contrast, North Africans have the lowest rates with around 10 per cent (figures from Tribalat, 1995, p. 130).

46 Through much of the 1990s, the key municipal player in the area other than the mayor was Bernard Roman, who was Mauroy's long-time first adjunct and prospective successor before the arrival of Martine Aubry in 1995 removed him from both positions. However, he remained informally in charge of Lille-Sud because he was close to the municipality's traditional working-class Socialist base, of which Lille-Sud was the stronghold. Martine Aubry became particularly active in the neighbouring area of Faubourg de Béthune.

47 He declared in the national weekly *L'Express*: 'en 2001, je me battrai pour que pas une voix des quartiers n'aille au PS' [in 2001, I will fight to take every vote from the neighbourhoods away from the Socialists], quoted in *La Voix du Nord*, 16/1/99.

48 Salah Djebien, interviewed in *Liberté Hebdo*, 15–21 January 1999.

49 Reported in *La Voix du Nord*, 31/5/93, my translation.

50 The 2001 municipal elections did not indicate such a change, but it may yet happen.

6 ROUBAIX, 1980S–2001: INCLUSION THROUGH NEIGHBOURHOOD GROUPS AND AN OPEN MUNICIPAL GAME

1 Jules Guesdes, quoted by Piat, 1981, p. 43.

2 My account of Roubaix's history is based primarily on Piat, 1981; Hilaire, 1984; and Florin, 1985.

3 To the extent that an official document from the city council characterizes the city as an example of 'durable non-development': 'No coherent urban develop-

ment plan, no real city centre, a lack of urban quality, an old and insanitary housing stock and a poorly trained population' (Observatoire Urbain de Roubaix, 1998, p. 4, my translation).

4 An indication of this is that in 1998, the number of jobs in Roubaix (45,000) was higher than the number of inhabitants employed or seeking a job (38,000) (Observatoire Urbain de Roubaix, 1998, p. 10).

5 Bataille, 1994, p. 51, notes that six of Roubaix's seven collèges are classified as ZEPs (*zones d'éducations prioritaires*), which are disadvantaged schools for which extra funds are earmarked by the ministry of education. Observatoire Urbain de Roubaix, 1998, pp. 6–13, has an exhaustive list of negative social economic indicators.

6 For a history of Roubaix's housing and the decay of its housing stock, see Cornuel and Duriez, 1986.

7 *Habitations à loyers modérés*, low-rent housing part controlled by city councils and part independent.

8 All figures on residential concentrations of foreigners in this paragraph are taken from Ville de Roubaix, *Vade Mecum: exploitation du recensement par quartier*, Roubaix, based on the 1990 INSEE data.

9 Campaign leaflet of Jean-Pierre Gendron (Front National) for the first round of the 1989 municipal election, my translation.

10 In his report, Bataille notes that ethnicity should be understood as a harmonious combination of three elements that were recurrent among the youths of Roubaix of recent immigrant background: protest against the degradation of the conditions of daily life, respect of certain fundamental traits such as religion, and demands for political representation (Bataille, 1994, p. 81, my translation).

11 The then Socialist government also organized the Assises de la Citoyenneté, a national meeting with concerned associations, in Paris on 18 and 19 March 2000 to consult over potential anti-discrimination policies (*Libération*, 20/03/00).

12 At the seminar 'Discrimination et Emploi, Normes et Réalités', Centre des Archives du Monde du Travail, Roubaix, 30–31 March.

13 The APU was very influential in the early 1980s, encouraging similar experiments in participative politics in other parts of the city and reinforcing the culture of neighbourhood participation that already existed in the city. For details on the politics of the APU, see Hatzfeld, 1986.

14 Marie Féraud, *Histoires Maghrébines vues de France* (Paris: Karthala, 1985).

15 Both quotes from Verfaillie, 1996, p. 38, my translation.

16 Cantonal elections are elections to the Conseil Général (the assembly that manages the *département*) and are fought in cross-commune districts, the cantons. They are less publicized and attended to by voters than municipal elections, which makes it all the more remarkable that ethnic minority voters, who tend to have higher rates of abstention than others, should bother to come out and vote in noticeable numbers when the candidate is of North African background.

17 See Giblin-Delvallet, 1990, ch. 10, 'Roubaix dans la main des patrons du textile', under the section headed 'La précocité du diagnostic'.

18 This was also the case in many other cities in the region, including Lille. However, nowhere did it have as lasting an impact as in Roubaix. In Lille, the Catholic heritage faded away in the 1960s, and the void left has been filled by the Socialist Party and urban regeneration programmes.

19 Research based on the mayor's archives from the 1930s reveals that a large proportion of the mayor's post-bag came from foreigners living in the city, asking for help in finding jobs and accommodation, and that the mayor's office was often very assiduous in providing help by accelerating administrative procedures (De Barros, 2000, p. 133).

20 Sociologist Philippe Bataille notes in his report: 'In Roubaix, all economic indicators point to the gravity of the crisis in the last ten years. The risk of riots increases daily. Yet these situations have always been controlled, precisely because in this town there are political and institutional actors who have spared no effort to maintain active contact with the youths who are victims of the crisis' (Bataille, 1994, pp. 7–8, my translation).

21 For extensive analyses of the instrumentalization of territorial identities in Roubaix by the current mayor, see Lefebvre, 1997, 'Être maire à Roubaix: la prise de rôle d'un héritier' ('Being a mayor in Roubaix: an heir learns his role').

22 As shown by the names of the largest and best established, which each refer to a particular neighbourhood: Loisirs Saint Michel, Hommelet Sport et Culture, Association Sportive et Culturelle Cartigny-Oran.

23 The importance of neighbourhoods as a basis for the creation of communities in French cities is often noted by French sociologists and anthropologists; on Roubaix, see Neveu, 1998; for an anthropological point of view, see Abélès, 1991.

24 Independent associations which run community centres in deprived neighbourhoods, offering leisure and educational activities to the area's inhabitants.

25 The municipality maintains a balanced relationship with the *centres sociaux*, with municipal representatives on their boards but no overwhelming control over them, as codified by a charter in 1997 (interview with urban regeneration manager).

26 See Neveu, 1998, p. 216, concerning the relationship between the young leaders of the FAJ with the *comités de quartier*.

27 As confirmed by the increase in the number elected as city councillors in the 2001 municipal elections.

28 Indeed, with 17.9 per cent of the vote going to the FN list in the first round, they proved impossible to ignore.

29 Although many of the youths in Roubaix are of Harki background as well.

30 Harkis are Algerians who fought on the French side in the war of Algerian independence (1954–62) and who subsequently fled Algeria to take refuge in France. Harkis are traditionally supporters of the right in French politics.

31 A newspaper article in 1998 proclaimed: 'Zora Zarouri: the delegation to women's rights is not just a gimmick' (*Nord-Éclair*, 21/02/98, my translation).

32 Which required all parties to present at least 50 per cent women candidates.

CONCLUSION

1 The 2001 municipal elections confirmed this trend, with the low-income vote for the Socialists showing new signs of erosion (*Le Monde*, 21/03/01)

Bibliography

Abélès, Marc, 1991, *Quiet Days in Burgundy: A Study of Local Politics*, Cambridge University Press, Cambridge.

Adolino, Jessica, 1998, *Ethnic Minorities, Electoral Politics and Political Integration in Britain*, Pinter, London and Washington.

Anwar, Muhammad, 1979, *The Myth of Return*, Heinemann, London.

——, 1980, *Votes and Policies: Ethnic Minorities and the General Election 1979*, Research Report, Commission for Racial Equality, London.

——, 1986, *Race and Politics: Ethnic Minorities in the British Political System*, Tavistock, London.

——, 1990, 'Ethnic minorities and the electoral process: Some recent developments', in Harry Goulbourne, ed., *Black Politics in Britain*, Gower, Aldershot, pp. 33–47.

——, 1991, 'Ethnic minority representation: Voting and electoral politics in Britain', in Muhammad Anwar and Pnina Werbner, eds, *Black and Ethnic Leaderships: The Cultural Dimension of Political Action*, Routledge, London and New York, pp. 41–62.

——, 1994, *Race and Elections: The Participation of Ethnic Minorities in Politics*, Centre for Research in Ethnic Relations, University of Warwick, Coventry.

——, 1998, *Ethnic Minorities and the British Electoral System: A Research Project*, Centre for Research in Ethnic Relations, University of Warwick and Operation Black Vote, Coventry.

—— and Pnina Werbner, eds, 1991, *Black and Ethnic Leaderships: The Cultural Dimension of Political Action*, Routledge, London and New York.

Ashford, Douglas, 1982, *French Pragmatism and British Dogmatism: Central–Local Policy-making in the Welfare State*, Allen and Unwin, London.

Bachman, Christian, and Nicole Le Guennec, 1996, *Violences urbaines: ascension et chute des classes moyennes à travers cinquante ans de politique de la ville*, Albin Michel, Paris.

Back, Les, and John Solomos, 1994, 'Labour and racism: Trade unions and the selection of parliamentary candidates', *Sociological Review*, 42(2), pp. 165–201.

Ball, Wendy, and John Solomos, eds, 1990a, *Race and Local Politics*, Macmillan, London.

——, 1990b, 'Racial equality and local politics', in Wendy Ball and John Solomos, eds, *Race and Local Politics*, Macmillan, London.

Balme, Richard, 1987, 'La participation aux associations et le pouvoir municipal: capacités et limites de mobilisation par les associations culturelles dans les communes de banlieue', *Revue Française de Sociologie*, 27(4), pp. 601–40.

——, Alain Faure and Albert Mabileau, eds, 1999, *Les Nouvelles Politiques locales: dynamiques de l'action publique*, Presses de Sciences Po, Paris.

Barnekov, Timothy, Robin Boyle and Daniel Rich, 1989, *Privatism and Urban Policy in Britain and the United States*, Oxford University Press, Oxford.

Bataille, Philippe, 1994, *Diagnostic du Schéma Local d'Intégration de la Ville de Roubaix*, FAS/État/Mairie de Roubaix, Roubaix.

——, 1997, *Le Racisme au travail*, La Découverte, Paris.

Battegay, Alain, 1990, 'La déstabilisation des associations Beurs en région Rhône-Alpes', *Hommes et Migrations*, 49, pp. 104–13.

Beazley, Michael, and Patrick Loftman, 1998, *Race and Regeneration: A Review of the Single Regeneration Budget*, Local Government Information Unit, London.

Beetham, David, 1970, *Transport and Turbans: A Comparative Study of Local Politics*, Oxford University Press, London.

Ben Tovim, Gideon, John Gabriel, Ian Law and Catherine Streddler, 1986, *The Local Politics of Race*, Macmillan, Basingstoke and London.

Biarez, Sylvie, 1989, *Le Pouvoir local*, Economica, Paris.

Birmingham City Council, 1991, *Facing the Challenge in Birmingham*, East Birmingham City Challenge, Economic Development Department, Birmingham.

Bleich, Erik, 1997, *Changing the Natives: Anti-discrimination Legislation in Britain and France*, paper prepared for the Centre d'Études des Politiques d'Immigration et de Citoyenneté research workshop, Institut d'Études Politiques de Paris, 2 April, Paris.

——, 2003, *Race Politics in Britain and France: Ideas and Policymaking since the 1960s*, Cambridge University Press, Cambridge.

Bleitrach, Danielle, Jean Lojkine, Ernest Oary, Roland Delacroix and Christian Mahieu, 1981, *Classe ouvrière et social-démocratie: Lille et Marseille*, Éditions Sociales, Paris.

Bobo, Lawrence, and Franklin D. Gilliam, Jr, 1990, 'Race, sociopolitical participation, and black empowerment', *American Political Science Review*, 84(2).

Boddy, Colin, and Martin Fudge, 1984, *Local Socialism? Labour Councils and New Left Alternatives*, Macmillan, Basingstoke and London.

Body-Gendrot, Sophie, 2000, *The Social Control of Cities: A Comparative Perspective*, Blackwell, Oxford and Malden, Mass.

——, Bernard D'Hellencourt and Michel Rancoule, 1989, 'La législation sur l'immigration en France, au Royaume-Uni et aux USA', *Revue Française de Science Politique*, 39(1), pp. 50–74.

——and Martin Schain, 1992, 'National and local politics in the development of immigration policy in the US and France: A comparative analysis', in Daniel

Horowitz and Gérard Noiriel, eds, *Immigrants in Two Polities: French and American Experiences*, New York University Press, New York, pp. 411–38.

—— and Marco Martiniello, eds, 2000, *Minorities in European Cities: The Dynamics of Social Integration and Social Exclusion at the Neighbourhood Level*, Macmillan, Basingstoke and London.

—— and Catherine Wihtol de Wenden, 2003, *Police et discriminations raciales: le tabou français*, Éditions de l'Atelier/Éditions Ouvrières, Paris.

Bouamama, Said, 1991, *Vers une nouvelle citoyenneté*, La Boîte de Pandore, Liège.

——, 1994, *Dix ans de marches des Beurs: chronique d'un mouvement avorté*, Deslée de Brouwer, Seuil, Paris.

——, Albano Cordeiro and Michel Roux, 1992, *La Citoyenneté dans tous ses états, de l'immigration à la citoyenneté*, CIEMI/L'Harmattan, Paris.

Bousetta, Hassan, 1997, 'Citizenship and political participation in France and the Netherlands: Reflections on two local cases', *New Community*, 23(3), pp. 215–31.

——, 2000, 'Institutional theories of immigrant ethnic mobilization: Relevance and limitations', *Journal of Ethnic and Migration Studies*, 26(2), pp. 229–45.

——, 2001, *Immigration, Post-immigration Politics and the Political Mobilization of Ethnic Minorities: A Comparative Case Study of Moroccans in Four European Cities*, Doctoral Dissertation, Catholic University, Brussels.

Briggs, Asa, 1952, *History of Birmingham*, Oxford University Press, London.

Browning, Rufus P., Dale Rogers Marshall and David H. Tabb, 1984, *Protest is Not Enough: The Struggle of Blacks and Hispanics for Equality in Urban Politics*, University of California Press, Berkeley.

——, 1990, *Racial Politics in American Cities*, Longman, White Plains, NY.

——, 1997, *Racial Politics in American Cities*, 2nd edition, Longman, White Plains, NY.

Brubaker, Rogers, 1992, *Citizenship and Nationhood in France and Germany*, Harvard University Press, Cambridge, Mass.

Bruyelle, Pierre, 1993, *La Communauté Urbaine de Lille, Métropole du Nord-Pas-de-Calais*, Cahier de la Documentation Française no. 4936, Documentation Française, Paris.

Bulpitt, Jim, 1986, 'Continuity, autonomy and peripheralization: The anatomy of the centre's race statecraft in England', in Zig Layton-Henry and Paul Rich, eds, *Race, Government and Politics*, Macmillan, London, pp. 17–44.

Carter, Bob, Clive Harris and Shirley Joshi, 1987, 'The 1951–1955 Conservative government and the racialization of black immigration', *Immigrants and Minorities*, 6(3).

Cashmore, Ellis, 1992, 'The new black bourgeoisie', *Human Relations*, 45(12), pp. 1241–58.

Castles, Stephen, 1995, 'How nations respond to immigration and ethnic diversity', *New Community*, 21(3), July, pp. 293–308.

——, and Godula Kozack, 1973, *Immigrant Workers and Class Structure in Western Europe*, Oxford University Press/Institute of Race Relations, London.

Césari, Jocelyne, 1993, 'Les leaders associatifs issus de l'immigration maghrébine: intermédiaires ou clientèles?', *Horizons Maghrébins*, special issue, 'Le Droit à la mémoire, élites maghrébines de France', 20/21, pp. 80–95.

——, ed., 1998, *Musulmans et républicains, les jeunes, l'Islam et la France*, Complexe, Paris.

Codaccioni, F., A. Derville, Louis Trenard and Pierre Léman, 1977, *Histoire d'une métropole: Lille, Roubaix, Tourcoing*, Privat, Toulouse.

Cole, Alistair, and Peter John, 1997, 'Urban regimes in Britain and France? The cases of Leeds and Lille', in *Gouvernance locale, pauvreté et exclusion dans les villes anglo-saxonnes, Frontières*, no. 9, Paris, pp. 37–50.

Commissariat Général au Plan, 1988, *Immigrations: le devoir d'insertion*, Government Report, Paris.

Community Relations Commission, 1975, *The Participation of Ethnic Minorities in the General Election of October 1974*, Research Report, London.

Cordeiro, Albano, 1996, 'Pratiques associatives, pratiques citoyennes', *Hommes et Migrations*, 1182, pp. 17–21.

——, 2001, 'Vie associative et action citoyenne', *Hommes et Migrations*, 1229, pp. 1–75.

Cornuel, Daniel, and Bernard Duriez, 1986, *Le Mirage urbain: histoire du logement à Roubaix*, Anthropos, Paris.

Correau, Laurent, 1995, *L'Identité des enfants de mineurs marocains, figures de l'immigration dans le Douaisis*, Mémoire DEA Études Politiques, Université Lille II, Lille.

Crewe, Ivor, 1983, 'Representation and ethnic minorities in Britain', in Nathan Glazer and Ken Young, eds, *Ethnic Pluralism and Public Policy*, London, Heinemann, pp. 258–84.

Cross, Malcolm, and Han Entzinger, eds, 1988, *Lost Illusions: Caribbean Minorities in Britain and the Netherlands*, London, Routledge.

Crowley, John, 1991, 'Ethnicité, nation, et contrat social', in Pierre André Taguieff and G. Delannoi, eds, *Théories du nationalisme*, Kimé, Paris, pp. 178–218.

——, 1992a, 'Consensus et conflit dans la politique de l'immigration et des relations raciales du Royaume-Uni', in Janine Costa-Lascoux and Patrick Weil, eds, *Logiques d'état et immigration*, Kimé, Paris, pp. 73–110.

——, 1992b, 'Immigration, racism, and integration: Recent French writing on immigration and race relations', *New Community*, 19(1), pp. 134–52.

——, 1993, 'Paradoxes in the politicization of race: A comparison of the UK and France', *New Community*, 19(4), pp. 627–43.

——, 1994, *Immigration, 'relations raciales', et mobilisations minoritaires au Royaume Uni*, Thèse de Doctorat, Institut d'Études Politiques de Paris, Paris.

——, and Patrick Weil, 1994, 'Integration in theory and practice: A comparison of France and Britain', *West European Politics*, 94, pp. 110–26.

CUDL, 1990, 'Contrat d'Agglomération de Lille–Roubaix–Tourcoing–Villeneuve d'Asq et de la CUDL', CODRA, Lille.

Deakins, David, and Monder Ram, 1996, 'African-Caribbeans in business', *New Community*, 22(1), pp. 67–84.

De Barros, Françoise, 2000, *Contribution à une sociologie politique des processus de catégorisation des étrangers, l'étranger et le local, genèse d'un débat sur la mixité sociale: la gestion des étrangers par quatre communes durant l'entre-deux-guerres*, Rapport Final pour le PUCA, le Ministère de l'Équipement, des Transports et du Logement et l'Université de la Rochelle, La Rochelle.

De Rudder, Véronique, 1992, 'Immigration, housing and integration in French cities', in Gérard Noiriel and Daniel Horowitz, eds, *Immigrants in Two Polities: French and American Experiences*, New York University Press, New York, pp. 247–67.

——, Christian Poiret and François Vour'ch, 2000, *L'Inégalité raciste: l'universalité républicaine à l'épreuve*, Presses Universitaires de France, Paris.

DiMaggio, Paul, and Walter Powell, 1991, *The New Institutionalism in Organizational Analysis*, University of Chicago Press, Chicago.

Dion, Stéphane, 1986, *La Politisation des mairies*, Economica, Paris.

Dolez and Laurent, 2002, *Le Vote des villes: les élections municipales des 11 et 18 mars 2001*, Presses de Sciences Po, Paris.

Donzelot, Jacques, and Philippe Estebe, 1994, *L'État animateur: essai sur la politique de la ville*, Esprit, Paris.

——, with Catherine Mével and Anne Wyvekens, 2003, *Faire société: la politique de la ville aux États-Unis et en France*, Seuil, Paris.

Dowding, Keith, et al., 1999, 'Regime politics in London local government', *Urban Affairs Review*, 34(4), pp. 515–45.

Dubet, François, Adil Jazouli and Didier Lapeyronnie, 1985, *L'État et les jeunes*, Éditions Ouvrières, Paris.

Dunleavy, Patrick, 1981, *The Politics of Mass Housing in Britain 1945–1975: A Study of Corporate Power and Professional Influence in the Welfare State*, Clarendon Press, Oxford.

Duprez, Dominique, 1997, 'Entre discrimination et désaffiliation: l'expérience des jeunes issus de l'immigration maghrébine', *Annales de la Recherche Urbaine*, 76 (September/October).

——, Michèle Leclerc-Olive and Michel Pinet, 1996, *Vivre ensemble: la diversité des quartiers sensibles à l'épreuve de la vie quotidienne*, Rapport de Recherche, IFRESI/CNRS, Lille.

Duyvendak, Jan Willem, 1995, *The Power of Politics: New Social Movements in France*, Westview, Oxford.

Eade, John, 1989, *The Politics of Community: The Bangladeshi Community in East London*, Gower, Aldershot.

Edwards, J., and R. Batley, 1978, *The Politics of Positive Discrimination: An Evaluation of the Urban Programme, 1967–1977*, Tavistock, London.

Esman, Milton, 1973, 'The management of ethnic conflict', *Public Policy*, 21, pp. 49–78.

Etchebarne, Serge, 1983, 'L'urne et le xénophobe: à propos des élections municipales à Roubaix en mars 1983', *Espace, Population, Société*, 2, pp. 133–8.

——, 1996, 'Le FN dans le Nord ou les logiques d'une implantation electorale', in Nonna Mayer and Pascal Perrineau, eds, *Le Front National à découvert*, Presses de Sciences Po, Paris, pp. 284–306.

FAS, 1997, *Les Schémas Locaux d'Intégration dans la Région Nord-Pas-de-Calais*, Working Paper, Lille.

Favell, Adrian, 1998, *Philosophies of Integration: Immigration and the Idea of Citizenship in France and Britain*, Macmillan, Basingstoke and London.

Feldblum, Myriam, 1993, 'Paradoxes of ethnic politics: The case of Franco-Maghrebis in France', *Ethnic and Racial Studies*, 16(1), pp. 52–73.

Fitzgerald, Marian, 1986, *Section 71 of the Race Relations Act: A Case Study*, Commission for Racial Equality and Ealing Community Relations Council, London.

——, 1987, *Black People and Party Politics in Britain*, Runnymede Trust, London.

——, 1988, 'There is no alternative . . . black people and the Labour Party', *Social Studies Review*, 4(1), pp. 20–3.

——, 1990, 'The emergence of black councillors and MPs in Britain: Some underlying questions', in Harry Goulbourne, ed., *Black Politics in Britain*, Avebury, Aldershot, pp. 17–32.

Florin, Jean-Pierre, 1985, 'Roubaix: 70 ans de socialisme municipal (1912–1983), esquisse d'un bilan, in De Franse Nederlanden', Les Pays-Bas Français.

Foot, Paul, 1965, *Immigration and Race in British Politics*, Penguin, Harmondsworth.

France Plus, 1989, 'Vivre en France toutes générations confondues: le point de vue de France Plus', *Hommes et Migrations*, 1118, pp. 9–12.

Freeman, Gary, 1979, *Immigrant Labor and Racial Conflict in Industrial Societies: The French and British Experience, 1945–1975*, Princeton University Press, Princeton, New Jersey.

Frybes, Marcin, 1992, 'France, un équilibre pragmatique fragile', in Didier Lapeyronnie, *Immigrés en Europe: politiques locales d'intégration*, Documentation Française, Paris.

Gabriel, Oscar W., and Vincent Hoffman-Martinot, 1999, *Démocraties urbaines: l'état de la démocratie dans les grandes villes de 12 pays industrialisés*, L'Harmattan, Paris.

Gaffney, John, 1987, *Interpretations of Violence: The Handsworth Riots of 1985*, Policy Paper in Ethnic Relations no. 10, Centre for Research in Ethnic Relations, University of Warwick.

Garraud, Philippe, 1988, 'La sélection du personnel politique local', *Revue Française de Science Politique*, 38(3), pp. 402–32.

——, 1989, *Profession homme politique: la carrière politique des maires urbains*, L'Harmattan, Paris.

Geddes, Andrew, 1993, 'Asian and African-Caribbean representation in elected local government in England and Wales', *New Community*, 20(1), pp. 43–57.

——, 1998, 'Inequality, political opportunity and ethnic minority parliamentary candidacy', in Saggar Shamit, ed., *Race and British Electoral Politics*, University College Press, London, pp. 145–73.

——, and Virginie Guiraudon, 2002, 'The anti-discrimination policy paradigm in France and the UK: Europeanization and alternative explanations to policy change', in Lionel Arnaud, ed., *Les Minorités ethniques dans l'Union Européenne: politiques et identités*, Final Report of the CNRS programme 'L'Identité Européenne en Question', CRAPE-CNRS, Rennes.

Geisser, Vincent, 1993, 'Les Élus issus de l'immigration maghrébine: l'illusion de médiation politique', *Horizons Maghrébins*, special issue, 'Le Droit à la mémoire, élites maghrébines de France', 20/21, pp. 60 79.

——, 1995, 'Des opérateurs symboliques d'intégration', *Migration*, 27, pp. 15–46.

——, 1997, *Ethnicité républicaine: les élites maghrébines dans le système politique français*, Presses de Sciences Po, Paris.

——, and Paul Oriol, 2001, 'Les Français "d'origine étrangère" aux élections municipales de 2001: vers une normalisation de leur présence parmi les candidats et les élus?', *Migrations et Sociétés*, 13(77), September/October , pp. 41–55.

——, 2002, 'Les élus "d'origine étrangère" aux élections municipales de 2001: Paris, Lyon, et Marseille', *Migrations et Sociétés*, 14(83), September/October , pp. 27–38.

GELD (Groupe d'Études et de Lutte contre les Discriminations), 2001, *Discriminations raciales et ethniques dans l'accès au logement*, Research Report, Paris.

Genty, Jean-René, 1999, *L'Immigration algérienne dans le Nord-Pas-de-Calais, 1909–1962*, L'Harmattan, Paris.

Ghemmaz, Malika, 2002, 'Les politiques publiques de lutte contre les discriminations "raciales" à l'embauche: les politiques de l'aléa', *Migrations et Sociétés*, 14(80), pp. 9–20.

Giblin-Delvallet, Béatrice, 1987, *Géopolitique du Nord-Pas-de-Calais*, Fayard, Paris.
——, 1990, *La Région, territoires politiques, le Nord-Pas-de-Calais*, Fayard, Paris.
——, 1992, 'Roubaix-Tourcoing: les conséquences d'une stratégie patronale', *Hommes et Migrations*, 1157, pp. 10–14.
Glazer, Nathan, and Daniel Moynihan, 1963, *Beyond the Melting Pot*, Harvard University Press, Cambridge, Mass.
Goulbourne, Harry, ed., 1990, *Black Politics in Britain*, Avebury, Aldershot.
——, 1991, 'Varieties of pluralism: The notion of pluralist, post-imperialist Britain', *New Community*, 17(2), pp. 211–28.
——, 1998, *Race Relations in Britain since 1945*, St. Martin's Press, London.
Grémion, Pierre, 1976, *Le Pouvoir périphérique*, Seuil, Paris.
Guiraudon, Virginie, 1996, 'The reaffirmation of the republican model of integration: Ten years of identity politics in France', *French Politics and Society*, 14(2), pp. 47–57.
——, 2000, *Les Politiques d'immigration en Europe: Allemagne, France, Pays-Bas*, L'Harmattan, Paris.
Gyford, John, 1985, *The Politics of Local Socialism*, Allen and Unwin, London.
——, et al., 1989, *The Changing Politics of Local Government*, Unwin Hyman, London.
Hall, Peter, 1986, *Governing the Economy: The Politics of State Intervention in Britain and France*, Polity Press, Cambridge.
——, and Rosemary Taylor, 1996, 'Political science and the three new institutionalisms', *Political Studies*, 44(5), pp. 936–57.
Hansen, Randall, 1998, 'Institutionalism and the three orders of feedback effect: Colonial immigration to France and the United Kingdom', paper presented at the eleventh annual conference of Europeanists, Baltimore, MD, 26–8 February.
——, 2000, *Citizenship and Immigration in Post-war Britain*, Oxford University Press, Oxford.
Hargreaves, Alec, 1995, *Immigration, Race and Ethnicity in Contemporary France*, Routledge, London and New York.
——, 2000, 'Half-measures: Antidiscrimination policy in France', *French Politics, Culture and Society*, 18(3), pp. 83–101.
Hartley-Brewer, Michael, 1965, 'Smethwick', in Nicholas Deakins, ed., *Colour and the British Electorate in 1964: Six Case Studies*, Pall Mall, London, pp. 77–105.
Hattersley, Roy, 1995, *Who Goes Home? Scenes from a Political Life*, Little, Brown, London.
Hatzfeld, Hélène, 1986, 'Municipalités socialistes et associations, Roubaix: le conflit de l'Alma-Gare', *Revue Française de Science Politique*, 3 (June), pp. 374–93.
Haut Conseil à l'Intégration, 1998, *Lutte contre les discriminations: faire respecter les principes d'égalité*, Rapport au Premier Ministre, Documentation Française, Paris.
Hilaire, Yves-Marie, 1984, *Histoire de Roubaix*, Éditions des Beffrois, Lille.
Hill, Ruth, and Michael Issacharoff, 1971, *Community and Race Relations: A Study of Community Relations Committees in Britain*, Oxford University Press, London.
Hodgins, Henry, 1985, 'Planning permission for mosques: The Birmingham experience', in *Islam in English Law and Administration: A Symposium, Muslims in Europe*, 9 (1981), Centre for the Study of Islam and Christian–Muslim Relations, Selly Oak Colleges, Birmingham.

Hollifield, James, 1991, 'Immigration and modernization', in James Hollifield and George Ross, *Searching for the New France*, Routledge, New York and London, pp. 143–76.

——, 1994, 'Immigration and republicanism in France: The hidden consensus', in Wayne A. Cornelius, Philip L. Martin and James Hollifield, *Controlling Immigration*, Stanford University Press, Stanford, Calif., pp. 143–76.

Holsten, James, and Arjun Appadurai, 1996, 'Cities and citizenship', *Public Culture*, 8, pp. 178–204.

Hooghes, 1996, *Cohesion Policy and European Integration*, Clarendon Press, Oxford.

Horowitz, Daniel, 1985, *Ethnic Groups in Conflict*, University of California Press, Berkeley.

Ireland, Patrick, 1994, *The Policy Challenge of Ethnic Diversity*, Harvard University Press, Cambridge, Mass.

Jazouli, Adil, 1986, *L'Action collective des jeunes Maghrébins en France*, L'Harmattan, Paris.

Jeffers, Sydney, 1991, 'Black sections in the Labour Party: The end of godfather politics?', in Muhammad Anwar and Pnina Werbner, eds, *Black and Ethnic Leaderships: The Cultural Dimension of Political Action*, Routledge, London and New York, pp. 63–83.

Johnson, Mark, 1990, 'Ressources locales en matière de services de protection sociale pour les minorités ethniques en Grande-Bretagne', paper presented at the conference 'L'Intégration des Minorités Immigrées en Europe', Colloque International, Paris, 8–9 October.

Johnston, M. R. D., 1988a, 'Resurrecting the inner city: A new role for the Christian churches', *New Community*, 15(1), pp. 91–102.

——, 1988b, 'The spirit still moves in the inner city: The churches and race', *Ethnic and Racial Studies* 11(3), pp. 306–73.

——, 1991, 'The churches, leadership, and ethnic minorities', in Muhammad Anwar and Pnina Werbner, eds, *Black and Ethnic Leaderships: The Cultural Dimension of Political Action*, Routledge, London and New York, pp. 277–95.

Joly, Danièle, 1992, 'Grande-Bretagne, minorités ethniques et risques de ségrégation', *Notes et Études Documentaires* (4952), pp. 111–46.

——, 1995, *Britannia's Crescent: Making a Place for Muslims in British Society*, Aldershot, Avebury.

——, and Mano Candappa, 1994, *Local Authorities, Ethnic Minorities and Pluralist Integration: A Study in Five Local Authorities*, Centre for Research in Ethnic Relations, University of Warwick, Coventry.

Jones, Philip N., 1967, *The Segregation of Immigrant Communities in Birmingham, 1961*, Occasional Papers in Geography, University of Hull Press, Hull.

Jones-Correa, Michael, ed., 2001, *Governing American Cities: Interethnic Coalitions, Competition, and Conflict*, Russell Sage Foundation, New York.

Joppke, Christian, ed., 1998, *Challenge to the Nation-state: Immigration in Western Europe and the United States*, Oxford University Press, Oxford.

——, 1999, *Immigration and the Nation-state: The United States, Germany, and Great Britain*, Oxford University Press, Oxford.

Judd, Denis R., and Todd Swanstrom, 1998, *City Politics, Private Power and Public Policy*, 2nd edition, Longman, New York.

Juhem, Philippe, 1998, *SOS Racisme, histoire d'une mobilisation 'a-politique', contribution à l'analyse des transformations des représentations politiques après 1981*, Thèse de Doctorat, Université de Nanterre, Nanterre.

Kaltenbach, Jeanne-Hélène, and Michèle Tribalat, 2002, *La République et l'Islam, entre crainte et aveuglement*, Gallimard, Paris.

Kastoryano, Riva, 1996, *La France, l'Allemagne et leurs immigrés, négocier l'identité*, Paris, Colin.

Kato, Junko, 1996, 'Institutions and rationality in politics: Three varieties of neo-institutionalists', Review article, *British Journal of Political Science*, 26, pp. 553–82.

Katznelson, Ira, 1973, *Black Men, White Cities: Politics and Migrations in the United States, 1900–1930 and Great Britain, 1948–1968*, Oxford University Press, Oxford.

Kavanagh, Dennis, 1985, 'Whatever happened to consensus politics?', *Political Studies*, 33(4), pp. 529–46.

Keating, Michael, 1988, *The City that Refused to Die: Glasgow, The Politics of Urban Regeneration*, Aberdeen University Press, Aberdeen.

——, 1991, *Comparative Urban Politics: Power and the City in the United States, Canada, Britain, and France*, Aldershot, Elgar.

——, 1998, *The New Regionalism in Western Europe: Territorial Restructuring and Political Change*, Edward Elgar, Cheltenham.

——, Roger Levy, Jack Geekie and Jack Brand, 1989, *Labour Elites in Glasgow*, Strathclyde Papers on Government and Politics, University of Strathclyde, Glasgow.

Kelfaoui, Schérazade, 1996, 'Un vote maghrébin en France? Périls géopolitiques en France', *Hérodote*, 1(80), pp. 130–55.

Kepel, Gilles, 1991, *Les Banlieues de l'Islam*, Seuil, Paris.

——, 1994, *À l'ouest d'Allah*, Seuil, Paris.

King, Desmond, 1989, 'Political centralization and state interests in Britain: The 1986 abolition of the GLC and MCCs', *Comparative Political Studies*, 21(4), pp. 467–94.

King, John, 1994, *Three Asian Associations in Britain*, Monograph in Ethnic Relations, Centre for Research in Ethnic Relations, University of Warwick, Coventry.

Kirp, David, 1979, *'Doing Good by Doing Little': Race and Schooling in Britain*, University of California Press, Berkeley.

Kitschelt, Herbert, 1997, 'European party systems: Continuity and change', in Martin Rhodes, Paul Heywood and Vincent Wright, eds, *Developments in West European Politics*, Macmillan, Basingstoke, pp. 131–49.

Koelble, Thomas A., 1995, 'The new institutionalism in political science and sociology', Review article, *Comparative Politics*, 27(2), pp. 231–43.

Koopmans, Ruud, and Paul Statham, eds, 2000a, *Challenging Immigration and Ethnic Relations Politics: Comparative European Perspectives*, Oxford University Press, Oxford.

——, eds, 2000b, 'Challenging the liberal nation-state? Postnationalism, multiculturalism, and the collective claims-making of migrants and ethnic minorities in Britain and Germany', in Ruud Koopmans and Paul Statham, eds, *Challenging Immigration and Ethnic Relations Politics: Comparative European Perspectives*, Oxford University Press, Oxford, pp. 189–232.

——, 2000c, 'Migrant mobilization and political opportunities: An empirical assessment of local and national variation,' paper presented at the international conference 'Explaining Changes in Migration Policy: Debates from Different Perspectives', University of Geneva, Geneva, 27–8 October.

Kraal, Karen, Rinus Penninx, Marco Martiniello and Steve Vertovec, 2004, *Citizenship in European Cities: Immigrants, Local Politics and Integration Policies*, Ashgate, Aldershot.

Lagroye, Jacques, and Vincent Wright, 1982, *Les Structures locales en France et en Grande-Bretagne*, Notes et Études Documentaires, Documentation Française, October.

Lapeyronnie, Didier, 1987, 'Assimilation, mobilisation et action collective chez les jeunes de la seconde génération de l'immigration maghrébine', *Revue Française de Sociologie*, 27(2), pp. 287–318.

———, 1993, *L'Individu et les minorités: la France et la Grande-Bretagne face à leurs immigrés*, Presses Universitaires de France, Paris.

Layton-Henry, Zig, 1986, 'Race and the Thatcher government', in Zig Layton-Henry and Paul Rich, eds, *Race, Government and Politics in Britain*, Macmillan, London, pp. 73–99.

———, 1992, *The Politics of Immigration: Immigration, Race, and 'Race Relations' in Post-war Britain*, Blackwell, Oxford.

———, and Donley Studlar, 1985, 'The political participation of black and Asian Britons: Integration or alienation?', *Parliamentary Affairs*, 38(3), pp. 307–18.

Le Cour de Grandmaison, Olivier, and Catherine Wihtol de Wenden, 1993, *Les Étrangers dans la cité: expériences européennes*, La Découverte, Paris.

Lefebvre, Rémy, 1997, 'Être maire à Roubaix: la prise de rôle d'un héritier', *Politix*, 38, pp. 66–87.

———, 1999, *Le Socialisme des beffrois: état des lieux et pistes de recherches*, Acte des Journées de Recherche de l'IFRESI, Lille.

Le Galès, Patrick, 1988, 'Grande-Bretagne: le gouvernement contre les villes', *Annales de la Recherche Urbaine*, 38, pp. 53–62.

———, 1990, 'Crise urbaine et développement économique local en Grande-Bretagne: l'apport de la nouvelle gauche urbaine', *Revue Française de Science Politique*, 40(5), pp. 714–34.

———, 1993, *Politique urbaine et développement économique local: une comparaison franco-britannique*, L'Harmattan, Paris.

———, 1995, 'Politique de la ville en France et en Grande-Bretagne: volontarisme et ambiguïté de l'état', *Sociologie du Travail*, 37(2), pp. 249–75.

———, 2003, *Le Retour des villes européennes, sociétés urbaines, mondialisation, gouvernement et gouvernance*, Presses de Sciences Po, Paris.

Le Lohé, Michel, 1998, 'Ethnic minority participation and representation in the British electoral system', in Shamit Saggar, ed., *Race and British Electoral Politics*, University College Press, London, pp. 73–95.

Leveau, Rémi, 2000, 'Les Beurs, nouveaux citoyens', in *Le Citoyen: mélanges offerts à Alain Lancelot*, Presses de Sciences Po, Paris, pp. 267–81.

LGIU, 1996, *Report on the First All-party Convention of Black, Asian, and Ethnic Minority Councillors*, London.

Lochak, Danièle, 1989, 'Les minorités et le droit public français: du refus des différences à la gestion des différences', in Alain Fenet and Gerard Soulier, eds, *Les Minorités et leurs Droits depuis 1798*, L'Harmattan, Paris, pp. 111–84.

Loftman, Patrick, and Brendan Nevan, 1992, *Urban Regeneration and Social Equity: A Case Study of Birmingham 1986–1992*, Research Paper no. 8, research paper series, Faculty of the Built Environment, University of Central England, Birmingham.

——, and Mike Beazley, 1998, *Race and Regeneration: A Review of the Single Regeneration Budget*, Challenge Fund, LGIU, London.

Lojkine, Jean, Roland Delacroix and Christian Mahieu, 1978, *Politique urbaine et pouvoir local dans l'agglomération lilloise*, CRAPS, Lille.

Lorreyte, Bernard, 1989, ed., *Les Politiques d'intégration des jeunes issus de l'immigration*, L'Harmattan, Paris.

Lowndes, Vivien, 1995, 'Citizenship and urban politics', in David Judge, Gerry Stoker and Harold Wolman, *Theories of Urban Politics*, Sage, London, pp. 160–80.

Mabileau, Albert, 1985a, 'Les Institutions locales et les relations centre–periphérie', in Madeleine Grawitz and Jean Leca, *Traité de sciences politiques*, volume 2, Presses Universitaires de France, Paris, pp. 553–98.

——, 1985b, 'De la monarchie municipale à la française', *Pouvoirs*, 73, pp. 7–18.

——, 1994, *Le Système local en France*, 2nd edition, Montchréstien, Paris.

——, George Moyser, Geraint Parry and Patrick Quantin, eds, 1989, *Local Politics and Participation in Britain and France*, Cambridge University Press, Cambridge.

March, James G., and Johan P. Olsen, 1989, *Rediscovering Institutions: The Organizational Basis of Politics*, Free Press, New York.

Masclet, Olivier, 2003, *La Gauche et les cités: enquête sur un rendez-vous manqué*, La Dispute, Pratiques Politiques, Paris.

Mauroy, Pierre, 1994, *Parole de lillois*, Lieu Commun, Paris.

Mayer, Nonna, 2003, 'Le Pen's comeback: The 2002 French presidential election', *International Journal of Urban and Regional Research*, 27(2), pp. 455–9.

Mény, Yves, 1985, 'Les politiques des autorités locales', in Madeleine Grawitz and Jean Leca, *Traité de sciences politiques*, volume 4, Presses Universitaires de France, Paris, pp. 423–66.

——, 1995, 'Modèles présidentiels et éxécutifs locaux', in Nicholas Wahl and Jean-Louis Quermonne, eds, *La France présidentielle: l'influence du suffrage sur la vie politique*, Presses de Sciences Po, pp. 195–206.

Messina, Anthony, 1989, *Race and Party Competition*, Oxford University Press, Oxford.

Miller, Mark J., 1981, *Foreign Workers in Western Europe: An Emerging Political Force?* Praeger, New York.

Ministère des Affaires Sociales et de la Solidarité Nationale, 1986, *Une Nouvelle Politique de l'immigration, 1981–1986*, report for Georgina Dufoix, Paris.

Minkin, Lewis, 1991, *The Contentious Alliance: Trade Unions and the Labour Party*, Edinburgh University Press, Edinburgh.

Modood, Tariq, 1994, 'Political blackness and British Asians', *Sociology*, 28(4), November, pp. 859–76.

——, 2000, 'La Place des Musulmans dans le multiculturalisme laïc en Grande-Bretagne', *Social Compass*, 47(1), pp. 41–55.

——, Richard Berthoud et al., 1997, *Ethnic Minorities in Britain: Diversity and Disadvantage*, Policy Studies Institute, London.

Mouriaux, René, and Catherine Wihtol de Wenden, 1987, 'Syndicalisme français et Islam', *Revue Française de Science Politique*, 37(6), December, pp. 794–819.

Negrouche, Ralph, 1992, 'L'Échec des associations franco-maghrébines issues de l'immigration (1980–1990)', *Esprit*, pp. 41–52.

Neveu, Catherine, 1993, *Communauté, nationalité, et citoyenneté, de l'autre coté du miroir: les Bangladeshis de Londres*, Karthala, Paris.

——, 1998, 'Dans notre pays et au-delà dans notre ville', *Citoyenneté, appropriation et territoire à Roubaix*, Rapport Final pour le PIR-Villes CNRS, Roubaix.

Newton, Kenneth, 1976, *Second City Politics: Democratic Processes and Decision-making in Birmingham*, Clarendon Press, London.

Nielsen, Jorgen, 1995, *Muslims in Western Europe*, 2nd edition, Edinburgh University Press, Edinburgh.

Noiriel, Gérard, 1986, *Le Creuset français: histoire de l'immigration, XIXᵉ–XXᵉ siècles*, Seuil, Paris.

Nordlinger, Eric, 1972, *Conflict Regulation in Divided Societies*, Centre for International Affairs, Harvard University, Cambridge, Mass.

Norris, Pippa, and Joni Lovenduski, 1995, *Political Recruitment: Gender, Race and Class in the British Parliament*, Cambridge University Press, Cambridge and New York.

Observatoire Urbain de Roubaix, Ville de Roubaix, 1998, *La Ville de Roubaix: un exemple de développement non-durable confronté à une crise urbaine unique en France.*

Oriol, Paul, 1991, 'Résidents étrangers et scrutins locaux', *Migrations et Sociétés*, 3(18), pp. 9–18.

——, 1998, 'Les immigrés et les élections municipales de 1995', *Migrations et Sociétés*, 10(56), pp. 5–17.

——, 2003, *Résident, étrangers, citoyens! Plaidoyer pour une citoyenneté européenne de résidence*, Presse-Pluriel, Paris.

Ouseley, Herman, 1981, *The System*, Runnymede Trust, London.

——, 1984, 'Local authority race initiatives', in Martin Boddy and Colin Fudge, eds, *Local Socialism: Labour Councils and New Left Initiatives*, Macmillan, London, pp. 133–59.

Parekh, Bikhu, 2001, 'The future of multi-ethnic Britain: Reporting on a report', *The Round Table*, 362, pp. 691–700.

Paul, Kathleen, 1997, *Whitewashing Britain: Race and Citizenship in the Postwar Era*, Cornell University Press, Ithaca, New York.

Perrineau, Pascal, 1997, *Le Symptome Le Pen*, Fayard, Paris.

Piat, Jean, 1981, *Roubaix, histoire d'une ville socialiste – période 1819–1945*, Roubaix, Ville de Roubaix.

Plant, M., 1971, 'The attitudes of coloured immigrants in two areas of Birmingham to the concept of dispersal', *Race*, 12, pp. 323–8.

Poinsot, Marie, 1991, 'L'intégration politique des jeunes maghrébins: deux stratégies associatives dans la région lilloise', *Revue Européenne des Migrations Internationales*, 7(3), pp. 119–34.

——, 1993, 'Competition for political legitimacy at local and national levels among young North Africans in France', *New Community*, 20(1), pp. 69–82.

——, 1994, *L'Intégration politique des jeunes issus de l'immigration: du débat d'idées aux actions collectives dans la région lilloise*, Thèse de Doctorat, Institut d'Études Politiques de Paris, Paris.

Pouvoirs, 60, 1992, special issue on decentralization.

Préfecture du Nord, 1998, *Le Nord, un département dont les caractéristiques requièrent un déploiement de la politique de la ville*, Rapport Administratif, Lille.

Race Relations Unit, 1995, *Directory of Black and Ethnic Minority Organizations in Birmingham*, Birmingham City Council, Birmingham.

Ratcliffe, Peter, 1979, *Race and Reaction: A Study of Handsworth*, Routledge and Kegan Paul, London.

Rex, John, 1991, *Ethnic Identity and Ethnic Mobilization*, Centre for Research in Ethnic Relations, University of Warwick, Coventry.

——and Robert Moore, 1967, *Race, Community and Conflict: A Study of Sparkbrook*, Oxford University Press, London.

——and Sally Tomlinson, 1979, *Colonial Immigrants in a British City: A Class Analysis*, Routledge and Kegan Paul, London.

——and Yunas Samad, 1996, 'Multiculturalism and political integration in Birmingham and Bradford', *Innovation*, 9(1), pp. 11–31.

Rich, Daniel, and Robin Boyle, 1984, *In Pursuit of the Private City: A Comparative Assessment of Urban Policy Orientations in Britain and the United States*, Strathclyde Papers on Planning, University of Strathclyde, Department of Urban and Regional Planning, Glasgow.

Richard, Jean-Luc, 1998, 'Rester en France, devenir Français, voter: trois étapes de l'intégration des enfants d'immigrés', *Économie et Statistique*, 316–317, pp. 151–162.

——, 1999, *Comment votent les jeunes Français issus de l'immigration? Ville, école, et intégration*, CNDP, dossier Citoyenneté, Paris.

Rogers, Alisdair, and Jean Tillie, 2001, *Multi-cultural Policies and Modes of Citizenship*, Ashgate, Aldershot.

Rose, Eliot Joseph Benn et al., 1969, *Colour and Citizenship: A Report on British Race Relations, London*, Oxford University Press, Oxford.

Rosenhek, Zev, 1999, 'The politics of claims-making in Israel', *Journal of Ethnicity and Migration Studies*, 25(4), pp. 575–95.

Saggar, Shamit, 1991a, 'The changing agenda of race issues in local government: The case of a London borough', *Political Studies*, 39, pp. 100–21.

——, 1991b, *Race and Public Policy*, Avebury, Aldershot.

——, ed., 1998a, *Race and British Electoral Politics*, University College Press, London.

——, 1998b, 'Analysing race and elections in British politics: Some conceptual and theoretical concerns', in Shamit Saggar, ed., *Race and British Electoral Politics*, University College Press, London, pp. 11–46.

——, 1998c, 'Smoking guns and magic bullets: The "race card" debate revisited in 1997', *Immigrants and Minorities*, 17(3), pp. 1–21.

Sawicki, Frédéric, 1997, *Les Réseaux du Parti Socialiste: sociologie d'un milieu partisan*, Belin, Paris.

Scavennec, Cécile, 1998, *Connaissance et reconnaissance de la culture arabo-musulmane à Roubaix*, IEP Lyon, Mémoire de DESS.

Schain, Martin, 1990, 'Immigration and politics,' in Peter A. Hall, Jack Hayward and Howard Machin, eds, *Developments in French Politics*, Macmillan, London.

——, 1993, 'Policy-making and defining ethnic minorities: The case of immigration in France', *New Community*, 20(1), pp. 59–77.

——, 1995, 'Policy and policy-making in France and the US: Models of incorporation and the dynamics of change', *Modern and Contemporary France*, 3(4), pp. 401–13.

——, 1996, 'Minorities and immigrant incorporation in France: The state and the dynamics of multiculturalism', paper prepared for delivery at the conference on 'Multiculturalism, Minorities and Citizenship', European University Institute, Florence, 18–23 April.

——, 2000, 'The impact of the extreme right on immigration policy', paper prepared for the conference 'Explaining Change in Migration Policies: Debates on Different Perspectives', University of Geneva, Geneva, 20–1 October.

——, 2002, 'The impact of the French National Front on the French political system', in M. Schain, A. Zolberg and P. Hossay, eds, *Shadows Over Europe: The Development and Impact of the Extreme Right in Western Europe*, Palgrave, Houndmills, Basingstoke.

Schnapper, Dominique, 1991, *La France de l'intégration: sociologie de la nation en 1990*, Gallimard, Paris.

——, 1992, *L'Europe des immigrés*, François Bourin, Paris.

Sewell, Terri, 1993, *Black Tribunes: Black Political Participation in Britain*, Lawrence and Wishart, London.

Seyd, Patrick, 1987, *The Rise and Fall of the Labour Left*, St Martin's Press, New York.

——, and Paul Whiteley, 1992, *Labour's Grass Roots: The Politics of Party Membership*, Clarendon Press, Oxford.

——, 2002, *New Labour's Grassroots: The Transformation of the Labour Party Membership*, Palgrave Macmillan, London.

Shukra, Kalbir, 1990, 'Black sections in the Labour Party', in Harry Goulbourne, ed., *Black Politics in Britain*, Aldershot, Ashgate.

——, 1998a, *The Changing Patterns of Black Politics in Britain*, Pluto Press, London.

——, 1998b, 'New Labour debates and dilemmas', in Shamit Saggar, ed., *Race and British Electoral Politics*, University College Press, London, pp. 117–44.

Shuttleworth, Alan, 1965, 'Sparkbrook', in Nicholas Deakins, ed., *Colour and the British Electorate in 1964: Six Case Studies*, Pall Mall, London, pp. 64–76.

Simons, John, 1974, 'Great Britain', in Bernard Berelson, ed., *Population Policies in Developed Countries*, McGraw-Hill, New York.

Singham, A. W., 1965, 'Immigration and the election', in D. E. Butler and Anthony King, *The British General Election of 1964*, Macmillan, London, pp. 360–8.

Skocpol, Theda, 1979, *States and Social Revolutions: A Comparative Analysis of France, Russia and China*, Cambridge University Press, Cambridge.

Smith, Graham, et al., 1999, 'Social capital and urban governance: Adding a more contextualized "top-down" perspective', unpublished paper.

Sociétés Contemporaines, 1999, *Immigration et politique de l'habitat*, 33–34.

Solomos, John, 1993, *Race and Racism in Britain*, Macmillan, London.

——, 1998, *Black Youth, Racism and the State: The Politics of Ideology and Policy*, Cambridge University Press, Cambridge.

——, and Les Back, 1995, *Race, Politics and Social Change*, Routledge, London.

Soysal, Yasemin, 1994, *Limits of Citizenship: Migrants and Postnational Membership in Europe*, Chicago University Press, Chicago.

Steinmo, Sven, Kathleen Thelen, and Frank Longstreth, eds., 1992, *Structuring Politics: Historical Institutionalism in Comparative Analysis*, Cambridge University Press, Cambridge.

Stoker, Gerry, 1991, *The Politics of Local Government*, Macmillan, London.

Stora, Benjamin, 1992, *Ils venaient d'Algérie: l'immigration algérienne en France, 1912–1992*, Paris, Fayard.

Studlar, Donley, 1985, 'Race in British politics', *Patterns of Prejudice*, 19(1), January, pp. 3–16.

——, 1986, 'Non-white policy preferences, political participation and the political agenda in Britain', in Zig Layton-Henry and Paul Rich, eds, *Race, Government and Politics in Britain*, Macmillan, London, pp. 159–86.

——and Susan Welch, 1990, 'Voting for ethnic minority candidates in local British and American elections', in Anthony Messina, *Ethnic and Racial Minorities in Advanced Industrialized Democracies*, Westwood Press, Westport, Conn., pp. 143–60.

Sueur, Georges, 1971, *Lille, Roubaix, Tourcoing, métropoles en miettes*, Stock, Paris.

Sutcliffe, Anthony, and Roger Smith, 1974, *History of Birmingham, Volume 3: 1939–1970*, Oxford University Press, London.

Todd, Emmanuel, 1994, *Le Destin des immigrés, assimilation et ségrégation dans les démocraties occidentales*, Seuil, Paris.

Tribalat, Michèle, 1995, *Faire France: une enquête sur les immigrés en France*, La Découverte, Paris.

Venel, Nancy, 2004, *Musulmans et citoyens*, Presses Universitaires de France, Paris.

Verbunt, Gilles, 1980, *L'Intégration par l'autonomie*, CIEMI, Paris.

Verfaillie, Bertrand, 1996, *Roubaix, chants de briques, paroles d'hommes*, Desclée de Brouwer, Paris.

Vertovec, Steve, 1994, 'Multicultural, multi-Asian, multi-Muslim Leicester: Dimensions of social complexity, ethnic organization and local government interface', *Innovation*, 7(3), pp. 259–76.

——, 1998, 'Politiques multiculturelles et citoyenneté dans les villes européennes', *Revue Internationale des Sciences Sociales*, 156, pp. 211–24.

Viet, Vincent, 2004, *Histoire des Français venus d'ailleurs, de 1850 à nos jours*, Éditions Perrin, Paris.

Ville de Lille, 1998, *Rapport d'étape sur l'étude-diagnostic portant sur l'intégration et sa mise en œuvre dans le cadre du SLI*, Lille.

——, 1999, *Schéma Local d'Intégration, février 1998–février 1999*, Rapport d'Activité, Lille.

Ville de Roubaix, *Exploitation du recensement par quartier, Vade Mecum* (based on 1990 INSEE census data), Roubaix.

Ware, Alan, 1996, *Political Parties and Party Systems*, Oxford University Press, Oxford.

Webman, Gerry, 1981, 'Centralization and implementation: Urban renewal in Great Britain and France', *Comparative Politics*, January, pp. 127–48.

Weil, Patrick, 1990, *La Politique française d'immigration: au-delà du désordre*, Documentation Francaise, Paris.

——, 1991, 'Immigration and the rise of racism in France: The contradictions of Mitterand's policies', *French Politics and Society*, 9(3–4), pp. 82–100.

——, 1995a, *La France et ses étrangers: l'aventure d'une politique de l'immigration de 1938 à nos jours*, Gallimard, Collection Folio, Paris.

——, 1995b, *Pour une nouvelle politique d'immigration*, Fondation St Simon, Paris.

——, 2001, 'The politics of immigration', in Alain Guyomarch, Howard Machin, Peter A. Hall and Jack Hayward, eds, *Developments in French Politics 2*, Palgrave, Basingstoke, pp. 211–26.

——, 2002, *Qu'est-ce qu'un Français? Histoire de la nationalité française depuis la Révolution*, Grasset, Paris.

——, 2003a, 'La crise du principe d'égalité dans la société française', *Recherche Socialiste*, 23, June, pp. 5–16.

———, 2003b, 'The evolution of state practices in Europe and the United States from the French Revolution to the inter-war period', in Andreas Fahrmeir, Olivier Faron and Patrick Weil, eds, *Migration Control in the North Atlantic World: The Evolution of State Practices in Europe and the United States from the French Revolution to the Inter-war Period*, Berghahn Books, New York and Oxford, pp. 271–97.

Werbner, Pnina, 1991, 'Black and ethnic leadership in Britain', in Muhammad Anwar and Pnina Werbner, eds, *Black and Ethnic Leaderships: The Cultural Dimension of Political Action*, Routledge, London and New York, pp. 15–40.

Wihtol de Wenden, Catherine, 1988, *Les Immigrés et la politique*, Presses de la FNSP, Paris.

———, and Rémy Leveau, 2001, *La Beurgeoisie, trois générations d'associations maghrébines*, Presses du CNRS, Paris.

Woods, R., 1979, 'Ethnic segregation in Birmingham in the 1960s and 1970s', *Ethnic and Racial Studies*, 2(4), 455–76.

Young, Ken, 1981, *Policy and Practice in the Multiracial City*, Policy Studies Institute, London.

———, 1982, 'An agenda for Sir George: Local authorities and the promotion of racial equality', *Policy Studies*, 3, pp. 54–70.

———, 1990, 'Approaches to policy developments in the field of equal opportunities', in Wendy Ball and John Solomos, eds, *Race and Local Politics*, Macmillan, London, pp. 22–42.

Zollberg, Aristide, 1981, 'International migrations in political perspective', in M. Kritz, C. Keely and S. Tomasi, eds, *Global Trends in Migration*, Centre for Migration Studies, New York.

Index

Abélès, Marc 239n
Adolino, Jessica 7, 58, 109, 224n
African populations *see* North African
    populations
African-Caribbean population 5, 12, 29,
    40, 99, 101, 108, 128
    church organizations 12, 22, 118–19,
    132
    community associations and organizations
    12, 22, 118–19, 132
    housing 43
    political alliances 31
    upward mobility 101
Ahsan, Raghib 133, 139
Algerian population 5, 10, 12, 14, 29, 40,
    68, 75, 149
    attempted repatriation xi–xii
    management by central state 69–70
    religion 17
    Roubaix 189–91
    see also North African populations
anti-immigrant movement, Britain 22, 40,
    46, 51
anti-racism movement
    Britain 22, 45, 52, 57, 60
    France 76
anti-Semitism 16
Anwar, Muhammad 21, 98, 112, 115,
    224n, 225n

Appadurai, Arjun 2
Ashford, Douglas 33
Asian populations *see* Bangladeshi
    population; Indian population; Pakistani
    population; Sikhs
Asian Workers' Union 118
assimilation 5
    republican assimilation 15, 32, 82–4
assimilationist model 5, 15, 16, 17
    Britain 17
    France 5, 15, 16, 18, 34
Association de Maliens de Lille 181
associations *see* community associations and
    organizations
ATACAFA 181
Atelier Populaire d'Urbanisme (APU)
    195–6, 203, 238n
Aubry, Martine 146, 175, 181, 194, 236n,
    237n
auto-gestion 165, 166

Bachman, Christian 75, 164, 169
Back, Les 93, 94, 109, 111, 122, 126,
    127–8, 129, 133, 136, 138, 230n, 231n,
    232n
Bagla, Nam Dev 233n
Baker, Kenneth 51
Ball, Wendy 58
Balladur, Edouard 86

Balme, Richard 173, 176
Bangladeshi population 5, 97, 99, 101, 108
  economic disadvantage 101–2
  mobilization 22
  unemployment 102
  upward mobility 101
Barnekov, Timothy 106
Barre, Raymond 235n
Bataille, Philippe 194, 201, 238n, 239n
Battegay, Alain 180
Beazley, Michael 49
Beckett, Margaret 233n
Beetham, David 11
Belgian population 198, 200
Bella, Rachid 202–3, 208
Bélorgey, Jean-Michel 235n
Ben-Tovim, Gideon 24, 31, 60, 225n
Benn, Tony 134, 233n
Berthoud, Richard 5, 43, 224n
Beur, meaning 224n
Beur movement 22, 67, 73, 76–8, 84, 90
  British movements compared 11, 14
  citizenship and 14, 76, 77
  failure of 14, 78, 88, 164–9, 187, 216, 217
  Lille 146, 148, 160, 177
  Roubaix 195
  Socialist Party and 74, 76–8, 215, 216
Biarez, Sylvie 233n
biracial electoral alliance 23, 24
Birmingham 19, 24, 29–32, 41, 62, 92–143, 218, 219
  1948–81 104–5
  alliances 31, 33
  church organizations 12, 22, 118–19, 132
  committees 96–7, 108, 109
  community organizations 117–21
  Conservative Party 103, 104, 105, 110, 111, 113, 114, 117, 142
  co-optation at ward level 93, 103, 112, 125–42: ethnic community model 135–42, 143; patronage model 125, 126–30, 142, 143; radical activist model 125, 130–5, 142–3
  council workforce 107–8
  Democratic Party 137
  education policies 106, 107
  electoral turnouts 123
  Equalities Unit 107

ethnic minority population 97–103
ethnic residential concentration 99–101, 179
history 95–7
history of migration and ethnic groups 97–9
independent candidates 135, 139–41, 143
industry 96
Justice for Kashmir Party 140, 141, 142
Labour Party 29, 31, 94, 102, 103, 109, 115, 212: black sections 127, 133–5, 137, 140; co-optation at ward level 93, 103, 112, 125–42; disillusion with 61–2, 139–42, 143; Pakistani candidates 132–3, 135–42, 212; party structure 122–5; penetration by ethnic minorities 116–42; pro-minority regime 105–8; proactive race relations policies 106–8
Liberal Democrat Party 31, 35, 105, 110, 111, 117, 135, 141, 142, 143, 213
local political system 34–5
mosques 121
Muslim religious organizations 120–1
political institutions 122–5
political system 96–7
Race Relations Unit 107, 114
reform of local government 97
Riyaz and Qayum cases 139–40
socio-economic disadvantage 101–3
Standing Consultative Forum (SCF) 107, 121, 231n
trade unions 116, 118, 119, 132
unemployment 102, 103, 106
urban regeneration 105, 106, 107
white–black and Asian liberal alliance 108–10: electoral dynamics 110–14; rationale for 114–16
youth of ethnic population 101, 103
Birmingham Citizen Association 104
Birmingham Immigration Control Association 104
black sections 127, 133–5, 137, 140
Black Workers' Union 132
Blair, Tony 7, 53, 61, 135, 143, 212, 215, 218
Bleich, Erik 2, 16, 21, 47, 88, 211
Bleitrach, Danielle 150, 151
Bleu d'Ailleurs 181

Blunkett, David   17, 227n, 233n
Boateng, Paul   233n
Bobo, Lawrence   8–9, 223n
Boddy, Colin   60
Body-Gendrot, Sophie   65, 87, 120, 223n
Bore, Albert   97, 131
Bosworth, Neville   113
Bouamama, Said   67, 77, 78, 164, 166–7,
    195, 196, 228n, 236n
Bousetta, Hassan   18, 20, 181, 182, 211,
    223n, 237n
Bradford   17, 24, 41, 56, 59
Briggs, Asa   96, 229n
British Nationality Act 1948   11, 39, 40, 49
British Nationality Act 1981   11, 51, 53, 54
Browning, Rufus   23, 109, 223n
Brubaker, Rogers   6, 15, 26
Bruyelle, Pierre   151, 189
Bulpitt, Jim   39, 48, 54
Burnett, Alton   109, 131–2
Burnley   17

Campaign Against Racial Discrimination
    (CARD)   16
Candappa, Mano   24, 58, 59, 61, 96, 113
Cantle Report   17
Cap 95   183, 184
Cardiff   98
Carette, Henri   198
Carignon, Alain   24
Carton, Bernard   207
Cashmore, Ellis   12
Castles, Stephen   5, 15, 26, 223n
Césari, Jocelyne   169, 184
Ceyrac, Pierre   156
Chagah, Malek   183
Chamberlain, Joseph   119, 130
Cherifi, Mohammed   208
Chevalier de Roubaix, Les   192, 200
Chevènement, Jean-Pierre   87–8
Chinese population   99, 102
Chirac, Jacques   77, 80, 82, 208, 228n,
    235n
church organizations   12, 22, 118–19,
    132
Citizens of the Independent Commonwealth
    Countries (CICCs)   39
Citizens of the United Kingdom and
    Colonies (CUKCs)   39

citizenship   xi–xii, 2, 6
    Beur movement and   14, 76, 77
    Britain   11–12, 15, 17, 32–3, 49, 51
    'citizenship framework'   20
    France   11–12, 15, 64, 70, 76, 77, 83,
        87–8, 214
    see also nationality
city councils   1–3
    levels of representation and modes of
        access   6–13
class   12, 43, 60, 116
Codaccioni, Colette   156, 171
Cole, Alistair   146, 151
Collett, Charles   104
Colonial Office   44
Commission Extra Municipale aux
    Étrangers (CEM)   192
Commission for Racial Equality (CRE)   17,
    51, 87, 88, 115
Commissions Départementales d'Accès à la
    Citoyenneté (CODACS)   88, 206
Committee on Racial Discrimination
    (CARD)   47
Commonwealth Immigrants Acts 1962 and
    1968   38, 46–7, 98
Communist Party   16, 66, 83, 122, 168,
    198, 217, 218
community associations and organizations
    16–17, 22, 117–21
    African-Caribbean population   12, 22,
        118–19, 132
    Beur movement   22
    church organizations   12, 22, 118–19,
        132
    Conservative Party   22
    Lille   172, 173, 177, 179–85
    Pakistani population   118, 119–21
    Roubaix   199–206, 219
    sports clubs   182, 202, 205
Community Relations Commission   11, 51
community relations councils (CRCs)   48,
    49, 57
Community Relations Movement   48
Confédération Française du Travail (CFDT)
    165
Conseil Français du Culte Musulman
    (CFCM)   17
Conservative Party   38, 39, 45, 50–1, 54
    in Birmingham see Birmingham

community associations 22
Immigration Acts 40
immigration policy 41, 43, 45, 54–5
minority support for 54, 59, 60
Convergence 84 movement 76
co-optation 19, 23–4
Birmingham 93, 103, 112, 125–42, 143
ethnic community model 135–42, 143
patronage model 125, 126–30, 142, 143
radical activist model 125, 130–5, 142–3
Cordeiro, Albano 162, 172, 236n
Cornuel, Daniel 238n
Coventry 24, 96
Craignos, Les 164–5, 167–9, 172, 195
Crewe, Ivor 52
Cross, Malcolm 119
Crowley, John 13–15, 83, 91, 162, 226n

Darragh, John 229n
De Barros, Françoise 200, 239n
de Gaulle, Charles 193, 234n
De Rudder, Véronique 83, 233n
Deakins, David 12
Decocq, Christian 155
Deferre, Gaston 235n
Delacroix, Roland 150, 217
Delgrange, Bouziane 167, 168
Delorme, Father 77
depoliticization of immigration
Britain 37, 44–6, 48, 49, 61, 80
France 78–80
Désir, Harlem 77
Deuxième Gauche 165
D'Hellencourt, Bernard 65
differential exclusion model 5, 15
Dijoud, Paul 71
Diligent, André 187, 192, 193, 195, 198,
199, 202, 203, 206, 207, 208, 209
DiMaggio, Paul 213
Dion, Stéphane 86
Ditta, Allah 139–40, 141
Djebien, Salah 236n, 237n
Donzelot, Jacques 75, 80
Doolan, Ed 112
Douste-Blazy, Philippe 225n
Dowding, Keith 155
Dray, Julien 77
Dubet, François 75
Dunleavy, Patrick 42

Duprez, Dominique 153, 154, 157
Duriez, Bernard 238n
Duyvendak, Jan Willem 76

Eade, John 225n
education
Britain 43, 106, 107
zones d'éducation prioritaire 75, 83, 238n
Edwards, J. 49
electoral systems 28
France 85, 89
levels of representation and modes of
access 6–13, 18
Ellahi, Fazal 132, 232n
Entzinger, Han 119
Equal Opportunities Committees and Units
57–8, 59, 107
equal opportunities policies 57–9
Esman, Milton 21
Estebe, Philippe 75
Etchebarne, Serge 155–6, 191, 235n
ethnic community model of co-optation
135–42
ethnic diversity 2, 18, 38, 76, 132

Fabius, Laurent 77, 81, 228n
family unification
Britain 98
France 71, 72
Faure, Alain 176
Favell, Adrian 3, 21, 83, 211
Fédération des Associations de Jeunes (FAJ)
201, 202–3, 205, 206
Feldblum, Myriam 83
Féraud, Marie 238n
Fitzgerald, Marian 53, 57, 112, 116, 225n
Florin, Jean-Pierre 189, 198, 206, 237n
Fonds d'Action et de Soutien pour
l'Intégration et la Lutte contre les
Discriminations (FASILD) 236n
Fonds d'Action Sociale (FAS) 69–70, 76,
90, 173, 174, 176, 194, 236n
funding 178
Foot, Paul 229n
Français de papiers 68
France Plus 9, 77, 78, 85, 166, 235n
Franche-Comté 148
Freeman, Gary 12, 17, 67, 69, 70, 71–2,
224n, 226n

French Council of the Muslim Faith 17
French League for Human Rights 192
Front de Libération Nationale (FLN) 12
Front National (FN) 22, 33, 34, 63, 64, 68,
  73–4, 77, 78, 84, 216
  internal crisis 87
  Lille 35, 155–6
  repatriation xii
  rise of 73, 74, 78, 80–2, 155, 172, 236n
  Roubaix 36, 191–5, 200, 207, 209, 219
  success of 13, 35, 90
  temporary weakening 91
Frybes, Marcin 4
Fudge, Martin 60

Gabriel, Oscar W. 84, 161, 162
Gaffney, John 103, 230n
Gaitskell, Hugh 45
Garraud, Philippe 161, 170, 218
Gaullists
  Lille 145, 155, 156, 168, 171
  Roubaix 194, 199, 207
  see also Rassemblement pour la
    République (RPR)
Geddes, Andrew 7, 122, 223n, 233n
Geisser, Vincent 9–10, 24, 67, 78, 85, 88,
  160, 224n, 225n
Gendron, Jean-Pierre 207, 238n
gentrification 150–2, 163, 170, 174
Genty, Jean-René 12, 159
Germany 6, 15, 50, 71
Ghemmaz, Malika 90
Giblin-Delvallet, Béatrice 146, 147, 149,
  150, 151, 198, 234n, 238n
Gilliam, Franklin D. 8–9, 223n
Giscard d'Estaing, Valéry xi, xii, 72, 75
Glasgow 106
Glazer, Nathan 223
Godsiff, Roger 140
Gordon Walker, Patrick 45
Goss, S. 232n
Goulbourne, Harry 15, 16, 17, 116
Greater London Council (GLC) 56, 57, 60,
  92
Greens 15, 123
  Lille 168, 185
  Roubaix 195, 196, 203, 204, 207, 208,
    209, 217
Grémion, Pierre 84
Grenoble 24

Griffiths, Peter 45, 104
group particularism 15
Groupe d'Études et de Lutte contre les
  Discriminations (GELD) 88, 233n
Guesdes, Jules 197–8, 237n
Guiraudon, Virginie 21, 83
Gyford, John 43, 218

Hague, William 230n
Hain, Peter 233n
Hall, Peter 25, 26, 226n
Hamlaoui, Riad 180
Hansen, Randall 21, 27, 39, 40, 41, 45,
  50, 51, 214, 225n, 226n
Hargreaves, Alec 40, 68, 88, 236n
Harkis 208, 239n
Harris, Clive 214
Hattersley, Roy 46, 126, 127, 131, 133–4,
  137, 232n
Hatzfeld, Hélène 238n
Haut Conseil à l'Intégration 87, 88
Haute Autorité de Lutte contre les
  Discriminations et l'Exclusion (HALDE)
  17
Heath, Edward 51
Hilaire, Yves-Marie 237n
Hill, Ruth 22, 44, 104, 226n, 230n
historical institutionalism (HI) 19, 21–2,
  25–6
  central and local factors 26–7
  definition of institutions 25
  local frameworks 27–8
  national frameworks 27
  strategies of management of ethnic
    conflict 21–5, 30
  strengths and limitations 211–13
Hoffman-Martinot, Vincent 84, 161, 162
Hollifield, James 65, 83
Holsten, James 2
Horowitz, Daniel 21
housing
  Britain 42, 43, 107, 120
  France 151, 153, 154, 188, 189, 198,
    199, 233n
Howell, Denis 126
Hunt, James 128
Hussain, Mahmood 132, 232n

Ifri, Malik 167, 168
Immigration Acts 10, 11, 39–40

Commonwealth Immigrants Acts 1962
    and 1968   38, 46–7, 98
  Immigration Act 1971   54
  see also Race Relations Acts
immigration restriction
  Britain   45–6, 49
  France   70–1
incorporation   8–9
  by assimilation   15
  'incorporation frameworks'   5, 15
  partial   23
independent candidates   135, 139–41, 143
Indian population   12, 29, 40, 97, 101, 107
  accommodation   42
  social class   12
  upward mobility   101
Indian Workers' Association   12, 47
Indian Workers' Union   118
industrial action   66
institutional channelling   20
  see also historical institutionalism
'institutional racism'   107–8
institutionalism   25
  see also historical institutionalism
institutions   26
  definition   25
  local   27–8
  national   27
Iraq war, effects of   xii, 6, 53, 142, 212, 219
Ireland, Patrick   18, 20, 83, 192, 193, 212,
    223n
Issachoroff, Michael   22, 44, 104, 226n,
    230n
Italian population   74, 148, 152

Jazouli, Adil   67, 75, 77, 164, 169, 225n
Jeffers, Sydney   133, 227n
Jenkins, Roy   48, 49, 127
Jeunes Arabes de Lyon et sa Banlieue (JALB)
    235n
Jeunesse et Avenir   183
Jeunesse Ouvrières Chrétiennes (JOC)
    204
John, Peter   146, 151
Johnson, Mark   43
Johnston, M. R. D.   119, 231n
Joly, Danièle   24, 40, 58, 59, 60, 96, 106,
    113, 120, 121, 213
Jones, Philip N.   42
Jones-Correa, Michael   18, 20

Joppke, Christian   1, 15, 24, 44, 57, 223n,
    226n
Joshi, Shirley   214
Jospin, Lionel   64, 77, 80, 86, 235n, 236n
Judd, Denis R.   109, 163, 227n
Juhem, Philippe   164
Juppé, Alain   82, 86, 87, 156, 236n
Justice for Kashmir Party   140, 141, 142

Kacet, Salem   207, 208
Kaltenbach, Jeanne-Hélène   224n
Kato, Junko   226n
Katznelson, Ira   41, 44, 45, 46, 223n, 225n,
    227n
Kazi, Mohammed   132, 139, 232n, 233n
Keating, Michael   2, 106, 161–2
Kelfaoui, Schérazade   14, 21
Kepel, Gilles   69, 70, 71
Kerrouche, Djamel   203, 208
Khan, Amir   129, 131, 134, 140, 232n
Khan, Tariq   141
King, Desmond   227n
King, John   231n
Kinnock, Neil   135
Kitschelt, Herbert   3
Knowles, Sir Richard   113, 130, 131, 230n
Koelble, Thomas A.   25, 26, 226n
Koopmans, Ruud   17, 18, 41–2, 50
Kozack, Godula   26, 223n
Kraal, Karen   25

Labour Party   xii, 7, 212
  in Birmingham *see* Birmingham
  black sections   127, 133–5, 137, 140
  conflict in   55
  co-optation at ward level   93, 103, 112,
    125–42
  disillusion with   61–2, 139–42, 143
  Immigration Acts   40
  Iraq war and   xii, 6, 53, 142, 212, 219
  local activism   54–6
  mass migration   41, 45
  as minorities' party   51–4, 112
  municipal socialism   43
  New Labour   53
  organization   33
  Pakistani candidates   132–3, 135–42, 212
  proactive race relations policies   106–8
Lal, Shaman   132, 232n
Lambeth   56, 60

Lang, Carl 156
Lang, Jack 77
Lapeyronnie, Didier 3, 6, 11, 13, 75, 77, 164, 217, 223n, 225n
Lasfar, Amar 180, 237n
Laurent, Augustin 145, 234n
Lawrence, Stephen 230n
Layton-Henry, Zig 33, 45, 51, 52, 54, 225n
Le Cour de Grandmaison, Olivier 14–15
Le Galès, Patrick 22, 33, 49, 56
Le Guennec, Nicole 75, 164, 169
Le Lohé, Michel 7, 8, 59, 108, 123, 227n, 231n
Le Pen, Jean-Marie 13, 80, 81, 87, 235n
Lebas, Jean 198, 200
Leclerc-Olive, Michèle 153
Leeds 41, 56
Lefebvre, Rémy 178, 193, 198, 235n, 239n
Leicester 23, 24, 41, 53, 54, 62
Leveau, Rémi 67, 195, 224n, 228n
levels of representation and modes of access 6–13, 18
Liberal Democrat Party
  in Birmingham *see* Birmingham
  minority support for 53–4, 59, 60, 141–2
Ligue des Droits de l'Homme 192
Lille 19, 29–32, 86, 147–86, 218, 219, 220
  abstention 155–6
  aggregation of ethnic minority interest 158–9
  associations 172, 173, 177, 179–85
  avoidance of ethnicity issues 156–8
  Beur movement 146, 148, 160, 177: failure of 164–9
  community associations and organizations 172, 173, 177, 179–85
  conseils de quartier 176, 177, 178–9
  Craignos, Les 164, 165, 167–9, 172, 195
  election 1995, failure of attempted participation 181–5
  Front National 35, 155–6
  Gaullists 145, 155, 156, 168, 171
  gentrification policy 150–2, 163, 170, 174
  housing 151, 153, 154
  isolation of community politics 171–3
  list system 132–3, 162
  local political system 35, 124–5

mosques 157, 180–1, 182, 237n
municipal institutions 146, 161–4
municipal machine 170–1
North African population 147–86
organization of political networks 176–9
residential concentration 153–5
Roubaix compared 144–5, 151, 163–4, 171–3, 179
secular groups 181–5
social and ethnic problem 152–5
Socialist Party 29, 145–6, 159, 162–5, 168, 174–6, 178, 185, 186, 218, 219: 'machine' 162–4, 174–6
sports clubs 182
subordination of associations to municipalities 173–4
Texture 164, 165–7, 168, 172, 183, 185, 195
unemployment 146, 152, 153–4, 157
urban regeneration 151, 156–8, 176
Liverpool 56, 60, 98, 130
Livingstone, Ken 57, 60, 134, 233n
local political systems 28, 34–6
Lochak, Danièle 83
Loftman, Patrick 49, 105, 106
Lojkine, Jean 150, 217
London 7, 24, 41, 42, 56
Longstreth, Frank 25, 226n
Lorraine 148
Lorreyte, Bernard 75
Lougrada, Saadi 208, 209
Lovenduski, Joni 116, 123
Lowndes, Vivien 2
Lutte Ouvrière 185
Lyon 9, 10, 24, 148

Mabileau, Albert 172, 173, 176, 233n, 235n
McPherson Report 108, 230n
Maghrebi population 9, 10, 68, 195, 216
  see also North African populations
Mahieux, Christian 150, 217
Mahmood, Khalid 93, 233n
Manchester 24, 41, 56, 106
Manku, Gurdev 132, 232n
March, James G. 25, 226n
Marseille 10, 86, 148
Marshall, Dale Rogers 23, 223n
Martiniello, Marco 120, 223

Masclet, Olivier 225n
mass migration
  Britain 4, 39–44
  France 4, 40, 64–5, 68–9
  local agitation 41–4
  national apathy 41–4
Mauco, Georges 65, 228n
Mauroy, Pierre 32, 35, 78, 145–6, 150,
  151, 155, 156, 162, 168, 169, 175, 177,
  178, 184, 218, 228n, 235n, 237n
Mayer, Nonna 87
Mégret, Bruno 87
Mény, Yves 233n, 235n
Mermaz, Louis 77
Messina, Anthony 40, 41, 45, 46, 47, 48,
  50, 51, 53, 225n, 226n
Militant 60
Miller, Mark J. 66
Minkin, Lewis 123
Mitterrand, François 73, 77, 81, 82, 84,
  236n
modèle français d'intégration, le 83
modes of election 6–13, 18
Modood, Tariq 5, 43, 223n, 224n, 229n
Moore, Robert 16, 25, 42, 43, 48, 93,
  225n, 226n
Moroccan population 12, 14, 29, 40, 68,
  75, 149, 157
  religion 17
  Roubaix 189
  see also North African populations
'Motivé-e-s' 24
Moussawi, Hussein 192
Mouvement Autonome 183
Mouvement National Algérien (MNA) 12
Mouvement National Républicain (MNR)
  87
Moynihan, Daniel 223
multiculturalism
  Britain 18, 40, 49, 50, 56, 106
  France 71, 74
Murphy, Philip 131, 133, 135, 232n
Muslim Public Affairs Committee (MPAC)
  54

National Commission on Commonwealth
  Immigrants (NCCI) 47–8
National Federation of Pakistani Associations
  47

national frameworks 27
National Front 22, 51, 52, 80, 104
Nationalist Association 104
nationality 6, 17
  Britain 17, 39
  France 18, 50, 64, 65–6, 67, 82, 83,
  87–8
  see also citizenship
naturalization 65–6, 67
Negrouche, Ralph 77
Nevan, Brendan 105, 106
Neveu, Catherine 199, 202, 204, 239n
New Commonwealth population 6, 10, 11,
  70, 98
New Labour 53
new pluralism 15
Newton, Kenneth 104, 105, 115, 116
Nice 86
Nielsen, Jorgen 121
Noiriel, Gérard 83
Nordlinger, Eric 21
Norris, Pippa 116, 123
North African populations 9, 11–12, 65,
  66, 75, 88
  Lille 147–86
  management by central state 69–70
  residential concentration 153–5
  voting rights 14, 67–8, 73
  see also Algerian population; Beur
  movement; Maghrebi population;
  Moroccan population; Tunisian
  population
Nottingham 59

oath of allegiance 17
Office National de l'Immigration (ONI)
  66, 68
Oldham 17
Olsen, Johan P. 25, 226n
Operation Black Vote (OBV) 227n
Oriol, Paul 9–10, 84, 88, 173
Ouseley, Herman 31, 57, 60

Pakistani population 5, 12, 29, 40, 97, 99,
  101, 107, 108
  accommodation 42
  community associations and organizations
  118, 119–21
  economic disadvantage 101–2

Pakistani population (*cont'd*)
  economic status   13
  independent candidates   135, 139–41,
    143
  kinship   120
  Labour Party candidates   132–3, 135–42,
    212
  Liberal Democrat Party   141
  mobilization   22
  political alliances   31
  religious organizations   120–1
  trade unionism   119, 132, 232n
  unemployment   102
  upward mobility   101
Parekh, Bikhu   223n
Paris   9, 10, 86, 148
Parti Socialiste Unifié (PSU)   165
party organization   28
party politics   28
Pasqua, Charles   82
patronage model of co-optation   125,
  126–30
Paul, Kathleen   38, 214
Perrineau, Pascal   78, 80, 81
Piat, Jean   237n
pluralist model   5, 15, 70: Britain   15, 17;
  new pluralism   15
Poinsot, Marie   76, 149, 164, 166, 167,
  168, 234n
Poiret, Christian   83
Polish population   148
Portuguese population   74, 148, 152
Powell, Enoch   13, 22, 38, 46, 51, 80, 93,
  104
Powell, Walter   213
proportional electoral system   81
protest and exclusion   23
Prouvost, Pierre   199
Provo, Victor   198
public disorder *see* riots and public disorder

Qayum case   139–40
Queshri, Mohammad   137

race relations   18, 50, 57–9
  local variations   59–61
  minority participation and   49–50
  policies   46–9
Race Relations Acts   16, 38, 51, 54
  1965 Act   16, 46, 47, 112

1968 Act   16, 46, 47, 48, 50, 112
1976 Act   16, 47, 51, 53, 54, 58, 106,
  112
Race Relations (Amendment) Act 2000
  47, 53, 230n
  see also Immigration Acts
Race Relations Board (RRB)   46, 47, 51, 52
Race Relations Committees and Units   38,
  57–8, 107, 114
racial discrimination laws
  Britain *see* Race Relations Acts
  France   16, 47
radical activist model of co-optation   125,
  130–5
Ram, Monder   12
Rancoule, Michel   65
Rashid, Abdul   233n
Rassemblement pour la République (RPR)
  74, 81, 155, 159, 168, 194, 199, 235n
  see also Gaullists
rational choice institutionalism   25
repatriation
  of bodies   121
  France   xi–xii, 72, 78, 79
republican assimilation   15, 32, 82–4
Rex, John   16, 42, 43, 47, 48, 92, 93, 103,
  104, 119, 121, 128, 225n, 231n
Rich, Daniel   106
Richard, Jean-Luc   21
riots and public disorder
  Britain   11, 17, 22, 29, 39, 44–5, 104,
    107, 230n
  France   16, 47, 66–7, 76–7, 164, 180–1,
    202, 225n, 236n
Riyaz case   139–40
RMI (*revenu minimum d'insertion*)   154, 189,
  234n
Rocard, Michel   165
Rogers, Alisdair   223
Roman, Bernard   175, 236n, 237n
Rose, Eliot Joseph Benn   16, 48
Roubaix   19, 29–32, 63, 187–210, 219–20
  activists, generations of   195–6
  Algerian population   189–91
  Belgian population   198, 200
  Beur movement   195
  comités de quartier   201, 203–5, 206, 207,
    208
  community associations and organizations
    199–206, 219

cross-party government 197–206
Front National 36, 191–5, 200, 207, 209, 219
Gaullists 194, 199, 207
Greens 195, 196, 203, 204, 207, 208, 209, 217
housing 151, 188, 189, 198, 199
identity 191–5
inclusion of migrants in municipal community 197–206
institutions 195–6
isolation of community politics 171–3
Lille compared 144–5, 151, 163–4, 171–3, 179
local political system 35–6, 124–5
North African minority 147–50
Polish community 148
political history 196–200
post-industrial crisis 188–9
pro-minority policies 191–5
Socialist Party 163–4, 199, 207–8, 209, 217
'third way' 198–9
urban regeneration 189, 193, 198, 209
Roubaix aux Roubaisiens 191
Rover plant 233n
Rushdie, Salman 127

Saad, Haroon 114
Saggar, Shamit 21, 33, 45, 52, 53, 55, 57, 60, 112, 115, 225n, 226n
Samad, Yunas 121
Sauvy, Alfred 65, 228n
Sawicki, Frédérick 174
Scally, Kevin 131, 134, 232n
Schain, Martin 23, 69, 70, 76, 80, 91, 173, 225n
Schéma Local d'Intégration (SLI)
Lille 181
Roubaix 209
Schnapper, Dominique 15, 26, 83
self-help movements 52
Sellani, Farid 183
Sewell, Terri 227n
Seyd, Patrick 55, 60, 124, 127, 218, 227n, 232n
Sharma, Paul 134, 137
Sheffield 56
Short, Clare 131, 134, 233n
Shukra, Kalbir 122, 133, 135, 138, 227n

Sikhs 11, 108, 119, 127
Simons, John 224n
Smith, Graham 107
Smith, John 135
Smith, Roger 104, 105, 229n
social class 12, 43, 60, 116
social services
Britain 43, 70, 107, 130
France 75
see also welfare provision
Socialist Party 29, 32, 81, 85, 112, 122, 218
Beur movement and 74, 76–8, 215, 216
gentrification policy 150–2, 163, 170, 174
internal politics 74
Lille 29, 145–6, 159, 162–5, 168, 174–6, 178, 185, 186, 218, 219
'machine' 162–4, 174–6
nationality and citizenship 86–8
Roubaix 163–4, 199, 207–8, 209, 217
voting rights for immigrants 15
sociological institutionalism 25
Solidarités des Femmes d'Ici et d'Ailleurs (SAFIA) 181
Solomos, John 58, 93, 94, 103, 109, 111, 122, 126, 127–8, 129, 133, 136, 138, 230n, 231n, 232n
SONACOTRA 67, 70, 90
SOS Racisme 77, 78, 82, 165, 166, 194, 235n, 236n
Soskice, Frank 48
Soysal, Yasemin 5, 16, 17
Spanish population 75, 148, 152
Spence, Sybil 109, 119, 132, 233n
sports clubs 182, 202, 205
Standing Consultative Forum (SCF) 107, 121, 231n
Statham, Paul 17, 18, 41–2, 50
Steinmo, Sven 25, 226n
Stewart, Theresa 109, 110, 129, 131, 135, 141, 143, 232n
Stoker, Gerry 43, 97, 123
Stora, Benjamin 12
Strasbourg 86
strategies of management of ethnic conflict 21–5, 30
student unions 132
Studlar, Donley 52
subjecthood 39, 70

Survey of Race Relations 1966   10
Sutcliffe, Anthony   104, 105, 229n
Swanstrom, Todd   109, 163, 227n
Sweden   5, 6
Switzerland   16

Tabb, David H.   23, 223n
Taylor, Rosemary   226n
Tebbit, Norman   51
Texture   164, 165–7, 168, 172, 183, 185, 195
Thatcher, Margaret   51, 56, 220, 230n
Thelen, Kathleen   25, 226n
Tillie, Jean   223
Tir, Slimane   195–6, 204, 207–8, 209
Todd, Emmanuel   83
Tomlinson, Sally   16, 92, 93, 103, 104, 119, 128, 225n, 231n
Tourcoing   29, 148, 149, 188, 193
trade unions   1, 6
   Asian Workers' Union   118
   Birmingham   116, 118, 119, 132
   Black Workers' Union   132
   Britain   55, 60, 110, 116, 118, 119, 132
   France   12, 66, 83
   Indian Workers' Union   118
   Pakistani population   119, 132, 232n
   Unison   110
Tribalat, Michèle   5, 223n, 224n, 225n, 237n
Tunisian population   10, 68, 69, 75
   see also North African populations
Turk, Alex   156, 168
Turkish population   17, 69, 75
Tyrell, John   133

Ugandan-Asian crisis   23
underclass   6, 26, 231n
unemployment
   Britain   6, 29, 102, 103, 106
   France   6, 29, 71, 80, 146, 152, 153, 157
Union de Défense de la France (UDF)   72, 74, 81, 155, 159, 199, 236n
Union des Organisations Islamiques de France (UOIF)   89
Union pour la Majorité Présidentielle (UMP)   228n

Unison   110
URBAN programme   193
urban regeneration
   Britain   38, 48–9, 105, 106, 107
   France   75, 151, 156–8, 176, 189, 193, 198, 209

Vandierendonck, René   199, 201, 203, 207, 208, 209, 226n
Vaz, Keith   227n, 233n
Verbunt, Gilles   67
Verfaillie, Bertrand   151, 191, 195, 200, 202, 238n
Vertovec, Steve   3, 120
Viet, Vincent   79, 81
voluntary liaison committees (VLCs)   43–4, 47, 48, 57
   see also community relations councils
voluntary organizations   16–17
   see also community associations and organizations
Vour'ch, François   83

Walden, Brian   126, 128
Wallace, Dorothy   132
Ware, Alan   175
weak minority mobilization   23
Webman, Gerry   33, 43
Weil, Patrick   6, 13–15, 16, 64, 65, 66, 69, 71, 72–3, 79, 82, 87, 228n
welfare provision   6, 106, 226n
   see also social services
Werbner, Pnina   112, 120
West Indian population *see* African-Caribbean population
Whiteley, Paul   124, 127, 218, 227n, 232n
Wihtol de Wenden, Catherine   15, 24, 87, 173, 195, 228n
Wilson, Harold   45
Wolverhampton   24, 29, 59, 60, 96
Woods, R.   98
work permits   66, 72, 73, 79

Young, Ken   57, 59, 60

Zollberg, Aristide   223n
zones d'éducation prioritaire (ZEPs)   75, 83, 238n